Adobe® Dreamweaver® CS3

The Professional Portfolio

Managing Editor: Ellenn Behoriam
Cover & Interior Design: Erika Kendra
Copy Editor: Laurel Nelson-Cucchiara
Proofreader: Angelina Kendra
Printing/Bindery: Prestige Printers

10   9   8   7   6   5   4   3   2

978-0-9764324-8-7 (spiral bound)

978-0-9815216-4-0 (perfect bound)

PO Box 260092, Tampa, Florida 33685
800-256-4ATC • www.againsttheclock.com

Acknowledgements

ABOUT AGAINST THE CLOCK

Against The Clock has been publishing computer arts educational materials for more than 15 years, starting out as a Tampa, Florida-based systems integration firm whose primary focus was on skills development in high-volume, demanding commercial environments. Among the company's clients were LL Bean, The New England Journal of Medicine, the Smithsonian, and many others. Over the years, Against The Clock has developed a solid and widely-respected approach to teaching people how to effectively utilize graphics applications while maintaining a disciplined approach to real-world problems.

Against The Clock has been recognized as one of the nation's leaders in courseware development. Having developed the *Against The Clock* and the *Essentials for Design* series with Prentice Hall/Pearson Education, the firm works closely with all major software developers to ensure timely release of educational products aimed at new version releases.

ABOUT THE AUTHORS

Erika Kendra holds a BA in History and a BA in English Literature from the University of Pittsburgh. She began her career in the graphic communications industry as an editor at Graphic Arts Technical Foundation before moving to Los Angeles in 2000. Erika is the author or co-author of more than fifteen books about graphic design software, including QuarkXPress, Adobe Photoshop, Adobe InDesign, and Adobe PageMaker. She has also written several books about graphic design concepts such as color reproduction and preflighting, and dozens of articles for online and print journals in the graphics industry. Working with Against The Clock for more than seven years, Erika was a key partner in developing the new Portfolio Series of software training books.

Gary Poyssick, co-owner of Against The Clock, is a well-known and often controversial speaker, writer, and industry consultant who has been involved in professional graphics and communications for more than twenty years. He wrote the highly popular *Workflow Reengineering* (Adobe Press), *Teams and the Graphic Arts Service Provider* (Prentice Hall), *Creative Techniques: Adobe Illustrator*, and *Creative Techniques: Adobe Photoshop* (Hayden Books), and was the author or co-author of many application-specific training books from Against The Clock.

CONTRIBUTING AUTHORS, ARTISTS, AND EDITORS

A big thank you to the people whose comments and expertise contributed to the success of these books:

- **Kara Hardin,** Pensacola Community College
- **Dean Bagley,** Against The Clock, Inc.
- **Debbie Davidson,** Sweet Dreams Designs
- **Lindsey Allen,** Austin Community College
- **Feroz Hassan** and **Sudha Iyer**, Teqnium Consultancy Services

Thanks also to Laurel Nelson-Cucchiara, editor, and Angelina Kendra, proofreader, for their help in making sure that we all said what we meant to say.

Walk-Through

PROJECT GOALS

Each project begins with a clear description of the overall concepts that are explained in the project; these goals closely match the different "stages" of the project workflow.

THE PROJECT MEETING

Each project includes the client's initial comments, which provide valuable information about the job. The Project Art Director, a vital part of any design workflow, also provides fundamental advice and production requirements.

PROJECT OBJECTIVES

Each Project Meeting includes a summary of the specific skills required to complete the project.

REAL-WORLD WORKFLOW

Projects are broken into logical lessons or "stages" of the workflow. Brief introductions at the beginning of each stage provide vital foundational material required to complete the task.

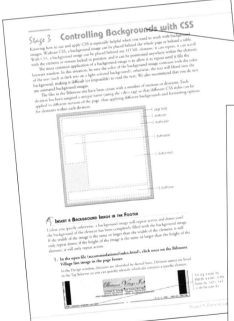

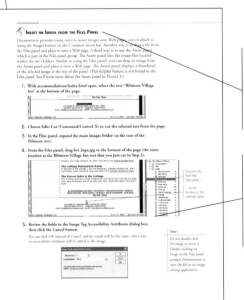

STEP-BY-STEP EXERCISES

Every stage of the workflow is broken into multiple hands-on, step-by-step exercises.

VISUAL EXPLANATIONS

Wherever possible, screen shots are annotated so students can quickly identify important information.

DREAMWEAVER FOUNDATIONS

Additional functionality, related tools, and underlying graphic design concepts are included throughout the book.

ADVICE AND WARNINGS

Where appropriate, sidebars provide shortcuts, warnings, or tips about the topic at hand.

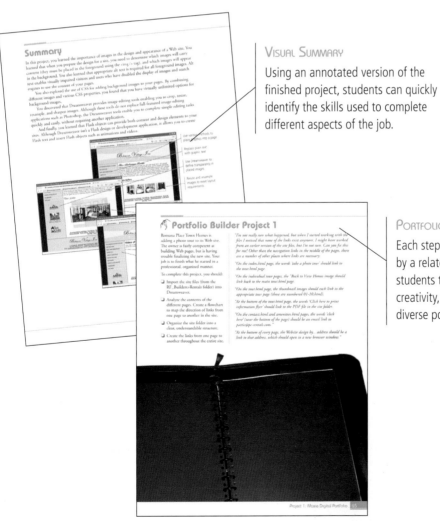

VISUAL SUMMARY

Using an annotated version of the finished project, students can quickly identify the skills used to complete different aspects of the job.

PORTFOLIO BUILDER PROJECTS

Each step-by-step project is accompanied by a related freeform project, allowing students to practice their skills and exercise creativity, resulting in an extensive and diverse portfolio of work.

Projects at a Glance

The Against The Clock *Portfolio Series* teaches graphic design software tools and techniques entirely within the framework of real-world projects; we introduce and explain skills where they would naturally fall into a real project workflow. For example, rather than including an entire chapter about printing (which most students find boring), we teach printing where you naturally need to do so — when you complete a print-based project.

The project-based approach in the *Portfolio Series* allows you to get in depth with the software beginning in Project 1 — you don't have to read several chapters of introductory material before you can start creating finished artwork.

The project-based approach of the *Portfolio Series* also prevents "topic tedium" — in other words, we don't require you to read pages and pages of information about marking up text (for example); instead, we explain text-related mark-up as part of a larger project (in this case, as part of a digital book chapter).

Clear, easy-to-read, step-by-step instructions walk you through every phase of each job, from creating a new file to saving the finished piece. Wherever logical, we also offer practical advice and tips about underlying concepts and graphic design practices that will benefit students as they enter the job market.

The projects in this book reflect a range of different types of Dreamweaver jobs, from creating a digital portfolio to developing a functional site template to building an online registration page. When you finish the eight projects in this book (and the accompanying Portfolio Builder exercises), you will have a substantial body of work that should impress any potential employer.

The eight Dreamweaver CS3 projects are described briefly here; more detail is provided in the full table of contents (beginning on Page viii).

Project 1

Moxie Digital Portfolio

- ❑ Exploring Existing Site Structure
- ❑ Organizing the Site Navigation
- ❑ Creating Image Links and Maps
- ❑ Creating Other Types of Links
- ❑ Naming Pages and Titling Documents

Project 2

Digital Book Chapter

- ❑ Preparing the Workspace
- ❑ Working with Special Markup
- ❑ Working with HTML Character Entities
- ❑ Creating Lists and Tables of Data
- ❑ Fitting a Page into an Existing Site

Project 3

Biltmore Web Site

- ❑ Working with Static Images
- ❑ Creating Image Links
- ❑ Controlling Backgrounds with CSS
- ❑ Editing Images in Dreamweaver
- ❑ Working with Flash Objects

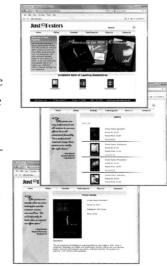
Some experts claim that most people use only a fraction — maybe 10% — of their software's capabilities; this is likely because many people don't know what is available. As you complete the projects in this book, our goal is to familiarize you with the entire tool set so you can be more productive and more marketable in your career as a graphic designer.

It is important to keep in mind that Dreamweaver is an extremely versatile and powerful application. The sheer volume of available tools, panels, and features can seem intimidating when you first look at the software interface. Most of these tools, however, are fairly simple to use with a bit of background information and a little practice.

Wherever necessary, we explain the underlying concepts and terms that are required for understanding the software. We're confident that these projects provide the practice you need to create sophisticated artwork by the end of the very first project.

Contents

PREREQUISITES

The entire Portfolio Series is based on the assumption that you have a basic understanding of how to use your computer. You should know how to use your mouse to point and click, as well as to drag items around the screen. You should be able to resize and arrange windows on your desktop to maximize your available space. You should know how to access drop-down menus, and understand how check boxes and radio buttons work. It also doesn't hurt to have a good understanding of how your operating system organizes files and folders, and how to navigate your way around them. If you're familiar with these fundamental skills, then you know all that's necessary to use the Portfolio Series.

RESOURCE FILES

All of the files that you need to complete the projects in this book are on the provided Resource CD in the RF_Dreamweaver folder. The main RF folder contains eight subfolders, one for each project in the book; you will be directed to the appropriate folder whenever you need to access a specific file. Files required to complete the related Portfolio Builder exercises are in the RF_Builders folder.

The Resource CD also includes a WIP folder, which you should copy to some location where you can save your work. At the beginning of each project, you will copy the files for that project from the RF_Dreamweaver folder on your CD to your WIP folder so you can work with files that can be saved without changing their location (in other words, on a writable disc).

For the project files to work as described in the exercises, they must be in the same relative location as other files for the same project; that's why we've provided a specific set of folders with known file names. Unless instructed otherwise, you should use the Save command rather than the Save As command.

SYSTEM REQUIREMENTS

As software technology continues to mature, the differences in functionality from one platform to another continue to diminish. The Portfolio Series was designed to work on both Macintosh or Windows computers; where differences exist do from one platform to another, we include specific instructions relative to each platform.

One issue that remains different between Macintosh and Windows is the use of different modifier keys (Control, Shift, etc.) to accomplish the same task. When we present key commands, we always follow the same Macintosh/Windows format — Macintosh keys are listed first, then a slash, followed by the Windows key command.

System Requirements for Adobe Dreamweaver CS3:

Windows

- Intel® Pentium® 4, Intel Centrino®, Intel Xeon®, or Intel Core™ Duo (or compatible) processor
- Microsoft® Windows® XP with Service Pack 2 or Windows Vista™ Home Premium, Business, Ultimate, or Enterprise (certified for 32-bit editions)
- 512MB of RAM
- 1GB of available hard-disk space
- 1,024×768 monitor resolution with 16-bit video card
- DVD-ROM drive

Macintosh

- PowerPC® G4 or G5 or multicore Intel® processor
- Mac OS X v10.4.8–10.5 (Leopard)
- 512MB of RAM
- 1.4GB of available hard-disk space
- 1,024×768 monitor resolution with 16-bit video card
- DVD-ROM drive

By default, the Dreamweaver Welcome Screen reappears when no files are open. Three columns comprise the main (upper) body of the Welcome Screen. The first column allows you to open a file you have worked on lately; as you work with an increasing number of files, the Recent Item list expands. The folder icon at the bottom allows you to quickly invoke a system-standard Open dialog box so you can open any file.

The second column offers a number of options for creating new documents. As you can see, there's a list of different types of files, including regular HTML documents as well as a number of programming-type files. The third column offers a list of **samples** or **templates** — predesigned layouts and formats that you can use as jumping-off points for your own work.

In the General category of the Dreamweaver Preferences (in the Dreamweaver menu on Macintosh and the Edit menu on Windows), you can turn the Welcome Screen on or off by checking or unchecking the Show Welcome Screen check box.

THE WORKSPACE

When you first launch Dreamweaver, you'll see the default user interface that Adobe defined as the basic toolset. Dreamweaver's WYSIWYG interface benefits new users who are learning Web design for the first time, graphic designers who are accustomed to creating their designs on screen, and experienced hand-coders who are familiar with writing HTML and other programming languages.

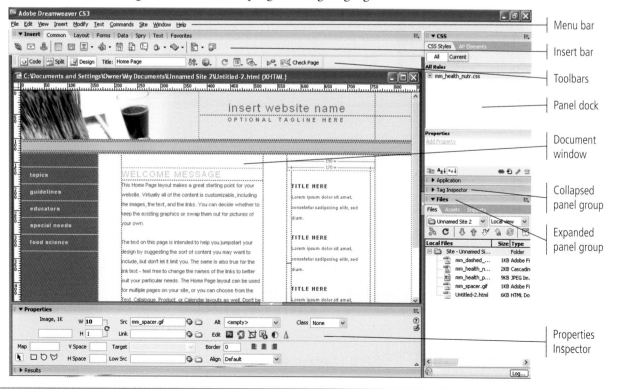

MENUS

Like most other applications, Dreamweaver has a menu bar across the top of the screen. In Dreamweaver, ten menus provide access to virtually all of the available options. (Macintosh users have two extra menus. The Apple menu provides access to system-specific commands. The Dreamweaver menu follows the Macintosh system-standard format introduced in OS X for all applications; this menu controls basic application operations such as About, Hide, Preferences, and Quit Dreamweaver.)

Some menu commands can be accessed using keyboard shortcuts. If a menu command has an associated shortcut, it is listed to the right of the specific command.

Most of the commands in the View and Window menus are **toggles**, which means the same command is used to turn an option on and off. If a toggle command shows a checkmark, that option is active or visible; if there's no checkmark, that option is off or hidden. If a menu command isn't available for a specific image or selection, it appears grayed out.

THE DOCUMENT WINDOW

There are three different options for working in the document window: Design view, Code view, and Split view. If you're visually oriented, you can ignore the underlying code that defines the page (Design view); if you're an experienced programmer, you can write code from scratch without ever looking at the page itself (Code view); or if you fall somewhere in between (like most people), you can view both the code and the design at the same time (Split view).

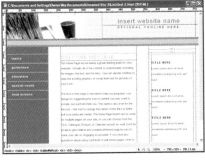
Design View

Code View

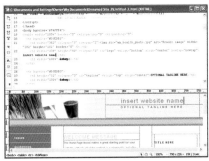
Split View

You can switch from one mode to another by simply clicking the buttons at the top of the document window. (If you don't see these buttons, choose View>Toolbars>Document to make them visible.) You can also choose a specific view in the View menu.

The top of the document window can display one or more toolbars, which are toggled on and off in the View>Toolbars submenu (the Coding option is only available when you're working in Code or Split view).

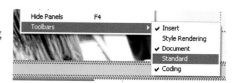

The **Standard toolbar** includes buttons for familiar file-access functions, as well as cut/copy/paste and undo/redo buttons.

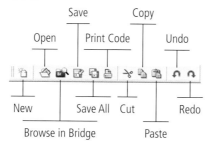

The **Document toolbar** includes buttons related to the specific page in the document window.

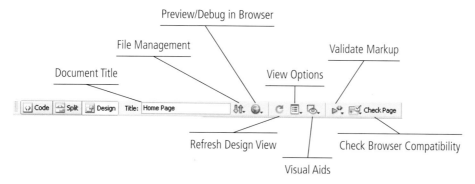

The **Style Rendering toolbar** includes buttons for previewing your design in different media types.

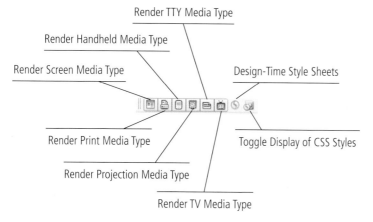

The **Coding toolbar** offers access to functions that facilitate working in and managing the Code window. This toolbar appears to the left of the Code window when working in Code or Split view.

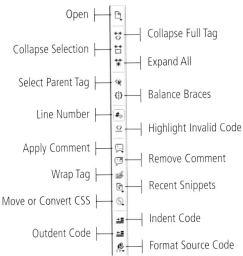

Open	Collapse Full Tag
Collapse Selection	Expand All
Select Parent Tag	Balance Braces
Line Number	Highlight Invalid Code
Apply Comment	Remove Comment
Wrap Tag	Recent Snippets
Move or Convert CSS	Indent Code
Outdent Code	Format Source Code

DOCUMENT STATUS

When you work in Design or Split view, you can use the options in the bottom-right corner of the document window to manage the document view.

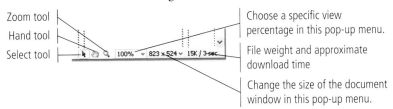

Zoom tool	Choose a specific view percentage in this pop-up menu.
Hand tool	File weight and approximate download time
Select tool	Change the size of the document window in this pop-up menu.

The Select tool is the primary tool in Dreamweaver; you can use it to place the insertion point in the document or to select existing objects or text. When you're zoomed in to a close view, you can use the Hand tool to drag the document around inside the document window. Clicking with the Zoom tool increases the document view to the next defined percentage, or you can choose a specific magnification in the view percentage pop-up window.

Note:

Pressing Option/Alt while using the Zoom tool allows you to reduce the view percentage to the next defined percentage.

DREAMWEAVER FOUNDATIONS

Adobe Bridge

Adobe Bridge, a standalone application that helps you browse and manage collections of files, is installed when you install Dreamweaver.

Bridge includes a Favorites area, where you can save quick links to specific locations on your system. The center displays thumbnail images of all files in the location you choose. File-specific information (such as a Preview, Metadata, and Keywords) appears in different panes on the left and right sides of the window.

If you have the entire Adobe CS3 Creative Suite, Bridge can be accessed from any of the applications to improve integration across the whole suite.

You can also change the size of the Dreamweaver document window to preview what users will see when using certain standard monitor sizes. Clicking the menu to the right of the View Percentage menu shows a list of predefined standard sizes, or you can choose Edit Sizes to add options to the list.

Note:

Choosing Edit Sizes opens the Status Bar pane of the Preferences dialog box, where you can manage the standard sizes that display in this pop-up menu.

The last piece of the status area shows the **weight** (file size) and approximate download speed of the page you're developing. The download size is based on the default connection speed defined in the Status Bar pane of the Preferences dialog box, which defaults to 56k per second.

Note:

You can also change the view percentage using the options at the top of the View menu.

THE INSERT BAR

The final Dreamweaver toolbar — the Insert bar — displays independently of the document window. By default, it appears above the document window, immediately below the menu bar. The Insert bar includes buttons for many of the commands and functions built into the application, divided into seven tabs or modes. (The word "Insert" is the name of the panel, not a modal tab.) The default view, the Common Insert bar, includes buttons for common features such as inserting hyperlinks and tables. You can access any of the other modes by clicking the appropriate named tab.

Click here to collapse the Insert bar.

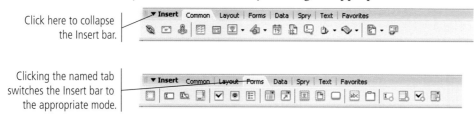

Clicking the named tab switches the Insert bar to the appropriate mode.

Note:

You can toggle the Insert bar on and off in the View>Toolbars submenu or by choosing Window>Insert.

You can also change the Insert bar from the default tabbed layout to a menu-style layout. Clicking the button in the top-right corner of the bar shows a list of options; you can change the Insert bar display, maximize the panel group if it's collapsed, or close the panel. (The other options in this menu, which are useful for managing other Dreamweaver panel groups, have no effect on the Insert bar, and they are grayed out.)

If you choose Show as Menu, the Insert bar switches to display a pop-up menu for the different modes. When viewing the Insert bar as a menu, you can change modes by clicking the pop-up menu and choosing from the different options. You can also switch back to the standard tabbed layout by choosing Show as Tabs from the bottom of the list.

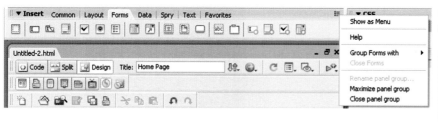

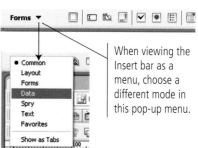

When viewing the Insert bar as a menu, choose a different mode in this pop-up menu.

PANELS

In addition to the options available in the Insert bar, Dreamweaver includes 19 panels that provide control over everything from the files in a site to CSS styles and server behaviors. In the default workspace, most of these panels are already opened in predefined groups and docked to the right side of your screen. You can collapse or expand panel groups by clicking the small black arrow to the left of the group name.

Panels can be toggled on and off in the Window menu. If you choose a panel that is already open as part of a group, that panel will become the active (visible) panel within the group. (Choosing a panel in a collapsed group expands the associated group, and then displays the panel you called.)

You can move individual panels out of a group by clicking the panel tab and dragging, or you can move entire groups out of the dock by dragging the button to the left of the group name. You can either drag away from the dock to make the panel a floating panel, or you can drag panels (or panel groups) to another location in the dock.

Note:

Toggle the visibility of all open panels by choosing Window>Show/Hide Panels or by pressing F4.

Note:

Choosing Window> Arrange Panels snaps all open panels and panel groups to the edges of your screen. If necessary, panels and groups will take up multiple columns on the right edge.

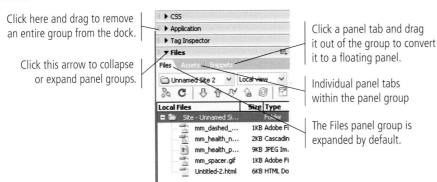

Click here and drag to remove an entire group from the dock.

Click this arrow to collapse or expand panel groups.

Click a panel tab and drag it out of the group to convert it to a floating panel.

Individual panel tabs within the panel group

The Files panel group is expanded by default.

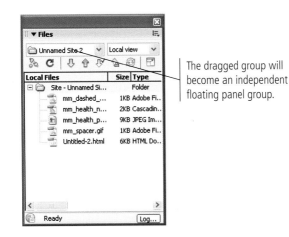

The dragged group will become an independent floating panel group.

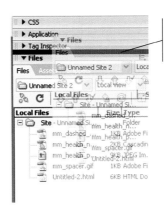

The black line indicates where the panel or group will be located.

Finally, you can move individual panels using the panel group options button. Most of the options in this contextual menu are related to the active panel in the group, so the options will be different depending on which panel is active/selected.

Several options, however, will be available for any panel or panel group. You can use the Group [Panel] With option to move the active panel into another panel group. You can also close the active panel, rename the panel group, maximize (expand) the panel group, or close the entire panel group.

(Even though the options button appears to be in the panel group name, most of the options are specific to the selected panel — not the panel group.)

Click here to access panel-specific options.

THE PROPERTIES INSPECTOR

The Properties Inspector is a special panel that appears by default at the bottom of your screen, below the document window. This panel is context sensitive, allowing you to change the attributes or properties (hence the name) of selected objects in the document window.

The following image shows the Properties Inspector when nothing is selected (top) and when text in a table cell is selected (bottom). As you can see, the second version has more potential options because there are properties related to the text and the table cell (instead of only the text in the first selection).

Note:

If you don't see the Properties Inspector, toggle it on in the Window menu or press Command/Control-F3.

For now, you don't need to know every available option in this panel; it's enough to recognize its modularity. You will use the Properties Inspector extensively to complete the projects in this book and for virtually every Dreamweaver project you build.

CUSTOMIZING THE WORKSPACE

Different workflows usually require a specific set of tools. As you become more familiar and comfortable with Dreamweaver, you'll develop a preference for specific panels in specific locations — and even different sets of panels for different types of jobs. To make your work easier and eliminate repeatedly opening, closing, and positioning specific panels, Dreamweaver includes the ability to save custom workspaces (Window>Workspace Layout>Save Current).

Note:

You can always return to the default Dreamweaver workspace by choosing Default (Macintosh) or Designer (Windows) from the Window>Workspace Layout menu.

Once you save a custom workspace, you can simply call it again in the Window>Workspace Layout menu. The same panels will reopen in the same positions as when you saved the workspace.

Note:

You can rename or delete existing layouts by choosing Window>Workspace Layout>Manage.

In addition to saving custom workspace layouts, Dreamweaver has sophisticated, built-in options for customizing the user interface, including the ability to define the keyboard shortcuts associated with menu commands and editing functions.

On a Macintosh computer, you can access and change keyboard shortcuts from the Dreamweaver menu; on Windows machines, the same option is available in the Edit menu. Once you've defined custom keyboard shortcuts, you can access the same custom choices again without having to redo the work.

Click here to access existing saved sets.

Click here to access different types of commands.

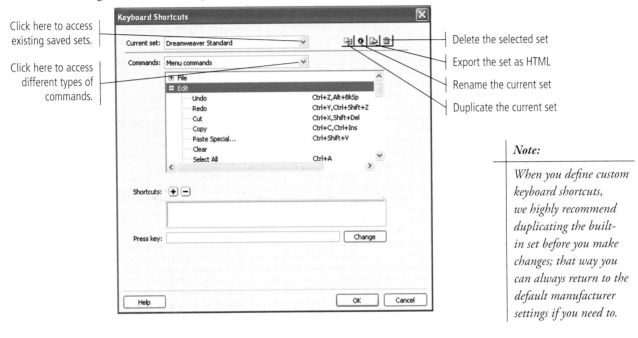

Delete the selected set

Export the set as HTML

Rename the current set

Duplicate the current set

Note:

When you define custom keyboard shortcuts, we highly recommend duplicating the built-in set before you make changes; that way you can always return to the default manufacturer settings if you need to.

PREFERENCES

In addition to customizing the user interface, you can also customize the way many different options work. The right side of the Preferences dialog box shows the options associated with the category selected in the left pane. As you work through the projects in this book, you will learn how — and why — to adjust the different preferences. For now, however, it's enough to know where to find these options.

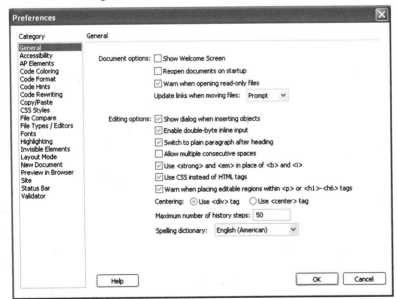

Note:

Preferences are accessed in the Dreamweaver menu on Macintosh; on Windows, they are accessed in the Edit menu.

Moxie Digital Portfolio

Your client, David Monroe, is the owner of Moxie Photographic Studios. He already has a basic Web site for his business, but he has hired you to organize and implement a new set of digital portfolio pages.

This project incorporates the following skills:

- ❏ Examining the existing and new site contents
- ❏ Creating, exporting, and removing site definitions in Dreamweaver
- ❏ Creating a flowchart to plan the new site organization
- ❏ Moving files around in a site root folder
- ❏ Creating relative links between pages in a site
- ❏ Defining absolute links to external sites and email addresses
- ❏ Creating image links and image maps
- ❏ Improving searchability with file names and titles
- ❏ Hiding site files from a Web server

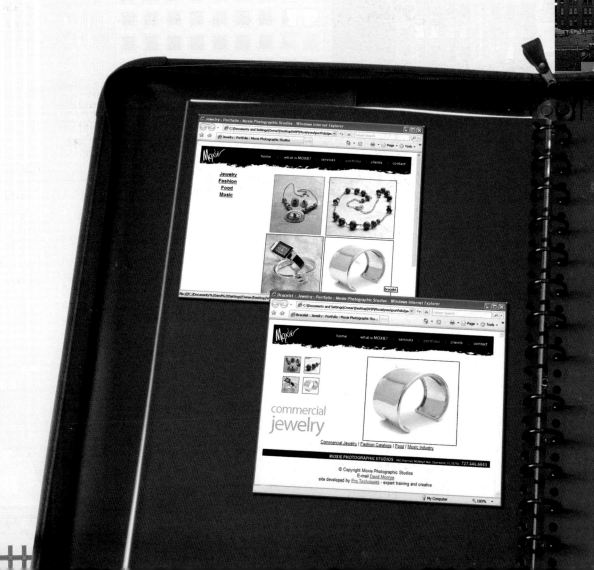

Client Comments

My basic Web site used to be enough of a digital presence, but lately I've been getting a lot of phone calls from potential clients, asking what types of photography I do and ordering samples of my work. Even though I think the physical prints have a stronger visual impact, it's getting expensive to send hard-copy samples in the mail — and a number of potential clients have specifically asked for a digital portfolio instead of prints.

I already created the Web pages for my new digital portfolio, but I don't know what links to use, and I'm not sure how to create them. I've also heard that there are certain things you should do to improve a site's search engine rating — which is obviously important for a small business like mine.

Art Director Comments

This project underscores the importance of a well-organized Web site. Moxie's existing site is simple, so you can drop everything into the root folder. But the more pages you add to a site, the more complex it becomes — until it's almost impossible to make sense of what you have where. All Web sites — even those with only a few pages — should be designed with a good organizational plan, making it much easier to add or modify pages later.

Once you have a handle on the organization, make sure the pages link to each other properly. Visitors get frustrated very quickly when they're forced to return to the home page every time they want to jump to a different set of pages. You need to build links between the different pages in the site, as well as add an external link and email link so that users can easily contact our client.

The last thing you should do is add page titles and change file names to give a better indication of what's on each page. That will make the site more accessible to people with screen-reader software, and it will also improve the site's ratings on search engines.

Moxie Photographic Studios

Root (/) folder – /index.html
/clients.html
/services.html
/contact.html
/whatis.html
/styles.css

/images/ folder – banner_clients.gif   banner_contact.gif
banner_index.gif   banner_port.gif
banner_svcs.gif   banner_what.gif
bottom_banner.gif   homewords.gif
MoxieLogo.gif   whatis.gif

/resources/ folder – portfolio notes.doc
portfolio images.psd

/portfolio/ folder – portfolio.html
/jewelry/ folder
/fashion/ folder
/food/ folder
/music/ folder
/images/ folder

Project Objectives

To complete this project, you will:

❏ Create a Dreamweaver site definition and export old site definitions

❏ Plan site organization using a flowchart

❏ Create new folders within the site root folder

❏ Use various methods to move files from one place to another within the site

❏ Create links between pages using several techniques available in Dreamweaver

❏ Differentiate between relative and absolute links

❏ Copy and paste uniform links from one page to another within the site

❏ Create image map hotspots and links

❏ Improve searchability and usability using page names and titles

❏ Cloak site files to hide them from the Web server

Stage 1   Exploring Existing Site Structure

When you start a new project that involves updating an existing site, your first task is to assess the file and folder structure. Doing so gives you a good idea of what the site contains.

A small site with only a few pages requires very little organization; in fact, you can usually place all of the files (Web pages and image files) in one folder. Larger sites, however, require careful organization of file names, Web pages, and image files. A good site design with excellent organization speeds development now, and also makes it much easier to update the site later.

CREATE A SITE DEFINITION

Web sites are designed so that all of the Web pages, image files, style sheets, and other resources are found under a common (**root**) folder. The root folder of a Web site is its base folder. For example, if you open your browser and go to CSSZenGarden.com, the page you see in your browser is found in the root folder of the Web site. Other folders can also be placed inside (below) the root folder of the Web site, such as an images folder.

1. **Copy the Moxie folder from the WIP folder on your resource CD to your WIP folder where you will save files.**

2. **Copy the contents of the RF_Dreamweaver>Moxie folder into your WIP>Moxie folder.**

   The files for this project need to be in a location where you can save changes, which is not possible when working directly from the resource CD. When you work through the exercises in this project, you should only access the files from your WIP>Moxie folder and not from the RF_Dreamweaver>Moxie folder.

3. **Launch Dreamweaver. If your screen does not look like the image shown below, choose Window>Workspace Layout>Default (Macintosh) or Window/Workspace Layout>Designer (Windows) to revert the interface to the default settings.**

Note:

If the Welcome Screen is not visible, you can choose Dreamweaver> Preferences (Macintosh) or Edit>Preferences (Windows), choose the General category, check the Show Welcome Screen option, and click OK. After you quit and then relaunch the application, the Welcome Screen will be visible.

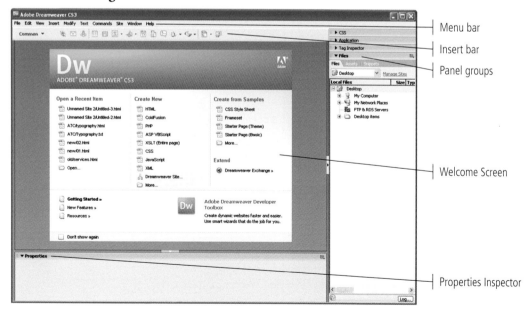

Menu bar

Insert bar

Panel groups

Welcome Screen

Properties Inspector

4. **In the Files panel, click Manage Sites or open the Directory menu and choose Manage Sites.**

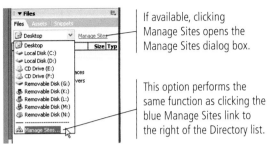

If available, clicking Manage Sites opens the Manage Sites dialog box.

This option performs the same function as clicking the blue Manage Sites link to the right of the Directory list.

Note:

In the Directory menu, sites that have already been defined appear below the drives on your computer and/or network. Simply choose from this list to switch to another site.

5. **In the Manage Sites dialog box, click the New button and choose Site from the pop-up list.**

6. **If the Site Definition dialog box appears in its basic form (as shown below), click the Advanced tab at the top of the dialog box.**

Dreamweaver offers two ways to create a site definition. The basic form offers only the basic functionalities, while the advanced form offers additional options. You will use the advanced form in this book.

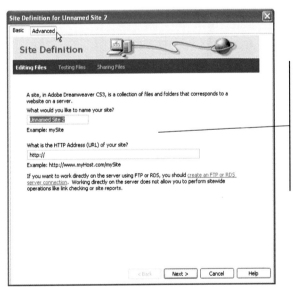

The basic version of the Site Definition dialog box uses a wizard-like method to help you define a new site. Although the basic version might be a little easier to configure for the first time, it does not offer any of the advanced options; once you have defined a site or two, it's faster to use the advanced version of the Site Definition dialog box.

7. **In the Site Name field, type "Moxie Old".**

The site name in Dreamweaver does not need to be the Web site's **URL** (uniform resource location, which is the Internet address of a Web site, Web page, image, style sheet, or any other Web resource file). The site name can be any name that will allow you to easily recognize the Web project.

This site name is only for the site identification within Dreamweaver. For example, you could use "Jimmy's Web site" as the site name within Dreamweaver to describe the Web site (bbq-tips.com) you are creating for your friend (Jimmy).

8. Click the folder icon to the right of the Local Root Folder field.

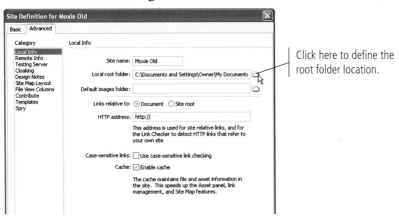

Click here to define the root folder location.

Part of the process of defining a site within Dreamweaver is to specify a particular folder as the root folder of the Web site. Clicking the Local Root Folder button opens a navigation dialog box where you can find the folder you want to use.

9. Navigate to the WIP>Moxie>old folder and click Choose/Select.

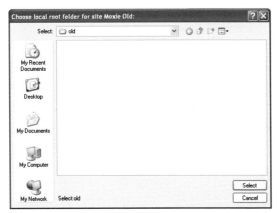

There is no default images folder defined in this exercise, so that portion of the Site Definition dialog box does not need to be set. You aren't required to insert the URL of the Web site either.

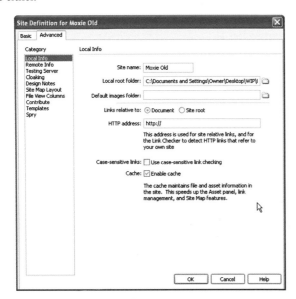

10. Click OK to close the Site Definition dialog box.

11. **In the Manage Sites dialog box, make sure the Moxie Old site appears in the list of sites, and then click Done.**

The Manage Sites dialog box can be used for more than just creating new site definitions. The most common uses are editing an existing site definition (to correct spelling or add new properties to the site definition) and removing a site definition once you've finished the site.

12. **Continue to the next exercise.**

Advanced Site Definition Categories

In addition to the local information (the site name, root folder location, etc.), you can define a large number of advanced options in the other categories of the Advanced Site Definition dialog box.

The **Remote Info** category allows you to specify the Web server on which the final version of the pages you create will be loaded. You enter the method of transfer such as **FTP** (File Transfer Protocol), as well as the password and username for uploading your site to the remote server.

The **Testing Server** category is used to specify the programming language used on a local server. In a corporate environment, your local computer is typically used for development purposes (a development server), and the remote server is the production server. In this environment, you use the Testing Server category to specify the location of the development server and its features.

The **Cloaking** category allows you to enable or disable cloaking and set cloaking file types. Cloaking is a feature of Dreamweaver that allows you to prevent certain files or folders from being uploaded to your Web server, such as files that contain preliminary information that you don't want site visitors to see.

The **Design Notes** category allows you to specify whether you want to keep and share design notes. Design notes contain information about a site, such as what changes are unfinished or how a particular price was set. These notes are meant to be shared with other designers; they do not upload to the Web site.

The **Site Map Layout** category allows you to manage the layout of the site map, which is an alternative to the Files panel; it displays the pages in your site and allows you to see links between the pages. When you view the files on your site using the expanded view, in addition to file names, you can also see other properties of the files such as file size and modified date. The File View Columns category allows you to enable and disable these and other columns, as well as change the column order.

Contribute is an Adobe application designed for organizations where many people contribute content to a Web site, but they are not responsible for its design. The Webmaster controls the permissions and the design of the site. The Contribute category enables compatibility of the site with the Contribute application.

The **Templates** category allows you to prevent Dreamweaver from changing the relative paths to files located in the Templates folder. This little-used feature has been added to the application in response to Dreamweaver users who encountered problems with their designs.

The **Spry** category allows you to define the default Spry assets folder location.

EXAMINE THE OLD SITE

One aspect of defining a Web site in Dreamweaver is that the application reads all of the pages in the site (a process that can take a few minutes in a large site) and notes the links between pages and which images are in which pages. These associations between files are stored in a cache that Dreamweaver creates when a new site is defined. When pages are either renamed or moved from one folder to another, Dreamweaver recognizes that other pages and image files are related to the moved or renamed files, and the program prompts you to update the links in all of the affected files.

Note:

When a browser downloads a Web page, it reads the code of the page, requests the image files from the defined locations, and displays them within the page for the visitor. In Project 3, you learn more about image files and how they are referenced in Web pages. For now, you should know that images in Web pages are not embedded into Web pages; they are merged into the Web page by the browser.

1. **With Moxie Old showing in the Directory menu of the Files panel, examine the files in the Moxie Old site folder.**

   If you can't see the list of files or the list does not match the one shown here, click the down arrow/+ to expand the site folder and show the file list.

   There are only 15 files in the root folder: 5 HTML documents, 9 GIF files (**GIF** is an acronym for Graphic Interchange Format, one of the Web-ready image file formats), and 1 CSS file (**CSS** is an abbreviation for Cascading Style Sheets, a file that sets the style and design properties of the Web site).

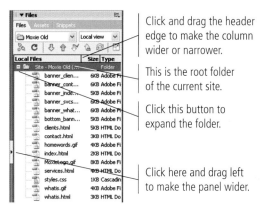

Click and drag the header edge to make the column wider or narrower.

This is the root folder of the current site.

Click this button to expand the folder.

Click here and drag left to make the panel wider.

Note:

When a site is defined in Dreamweaver, the Manage Sites link at the top of the Files panel is replaced by a menu that defaults to Local view. A series of buttons also appears below the two menus.

2. **Double-click index.html to open the file in Dreamweaver.**

3. **Choose File>Preview in Browser and select your preferred browser to preview the page.**

4. **Click the links in the top banner image to explore the old site.**

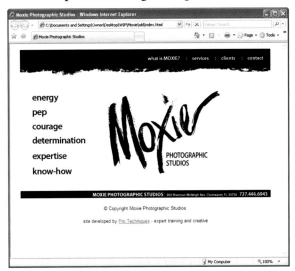

Note:

Press Option-F12/F12 to preview a page in your primary browser. Press Command/Control-F12 to preview the page in your secondary browser.

The Files Panel in Depth

By default, the Files panel displays the files on your local computer. You can also choose to view the files on the remote or testing servers by selecting those options from the View menu, or you can select Map view to see a graphic representation of your site structure.

The top of the Files panel also includes buttons that allow you to manage the files in your site.

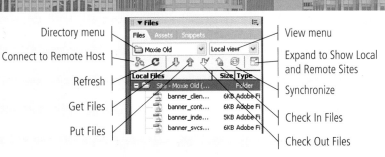

- Directory menu
- Connect to Remote Host
- Refresh
- Get Files
- Put Files
- View menu
- Expand to Show Local and Remote Sites
- Synchronize
- Check In Files
- Check Out Files

- The **Connect to Remote Host** button establishes a connection with the remote server (if you have defined it). Otherwise, clicking this button opens the Site Definition dialog box.

- The **Refresh** button refreshes the file list that is displayed in the panel.

- The **Get Files** button copies the selected files from the remote server to the local folder. If the Enable File Check In and Check Out option is active, the copied files are available on the local site in read-only mode, which means you can't modify them. You must click the Check Out Files button to edit the files.

- The **Put Files** button copies the selected files from the local folder to the remote server. If a new file is added to the server, and if the Enable File Check In and Check Out option is active, the file's status is Checked Out.

- The **Check Out Files** button copies the selected files from the remote server to the local folder and locks the files so only the user who checked out those files can edit them.

- The **Check In Files** button copies the selected files from the local folder to the remote server and makes the copied files read-only in the local folder. To edit these files, you need to select them and click the Check Out Files button.

- The **Synchronize** button synchronizes the files between the local folder and the remote server so the same version of the files appears in both places.

- The **Expand** button shows both local files and the remote site (if one has been defined). The expanded Files panel has two panes. The left pane displays the files on the remote or test server; the right pane displays the site files on the local computer.

5. **Close your browser and return to Dreamweaver.**

6. **In Dreamweaver, choose File>Close to close index.html.**

   You can also close a document in Dreamweaver by clicking the red Close button in the top-left corner (Macintosh) or the "X" Close button in the top-right corner (Windows) of the document window.

7. **Continue to the next exercise.**

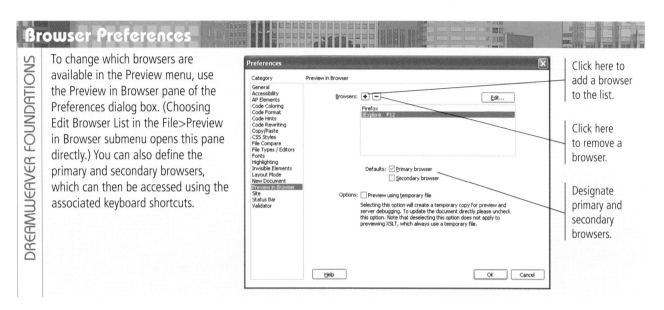

Browser Preferences

To change which browsers are available in the Preview menu, use the Preview in Browser pane of the Preferences dialog box. (Choosing Edit Browser List in the File>Preview in Browser submenu opens this pane directly.) You can also define the primary and secondary browsers, which can then be accessed using the associated keyboard shortcuts.

Click here to add a browser to the list.

Click here to remove a browser.

Designate primary and secondary browsers.

 EXPORT AND REMOVE A SITE DEFINITION

As you gain experience designing and developing Web sites, your site definition list will continue to grow — and a longer list becomes increasingly difficult to manage. To keep your list under control, you can remove or export old site definitions from the list.

When you remove a site definition, you are not deleting the actual files and folders from your computer; you are simply removing their registration from Dreamweaver's site definition list. This way, when you need to work on a site you created last year, for example, all you need to do is reinstate the appropriate site definition settings.

Rather than simply removing a site definition from Dreamweaver, you can export a site definition from the Advanced options in the Site Definition dialog box. When you export the site definition, you can later import that definition to restore the same settings and options that you already defined.

1. **With the Moxie Old site showing in the Directory menu of the Files panel, choose Manage Sites from the bottom of the panel Directory menu.**

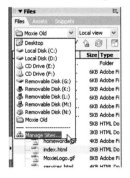

Note:

As you work through the projects in this book, you remove the site definitions for previous projects so that your site list remains manageable. You should also get into the habit of exporting site definitions before you remove them so you can quickly reinstate the site definitions if necessary.

2. **In the Manage Sites dialog box, click the Moxie Old site name, and then click the Export button.**

3. **Make sure the current folder is WIP>Moxie>old and click Save.**

   This function creates a ".ste" file that stores the Dreamweaver site definition settings.

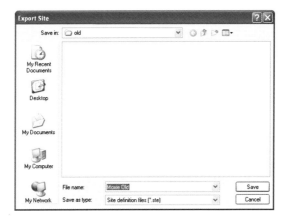

4. **In the Manage Sites dialog box, make sure Moxie Old is selected in the list, and then click Remove.**

5. **Click Yes to confirm the removal of the Moxie Old site definition.**

   After exporting the settings, you can easily remove the site definition from the list. Remember, you are not deleting the files from the site; you are simply removing the site definition from Dreamweaver.

6. **At the bottom of the Manage Sites dialog box, click Done.**

   When you want to reinstate the site definition, simply click the Import button, navigate to the root folder of the site you want to reinstate, and import the .ste file. All of the settings will be reinstated — saving you a great deal of time and effort.

7. **Continue to the next exercise.**

CREATE THE NEW SITE DEFINITION FOR MOXIE

As a Web site designer, you'll find that sites are in constant flux. The small changes you make will require little (if any) reorganization. When you make large changes, however, you must check to ensure that everything works properly, with no broken links or empty pages.

In this exercise, you'll see that the portfolio pages and files were simply dropped into the Web site's root folder — a very poor organizational choice when making such a large change to the site. Your job is to correct this organizational error.

1. **Choose Manage Sites from the Directory menu in the Files panel.**

2. **Click the New button at the top of the Manage Sites dialog box and choose Site.**

3. **Make sure the Advanced tab of the Site Definition dialog box is showing, and type "Moxie" in the Site Name field.**

   If no one has used your workstation since you completed the previous series of exercises, and if you haven't done anything else in Dreamweaver, the Site Definition dialog box automatically opens in Advanced mode; Dreamweaver remembers the last-used state of the dialog box.

4. **Click the button to the right of the Local Root Folder field. Navigate to the WIP>Moxie>new folder and click Choose/Select.**

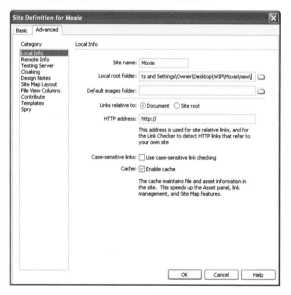

5. **At the bottom of the Site Definition dialog box, click OK.**

6. **At the bottom of the Manage Sites dialog box, click Done.**

7. **Continue to the next exercise.**

EXAMINE THE NEW SITE FILES

There are many files in the messy and disorganized Moxie New folder. The first step in organizing the new portfolio files is to examine the Web page files and understand what they contain.

1. **With the new Moxie site showing in the Directory menu of the Files panel, expand the site root folder and examine the files in the site.**

   There are 95 files in the root folder: 26 HTML files, 52 JPEG (an image file format) files, 14 GIF files, 1 CSS file, 1 Word document (.doc file), and 1 Photoshop image file (identified by the ".psd" extension). Except for the Word and Photoshop files, all of the files in the folder are Web-ready.

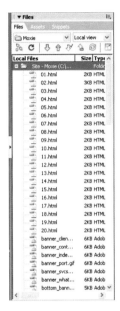

2. **Open portfolio.html by double-clicking the file name in the Files panel.**

   This page is identified as the portfolio page by its file name, as well as by the word "portfolio" in blue letters at the top of the page. (The designer of this site used blue to identify the current page.) This page is also the gateway page for the different photographic portfolios that your client wants to promote: commercial jewelry, fashion catalogs, food, and music industry. These words will serve as the links to the portfolio pages for these categories.

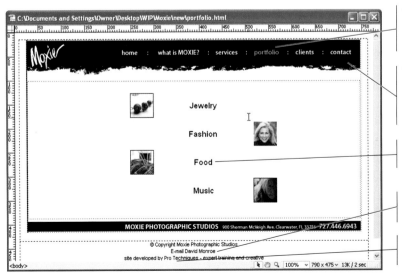

The word "portfolio" is blue, indicating that the current page is part of the portfolio group of pages.

The top banner image will be made into an image map, with each phrase defined as a hotspot link to a different page.

Each of these lines of text will be a link to the respective portfolio page.

"David Monroe" will become an email link to your client's email address.

"Pro Techniques" will be a link to the Web site of the original site designer.

3. **Close portfolio.html and open 01.html by double-clicking the file name in the Files panel.**

   This page is the gateway page to the jewelry photographs that David Monroe wants to display. From the appearance of the four images in the middle of the page, there are four jewelry photographs available for this portion of the portfolio. Each of the four lines of text in the top left of the page will be a link to another portfolio on the site.

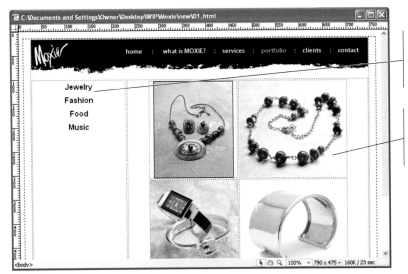

Each of these lines of text will be a link to the home page for that category of Monroe's portfolio.

Each of these images will be made into a link to open a page with a larger version of the associated photo.

4. **Close 01.html. One by one, open 02.html, 03.html, 04.html, and 05.html and examine the content of the files.**

   These four Web pages display larger photographs that make up the jewelry section of the portfolio.

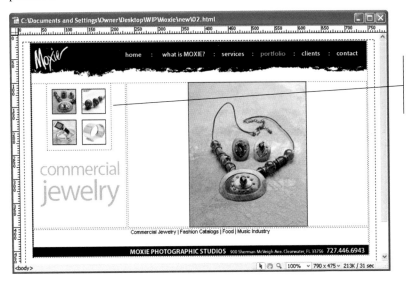

Each of these images will be made into a link to open the associated Web page.

5. **Close any open files from the previous step and, one by one, open 06.html, 11.html and 16.html.**

   These pages are the gateway pages to the fashion, food, and music collections of portfolio photographs. Similar to the jewelry collection, there are four photographs (and pages) for each portfolio collection.

6. **Close any open files, and then continue to the next exercise.**

DREAMWEAVER FOUNDATIONS

Many different file types can be found on the Internet. The basic document is an HTML file, which can have either .htm or .html as the file name extension. The most common image file types are **GIF** and **JPEG** (Joint Photographic Experts Group, with the extension of .jpg or .jpeg).

In addition to GIF and JPEG, **PNG** (Portable Network Graphics) image files are gaining in popularity.

The most recent image file type is **SVG** (Scalable Vector Graphics); code in an SVG file tells the browser how to draw shapes on screen. This format is supported only by recent versions of the Firefox and Opera browsers.

CSS (.css) files contain instructions that tell browsers how to display information in associated Web pages.

JavaScript (.js) files are similar to CSS files in that their content is not normally seen; instead, JavaScript content is responsible for the behaviors and animation effects that appear in a browser.

Many Web pages that appear to be HTML files have extensions such as .cfm, .php, .jsp, .asp, or .aspx. These extensions are reserved for Web pages generated by programming code—otherwise known as **dynamic pages**. For example, if you are a registered member of a particular Web site, you might see "Welcome back, Susan!" at the top of the page. The programming code in that particular page reads your browser's cookie, retrieves your name from

the members' database, and inserts your name into the appropriate place on the page. If you viewed the page code, it would appear to be standard HTML — and it is, except that parts of the page were generated by programming code that replaced "Welcome back $personal_name!" with "Welcome back, Susan!"

The extension .cfm is associated with the Cold Fusion programming language; .php is associated with the **PHP** (PreHypertext Processor) programming language; .jsp is associated with Java Servlet Pages (a language based on Java); and .asp and .aspx are associated with Microsoft Active Server Pages (ASP) and ASP.Net respectively.

Some file formats require browser **plugins** (accessory programs built into your browser). Flash (.fla) is an animation format that you can use to create basic animations, as well as play videos and interact with databases such as a hotel reservation system. Shockwave (.swf) is a relative of Flash, used to create Web-based games.

Various video formats (.wmv, Windows Media Video and .qt, Quicktime) and audio formats (.mp3) are also found on the Web. Some Web-based video and audio files can only be viewed (or heard) while your browser is connected to the Internet (known as streaming video or audio); other video and audio files must be downloaded before you can see/hear them. This is not related to the file type, but rather to the code that tells the Web page how to handle the files.

PLAN FOLDER ORGANIZATION

Although it is possible to put 95 files in the root folder of a Web site, managing the files this way would be very challenging. A well-organized site is an easy-to-manage site. Ideally, organization occurs before the site is constructed, but you can certainly add organization to sites that already exist.

There are no absolute rules to follow for organizing files and folders — other than the general principle of keeping related components together so you know where to find certain files when you need for them.

In this exercise, you use a paper and pencil to sketch out a plan for organizing the site's files. As you become more comfortable with this process, you will be able to complete this process in your head — but having a sketch allows you to clearly communicate your ideas to your client.

1. **With the Moxie site showing in the Directory menu of the Files panel, double-click index.html in the panel to open that file in a new document window.**

2. **Get a piece of paper and a pen or pencil and write "Moxie Photographic Studios" at the top of the paper.**

   The original pages of this site (home page, about us, contact us, etc.) serve the most important functions of the site: telling the reader who we are, what we do, what have we done before, and how to contact us. These basic pages form the root of the site, and should therefore appear within the root folder of the site.

3. **Write "Root (/) folder –" near the top of the paper. To the right of the hyphen, write the following list:**

> /index.html
>
> /clients.html
>
> /services.html
>
> /contact.html
>
> /whatis.html

Note:

The leading forward slash (/) is a standard representation for the root folder; all of these files appear within the root folder of the Web site.

4. **Below the last HTML file, write "/styles.css".**

   This **CSS** (Cascading Style Sheets) file describes the style properties of the pages in the site; the style file should also appear in the root folder of the site. While it is common practice to put the style file in the root folder of a site, if there are multiple CSS files, you typically create a styles folder to hold all of the CSS files for the site.

Note:

The file name "index.html" is the file-naming convention for the home page of the Web site or the default page of a specific folder.

5. **In Dreamweaver, examine the graphic images in the index page.**

   The animated image in the middle left and the large Moxie logo in the middle right are used in the index page.

   The bottom banner image appears in every root page.

   The top banner image is slightly modified for each root page.

   Other root pages (whatis.html, clients.html, etc.) include other images that are specific to those pages, so those images should be near the root pages.

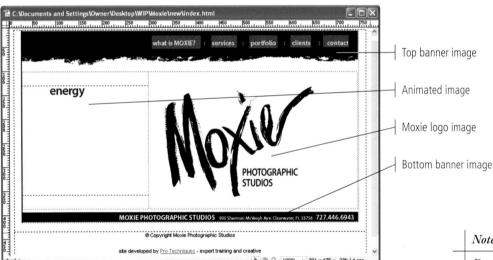

6. **Below the list of Web pages on your paper, write "/images/ folder –". To the right of the hyphen, list the images that appear in the root pages of the site.**

   The format **/images/** means an images folder will be created in the root folder of the site. By coincidence, all of the image files that are common to the root pages are in GIF format. (In fact, all GIF files in the site — with the exception of commjewelry.gif, fashioncat.gif, food.gif, and music.gif — will go into the root images folder.)

Note:

Dreamweaver does not allow animations to run, so only the first frame of the animation (the word "energy") is visible.

7. **Below the list of GIF image files on your paper, write "/resources/ folder –". To the right of the hyphen, list the Word file (portfolio notes.doc) and the Photoshop file (portfolio images.psd).**

The Word and Photoshop files contain preliminary information that helped the designer build the portfolio Web pages, but these files are not part of the Web site. While you might be tempted to simply delete these files, there are various techniques for keeping these background or resource files without including them within the Web site. You'll learn one of these methods later in this project.

8. **On the paper, write "/portfolio/ folder – ". To the right of the hyphen, write "portfolio.html".**

You might wonder why this page doesn't stay in the root folder. The reasons for keeping it in the root folder or moving it into its own folder are equally strong. Because there are many other portfolio pages with images of individual photos, the portfolio group of files is best placed within its own folder.

9. **Below portfolio.html, write (on separate lines):**

   /jewelry/ folder

   /fashion/ folder

   /food/ folder

   /music/ folder

   /images/ folder

Each portfolio category is assigned its own folder. The page **02.html** contains a jewelry photograph; when moved to its appropriate folder, the page will be located at **/portfolio/jewelry/02.html**. All of the portfolio images will be moved into the **/portfolio/images/** folder so that they all remain together.

This is how our organizational mockup looks:

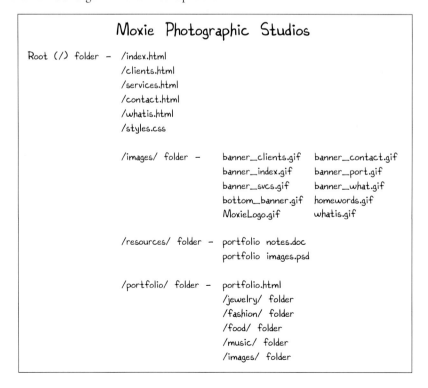

Note:

If the number of portfolio images grows to a much larger number, it might be beneficial to create an image folder for each portfolio category (such as /portfolio/jewelry/ images/). That way, the specific images for the pages in the /portfolio/ jewelry/ folder would be located nearby, making it easier to find and change the images or pages if necessary.

10. **Close index.html, and then continue to the next exercise.**

SEO (search engine optimization) is the art of improving the ranking of a Web site and its pages within **SERPs** (search engine results pages, or the pages that list the results of a search). Search engines certainly use the content of a page for ranking purposes, but they also use folder and file names. Putting portfolio pages within a portfolio folder improves the ranking of those pages.

Many content management systems (CMS) and blogs manipulate the URL of a page so that the URL contains the title of the article. For example, an article on WebStandards.org titled **Scared of the Dark?** can be found at http://www.webstandards.org/2006/05/10/scared-of-the-dark/. In addition to the article title, you can see in the URL that the article was created on May 10,

2006. Each portion of the URL in this example displays searchable content, and the URL provides meaningful information for search engines and users alike.

Compare the WebStandards.org URL with http://www.gov.on.ca/ont/portal/!ut/p/.cmd/cs/.ce/7_0_A/.s/7_0_24P/_s.7_0_A/7_0_24P/_l/en?docid=EC002001which (believe it or not) is the URL of the English homepage of the Government of Ontario Web site. To a search engine, this complicated URL doesn't mean anything, and therefore this type of URL doesn't rank highly in SERPs.

When planning the organization of a Web site, carefully consider the folder and file names so they are not a hindrance to good search engine ranking.

CREATE FOLDERS

Once you have mapped a clear plan for organizing your site, you can begin to implement that plan by creating new folders in Dreamweaver.

1. **With your Moxie site open in the Files panel, scroll to the top of the Files panel and click to select the site name at the top of the list.**

2. **Control/right-click the site name and choose New Folder from the pop-up menu.**

3. **Type "images" and press Return/Enter to apply the new folder name.**

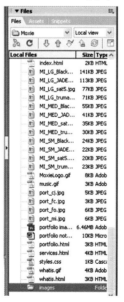

Note:

If after pressing Return/Enter, the folder name remains untitled, Control/right-click the untitled folder, choose Edit>Rename (or press F2), and correct the name.

4. **In the Files panel, click the Refresh button.**

   When folders and files are created, they appear at the bottom of their containing folders.

   On Macintosh, Dreamweaver alphabetizes folders along with all other files and folders; on Windows, Dreamweaver alphabetizes folders at the top of the list (above individual files); refreshing the site forces Dreamweaver to sort the files and folders into their preferred order.

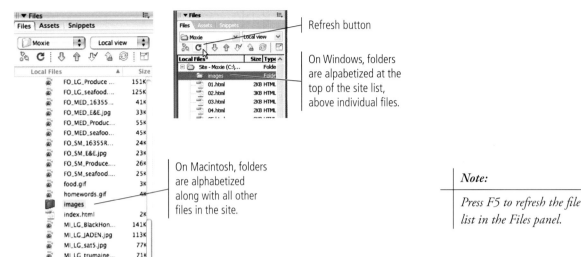

Refresh button

On Windows, folders are alpabetized at the top of the site list, above individual files.

On Macintosh, folders are alphabetized along with all other files in the site.

Note:

Press F5 to refresh the file list in the Files panel.

5. **Control/right-click the site folder at the top of the Files panel and choose New Folder again.**

6. **Type "resources" and press Return/Enter to apply the new folder name.**

7. **Add another new folder named "portfolio" to the site.**

8. **Control/right-click the new portfolio folder and choose New Folder. Type "images" and press Return/Enter.**

   By selecting an existing folder before creating a new folder, the new folder is created under the selected folder.

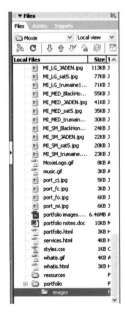

9. **Add four more folders to the portfolio folder: "jewelry", "fashion", "food", and "music".**

10. **Click the Refresh button at the top of the Files panel.**

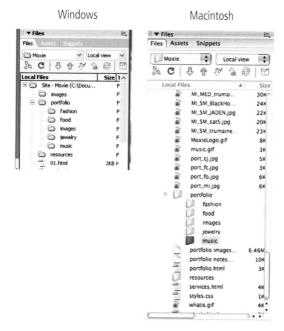

Windows   Macintosh

11. **Continue to the next exercise.**

 ## SORT AND MOVE IMAGE FILES

Now that you've created the required folder structure, you can begin to sort the various files into their appropriate folders. You can drag one image at a time, or you can move multiple images at once. In this exercise, you continue to reorganize the existing site by moving the images to the folders you created in the previous exercise.

1. **With your Moxie site open in the Files panel, click and drag banner_clients.gif into the main images folder in the root folder (not the /portfolio/images/ folder).**

   Make sure you drag the file over the name of the folder or folder icon; if you drag the file too far to the left or right, Dreamweaver will not move the file.

2. **Click Update to update the clients.html page with the new location for the banner_clients.gif image file.**

By using the Files panel to move the image file to another folder, Dreamweaver is able to check its cache, note that clients.html refers to banner_clients.gif, and request that you update the HTML file to use the new location of the image file.

If you chose Don't Update, the image will not appear in the clients.html page. If you had moved the image file using Windows Explorer or the Macintosh Finder, Dreamweaver would not be aware of the movement and you would not have the opportunity to automatically adjust the path to the image file in clients.html.

List of files affected by moving the image file

3. **Examine the images folder in the Files panel.**

The banner_clients.gif file is now stored in the images folder.

4. **Double-click clients.html to open the file, and then examine the top banner in the page.**

The top banner should appear as shown here. Dreamweaver adjusted the necessary code so the page can continue to use any of the moved image files.

5. **Close clients.html.**

6. **Drag bottom_banner.gif into the main images folder.**

7. **Click Update to update all of the files that use the bottom_banner.gif image file.**

All of the pages in this project use this image file, so all of the pages must be updated with the file's new location. The update process will take a while to complete because many files need to be updated.

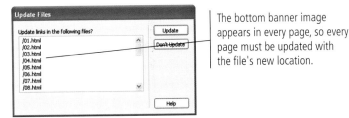

The bottom banner image appears in every page, so every page must be updated with the file's new location.

Note:

The same concept applies if you rename a file in the Files panel; you will have the opportunity to automatically update all references to the renamed file.

8. **Click banner_contact.gif, and then Shift-click banner_what.gif to select the five contiguous image files.**

   You can move multiple files into a folder at the same time. The trick is to learn how to select multiple files at once. To select files that are grouped together (contiguous), simply click the first one and then Shift-click the last one; all files between the first and last are selected too.

9. **Drag the selected image files to the images folder, and then click Update to update the Web pages affected by the move.**

10. **Click homewords.gif, Command/Control-click MoxieLogo.gif, and Command/Control-click whatis.gif to select the three files.**

    If files are separate (non-contiguous), click the first one, then Command/Control-click each additional file you want to select.

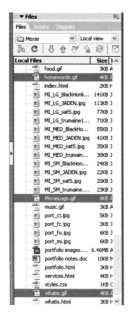

Note:

You can also use Command/Control-click to deselect a selected file. For example, if you select a file by accident, you can deselect it by Command/Control-clicking the file name.

11. **Drag one of the selected image files to the main images folder.**

    If you can't see the images folder at the top of the Files panel, drag the selected files to the top visible file name in the Files panel, and then the file list will scroll until the images folder becomes visible.

12. **Click Update when you see the Update Files dialog box.**

13. Open index.html by double-clicking the file name in the Files panel. Examine the page in Dreamweaver.

The index.html page contains four of the image files you moved: banner_index.gif, homewords.gif on the left (where the word "energy" appears), MoxieLogo.gif to the right, and banner_bottom.gif at the bottom.

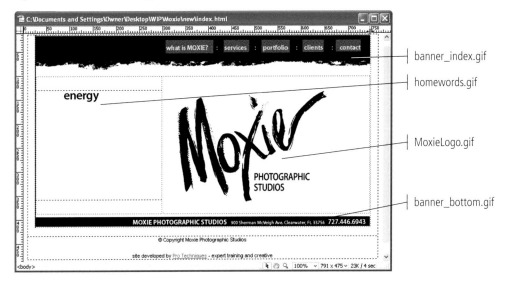

14. Close index.html.

15. In the Files panel, click the down-facing arrow (Macintosh) or the "−" symbol (Windows) to the left of the images folder name to collapse the folder.

On Macintosh, expanded folders show a down-facing arrow; clicking that arrow collapses the folder and changes the arrow to face to the right. You can click a right-facing arrow to expand a folder and show its contents.

On Windows, expanded folders show a "−" symbol; clicking that symbol collapses the folder and changes the "−" to a "+" symbol. You can click a "+" symbol to expand a folder and show its contents.

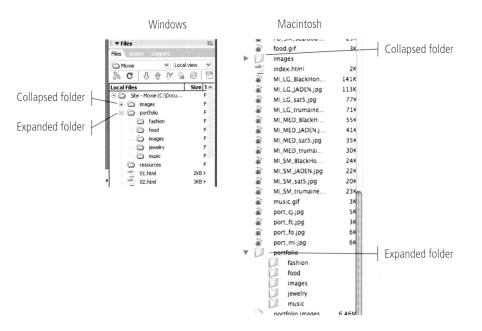

16. Continue to the next exercise.

CUT AND PASTE RESOURCE FILES

Just as there are multiple ways to select files, there are many ways to move files into or out of folders. In this exercise, you use the Cut and Paste functions to move files to new locations.

1. **With the Moxie site open in the Files panel, scroll to the bottom of the files list.**

2. **Click once to select portfolio images.psd, and then Shift-click to select portfolio notes.doc.**

3. **Control/right-click one of the selected files and choose Edit>Cut from the contextual menu.**

    The cut files will still be visible until you paste them in the next step.

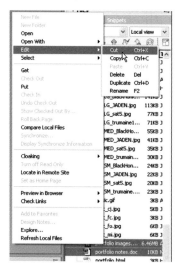

4. **Scroll to the top of the Files panel and click the resources folder to select it.**

5. **Control/right-click the resources folder and choose Edit>Paste to paste the cut files into the selected folder. Update links to the moved files when asked.**

6. **Click the Refresh button at the top of the Files panel.**

7. **Click the down-facing arrow (Macintosh) or "–" symbol (Windows) to collapse the Resources folder.**

8. **Continue to the next exercise.**

Note:

You can cut selected text, images, or files using Command/Control-X; copy using Command/Control-C; or paste using Command/Control-V.

Note:

Press F5 to refresh the file list.

ORGANIZE THE PORTFOLIO PAGES

Moving files from one folder to another is just as easily done in Dreamweaver's Files panel as it is using the file management software of your operating system. However, if you moved files using Finder (Macintosh) or Explorer (Windows), the links between pages and to image files would not be updated to accommodate the new paths.

1. **With the Moxie site open in the Files panel, move portfolio.html into the portfolio folder and click Update when prompted.**

2. **Move the files 01.html through 05.html into the portfolio/jewelry folder and update the links.**

   When you move files into a folder, that folder is automatically expanded in the Files panel.

3. **Collapse the jewelry folder.**

4. **Move 06.html through 10.html to the portfolio/fashion folder, update the links, and collapse the fashion folder.**

5. **Move 11.html through 15.html to the portfolio/food folder, update the links, and collapse the food folder.**

6. **Move 16.html through 20.html to the portfolio/music folder, update the links, and collapse the music folder.**

7. **Move all of the JPG image files beginning with CJ, FC, FO, and MI (48 image files in total) to the portfolio/images folder. Update the links.**

8. **Move the following files into the portfolio/images folder and update the links:**

commjewelry.gif	fashioncat.gif	food.gif	music.gif
port_cj.jpg	port_fc.jpg	port_fo.jpg	port_mi.jpg

9. Collapse the images folder.

From the folder structure alone, the Web site appears to be better organized. You now know what to expect when you open each folder.

10. Continue to the next stage of the project.

Stage 2 Organizing the Site Navigation

Virtually all Web pages have links to other Web pages. **Hyperlinks** (the official term for links) can be created to link pages on a site to other pages within the same site, or to pages in other sites. Although it is relatively easy to create links between pages of your site, you shouldn't go overboard by creating more links than necessary. For example, you don't need to include a link between every page on a site; using this method to set up a large site would result in thousands of links on every page. A much better plan is to decide which links on any given page will help the user better navigate your site. Exploring similar sites can provide some inspiration; but ultimately, you must carefully plan the flow of links and connections between pages—always keeping the reader's usability in mind.

 CREATE A FLOWCHART OF LINKS

Creating a flowchart of links between pages is an excellent exercise in planning the relationships between pages of a site. Organizing links is a simple application of a science called **information architecture**, which is the organization of a Web site to support not only usability, but also "findability." As you organize site links, remember that your goal is to enable visitors to see a pattern in your links, which will assist them in navigating through your site.

Not every link in a site can be planned ahead of time because some connections are irregular. For example, the history department of a university site provides links to the courses offered. Some of those courses have prerequisite courses. It would be very useful to link each course to its prerequisites; but because prerequisite courses are irregular, it might be difficult to accurately sketch them in a flowchart. Instead, you can establish a general principle that all courses with prerequisite courses must provide links to those prerequisite courses.

In this exercise, you create a basic flowchart of links between pages in your site. While it might seem simplistic to sketch links between pages, in fact, the more complicated your Web site becomes, the greater the need to create a flowchart.

Note:

*Creating flowcharts should not be considered a tool for novice designers. Flowcharts are often used to map complex software programming and Web site development. In fact, a language called **UML** (unified modeling language, a standardized graphical notation that can be used to create models of systems) has been developed by professionals specifically for this purpose.*

1. **On a sheet of paper, write "Moxie Photographic Studio" at the top.**

2. **On a line below, write "Home", "What Is", "Services", "Clients", "Portfolio", and "Contact".**

   These primary pages should be accessible from every page on the site, including the individual portfolio pages; the banner image at the top of every page provides these links.

3. **Draw arrows from "Home" to each of the other five page names.**

   You can't know how visitors will enter your site; they might enter from the home page, the contact page, or the portfolio page. For that reason, you should provide access to all of the primary pages from the other primary pages.

   To be technically thorough, you might also create lines from each root page to the other root pages. However, as you can see, that can get messy and nearly incomprehensible; the first set of arrows is enough if you understand the idea that all pages should link to all other pages at the same level.

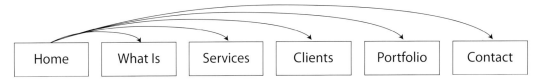

Moxie Photographic Studio

Home · What Is · Services · Clients · Portfolio · Contact

4. **From Portfolio, draw four arrows down; at the end of each, write "Jewelry", "Fashion", "Food", and "Music".**

   These are the four categories of portfolios that the client wants to display; they should all be accessible via links from the main portfolio page.

5. **Draw arrows from Jewelry to the six primary pages (including Portfolio).**

   A visitor should be able to navigate from each of the portfolio category pages to all of the primary pages. Technically, this step should be repeated for each of the portfolio category pages; but as long as you understand the principle, you don't need to draw those links.

6. **Draw arrows from Jewelry to the three other portfolio category pages.**

   A visitor should not be forced to go back to the main portfolio page (one step backward) to go to another portfolio category. Consider the portfolio category pages as siblings of one another. It is common practice to provide links between sibling pages.

7. **Under Jewelry, write "southwest", "costume", "watches", and "bracelet" to represent the four portfolio photographs within the jewelry category. Draw arrows from Jewelry to these pages.**

   Once a visitor has reached the Jewelry category, these links allow the visitor to explore the jewelry photographs.

8. **Draw arrows from each specific jewelry photograph to the other jewelry photographs.**

   Again, these pages (photographs) are siblings of one another; links between them allow visitors to explore all of the photographs within this category without having to return to the Jewelry category home page one level above.

Note:

Using the terms parent, child, and sibling is simply a way of describing relationships between pages. A large Web site cannot provide links to all of the pages from its home page. By grouping pages, grouping groups of pages, and so on, you create relationships of equality between pages that are grouped together, as well between groups that are grouped together.

9. **Draw arrows from the southwest page to each of the primary pages in the top row, including the Portfolio page.**

   Every page should be linked to the primary pages. Although this step could be repeated for each of the four jewelry pages and the twelve pages in the other three categories, as long as you understand the principle, the step is unnecessary.

10. **Draw arrows from the southwest page to the Jewelry, Fashion, Food, and Music pages.**

    The links to the main pages provide easy access to the other portfolio categories.

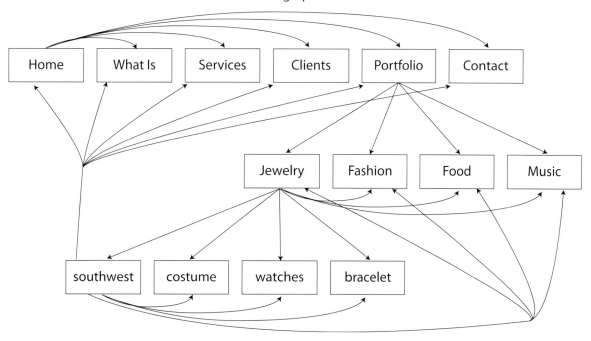

Moxie Photographic Studio

11. **Continue to the next exercise.**

 CREATE LINKS USING THE HYPERLINK BUTTON

The first step to completing the navigation outlined in the previous exercise is to create links between the main portfolio pages. In this exercise, you learn to create links between pages using the Hyperlink button on the Common Insert bar.

1. **With the Moxie site open in the Files panel, open 01.html from the /portfolio/jewelry folder.**

2. **Drag to select the word Jewelry in the top-left area of the page.**

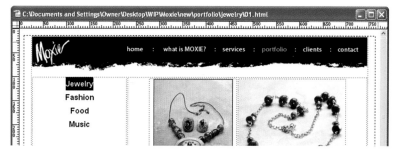

3. Click the Hyperlink button in the Common Insert bar.

The Common Insert bar contains many of the common functions you use to create Web pages. If a different Insert bar is showing, you can return to the Common Insert bar by simply clicking the Common tab.

Hyperlink button

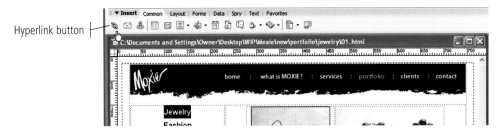

4. In the Hyperlink dialog box, click the Browse button to the right of the Link field.

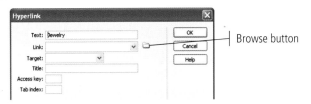

Browse button

Note:

You can also choose Hyperlink from the Insert menu to access this dialog box.

5. Navigate to the /portfolio/jewelry folder, select 01.html, and click Choose/OK.

The Hyperlink Dialog Box in Depth

In addition to specifying the link, the Hyperlink dialog box also allows you to determine how the link appears and how the link is accessed.

The text selected for creating a link appears in the **Text field** by default.

In the **Link field**, you can either select a file within the site you are creating, or you can type the URL of a location that is outside the Web site you're building.

You use the **Target field** to select where the linked file will open. By default, the linked file opens in the same window or frame as the one in which the link appears (this corresponds to the _self option in the menu). If you select _blank, the linked file opens in a new browser window. If you select _parent, and if the link appears in a frame within a frame, the linked file opens in the parent frame; if the link appears in a frame that is not within another frame, then the linked file opens in the full browser window. To open the linked file within the same browser window regardless of any existing frames, select _top.

You use the **Title field** to specify the text that appears when the cursor is placed over the link text.

To be able to access the link using the keyboard, you can either specify a key that a user can press, or the user can press Tab on the page until the link is selected. You can specify the key in the **Access Key field**, and you can use the **Tab Index field** to specify the number of times a user needs to press the Tab key to select the link.

DREAMWEAVER FOUNDATIONS

6. **Click OK in the Hyperlink dialog box to create the link.**

Note:

You can remove a link by selecting the linked text or object in the document and choosing Modify>Remove Link.

7. **Examine the link in the design window.**

   The text is now underlined. The link text does not change to blue because the style rules for this navigation bar state that the link text is to be bold and black.

8. **Save your work (File>Save) and continue to the next exercise.**

Note:

The most common links are text links where a word or group of words forms the link text. Commonly, text links are blue with an underline; but with the advent of CSS, many different styles are possible.

CREATE A LINK USING THE BROWSE FOR FILE FUNCTION

The Browse for File function in the Properties Inspector is similar to the Hyperlink button in the Insert bar. Like most applications, Dreamweaver often includes several different ways to achieve the same result. You should use the method that is most efficient at the time. For example, if you are using a different mode of the Insert bar, you can use Properties Inspector to create a link without switching modes in the Insert bar.

1. **With the Moxie site open in the Files panel, make sure 01.html is open in a document window.**

2. **Select the word "Fashion" below the Jewelry link you created in the last exercise.**

3. **Click the Browse for File button to the right of the Link field in the Properties Inspector.**

   If you don't see the Properties Inspector, choose Window>Properties. The Properties Inspector's primary purpose is to review and change the properties of the selected HTML element (such as a heading, paragraph, or table cell).

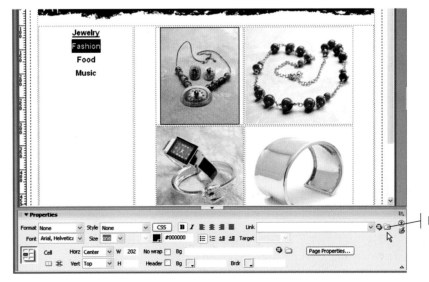

Browse for File button

The Common Insert Bar in Depth

The Insert bar appears directly below the main menu bar. The Common Insert bar contains buttons for objects that are most frequently used. To insert an object, click the corresponding button. (Some of the terms and functions in the following descriptions will make more sense as you use those tools to complete later projects.)

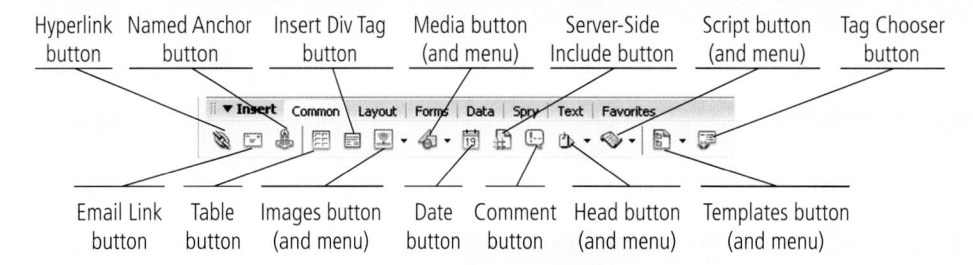

Hyperlink button · Named Anchor button · Insert Div Tag button · Media button (and menu) · Server-Side Include button · Script button (and menu) · Tag Chooser button

Email Link button · Table button · Images button (and menu) · Date button · Comment button · Head button (and menu) · Templates button (and menu)

- The **Hyperlink button** is used for linking text or images in a page to a file, either in the same Web site or in an external Web site.

- The **Email Link button** is used for providing links to email addresses. When a user clicks an email link, it opens the user's default email application with the email address in the To line.

- The **Named Anchor button** is used for marking locations within a page. Links can be provided to these locations from within the same page or from other pages of the same Web site or other Web sites.

- The **Table button** inserts a table within a page.

- The **Insert Div Tag button** is used for inserting new sections in a page. Each division in a page is marked by a dotted line in Dreamweaver; these dotted lines do not appear when the page is viewed in a browser. Sections are useful for inserting blocks of content that you want to format independently from other blocks.

- The **Images button** is used for inserting pictures. Click the arrow of this button to insert image-related objects such as images exported from the Adobe Fireworks application, navigation bars (containing links to other pages), rollover images (which change when the cursor is placed on them), and hotspots (sections of an image that can be linked to different targets). You can also insert an image placeholder, which reserves a portion of the page for inserting an object later.

- The **Media button** is used for inserting audio-visual files. These files could be in any format, but Dreamweaver also has functionality specific to inserting Flash, QuickTime, and Shockwave files; Java applets; and ActiveX controls.

- The **Date button** is used for inserting the date and time. An option is provided for updating the date and time whenever the file is saved.

- The **Server-Side Include button** is used for inserting a file within a page. In this case, the contents of the file are included in the page itself.

- The **Comment button** is used for inserting comments in the code that describe something about its use. These comments display only in Code view; they do not display in Design view or in the browser.

- The **Head button** is used for adding information about the page that will be used by browsers. This information is included in the properties of the page. Click the arrow to select the information you want to add.

- The **Script button** is used for adding code that will be used by the browsers to perform an action when the page is accessed. Click the arrow and choose Script from the menu to add the code. Some older versions of browsers might have the script-reading feature disabled; to display alternate content when browsers fail to read the script, choose No Script from the menu. You need to know programming languages to use this feature properly.

- The **Templates button** is used for creating a template based on the current document. Templates are useful when you need to create multiple documents based on a single layout.

- The **Tag Chooser button** is used for inserting tags in the code. Tags are elements in the code that determine the kind of content that can be included in them. Tags are included automatically when you edit pages in Design view.

4. **Navigate to the /portfolio/fashion folder, select 06.html, and click Choose/OK.**

Note:

You can change the destination of a link by selecting the linked text or object in the document and choosing Modify>Change Link. This menu command opens the same dialog box as the Browse for File button, where you can navigate to and select the new link destination.

5. **Save the file and continue to the next exercise.**

CREATE A LINK USING THE POINT TO FILE FUNCTION

The Point to File function is an excellent feature of Dreamweaver. To create a link, simply drag the Point to File button to a file in the Files panel, and a link is automatically created. This function has one minor drawback — the file must be visible in the Files panel. If the file is not visible, you must expand the folder first.

Note:

When a link to another page in the site is selected in the document, you can open the related page in Dreamweaver by choosing Modify>Open Linked Page.

1. **With 01.html (from the Moxie site) open, select the word "Food" below the Fashion link you created in the previous exercise.**

   This text will link to the 11.html page in the /portfolio/food folder, which is currently collapsed in the Files panel.

2. **Expand the /portfolio/food/ folder in the Files panel.**

3. **Click the Point to File button and drag to 11.html in the /portfolio/food/ folder.**

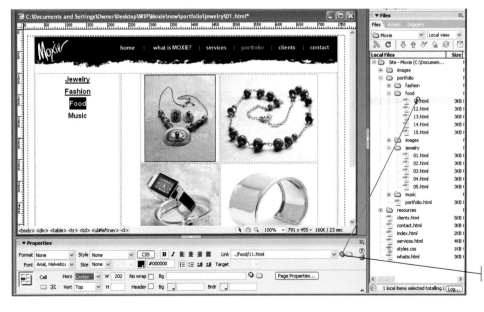

Point to File button

4. **Save the file and continue to the next exercise.**

SHIFT-DRAG TO CREATE A LINK

One final way to create a link between pages in a site does not require any buttons, toolbars, or panels. You can create a link directly from the document window by pressing Shift and dragging to the destination page in the Files panel.

1. **With 01.html (from the Moxie site) open, select the word "Music" below the Food link you created in the previous exercise.**

2. **Expand the music folder in the Files panel.**

3. **Press the Shift key, then click the selected text and drag to 16.html in the music folder.**

   You have to press the Shift key, and then click and drag to the link destination. If you try to click and drag before pressing the Shift key, this technique will not work.

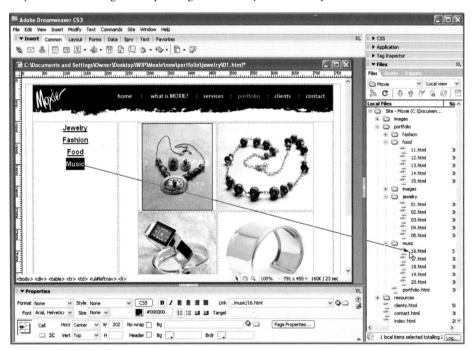

4. **Save the changes to 01.html and close the file.**

5. **Create the same links on 06.html (in the fashion folder), 11.html (in the food folder), and 16.html (in the music folder).**

   Link the word Jewelry to 01.html.

   Link the word Fashion to 06.html.

   Link the word Food to 11.html.

   Link the word Music to 16.html.

6. **Save and close any open files.**

7. **Continue to the next exercise.**

Note:

As you work in Dreamweaver, expand and collapse Files panel folders as necessary depending on your available screen space. We will not repeat instructions to collapse or expand folders unless it is necessary to perform a specific function.

Using Relative Paths in Links

By default, Dreamweaver uses relative paths when creating links (in the Hyperlink dialog box, Dreamweaver refers to this as "relative to the document"). The alternative is to create absolute paths; but unless your site is running on a Web server, you cannot test links that use absolute paths (Dreamweaver refers to absolute links as "relative to the site").

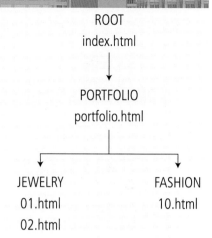

ROOT
index.html

↓

PORTFOLIO
portfolio.html

JEWELRY   FASHION
01.html   10.html
02.html

A path is the route taken through the folder structure to link one page to another. In the figure above, if the source and destination pages are in the same folder (**01.html** and **02.html** are both in the **jewelry** folder), then a link created between them simply states the file name of the destination page:

    <a href="01.html">Jewelry Home Page</a>

However, if the source and destination pages are in different folders, then the path to the destination page must be described. When you are drilling down into nested levels of folders, the source folder is not identified in the path; the link automatically works starting from the location of the link.

For example, to link from **portfolio.html** in the **/portfolio/** folder to **01.html** in the **/portfolio/jewelry/** folder, you have to include the nested folder in the path, but not the starting **/portfolio/** folder:

    <a href="jewelry/01.html">Jewelry Home Page</a>

To link from **index.html** in the root folder to **01.html** in the **/portfolio/jewelry/** folder, you have to include both folders in the path:

    <a href="portfolio/jewelry/01.html">Jewelry Home Page</a>

When the link is in an upward direction, the **../** notation is used to say "go up one folder". To link from **01.html** in the **/jewelry/** folder to **portfolio.html** in the **/portfolio/** folder means the link needs to take the visitor up one folder level:

    <a href="../portfolio.html">Portfolio</a>

To link from **01.html** in the **/portfolio/jewelry** folder to **/index.html** in the root folder, the link must take the visitor up two folder levels:

    <a href="../../index.html">Moxie Photography Home Page</a>

It's possible to combine the two methods. For example, to link from **/portfolio/jewelry/01.html** to **/portfolio/fashion/10.html**, the link must take the visitor up one folder level and then down to a different folder:

    <a href="../fashion/10.html">Sportswear</a>

 ## LINK PHOTO PAGES TO PORTFOLIO CATEGORY PAGES

When you created the linking plan, you drew lines from the photo pages to the portfolio category pages, showing that a visitor could jump from a specific photo to another category. In this exercise, you create the actual links.

1. **With the Moxie site open in the Files panel, open 02.html from the /portfolio/jewelry/ folder.**

2. **Select the words "Commercial Jewelry" below the photograph.**

3. **Using either the Point to File or Browse to File method, create a link from the selected text ("Commercial Jewelry") to 01.html in the Jewelry folder.**

Remember, you need to expand folders in the Files panel if you plan to use the Point to File method.

Note:

The Shift-Drag method will not work in this instance because each text link is only part of a single paragraph.

4. **Select the words "Fashion Catalogs" and create a link to 06.html in the /portfolio/fashion/ folder.**

5. **Select "Food" and create a link to 11.html in the /portfolio/food/ folder.**

6. **Select "Music Industry" and create a link to 16.html in the /portfolio/music/ folder.**

7. **With the Music Industry link selected, examine the link path in the Link field of the Properties Inspector.**

The path from /portfolio/jewelry/02.html to /portfolio/music/16.html requires you to go up one folder to the /portfolio/ folder, and then down to the /music/ folder to get to 16.html.

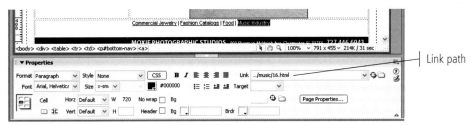

8. **One by one, click the Food and Fashion links in the document and review the paths in the Properties Inspector.**

In each case, the link goes up to the /portfolio/ folder, then moves down to the specific folder for the page that is linked.

9. **Click the Commercial Jewelry link and note the path.**

There is no folder path because both 01.html and 02.html are in the same folder.

10. **Save the file and continue to the next exercise.**

ADJUST THE MUSIC LINK

These links are present in all sixteen of the photo pages of the portfolio. If you copied this block of links to the other pages in the /portfolio/jewelry/ folder, they would all work. However, if you copied them to the pages in the /portfolio/music/ folder, the first link (to 01.html) would be broken because the path (or lack of one) would make the browser look for 01.html in the /portfolio/music/ folder. Rather than adjust these links for each of the new folders, in this exercise you change the link to 01.html so it will work in any of the portfolio photo pages.

1. **With the Commercial Jewelry link selected in 02.html (of the Moxie site), click the Link field and move the insertion point to the left of the existing path ("01.html").**

2. **Type "../jewelry/" to the left of 01.html.**

   This modification to the link takes the browser up to the /portfolio/ folder, and then back to the /portfolio/jewelry/ folder. This might seem like unnecessary effort, but it means that this link will work from any of the sixteen photo pages.

3. **Save the changes to the page.**

4. **Preview the page in your primary browser (File>Preview in Browser). Test the links by clicking them one at a time to ensure that the intended page opens from the link.**

   You must click the Back button in your browser to return to this page to check each link; the other pages don't yet have links to return you to this page.

5. **Close your browser, return to Dreamweaver, and continue to the next exercise.**

 ## COPY AND PASTE LINKS

Now that the bottom set of links has been configured to work from every photo page of the portfolio, it's time to copy and paste that paragraph to the rest of the photo pages in the portfolio.

1. **With 02.html (from the Moxie site) open, click within the paragraph of links, and then click the <p#bottom-nav> tag in the Tag Selector.**

   The Tag Selector, located in the status bar of the document window, shows the path of tags to the tag of the current selection or the current location of the insertion point.

   Clicking a tag in the Tag Selector selects all of the content contained within that tag. In the document window, the associated content is highlighted.

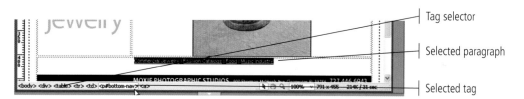

Note:

Dreamweaver is very good at creating the correct HTML code according to your instructions, but it's entirely possible for you to create a link to the wrong page, such as linking the text "Contact Us" to clients.html instead of contact.html. Although the code might be correct, the destination is incorrect. The best way to catch errors such as these is to preview the pages in your browser and test the links shortly after creating them.

2. Copy the selected content to the clipboard by choosing Edit>Copy or pressing Command/Control-C.

3. Close 02.html and open 03.html.

4. Click within the paragraph near the bottom of the page and click the <p#bottom-nav> tag in the Tag Selector to select the paragraph.

The selected content does not include links.

5. Paste the content from the clipboard by choosing Edit>Paste or pressing Command/Control-V.

The pasted content includes the links.

6. Save the changes to 03.html and close the file.

7. Repeat Steps 3 through 6 to paste the copied content (the links) into pages 04.html and 05.html in the /portfolio/jewelry/ folder.

8. Repeat Steps 3 through 6 to paste the same links into the following pages:

    07.html to 10.html in the /portfolio/fashion/ folder

    12.html to 15.html in the /portfolio/food/ folder

    17.html to 20.html in the /portfolio/music/ folder.

If you hadn't adjusted the link path to 01.html in the previous exercise, you would have to adjust the path each time you pasted to a page that was not in the /portfolio/jewelry/ folder. By adjusting the path so it would work each time, all you had to do was paste the same paragraph of links into each of the pages in all four category folders.

9. Save and close all files, and then continue to the next stage of the project.

Stage 3 Creating Image Links and Maps

Many Web sites use navigation bars in which the links are not live text but images of text; text graphics are often used because the appearance of the text can be modified to a much greater extent in graphics applications than is possible using CSS alone. And of course there are photo galleries, in which you click a thumbnail image to open a larger version of the photo.

You can use any of the methods you already learned to create image links, with one exception — you can't Shift-point to another file from an image in the document window. You can, however, use the Hyperlink button in the Common Insert bar, type a URL in the Link field, use the Browse for File button, or use the Point to File button in the Properties Inspector.

 ## CREATE IMAGE LINKS

In this exercise, you create links from the portfolio category pages to the photo pages with larger versions of the photos.

1. **With the Moxie site open in the Files panel, open 01.html from the /portfolio/jewelry/ folder.**

2. **Click the top-left portfolio image.**

3. **Examine the Properties Inspector, noting the position of the Link field, the Browse for File button, and the Point to File button.**

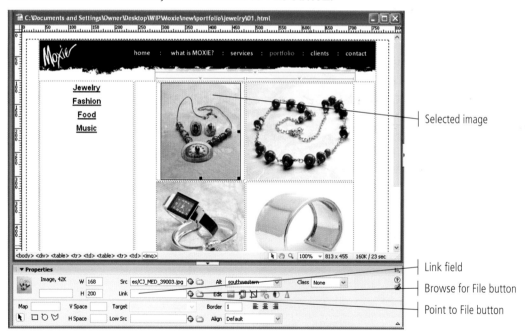

4. **Using the Browse for File method, link the selected image to 02.html in the /portfolio/jewelry/ folder.**

5. **Click the image in the top-right corner and use the Point to File method to link the selected image to 03.html.**

6. **Using any method you prefer, link the lower-left image to 04.html and link the lower-right image to 05.html.**

7. **Preview the page in your primary browser (click Yes to save the file if prompted) and check the links.**

8. **Close your browser and return to Dreamweaver.**

9. **Close 01.html and open 06.html from the /portfolio/fashion/ folder.**

10. **Working from left to right, top to bottom, link the four images to the four remaining pages in the /portfolio/fashion/ folder in numerical order, using whatever method you prefer. Save and close 06.html when finished.**

11. **Repeat Step 10 for 11.html in the /portfolio/food/ folder.**

12. **Repeat Step 10 for 16.html in the /portfolio/music/ folder.**

13. **Continue to the next exercise.**

COPY AND PASTE IMAGE LINKS

When a visitor clicks a link to jump to a specific portfolio image, the user should be able to explore other photos in the same category without being forced to first return to the main category page. Four thumbnail images in the left side of the page will provide this navigational structure. Once you've created links from the thumbnails in one page, you can copy and paste that group to the other pages in the same category — which reduces some of the effort.

1. **With the Moxie site open in the Files panel, open 02.html from the /portfolio/jewelry/ folder.**

2. **Click to select the top-left image in the top-left region of the page.**

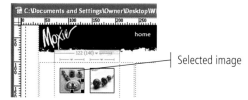

Selected image

3. **Link this image to 02.html.**

   This image creates a link to the current page. Some designers counsel against this practice; but when this block of links is copied to the other four pages in this folder, this image will link from other pages to this one.

4. **Working from left to right, top to bottom, link the remaining images to the last three pages in the /portfolio/jewelry/ folder in numerical order.**

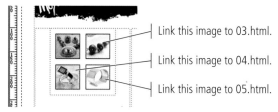

Link this image to 03.html.

Link this image to 04.html.

Link this image to 05.html.

5. **With any of the four thumbnail images selected, click the right-most (second) <table> tag in the Tag Selector to select the small table that encloses the four thumbnail image links.**

   The Tag Selector shows the "path of tags", leading to the selected <img> tag.

   When you click the <table> tag, the selection switches to the entire table that contains the originally selected image. The path of tags now ends at the selected <table> tag.

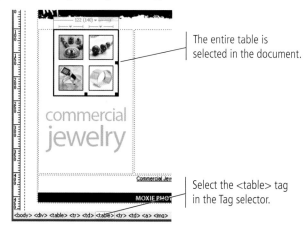

The entire table is selected in the document.

Select the <table> tag in the Tag selector.

6. **Choose Edit>Copy (or press Command/Control-C) to copy the selected table to the clipboard.**

7. **Save the changes to 02.html and close the file.**

8. **Open 03.html and click one of the thumbnail images.**

9. **Click the right-most <table> tag in the Tag Selector and paste the copied table (with the defined links) in place of the selected table (which has no links).**

10. **Save the changes to 03.html and close it.**

11. **Repeat Steps 8 through 10 on 04.html and 05.html.**

12. **Repeat this process for each category of photo pages:**
    - **Create the thumbnail links in one of the category pages.**
    - **Use the Tag Selector to select the table containing the thumbnail links.**
    - **Copy the linked thumbnail table.**
    - **Paste the linked thumbnail table, replacing the unlinked thumbnail table in the other pages of the same category.**

    By adding these links, a visitor can explore the other photos within the same category from each of the photo pages in that category.

13. **Save and close any open files, and then continue to the next exercise.**

CREATE IMAGE MAP LINKS

In addition to creating a link from a whole image, you can also create a link from a portion of an image. For example, an image of a map of the United States could have a link from each state to the government Web site for that state; or a group photograph could have a link from each person to a personal Web page. This type of image is known as an **image map**.

Image maps contain **hotspots**, which are specific areas of the image configured as links. Each hotspot on an image can have its own URL, which means a single image can have multiple URLs. Dreamweaver applies a semi-transparent, aqua-colored shape to represent the location, shape, and size of each hotspot area.

There are three basic shapes of hotspots: rectangular (including square), circular, and polygonal (any multi-pointed shape that isn't a rectangle). You can create any of these types of hotspots in Dreamweaver, although you create only rectangular hotspots in this project.

The top banner image of each page will be an image map that includes links to the primary pages of the site. The image map hotspots were already created in the old primary pages (index.html and the others), but not in any of the portfolio pages.

1. **With the Moxie site open in the Files panel, open 01.html from the /portfolio/jewelry/ folder and examine the top banner image.**

   The words in the banner image, with the exception of Moxie, will be links to the primary pages.

2. **Click once on the banner image and examine the bottom-left region of the Properties Inspector.**

   The field to the right of the word Map is for the image map name. The three aqua shapes below the field allow you to select the shape of the hotspot before drawing it on the image.

Map Name field
Rectangular Hotspot tool
Pointer tool
Oval Hotspot tool
Polygon Hotspot tool

3. **Type "primary" in the Map Name field.**

4. **Click the Rectangular Hotspot tool.**

5. **Drag to draw a rectangle around the word "home" in the banner image at the top of the document.**

   It's best to start from the top left and drag to the bottom right.

6. Click OK to dismiss the message dialog box.

After drawing a hotspot, you will see a message reminding you to define alt text for the image map. Alt text aids usability for disabled users who use screen-reader software. This is an extremely important issue, which you will learn about extensively in Project 3.

7. From the Properties Inspector, use either the Point to File or Browse for File method to create a link to index.html in the root folder of the site.

Because 01.html is two folders below index.html in the root folder, Dreamweaver inserts the required ../../ to direct the browser up two folders to index.html.

8. Using the Rectangular Hotspot tool, draw rectangles around each phrase in the image. Link each hotspot to the appropriate pages.

Most of these pages are in the root folder; the word "portfolio", however, links to portfolio.html in the /portfolio/ folder.

9. Save your changes to the page.

10. **Click once outside the banner image to disable the Rectangular Hotspot tool, and then click the banner image again to select the entire image.**

    This image map is the same for all pages within the portfolio group of pages. You can copy and paste the banner image to replace the banner images in the other pages; the image map links will be copied to those pages as well.

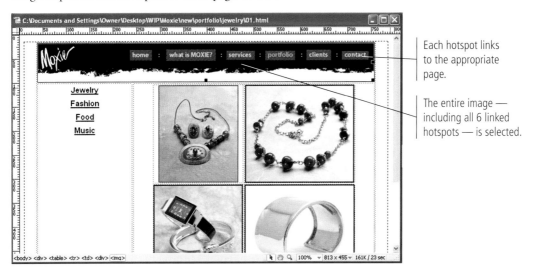

Each hotspot links to the appropriate page.

The entire image — including all 6 linked hotspots — is selected.

11. **Copy the image to the clipboard (Command/Control-C or File>Copy).**

12. **Close 01.html and open 02.html from the /portfolio/jewelry/ folder.**

13. **Click once on the banner image at the top of the page to select it, and then paste the copied image (including the image map links).**

14. **Click OK to dismiss the Image Description dialog box.**

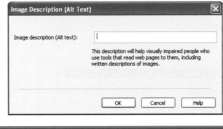

15. **Close 02.html after saving the changes.**

16. **Repeat Steps 12 through 15 for the remaining 18 portfolio pages.**

17. **Continue to the next stage of the project.**

Stage 4 Creating Other Types of Links

There are two other common types of links — external links and email links. An external link is a link to another Web site or a page on another Web site. An email link opens the site user's email application so the user can send an email to the address in the link. Both types of links can be text links, image links, or image map links.

Regardless of the type of link, the URL must begin with the appropriate protocol for that link. An external Web site link must begin with **http://**, followed by the site's domain name and, if necessary, the folder path and file name of the Web page to which you are linking. For example, the faculty page on the UCLA Web site is found at http://www.ucla.edu/audience/faculty.html. Dreamweaver cannot help you create an external link because it's outside the site definition; you must either type it manually or copy it from the original page and paste it into the Link field in Dreamweaver.

An email link must begin with **mailto:** followed by the address (e.g., **mailto:info@sony.com**). Similar to an external Web site link, Dreamweaver cannot provide much help with constructing an email link; you must manually type it or copy and paste it (although there is an email dialog box that you can use to create an email link).

CREATE A LINK TO AN EXTERNAL WEB SITE

The original Moxie Photographic Studios Web site was created for David Monroe by a company called Pro Techniques. For the purposes of marketing their products and services, Web design businesses often insert a link to their own Web sites on the pages of their clients' sites.

1. **With the Moxie site open in the Files panel, open portfolio.html and examine the bottom of the page, where you find the reference to Pro Techniques.**

2. **Drag to select the words "Pro Techniques."**

3. **In the Link field of the Properties Inspector, type "http://www.protechniques.com" and press Return/Enter.**

4. **Save and continue to the next exercise.**

CREATE AN EMAIL LINK

It's a good idea to include an email link to the owner or designer of the Web site on every page. This link makes it easy for a visitor to contact the owner/designer in case the visitor sees something of interest. (This doesn't eliminate the value of a contact page, which should contain the mailing address and other contact information.)

1. **In the open portfolio.html file, select the words "David Monroe" above the Pro Techniques link.**

2. **In the Common Insert bar, click the Email Link button.**

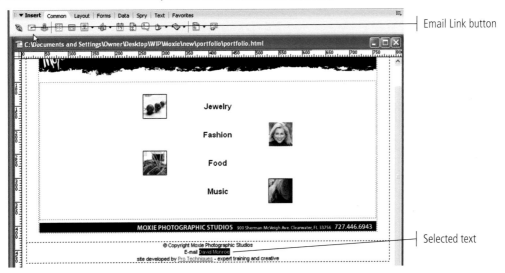

Email Link button

Selected text

3. **In the Email Link dialog box, type "Info@moxiestudios.com" in the E-Mail field.**

   By default, if you select text before clicking the Email Link icon, the Text field is completed for you from the selected text. Also, Dreamweaver remembers the last email address you entered into the E-Mail field; you might not need to complete that field if you insert the same email address multiple times.

Note:

You can access the same Email Link dialog box by choosing Insert>Email Link.

4. **Click OK to create an email link from the text David Monroe.**

5. **Examine the Link field in the Properties Inspector.**

   Dreamweaver automatically inserts the mailto: protocol.

6. **Save the changes to portfolio.html.**

   The rest of the portfolio pages do not yet contain these links. You have to copy this entire block of text to the rest of the pages in the portfolio section of the Web site.

7. **With the insertion point in the block of text containing the two links, click the <div#footer> tag in the Tag Selector.**

This tag identifies the section (or division) of the page named "footer", which is the area that contains the external page link and the email link.

Selected area corresponding to the selected tag

Selected tag

8. **Copy the selected content to the clipboard.**

9. **Close portfolio.html and open 01.html from the /portfolio/jewelry/ folder.**

10. **Click within the same block of text at the bottom of the page, and then click the <div#footer> tag in the Tag Selector.**

11. **With the footer section selected, paste the copied content (with the links) from the clipboard, replacing the original (unlinked) selection.**

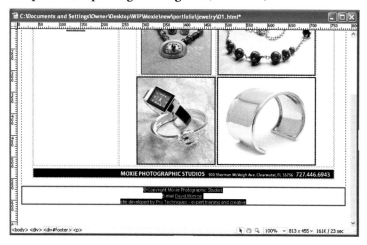

12. **Save the changes and close the 01.html file.**

13. **Repeat Steps 9 through 12 on the remaining 19 pages in the portfolio section of the Web site.**

14. **Continue to the next stage of the project.**

Named Anchors

A **named anchor** is used to mark a specific location on a page so it can be linked to from other locations within the same page or from other pages. Instead of forcing the reader to search for the information by scrolling or other means, you can create a hyperlink that points to the exact location of the information.

Named anchors can be especially useful on long Web pages. For example, on a page that contains many sections, you can include a table of contents at the top with links to each section. To help the reader return to the table of contents from any section of the page, it is considered good practice to include a link to the top of the page at the end of each section (such as "Back to Top").

To insert a named anchor, simply click the Named Anchor button on the Common Insert bar. When linking to the named anchor, type the number sign (#) followed by the name of the anchor in the Link field of the dialog box or Properties Inspector. If you are linking to the anchor from another page, type the name of the file containing the anchor, followed by the number sign and the name of the anchor.

Stage 5 Naming Pages and Titling Documents

The names of folders and files have an impact on search engine optimization (SEO). Creating appropriate folder and file names also improves usability; even though you can use /p/j/3.html for the path to the costume jewelry page, for example, /portfolio/jewelry/costume.html is much easier to understand for human visitors — and will also improve your SERP ranking.

Web servers (specially designed computers used to store and deliver Web pages over the Internet) are configured to deliver a default page if a specific page has not been requested. For example, if you browse to www.nytimes.com, you still see content — the home page — even though you haven't requested a specific page. When a Web server receives a request for a folder but not a specific page, the Web server delivers the default page for that folder; the default page is identified by its file name, which is most often index.html or index.htm.

When creating a link to the default Web page for a particular folder, you can choose not to include the file name, such as http://moxiephotographic.com/portfolio/ versus http://moxiephotographic.com/portfolio/index.html. Both URLs refer to the same page. Remember, however, that you can't test a link to a folder path on your local computer because your computer won't know what page to deliver. If you are running Web server software on your local computer, however, you can complete the test.

Note:

Some pages employ server-side programming languages such as PHP or ASP; their default names are index.php and default.asp, respectively.

Rename Default Pages

In this exercise, you rename the default pages for each folder. Dreamweaver recognizes when a file name has been changed and knows that links to the page must be adjusted.

1. **With the Moxie site open in the Files panel, Control/right-click /portfolio/portfolio.html and choose Edit>Rename.**

2. **Type "index.html", press Return/Enter, and then click Update to update all pages that link to this page.**

@ 3. **Open clients.html from the root folder of the site, click the hotspot for portfolio, and examine the URL in the Properties Inspector.**

The destination page changed from portfolio.html to index.html.

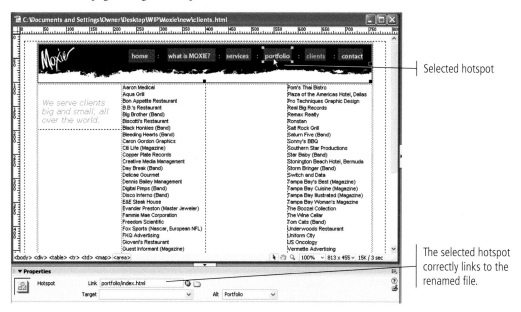

Selected hotspot

The selected hotspot correctly links to the renamed file.

4. **Close clients.html.**

5. **In the Files panel, rename the following files as "index.html". Click Update each time you are prompted.**

> **/portfolio/jewelry/01.html**
>
> **/portfolio/fashion/06.html**
>
> **/portfolio/food/11.html**
>
> **/portfolio/music/16.html**

These are the default pages for each of the portfolio category folders.

6. **Continue to the next exercise.**

Legal Characters in File Names

We could talk for hours about what characters are suitable (or "legal") for naming your Web pages. Suffice it to say that the safest way to name your pages is to limit the use of the available characters on your keyboard to just a few that are sure to work perfectly. Basically, you should limit the characters you use to:

- a through z (use only lowercase letters)
- 0 through 9
- Hyphen (-) character
- Underscore (as in great_site.com)

Consider everything else to be "illegal," including:

- Spaces — no Web site name can use a space
- Brackets of all kinds, including ( ), [ ], { }, and < >
- Symbols, including #, @, %, ~, |, *, and &
- Quotation marks, both double (" ") and single (' ')
- Slashes, both back slashes (\) and forward slashes (/)
- Punctuation marks, including commas, question marks, and exclamation marks
- Uppercase characters

In short, limiting the characters you use to lowercase alphanumeric characters plus the underscore and hyphen will save you a great deal of time, effort, and frustration later.

RENAME PORTFOLIO PAGES FOR IMPROVED USABILITY

The rest of the file names for the pages in the portfolio folders are essentially nonsense; numbers mean nothing and do not represent the content of the pages. The file names of these pages should be changed so the content or purpose of the page is clear.

When you want to use two or more words in a file name, you should know that the space character is illegal in UNIX and Linux file and folder names. Instead, you can use either the hyphen or underscore character to represent a space.

In some cases, people use **camelcase** (uppercase letters at the beginning of words within a file name, such as redHotChiliPeppers.html) file names instead of using hyphen or underscore characters to separate words. The problem with mixing the lettercase is that some Web server software is case-sensitive and some is not. Most Windows-based Web server software is not case-sensitive; but UNIX- and Linux-based Web server software is case-sensitive.

1. **With the Moxie site open in the Files panel, change the following file names in the /portfolio/jewelry/ folder. Click Update when prompted.**

Current name	New name
02.html	southwestern.html
03.html	costume.html
04.html	watches.html
05.html	gold-bracelet.html

2. **In the /portfolio/fashion/ folder, change the following file names (click Update when prompted).**

Current name	New name
07.html	fall.html
08.html	leisure.html
09.html	business.html
10.html	sports.html

3. **In the /portfolio/food/ folder, change the following file names (click Update when prompted).**

Current name	New name
12.html	breakfast.html
13.html	restaurant.html
14.html	fruits-vegetables.html
15.html	seafood.html

4. **In the /portfolio/music/ folder, change the following file names (click Update when prompted).**

Current name	New name
17.html	the-black-honkies.html
18.html	jaden.html
19.html	saturn-5.html
20.html	trumaine.html

5. **Continue to the next exercise.**

CREATE DOCUMENT TITLES FOR THE PORTFOLIO PAGES

When creating new pages for a site, applying appropriate document titles is another critical concern. The document title is important for both SEO and site visitors. While the document title does not appear within the Web page, it does appear in the title bar of the browser, as the name of the page in the Bookmarks or Favorites list, and as the page name in search-engine results pages.

The generally recommended format for a document title is to list the categories in which the page is found, similar to the folder path in which the page is located, ending with the Web site name. You should separate the components of the title with a colon (:) or pipe (|) character. For example, for the Jaden page of the /portfolio/music/ folder, the title could be Jaden : Music : Portfolio : Moxie Photographic Studios.

It might be tempting to list the Web site name first; but if a page title is long, the specific details of the page (such as Jaden in the example above) could be cut off. Also, in a SERP, it's easier to see if your search has provided suitable results if the specific information about the page is listed first. The following images show results from two Google searches. The blue underlined links (top lines) are the document titles — suggesting that the document titles are important to visitors looking for information using search engines.

In this exercise, you add document titles to all of the new pages. Doing so will increase the pages' rankings in search engines and improve usability for visitors who find the pages in search engines and in bookmarks. You also learn to use the Find and Replace function, which can greatly reduce the amount of effort required to create all of the document titles.

Note:

Unlike file names, document titles can use mixed lettercase and include spaces and other characters.

1. **With the Moxie site open in the Files panel, open index.html from the /portfolio/ folder**

2. **Make sure the Document toolbar is showing (View>Toolbars>Document) and examine the Document Title field above the design window.**

   When you create a new page in Dreamweaver, the default title is "Untitled Document".

3. **Close index.html.**

4. **With no documents open, choose Edit>Find and Replace.**

   Don't worry if your settings are different than what you see in our screen shot. You configure them in the next step.

5. **Change the Find In field to Folder, click the Browse button, and select the /portfolio/ folder.**

   All files within and below the /portfolio/ folder will be searched.

6. **Change the Search field to Source Code (from the pop-up menu).**

   The document title does not appear within the body of the page; so when you use Find and Replace, you must apply the change to the source code rather than the document text.

7. **In the Find field, type "Untitled Document".**

8. **In the Replace field, type "Portfolio : Moxie Photographic Studios".**

   All pages in the portfolio folder will include this block of text at the end of the document title. As more detail about the pages becomes available, it will be added to the left of the document title.

9. **Click Replace All.**

10. **When prompted to confirm whether you want to proceed with this function, click Yes.**

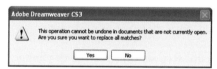

Like most applications, Dreamweaver has an Undo function that allows you to undo the most recently completed actions; however, this function only works if the document is open. Since you are using the Find and Replace function on the entire folder and not an open page, you are making changes in closed documents — which means you cannot use the Undo command.

After completing the Find and Replace function, Dreamweaver displays the results in the Results panel.

11. **Open index.html from the /portfolio/ folder and examine the Document Title field again.**

    As a result of the Find and Replace function, the document title has been changed. (The same change has been made in all of the portfolio pages.)

12. **Close index.html.**

13. **Open the Find and Replace dialog box again. Repeat this process to change the document title of all files in the portfolio/jewelry/ folder:**

    - **Set the Find In field to Folder and choose the portfolio/jewelry/ folder as the target.**

    - **Set the Search field to Source Code.**

    - **Change the Find field to "Portfolio :"**

    - **Change the Replace field to "Jewelry : Portfolio :".**

    - **Click Replace All. When prompted to confirm your action, click Yes.**

14. **Open the Find and Replace dialog box again. Repeat this process to change the document title of all files in the portfolio/fashion/ folder:**

    - **Set the Find In field to Folder and choose the portfolio/fashion/ folder as the target.**

    - **Set the Search field to Source Code.**

    - **Change the Find field to "Portfolio :"**

    - **Change the Replace field to "Fashion : Portfolio :".**

    - **Click Replace All. When prompted to confirm your action, click Yes.**

15. **Open the Find and Replace dialog box again. Repeat this process to change the document title of all files in the portfolio/food/ folder:**

   • **Set the Find In field to Folder and choose the portfolio/food/ folder as the target.**

   • **Set the Search field to Source Code.**

   • **Change the Find field to "Portfolio :"**

   • **Change the Replace field to "Food : Portfolio :".**

   • **Click Replace All. When prompted to confirm your action, click Yes.**

16. **Open the Find and Replace dialog box again. Repeat this process to change the document title of all files in the portfolio/music/ folder:**

   • **Set the Find In field to Folder and choose the portfolio/music/ folder as the target.**

   • **Set the Search field to Source Code.**

   • **Change the Find field to "Portfolio :"**

   • **Change the Replace field to "Music : Portfolio :".**

   • **Click Replace All. When prompted to confirm your action, click Yes.**

17. **Choose Window>Results to close the Results panel.**

18. **Continue to the next exercise.**

ADD SPECIFIC PAGE INFORMATION IN THE DOCUMENT TITLE

The current document titles contain only generic information that represents the broad portfolio categories. In this exercise, you add the most specific information in the document title for each page.

1. **With the Moxie site open in the Files panel, open southwestern.html from the /portfolio/jewelry/ folder.**

2. **In the Document Title field, click to place the insertion point to the left of the word Jewelry and type "Southwestern : ".**

3. **Save the changes to southwestern.html and close the file.**

4. **One by one, open the rest of the pages in the portfolio category folders and add the same text you used in the file name to the beginning (left) of the document title ("Saturn 5" and "Fruits and Vegetables", for example). Save and close each file after changing the document title.**

   Unlike file names, document titles can have spaces, so you can replace hyphens or underscores with spaces between words.

5. **Continue to the next exercise.**

 ## HIDE FILES FROM THE WEB SERVER

For all intents and purposes, the new portfolio pages are ready to upload to the Web server. Because there are more new files than there were old files, it makes the most sense to reload the complete site rather than select only the new files to upload to the Web server. However, not all of the new files are meant to be uploaded to the Web server — specifically, the Word document and Photoshop file in the /resources/ folder. (You should store them locally as source files or documentation for the work you completed.)

Dreamweaver provides a very useful function — called **cloaking** — that allows you to prevent certain files from uploading. There are two methods for cloaking files: by file extension and by folder. If you cloak by file extension, such as .psd (a Photoshop file), any .psd files in the site's folder will be cloaked. The disadvantage of cloaking by file extension is that if you want to upload some .psd files but not others, you can't uncloak some files while leaving other files cloaked. However, if you create a folder for files that you don't want uploaded, you can cloak the entire folder, no matter what type of files exist within that folder (including HTML files).

Cloaking a folder allows you to keep preliminary, source, draft, and other documents and files within the site, but prevent them from uploading to the Web server. By default, Dreamweaver has the cloaking function enabled; all you need to do is identify the folder you want to cloak.

1. **With the Moxie site open in the Files panel, collapse all open folders and expand only the resources folder.**

2. **Control/right-click the resources folder and choose Cloaking>Cloak.**

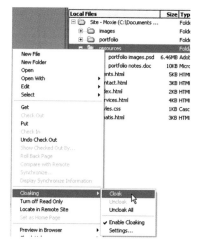

Notice the red slash through the resources folder icon and the icons for the two files in the resources folder. The red slash refers to the cloaking function only; it does not prevent you from working with the files, adding more files, or deleting any of the existing files.

Summary

In this project, you learned that creating a Web site requires a lot of detailed, upfront planning. You found that without proper planning, adding or renaming a file can cause serious problems that ripple throughout a site. You also learned the value of structuring your folders and applying appropriate file names and document titles. You discovered how to apply links within your pages, as well as to external pages and sites. You also learned about image maps and hotspots, and how they can be used as navigational aides within your Web sites.

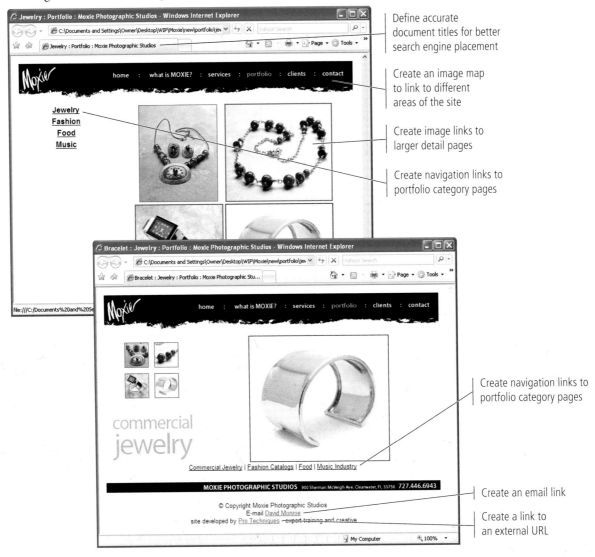

Define accurate document titles for better search engine placement

Create an image map to link to different areas of the site

Create image links to larger detail pages

Create navigation links to portfolio category pages

Create navigation links to portfolio category pages

Create an email link

Create a link to an external URL

Portfolio Builder Project 1

Romana Place Town Homes is adding a photo tour to its Web site. The owner is fairly competent at building Web pages, but is having trouble finalizing the new site. Your job is to finish what he started in a professional, organized manner.

To complete this project, you should:

❏ Import the site files (from the RF_Builders>Rentals folder) into Dreamweaver.

❏ Analyze the content of the different pages. Create a flowchart to map the direction of links from one page to another in the site.

❏ Organize the site folder into a clear, understandable structure.

❏ Create the links from one page to another throughout the entire site.

"I'm not really sure what happened, but when I started working with the files I noticed that none of the links exist anymore. I might have worked from an earlier version of the site files, but I'm not sure. Can you fix this for me? Other than the navigation links in the middle of the pages, there are a number of other places where links are necessary:

"On the index.html page, the words 'take a photo tour' should link to the tour.html page.

"On the individual tour pages, the 'Back to View Homes' image should link back to the main tour.html page.

"On the tour.html page, the thumbnail images should each link to the appropriate tour page (those are numbered 01-10.html).

"At the bottom of the tour.html page, the words 'Click here to print information flyer' should link to the PDF file in the site folder.

"On the contact.html and amenities.html pages, the words 'click here' (near the bottom of the page) should be an email link to pattic@pc-rentals.com."

"At the bottom of every page, the 'Website design by...' address should be a link to that address, which should open in a new browser window."

Digital Book Chapter

Your client, Against The Clock Inc., publishes textbooks for the graphic communications education market. The owner wants to provide a chapter excerpt on their corporate Web site, which will be offered free of charge so anyone can download and read it. ATC believes this offering will lead to increased sales of the full line of ATC titles. Your task is to structure the content appropriately, using HTML code.

This project incorporates the following skills:

❏ Incorporating text from external sources

❏ Working in both Design view and Code view to add appropriate HTML tags

❏ Organizing content with appropriate heading tags

❏ Properly formatting block quotes and citations

❏ Adding special characters that work in HTML code

❏ Creating lists and tables within text-based content

❏ Attaching a CSS file to the new pages

The Project Meeting

Client Comments

We publish a series of books, designed as companion titles to our application-specific training books (which is why it's called *The Companion Series*). The companions cover general topics that are important to graphic design students — including color, typography, and Web design concepts — but don't quite fit into an application-specific book.

Whenever we talk to people about these books, they always ask, "Why haven't I heard about these before?" — but the books have been available for several years. We're hoping the sample chapter will help get the word out about these books and ultimately improve sales.

We want to be sure of two things: First, this page needs to be instantly recognizable as part of our existing Web site, with the same layout and formatting. Second, the page must be searchable text.

Art Director Comments

The publisher emailed the text she wants to offer on the site. When you have this much text on a Web page — which isn't uncommon — it's very important that you format it with the proper structural tags. If you use Heading 2 because you think Heading 1 is too big, for example, you're causing problems for search engines and anyone with screen-reader software.

The client already has a corporate Web site. To create the new pages, you can use the existing template, as well as the CSS file that defines the appearance of the various structural elements. Once you apply the correct structural tags to the text in the new pages, you can attach the existing CSS file. This will ensure that the existing format maps to the structural tags in your new pages.

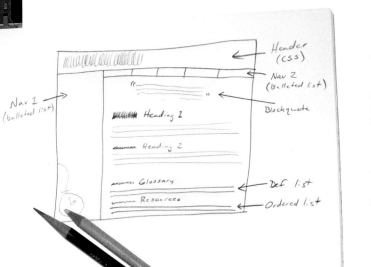

Project Objectives

To complete this project, you will:

- ❏ Paste text content from a text-only email
- ❏ Apply the appropriate heading and paragraph tags throughout the text
- ❏ Create block quotes and define quote citations
- ❏ Mark up abbreviations and acronyms for improved usability and accessibility
- ❏ Use the correct HTML tags to show emphasis
- ❏ Add special HTML characters throughout the text
- ❏ Create ordered, unordered, and definition lists
- ❏ Use a table to present ordered content
- ❏ Attach an existing CSS file to new pages

Stage 1 Preparing the Workspace

After working on several projects, the list of defined sites may have become quite long and unwieldy. To reduce the potential for confusion, it's a good idea to remove the defined sites of completed projects, leaving only the defined sites of current projects. Remember, however, that you should export site definitions before you remove them from the list. This stores the site definition settings in a file, so you can import the file and restore the settings later if necessary.

EXPORT AND REMOVE SITE DEFINITIONS

In the previous project, you exported and removed the site definition for the Moxie Old site, so you should be familiar with this process. It's a good idea to continue exporting and removing site definitions as you complete the projects in this book, as well as in on-the-job projects.

1. **With the Moxie site from Project 1 open in the Files panel, choose Manage Sites from the bottom of the Directory menu in the Files panel.**

2. **In the Manage Sites dialog box, choose the Moxie site name, and then click the Export button.**

3. **Navigate to WIP>Moxie>new and click Save.**

   The Export Site dialog box defaults to the current site's root folder. You can restore the site settings by importing the site definition file from this location.

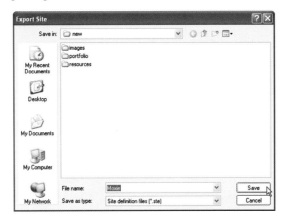

4. **In the Manage Sites dialog box, make sure Moxie is selected in the list and click Remove.**

5. **Click Yes to confirm the removal of the Moxie site definition.**

   Remember, you are not deleting the files from the site; you are simply removing the site definition from Dreamweaver.

6. **At the bottom of the Manage Sites dialog box, click Done.**

   You will repeat this task at the beginning of each project. Refer to this exercise if you need help exporting and removing a site definition.

 ## DEFINE THE ATC SITE

The procedure for defining the site is essentially the same for the ATC site as it was for the Moxie site in the previous project. Until you require **FTP** (file transfer protocol, a means of transferring files from your computer to a remote computer) or use a Web programming language such as **ASP** (Microsoft Active Server Pages), **PHP** (Pre-Hypertext Processor, a popular open-source language), or **ColdFusion** (a proprietary Web programming language from Adobe), the site definitions will be similar to what you've already seen.

1. **Copy the ATC folder from the WIP folder on the resource CD to your WIP folder where you are saving your work.**

2. **Copy the contents of the RF_Dreamweaver>ATC folder to your WIP>ATC folder.**

   As you complete the exercises in this project, you have to work with the files in your WIP folder.

3. **From the Files panel, choose Manage Sites, either by clicking the link to the right of the Directory menu, or by choosing the option at the bottom of the Directory menu.**

4. **In the Manage Sites dialog box, click the New button and choose Site from the pop-up list.**

5. **In the resulting Site Definition dialog box, type "ATC" in the Site Name field.**

   Make sure you are working with the Site Definition dialog box in Advanced mode.

6. **Click the folder icon to the right of the Local Root Folder field, navigate to your WIP>ATC folder, and click Choose/Select.**

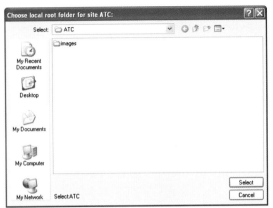

7. **Click OK to accept the Site Definition settings.**

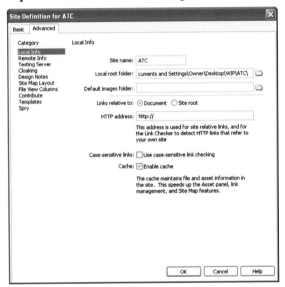

8. **In the Manage Sites dialog box, make sure the ATC site appears in the list of sites, and then click Done.**

9. **Continue to the next exercise.**

CREATE A NEW XHTML DOCUMENT

The content for the first excerpt page was sent to you in an email. The email message contains most of the content for the page, but it does not include the common navigation bar links, the common page header, or the common page footer. Although these common items already exist in other Web pages from the ATC site, you will create these items from scratch — which will give you a clear understanding of how to build these types of items.

1. **With the ATC site open in the Files panel, choose File>New.**

2. **In the New Document dialog box, choose Blank Page in the left pane. Choose HTML in the Page Type list, and choose <None> in the Layout list.**

   You can use this dialog box to create new files based on existing templates, or use the <None> option to create a new blank page.

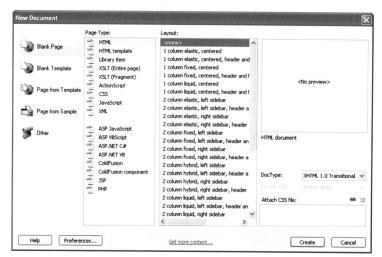

> *Note:*
>
> *As shown in the DocType menu, you're actually creating an XHTML document rather than an HTML document. XHTML is the default page format in Dreamweaver CS3, unlike previous Dreamweaver versions that defaulted to HTML 4.01.*

3. **Click Create to create the new blank file.**

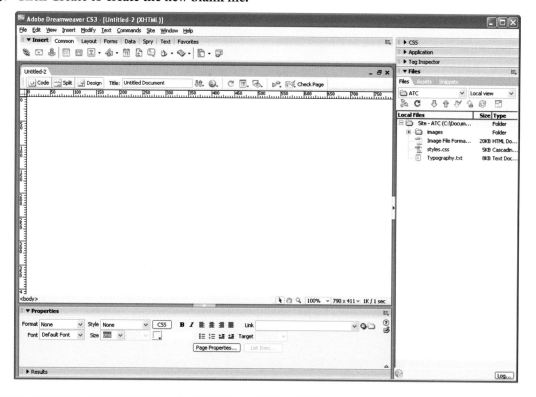

4. Switch to Split view by clicking the Split button in the Document toolbar.

If you don't see the View buttons, choose View>Toolbars>Document.

Even though the document appears to be blank in Design view, it contains some XHTML code in the background, which you can see in Code view.

5. Examine the code in the document window.

The **DTD** (Document Type Definition) tells the browser what version of HTML or XHTML is being used in the document. Some browsers might handle the document differently, depending on which version of (X)HTML is specified by the DTD.

Information in the head section of the HTML is not visible in the Web page (except for the content between the opening and closing <title> tags, which appears in the title bar of a browser, as the title of a bookmark, and as the text in search engine results). Content within the <head> element is beneficial to the document, but not visible to the user.

Web page content is created within the body section, between the opening and closing <html> and <body> tags.

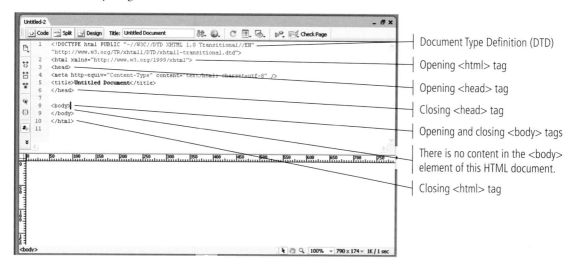

Document Type Definition (DTD)

Opening <html> tag

Opening <head> tag

Closing <head> tag

Opening and closing <body> tags

There is no content in the <body> element of this HTML document.

Closing <html> tag

DREAMWEAVER FOUNDATIONS

(X)HTML Versions

HTML was created in the early 1990s by Sir Tim Berners-Lee as a coding language used to apply structure (paragraphs, headings, and lists) to online documents. HTML has since evolved to include more structures, including tables and definition lists.

By 1996, the modern methods of document markup had outgrown the inflexible HTML, so the extensibility concept from **XML** (eXtensible Markup Language, a language similar to HTML but primarily used for data instead of documents) was added to HTML 4.01, making it much better suited to the evolving needs of Web designers.

Extensibility means that the language can incorporate structures that don't exist in HTML. For example, HTML supports six heading levels, from 1 to 6; the extensibility principle in XHTML allows designers to create heading level 7 if necessary.

Unless otherwise specified, whenever we refer to "HTML" in this book, we are actually referring to both XHTML and HTML.

6. **Select the words "Untitled Document" between the opening and closing \<title\> tags, press Delete, and type "Special Characters in Typography | Tutorials | Against The Clock".**

The pipe character (|) is created by pressing the Shift and backslash (\ ) keys.

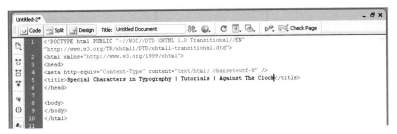

7. **Choose File>Save and save this blank document as an HTML file named "typography.html" in your WIP>ATC folder (the root of your site).**

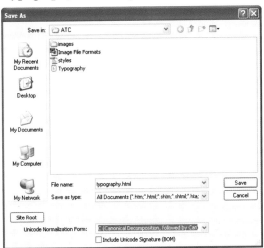

8. **Continue to the next exercise.**

PASTE CONTENT IN CODE VIEW

HTML is a coding language of structure; without HTML, the content between the opening and closing \<body\> tags would be completely unstructured. Web browsers depend on the structural markup of HTML to properly display a Web page so headings stand out from regular text and paragraphs are separated from one another. Without structure, all of the text would appear as a single, large block of text.

Content is often plain text without structural markup (paragraph returns do not quality as structure). Without structural markup, readers can assume that a short block of text is a heading and a long block is a paragraph. Browsers, however, can't make assumptions; they require structure so they know how to display content.

Most modern email applications allow you to change text styling such as typeface, color, and font size; some support structures such as headings. In most situations, however, you must add the structural markup to the text from within Dreamweaver.

1. **With typography.html open (from the ATC site in your WIP>ATC folder) in Split view, click to place the insertion point to the right of the opening \<body\> tag.**

If typography.html is not open in Dreamweaver, double-click that file in the Files panel to open the document.

2. Press Return/Enter once to create a new line between the opening and closing <body> tags.

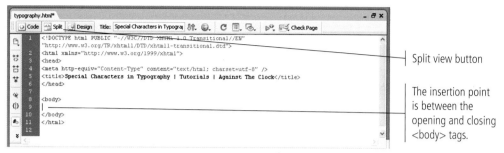

Split view button

The insertion point is between the opening and closing <body> tags.

3. Double-click Typography.txt in the Files panel to open that file.

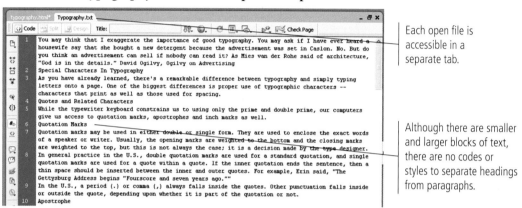

Each open file is accessible in a separate tab.

Although there are smaller and larger blocks of text, there are no codes or styles to separate headings from paragraphs.

Element Names, Tags, and Attributes

The **element name** is the text that identifies the tag, such as meta, title, head, or body.

A **tag** consists of the element name surrounded by angle brackets, such as <html>, <head>, or <body>.

An **element** is the tag plus its containing content, such as the title element <title>Untitled Document</title>.

Container tags consist of an opening tag (<title>) and a closing tag (</title>). The closing tag is the same as the opening tag, with the addition of the initial forward slash. For example:

<title>"Weather Forecast"</title>.

Empty tags (<meta />) do not have a separate closing tag. In an empty tag, the closing forward slash appears with the closing angle bracket of the tag. For example:

<img src="sun.gif" alt="sunny day" />.

Attributes add properties to HTML elements. For example, the cite attribute of the <blockquote> tag allows you to identify the URL of a quotation. Attributes appear in the opening tag only, and consist of the attribute name and the attribute value (for example, attribute="attribute value").

When marking up a short quotation, you would type:

<q cite="http://www.useit.com/alertbox/9710a.html">People rarely read Web pages word by word.</q>

In this example, the attribute name is cite and the attribute value is http://www.useit.com/alertbox/9710a.html.

Most attributes are optional, such as the cite attribute of the <blockquote> tag. Some attributes are required, such as the alt attribute of the <img> tag (which describes an image for visitors who can't see the images). Some attributes are unique to certain elements, such as the src attribute of the <img> element (which identifies the location of the image).

In HTML, some attributes do not require an attribute value, such as the checked attribute that allows you to pre-select a check box option. In XHTML, however, each attribute must have an attribute value (e.g., checked="checked").

Finally, attribute values in XHTML must be placed with quotes (e.g., width="130"); HTML allowed width=130.

DREAMWEAVER FOUNDATIONS

4. **Choose Edit>Select All, and then copy the selected content to the clipboard (Edit>Copy, or Command/Control-C).**

5. **Close Typography.txt.**

Note:

*Press Command/
Control-A to select all
content in the open file or
document.*

6. **In typography.html, place the insertion point in the empty line between the opening and closing <body> tags and paste the copied text.**

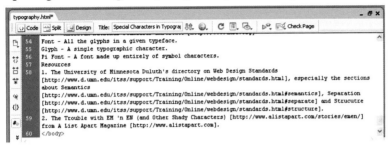

7. **Click Refresh in the Properties Inspector.**

When working in Split view, you have to click the Refresh button before changes in the Code pane are reflected in the Design pane.

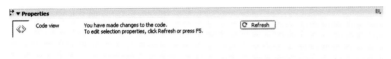

8. **Compare the appearance of the pasted text in the Design and Code panes.**

The Design view of the text content is perhaps more difficult to interpret than either the original text file or the Code view. Although Dreamweaver is not a true Web browser, it displays a Web page according to its structural markup. Without markup, there is no structure to the content of the page.

Note:

*Web browsers and
Dreamweaver ignore
extra spaces between
words and paragraph
returns between lines of
text. Properly displaying
Web page text requires
structural markup.*

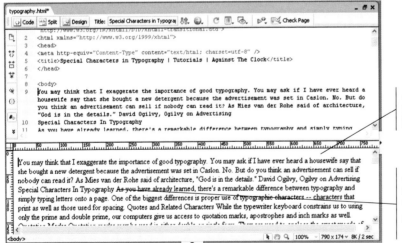

After refreshing, the pasted text appears in the Design pane.

Although lines are separated in the Code pane, there is not yet any code to separate paragraphs in the Design view.

9. **Choose File>Save to save the changes to the document.**

10. **Continue to the next stage of the project.**

Stage 2 Working with Special Markup

Many people have difficulty structuring documents — including word-processing files. Let's say, for example, that a user wants to create a heading. The user enters text, and then applies bold styling, increases the font size, a changes the text color. While this **local formatting** makes the text appear to be a heading, it is actually a styled paragraph. A document in digital form — whether a Web page, a **PDF** (portable document format) file, or a word-processing document — should make use of available document structures to enhance the document's usability. This is where HTML comes in.

Properly structured HTML documents provide a wide range of benefits to users: they are more accessible, they load quickly in a browser, they reduce bandwidth costs for high-traffic Web sites, they achieve high search engine rankings, and they are easy to style. As a Web designer, you should take full advantage of these benefits by converting the unstructured or poorly structured documents you receive from clients into properly structured HTML documents.

 FORMAT LINES OF TEXT AS PARAGRAPHS

Not all lines in the text document are paragraphs; some lines of text are headings and some are list items. Marking each line of text as a paragraph provides a starting point that you can modify later. To mark up a block of text as a paragraph, you simply insert the opening paragraph tag (<p>) at the beginning of the paragraph and the closing paragraph tag (</p>) at the end of the paragraph.

1. **With typography.html open (from your ATC site), switch to Code view and place the insertion point to the left of the word "You" on the line below the opening <body> tag.**

2. **Type an opening angle bracket "<" (Shift-Comma).**

   As you type the code in Code view, Dreamweaver provides code hints (a list of HTML tags) to assist you. The <p> tag is very short and requires little assistance; but for longer tags, Dreamweaver's code hints are very useful.

You are typing here, as shown by the location of the code hint list.

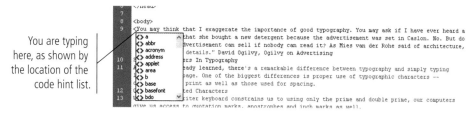

Structure is Visual Formatting Plus a Whole Lot More

When viewing an unstructured text-based document in a word-processing program such as Microsoft Word, sighted users assume that short blocks of text are headings and larger blocks of text are paragraphs. Even though the information is not formatted correctly, it is still intelligible. When the same unstructured text is viewed in a Web browser, however, the text loses all sense of perceived structure and appears as a single, unintelligible block of text.

Although many structures are identified by specific visual appearances (such as the text size of a Level 1 heading), do not use appearance as your guide when selecting a format. Use the structural elements as they were intended — that includes leaving their visual appearances unchanged (i.e., don't make a paragraph look like a heading) and using tags appropriately (i.e., use the <q> tag, even though you prefer the appearance of the <blockquote> tag).

Document structure is not for sighted users only. Screen-reader software (used by the visually impaired to "read" the content on a Web page) relies on the structure of a document to properly interpret the content. In short, proper structural markup within a document enables both sighted and screen-reader users to correctly interpret the content of a Web page.

3. Type the letter "p".

The code hints list scrolls to the first HTML tag beginning with the letter "p."

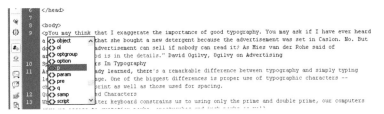

4. Type the closing angle bracket ">" (Shift-Period) to close the opening paragraph tag.

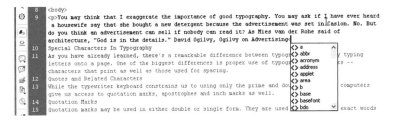

5. Press the End key to move the insertion point to the end of the current line and type "<".

Again, the code hints list of HTML tags appears.

Controlling Code Hints

Code hints display by default when you type code in Dreamweaver. You can display and refresh code hints by choosing Show Code Hints and Refresh Code Hints (respectively) in the Edit Menu. The Code Hint Tools submenu contains tools that automatically insert the code for colors, URLs, and font combinations.

You can also use the Code Hints pane of the Preferences dialog box to control which code hints display and how.

The **Close Tags** options can be used to close tags automatically.

- If you select **After Typing** "</", the nearest open tag closes when you type the forward slash after the opening carat. This option is selected by default.

- If you select **After Typing the Open Tag's** ">", Dreamweaver automatically closes a tag as soon as it opens; you can then enter the tag content between the opening and closing tags.

- You can select **Never** if you do not want tags to close automatically.

You can disable code hints by unchecking the **Enable Code Hints** box. The **Delay** bar determines how soon code hints display when you open a tag. The **Menus** options list code categories for which hints can display. All options are selected by default.

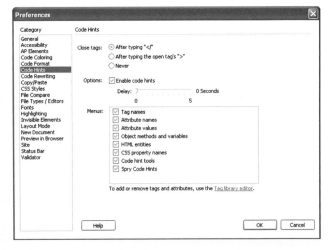

DREAMWEAVER FOUNDATIONS

---

6. **Type the forward slash "/".**

   All HTML container tags have virtually identical opening and closing tags. In opening tags, the HTML element name is specified between opening and closing angle brackets. In closing tags, the forward slash precedes the element name (in this case, the "p").

   This step shows you another of Dreamweaver's code assistance functions, which is to automatically close the nearest unclosed tag when "</" is typed.

   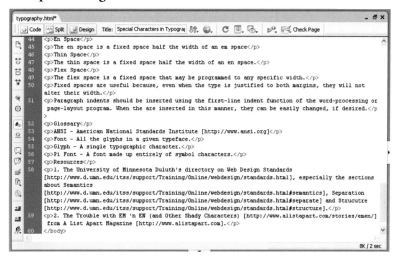

7. **Press the Right Arrow key to move the insertion point to the beginning of the next line.**

8. **Repeat Steps 2 through 7 for each line in the document.**

   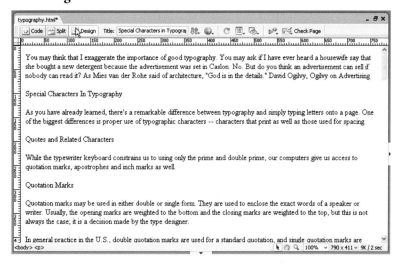

9. **Switch to Design view.**

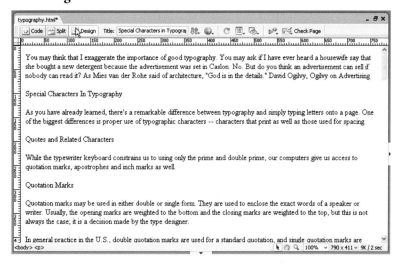

Note:

Now that the HTML document has structural tags (even if they are all paragraph tags), the text is much easier to read in Design view.

10. **Switch to Split view, and then move the insertion point to the beginning of the second body paragraph.**

11. **Press Delete/Backspace to bring the second paragraph up to the end of the first paragraph, then click the Refresh button in the Properties Inspector.**

Despite the fact that the first and second paragraphs are on the same line in the code, the two paragraphs remain separate in Design view (and would appear the same way in a Web browser). Again, this supports the concept that browsers display Web pages according to their structural markup — in other words, the code controls the appearance of content when viewed in Design view or a browser window.

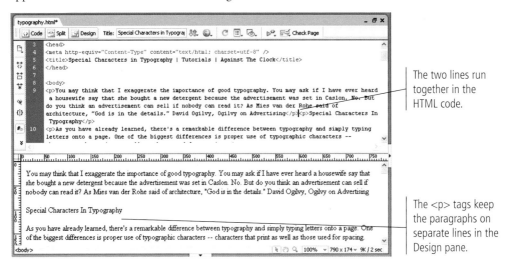

The two lines run together in the HTML code.

The <p> tags keep the paragraphs on separate lines in the Design pane.

12. **Choose Edit>Undo to return the second paragraph to its own line in the Code pane.**

13. **Save the file and continue to the next exercise.**

 ## CREATE A HEADING IN CODE VIEW

Headings speed up the skimming process and help readers find the information they need. For visual users, a heading is effective as long it looks like a heading; it doesn't matter if it's a properly structured heading or a short paragraph styled to look like a heading.

This is not the case for visually impaired users who rely on screen-reading software to skim Web pages. Screen-reading software and some browsers have keystroke combinations that allow users to skip forward and backward through the headings — effectively skimming the Web page. For these reasons, it is important to use proper headings rather than styled paragraphs.

There are six heading levels, <h1>, <h2>, <h3>, and so on to <h6>. Heading level 1 is the largest and most important; it should be used only once per page to describe the purpose or title of the Web page. Because every Web page has a purpose, every page should have a level 1 heading. The rest of the headings can be used multiple times, but they should be used in a branch-like pattern or hierarchy.

Many new Web designers complain that heading level 1 appears too large, so they apply heading level 2 or 3 instead. This is a structural mistake. In a later project, you learn to use Cascading Style Sheets (CSS) to apply style and appearance to Web pages; using CSS, you can style heading level 1 text to be smaller, balancing the need for proper structure with concerns about the appearance of the heading level 1 text.

1. With **typography.html** (from your ATC site) open in Split view, move the insertion point to the second paragraph (line 10) in the Code pane.

2. Delete the **<p>** tag from the beginning of the line and the **</p>** tag from the end of the line.

Note:

You cannot wrap the paragraph tags with heading tags; instead, you have to replace the <p> and </p> tags with the appropriate heading tags.

3. Move the insertion point to the beginning of the line, type "**<h**", press Return/Enter to accept "**h1**" and type "**>**".

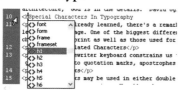

4. Move the insertion point to the end of the line and type "**</**" (Dreamweaver will complete the closing tag for you).

5. Click Refresh in the Properties Inspector.

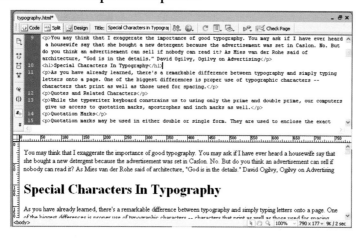

6. Save the changes to **typography.html** and continue to the next exercise.

Headings and Search Engines

When reviewing the content of a page and its relevance to a particular topic, search engine software uses headings and heading levels (among other criteria) to make evaluations.

For example, if two pages have a similar discussion about Goldendoodle dogs, and one page formats "Goldendoodle" using heading level 1, and the other page formats "Goldendoodle" as a simple paragraph but styles it to appear the same as heading level 1, the search engine will rank the heading 1 page higher than the "faked" heading 1 page. To ensure that visitors can find your content, always use proper headings. This requires very little effort, and it significantly improves the rankings of your pages.

Of course, you shouldn't overuse headings either. We have seen Web pages in which all of the content was marked as heading level 1, then styled differently using CSS. This is one of many methods that can be used to fool a search engine into ranking the page higher than others with similar content. This technique is known as "spamdexing" — it generally results in the page being banned from search engines.

Using proper heading markup helps all visitors to your site, ignoring the benefits of proper headings reduces page ranking, and abusing markup can get the page banned. What better reasons are there for learning about proper markup and applying it correctly?

FORMAT HEADING LEVELS IN THE PROPERTIES INSPECTOR

The page you're building discusses a number of special characters in typography and groups the characters into related groups and subgroups. A heading precedes each of these discussions. Your task is to determine what heading level is appropriate for each discussion/section. If the text (or copy) was written by a qualified copywriter, you will probably see a pattern in the structured text that you receive; this will allow you to quickly determine the appropriate heading level. If you receive poorly structured copy, you might need to contact the author or make the assessments yourself.

1. **With typography.html open in Design view, examine the short paragraphs following the heading level 1 text.**

   The text "Quotes and Related Characters" appears to be a heading. Because the only heading level before it is level 1, this heading should be formatted as heading level 2.

   The next short paragraphs below, "Quotation Marks," "Apostrophe," and "Inch and Foot Marks" describe different forms of quote characters. These are subordinate headings to the

Understanding the Code View Formatting

Code can be difficult to read because it interferes with, and is interrupted by, the content of the page. To overcome this problem, you can format the code using the Code Coloring and Code Format panes of the Preferences dialog box. You can assign different colors to each part or type of code, as well as indent the text so that each block of code appears distinct.

The Code View Options

The Code View options, which can be toggled on or off in the View menu, determine how code displays.

- **Word Wrap** ensures that the code does not extend beyond the available width of the window. This option only affects the appearance of code in the Code pane; it does not insert actual line breaks in the code or content (unlike the Automatic Wrapping After Column option of the Code Format pane).

- **Line Numbers** displays line numbers in a column to the left of the page code.

- **Hidden Characters** displays characters such as line-break markers, which would not otherwise display.

- **Highlight Invalid Code** displays incorrect code (such as a tag that has not been closed) in yellow.

- **Syntax Coloring** displays the code in defined colors.

- **Auto Indent** indents every new line of code to the same position as the previous line. A new line is inserted each time you press Return/Enter.

The Code Coloring Pane

By default, HTML tags appear in blue. To change the color of all or some of these tags, as well as any other part of the code, you can use the options in the Code Coloring pane of the Preferences dialog box.

The **Document Type** box lists the various types of code that Dreamweaver supports. (The code type used in your document is selected by default in the list.) When you click the Edit Coloring Scheme button, a secondary dialog box displays a list of all the possible parts of the code. When you select a part, its text and background colors display to the right of the list, and a preview is available at the bottom. Buttons are available under the text and background color boxes to make the code bold, italic, and/or underlined.

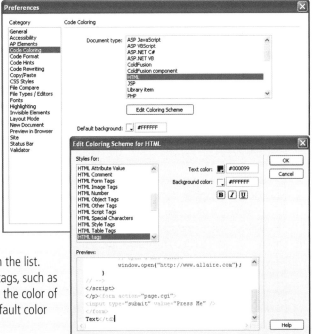

You can set colors for all tags by selecting HTML Tags from the list. You can also set different colors for specific categories of tags, such as HTML Table Tags or HTML Image Tags. If you don't change the color of a specific category of tag, those tags will appear in the default color assigned to HTML tags.

"Quotes and Related Characters" heading and should be formatted as heading level 3.

"Hyphens and Dashes" is not related to "Quotes and Related Characters"; rather, it is a new level 2 heading.

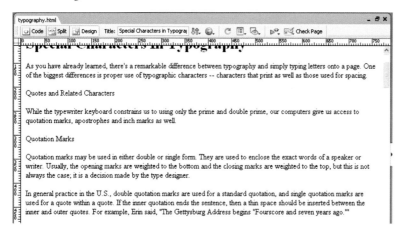

DREAMWEAVER FOUNDATIONS

The Code Format Pane

The Code Format pane of the Preferences dialog box allows you to specify rules to determine how the code will be structured. This does not affect how the content appears in a browser; the sole purpose of this pane is to make it easier for you to read code.

Code structuring pertains primarily to the positioning of text within tags and the case (upper or lowercase) of tags and attributes. All code-formatting preferences (except the Override Case Of option) are automatically applied to new documents, but not to existing documents. To apply any change in the preferences to existing documents, you must choose Commands>Apply Source Formatting. To apply changes to only part of a document, select the part you want to change, and then choose Commands>Apply Source Formatting to Selection.

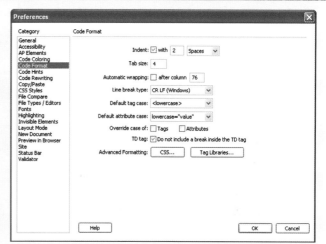

- **Indent With** indents the text that appears within tags. When used with the Auto Wrapping (After Column) option, this option indents content within each tag so that you can easily identify each block of code. You can indent by character spaces or by tabs.

- **Tab Size** specifies the number of spaces that each tab character contains. For example, if you type "4" in this box, each time you press the Tab key, space equivalent to four characters is inserted.

- **Automatic Wrapping (After Column)** inserts line breaks to prevent the code from extending beyond the specified column. To avoid a change in the appearance of the content in a browser, the line breaks cannot be inserted at the same point for each line.

- **Line Break Type** ensures the line breaks inserted by Dreamweaver are compatible with the operating system of the remote server on which your site will be hosted.

- **Default Tag Case** changes the case of tags, and **Default Attribute Case** changes the case of attributes. We highly recommend lowercase tags and attributes because XHTML does not support uppercase tags. (HTML supports tags of both cases.)

- **Override Case of Tags and Override Case of Attributes** change the case of tags and attributes to the options selected in this pane, even if a different case is defined for them in Tag Libraries.

- The **TD Tag** option prevents a line break or white space from being inserted directly after a <td> (table cell) or directly before a </td> tag. Such line breaks and white spaces within the tag cause problems in older browsers.

- In Advanced Formatting, the **CSS** button allows you to change the code formatting definitions in the cascading style sheet (CSS) used by the document. (You will learn about designing with style sheets in Project 5.)

- Use the **Tag Libraries** button to define formatting features for each tag and its associated attribute.

2. **Switch to Split view and move the insertion point to the "Quotes and Related Characters" paragraph (line 12).**

3. **In the Code pane, click the line number to the left of the paragraph to select the entire line of text and code.**

Clicking the line number selects the entire line of code.

The related text is also selected in the Design pane.

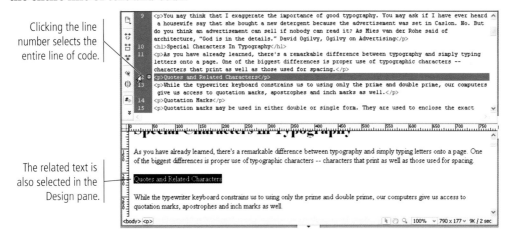

4. **In the Properties Inspector, choose Heading 2 from the Format list.**

Click the arrow to open the Format list, and then click to choose the format you want to assign.

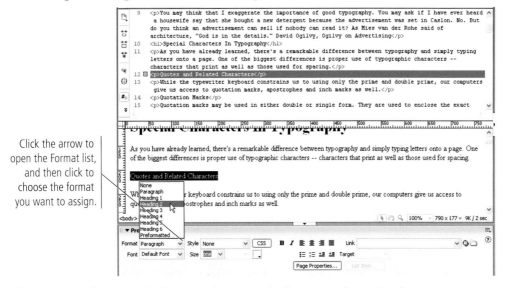

After choosing a format in the Properties Inspector, the Code pane shows that the <p> and </p> tags have been replaced with <h2> and </h2> tags, respectively.

The <p> tags have been replaced in the selected text.

The default <h2> formatting is applied in the Design pane.

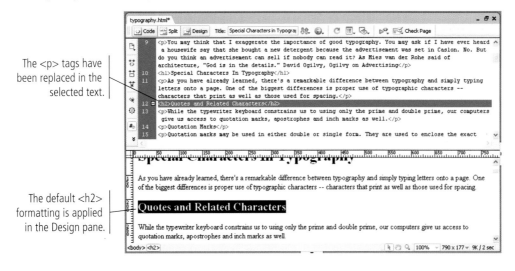

5. Using the same technique from Steps 3 and 4, format lines 14 (Quotation Marks), 18 (Apostrophe), and 20 (Inch and Foot Marks) as Heading 3. Review the results in the Design view.

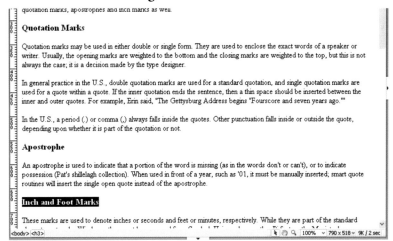

6. Switch to Code view, and then repeat Step 5 as follows:

Line Number	Content	Heading Level
22	Hyphens and Dashes	2
24	Hyphen	3
27	En Dash	3
29	Em Dash	3
31	Special Characters	2
32	Multiplication Sign	3
34	Copyright Symbol	3
36	Registered Trademark Symbol	3
38	Spacing Options	2
40	Non-breaking Space	3
42	Em Space	3
44	En Space	3
46	Thin Space	3
48	Flex Space	3
52	Glossary	2
58	Resources	2

Note:

When you're working in Design view, you can apply paragraph structure and heading levels by choosing from the Text>Paragraph Format menu.

7. Switch to Design view and examine the page.

The organized content is easier to understand and would enable users, sighted or otherwise, to scan headings and determine whether the page content meets their needs.

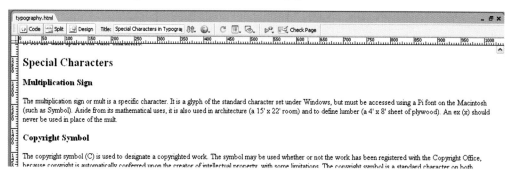

8. Save the file and continue to the next exercise.

Formatting Text with the Properties Inspector

The Properties Inspector (Window>Properties, or Command/Control-F3) appears directly below the page area. Use this panel to view and modify the properties of the text and page you're building. When you're working with text, you have access to a number of different properties, as shown below.

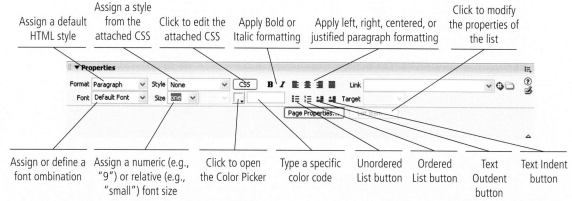

- The **Format** menu contains the default HTML paragraph and heading styles that you can apply to any paragraph. The Preformatted option in this menu allows you to include more than a single space between words and does not automatically wrap the contents.

- The **Style** menu contains the list of style classes defined in the style sheet that is attached to the page. If no style sheet is attached, you can select the Attach Style Sheet option in this menu to attach one. You can also rename an attached style sheet from this list. To edit the attached CSS, click the CSS button.

- You can select a font and size using the related menus in the Properties Inspector. Instead of selecting a single font, you normally select a combination of fonts, which enable a browser to use whichever font in the list that is available on the user's computer. The fonts are arranged in the combination according to their priority; if the user's computer doesn't have the first listed font, the browser will try to use the second font in the list, and so on. You can also change the combinations provided here, or you can add a new one.

- You can select a color for the text from the Color Picker, or you can type the HTML color code in the field next to the color swatch.

- You can use the buttons in the first line to make the text bold or italic, and you can select a paragraph alignment option for the selected text.

- The **Unordered List** button formats selected paragraphs into a bulleted list. The **Ordered List** button arranges the paragraphs in a numbered list. Each paragraph in the selection is a separate bulleted or numbered list item.

- The **Text Outdent** and **Text Indent** buttons are used for indenting paragraphs. (The Text Indent button uses the blockquote tag to make text appear indented.)

- The **Link** field displays the URL to which the selected text is linked. The Point to File and Browse for File buttons help you locate the files to which you want to attach links.

- The **Target** menu determines where the linked file will open (new window, parent frame, etc.).

FORMAT A BLOCK QUOTE AND INLINE QUOTES

HTML has three tags that provide formatting for quotation-related structures — <blockquote>, <q>, and <cite>.

The **blockquote element** formats a quotation as a block of text that is indented from the left and right margins and separated from surrounding text by white space above and below it. The blockquote element requires at least one paragraph element to be nested within it, such as <blockquote><p>quotation goes here</p></blockquote>.

The blockquote element has an optional cite attribute designed to identify the URL of the quote source. The URL is not clickable or visible (although in Firefox, you can view the cite URL via the properties of a blockquote or q element).

1. **With typography.html open in Design view, click in the top paragraph (above the heading level 1 text).**

2. **Click the Text Indent button in the Properties Inspector.**

   Clicking the Text Indent button in the Properties Inspector applies the blockquote element to the selected paragraph.

   In the Tag Selector, the <p> tag appears to the right of the <blockquote> tag, indicating that the <p> tag has been nested within a <blockquote> tag. In the Design window, the blockquote content has been indented from both the left and right margins.

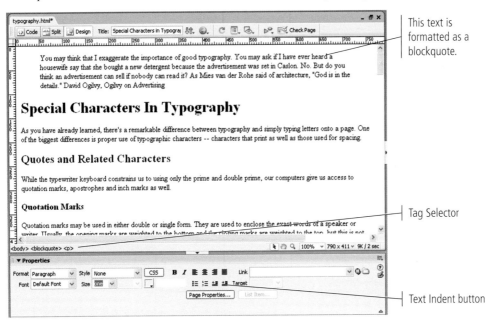

This text is formatted as a blockquote.

Tag Selector

Text Indent button

3. **Save the file and continue to the next exercise.**

FORMAT A CITATION

If the source of a quotation is a URL, you can add the URL as the cite attribute of either the blockquote or q element. If the source of the quotation is not a URL, you should use the cite element.

1. **With typography.html open in Design view, scroll to the top of the page and select "David Ogilvy, Ogilvy on Advertising" at the end of the block quote.**

2. **Control/right-click the selected text and choose Quick Tag Editor from the contextual menu.**

   The Quick Tag Editor allows you to work temporarily with code, while still working in the Design view.

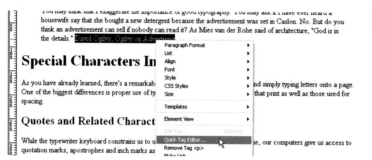

Note:

You can also open the Quick Tag Editor by choosing Modify>Quick Tag Editor.

Formatting Inline Quotes with the q Element

The **q element** is used for marking quotations that are part of a sentence or paragraph, rather than separate paragraphs. (Like the blockquote element, you can also define an optional cite attribute for q element text.)

Firefox, Safari, and Opera browsers automatically place quotation marks around q element text, eliminating the need to insert them as characters in the page content. Internet Explorer, however, does not add the quotation marks to the tagged text. This different browser behavior presents a problem.

If you use the q element, you have to decide which method you prefer — leaving the manually typed quotation marks so that quotes display properly in IE but as double marks in other browsers (Opera, Firefox, and Safari), or removing the manual quotes so that tagged q elements appear properly in all browsers except IE. Alternatively, you could simply leave inline quotes untagged, which is technically unstructured but the straight quote marks will appear properly in every browser.

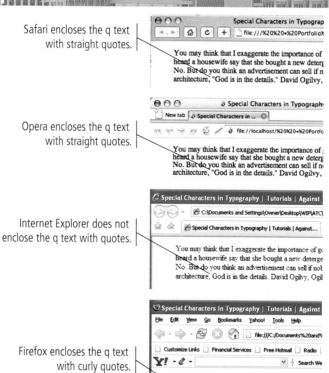

Safari encloses the q text with straight quotes.

Opera encloses the q text with straight quotes.

Internet Explorer does not enclose the q text with quotes.

Firefox encloses the q text with curly quotes.

3. Type "ci".

Cite is selected in the code hint list because it is the first element name beginning with "ci." (In fact it is the only element beginning with "ci.") When using this tool for other elements, you might need to type a third letter to find the element you want.

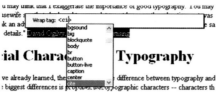

There are no buttons in the Dreamweaver interface to insert a q element for an inline quote. Fortunately, Dreamweaver provides alternate access for all elements — including the less common ones — in the Tag Chooser. You can access the Tag Chooser by clicking the associated button in the Common Insert bar; when you open the Tag Chooser, the document window automatically switches to Split view.

In the Tag Chooser dialog box, you can select a specific category of tags in the left pane, and then choose a specific tag from the selected category in the right pane.

When you click Insert in the Tag Chooser dialog box, the Tag Editor dialog box automatically presents additional options related to the selected tag. For the q tag, you can define the cite attribute (other options are also available by clicking a different category in the left pane). The browse button to the right of the Cite field allows you to select a page from your current site in Dreamweaver as the source of the quotation. If the source of your quotation is a page from another cite, you must type the URL into the Cite field. (If the source of your quotation is not a URL, enter nothing in the Cite field.)

The Tag Chooser provides help for more tags than just HTML tags.

Clicking OK in the Tag Editor dialog box returns you to the Tag Chooser. Clicking Close in the Tag Chooser dialog box returns you to the document window; the q tag is added to the selected text, which you can see in the Code view:

```
t I exaggerate the importance of good t
say that she bought a new detergent bec
think an advertisement can sell if nobc
ure, "<q>God is in the details.</q>" Da
```

Nested Inline Quotes

Although uncommon, it is possible to find a quotation within a quotation. The markup follows the same basic procedure as for a "normal" quotation: mark up the outer quotation with the q element, and then mark up the inner quotation with another q element (the order in which you place the q elements doesn't matter). According to typographic convention, the outer quotation is surrounded with double curly quotes and the inner quotation is surrounded with single curly quotes.

```
18  <p>In general practice in the U.S., double quotation marks are used for a standard quotation, and
    single quotation marks are used for a quote within a quote. If the inner quotation ends the
    sentence, then a thin space should be inserted between the inner and outer quotes. For example,
    Erin said, <q>The Gettysburg Address begins <q>Fourscore and seven years ago.</q></q></p>
```

In general practice in the U.S., double quotation marks are used for a standard quotation, and single quotation marks are used for a quote within a quote. If the inner quotation ends the sentence, then a thin space should be inserted between the inner and outer quotes. For example, Erin said, "The Gettysburg Address begins 'Fourscore and seven years ago.'"

Remember, however, that Internet Explorer does not format q text elements — including nested ones — with curly quotes.

4. Press Return/Enter to choose "cite" from the list of tags.

5. Press Return/Enter again to apply the cite tag to the selected text.

The default appearance of cite element text is italic.

You may think that I exaggerate the importance of good typography. You may ask if I have ever heard a housewife say that she bought a new detergent because the advertisement was set in Caslon. No. But do you think an advertisement can sell if nobody can read it? As Mies van der Rohe said of architecture, "God is in the details." *David Ogilvy, Ogilvy on Advertising*

Special Characters In Typography

6. Save your changes and continue to the next exercise.

MARK UP ABBREVIATIONS IN CODE VIEW

Both abbreviations and acronyms are shortened forms of words or phrases. The basic difference between the use of the abbr and acronym elements is that if you spell out the short form (such as HTML), you mark it with an abbr element. If you sound it out like a word (such as NATO), you mark it with an acronym element. Some abbreviations are read both ways; SQL, for example, is sometimes spelled out and sometimes spoken as "sequel."

The title attribute plays a useful role in the abbr and acronym elements. Any text you insert into the title attribute appears as a tool tip when you hover the mouse over the titled element. In the case of abbr and acronym elements, you enter the full text of the abbreviation or acronym in the title attribute so the tool tip displays the expanded form. People who use screen-reader software also benefit from the title attribute because the software can be set up to read the title text in place of the abbreviation.

Dreamweaver's code hints help with HTML attributes. In some cases (such as alignment options), the attribute values are limited so code hints provide a list of available attributes. In other cases, Dreamweaver cannot provide a list of options and simply allows you to type either the cite URL or the title text.

1. With typography.html open in Split view, select "U.S." in the first line of the second paragraph after the Quotation Marks heading (in the Design window).

The text selected in Design view is also selected in Code view. This is a useful way to locate specific text in code (or vice versa).

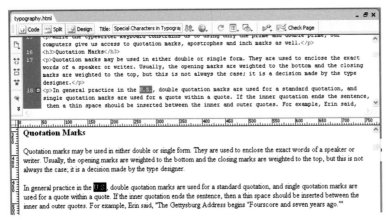

Note:

Unfortunately, IE supports neither the abbr nor the acronym element; IE doesn't support CSS styling of either element, and tool tips do not appear. Although this seems to reduce the value of these two elements, remember that not everyone uses IE. Also, IE will improve in future versions; marking up the document properly now means you don't have to modify the file later.

2. Click the Code pane to make it the active pane.

When working in either window of Split view, you have to click the other window to bring it into focus (make it active) before you can make changes there.

3. Place the insertion point before the previously highlighted text, and then type "<ab".

The abbr tag will be selected in the code hint list.

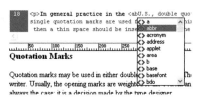

Note:

When you click the Code pane to bring it into focus, the highlight text is no longer highlighted.

4. Press Return/Enter to accept abbr.

By pressing Return/Enter, you select the <abbr> tag. After adding the tag, the insertion point flashes after the tag so you can type to add attributes of the tag.

The insertion point is ready
for you to type and add
attributes of the new tag.

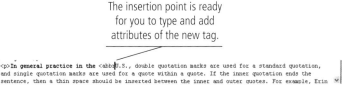

5. Press the Spacebar, and type "t".

Inserting a space after the abbr element name within the tag prompts Dreamweaver to open code hints and present a list of valid attributes for the current tag.

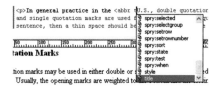

6. Press Return/Enter to accept the title attribute.

When you add the title attribute, the insertion point is automatically placed between quotation marks so you can type a value for the attribute.

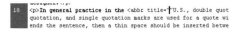

7. Type "United States" between the quotation marks.

8. Move the insertion point to the right of the closing quotation mark and type ">" to close the tag.

Attribute values must always be quoted; when you select the attribute in the code hint list, Dreamweaver follows the attribute with = " " and places the insertion point between the two quotation marks so you can immediately type a value for the attribute.

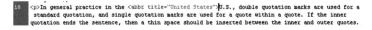

Note:

After pressing Return/ Enter to accept an attribute name that has limited options, Dreamweaver presents a list of valid attribute values, instead of leaving you with an empty pair of quotation marks.

9. **Move the insertion point to the right of "U.S." and type "</".**

   Dreamweaver closes the abbr tag for you.

   ```
   18  <p>In general practice in the <abbr title="United States">U.S.</abbr>, double quotation marks are
       used for a standard quotation, and single quotation marks are used for a quote within a quote. If the
       inner quotation ends the sentence, then a thin space should be inserted between the inner and outer
   ```

10. **Select all of the code for the marked up U.S. abbreviation and copy it to the clipboard (Command/Control-C).**

    ```
    18 □ <p>In general practice in the <abbr title="United States">U.S.</abbr>, double quotation marks are
         used for a standard quotation, and single quotation marks are used for a quote within a quote. If the
         inner quotation ends the sentence, then a thin space should be inserted between the inner and outer
         quotes. For example, Erin said, "The Gettysburg Address begins "Fourscore and seven years ago.""</p>
    19   <p>In the U.S., a period (.) or comma (,) always falls inside the quotes. Other punctuation falls
         inside or outside the quote, depending upon whether it is part of the quotation or not.</p>
    ```

    Note:

    You can also add abbreviation and acronym tags — and a number of other options — by using the Insert>HTML>Text Objects submenu.

11. **Select the second instance of the abbreviation "U.S." in the next paragraph (line 19) and paste the copied code.**

    ```
    18   <p>In general practice in the <abbr title="United States">U.S.</abbr>, double quotation marks are
         used for a standard quotation, and single quotation marks are used for a quote within a quote. If the
         inner quotation ends the sentence, then a thin space should be inserted between the inner and outer
         quotes. For example, Erin said, "The Gettysburg Address begins "Fourscore and seven years ago."</p>
    19   <p>In the <abbr title="United States">U.S.</abbr>, a period (.) or comma (,) always falls inside the
         quotes. Other punctuation falls inside or outside the quote, depending upon whether it is part of the
         quotation or not </p>
    ```

12. **On line 39, mark "U.S." as an abbreviation (it's farther along the line).**

13. **On line 43, mark up "St." (of St. Louis) as an abbreviation of "Saint".**

    ```
    43   <p>The non-breaking space, like the non-breaking hyphen, is used to keep two words together. For
         example, you may want to ensure that <abbr title="Saint">St.</abbr> Louis always appears as a unit,
         rather than falling on two lines. A non-breaking space is variable in width when type is justified to
         both margins.</p>
    ```

14. **On line 45, mark up both instances of "pt." as abbreviations of "point".**

    ```
    45   <p>The em space is a fixed space the width of the point size. An em in 12-<abbr title="point">pt.</abbr>
         type is 12 points wide; an em in 10-<abbr title="point">pt.</abbr> type is 10 points wide.</p>
    ```

15. **Preview the page in your browser (save if prompted) and look for any differences in appearance between abbr elements and regular paragraph text.**

    In Internet Explorer and Safari, you will see no obvious difference in text that is tagged as an abbreviation. Firefox and Opera browsers display a dotted line under abbr element text. When you move your mouse pointer over abbr element text, however, the title text appears as a tool tip in all but Safari.

Safari does not show any visual indication that the text is tagged as an abbreviation, nor does it show the title in a tool tip.	In general practice in the U.S., double quotatio marks are used for a quote within a quote. If th inserted between the inner and outer quotes. Fo and seven years ago."" In the U.S., a period (.) or comma (,) always fa quote, depending upon whether it is part of the	In general practice in the U.S., double quota and single quotation marks a United States qu the sentence, then a thin space should be ins example, Erin said, "The Gettysburg Addres In the U.S., a period (.) or comma (,) alway	Internet Explorer does not underline the abbreviation, but the expanded form of the abbreviation does appear in a tool tip.
Opera displays a dotted line under abbr elements. When you hover your mouse pointer over U.S., the text in the title attribute appears.	In general practice in the U.S., double quotatio quotation marks are used for a quote within a c space should be inserted betv Title: United States ic Address begins "Fourscore and seven years ag In the U.S., a period (.) or comma (,) always fa the quote, depending upon whether it is part of	In general practice in the U.S., double quota and single quotation marks are used for a qu the sentence, then a thin spac United States inst example, Erin said, "The Gettysburg Addres: In the U.S., a period (.) or comma (,) always	Firefox displays a dotted line under abbr elements. When you hover your mouse pointer over U.S., the text in the title attribute appears.

16. **Return to Dreamweaver and continue to the next exercise.**

Mark Up Acronyms in Design View

Except for the specific tag being used, the basic process of marking up acronyms is the same as for marking up abbreviations. In both cases, the title attribute is used for the long form of the word or phrase. There are two ways to insert acronym (and abbr) elements from Design view: the Quick Tag Editor or the Text Insert bar.

1. **With typography.html open in Split view, select "ANSI" near the end of the paragraph following the Copyright Symbol heading.**

2. **Control/right-click the selected word and choose Quick Tag Editor from the contextual menu.**

3. **Type "ac" and press Return/Enter to choose acronym from the list.**

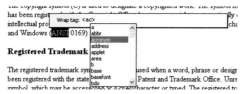

4. **Press the Spacebar, type "t", press Return/Enter to choose the title attribute.**

5. **Type "American National Standards Institute" between the quotation marks in the code, then press Return/Enter to insert the tag.**

6. **In the paragraph after the Registered Trademark Symbol heading, select "ANSI" near the end of the paragraph.**

7. **In the Insert bar, click the Text tab to switch to the Text Insert bar.**

8. **Click the Acronym button on the Text Insert bar.**

   The symbol on the button, W3C, is supposed to represent an acronym, but the developers of Dreamweaver made a mistake: W3C is actually an abbreviation. However, clicking the button inserts the <acronym> tag, just as the button tool tip suggests.

9. **In the Acronym dialog box, type "American National Standards Institute" in the Full Text field and click OK.**

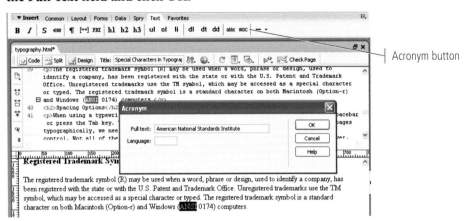

Acronym button

10. **Preview the page in your browser (saving when prompted).**

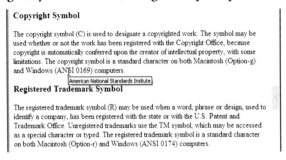

Copyright Symbol

The copyright symbol (C) is used to designate a copyrighted work. The symbol may be used whether or not the work has been registered with the Copyright Office, because copyright is automatically conferred upon the creator of intellectual property, with some limitations. The copyright symbol is a standard character on both Macintosh (Option-g) and Windows (ANSI 0169) computers.

American National Standards Institute

Registered Trademark Symbol

The registered trademark symbol (R) may be used when a word, phrase or design, used to identify a company, has been registered with the state or with the U.S. Patent and Trademark Office. Unregistered trademarks use the TM symbol, which may be accessed as a special character or typed. The registered trademark symbol is a standard character on both Macintosh (Option-r) and Windows (ANSI 0174) computers.

11. **Return to Dreamweaver and continue to the next exercise.**

 FORMAT WITH STRONG AND EM ELEMENTS

Two HTML elements can be used to show emphasis — em and strong. The em element is used when light emphasis is needed, such as "you should go to your brother's game to support him." For stronger emphasis, use the strong element, such as "Don't touch the stovetop, it is hot!"

Text marked up with the em element appears in italic; text marked up with the strong element appears in bold. Visually, it is the same as using the <i> and <b> tags (italic and bold, respectively) but the i and b elements are presentational — not structural — HTML. Screen-reader software changes the tone of voice when it finds em and strong element text, but not when it finds i or b element text.

Current Web design software, including Dreamweaver, inserts a strong or em element when you apply bold or italic styling (respectively) through format menus or other means. Don't assume, however, that there is a direct relationship between b and strong elements and i and em elements. Remember: b and i elements are for presentational purposes only, and strong and em elements are for structural purposes.

1. **With typography.html open, open the Preferences dialog box (Dreamweaver menu on Macintosh or Edit menu on Windows) and show the General category.**

2. **In the Editing Options group, make sure the "Use <strong> and <em>" option is checked.**

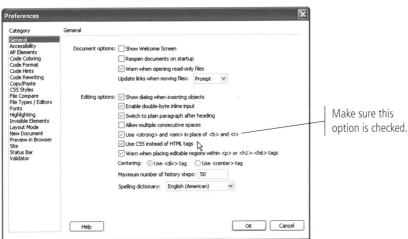

Make sure this option is checked.

Note:

As you work through this book, remember that preferences are accessed in the Dreamweaver menu on Macintosh and the Edit menu on Windows.

3. **Click OK to close the Preferences dialog box.**

Now when you select bold or italic, Dreamweaver will automatically insert strong or em elements. It might appear that you have lost the ability to format text as bold or italic (or both) because the visual-only formatting is no longer available (unless you disable the preferences option), but that's okay. Remember that the b and i elements are for presentation/visual purposes only; they have no structural impact on the document.

Using the Text Insert Bar

The Text Insert bar provides a convenient way of inserting common tags in your pages. The following explains the buttons (left to right).

- **Bold** and **Strong** insert the <strong> tag, which makes the selected text appear bold.
- **Italic** and **Emphasis** insert the <em> tag, which makes the selected text italic.
- **Paragraph** inserts the <p> tag, which defines the selected text as a paragraph.
- **Blockquote** inserts the <blockquote> tag, which indents the selected text and identifies it as a quote.
- **Preformatted** inserts the <pre> tag, which allows you to include more than a single space between words and does not automatically word-wrap the contents.
- **Headings** (h1, h2, and h3) insert <h> tags (<h1>, <h2>, and <h3>, respectively), which define the selected text as a heading.
- **Unordered List** inserts the <ul> tag, which converts the selected text into a bulleted list item.
- **Ordered List** inserts the <ol> tag, which converts the selected text into a numbered list item.
- **List Item** inserts the <li> tag, which converts the selection to an unordered list item.

- **Definition List** inserts the <dl> tag, which is used for creating a list of definitions. This does not alter the appearance of the page, but it is meant to contain terms and their descriptions.
- **Definition Term** inserts the <dt> tag, which marks the text as a term whose description follows.
- **Definition Description** inserts the <dd> tag, which marks the selected text as a description for the preceding text.
- **Abbreviation** inserts the <abbr> tag, which marks the selected text as an abbreviation. You enter the full text of the abbreviation using the title attribute; the expanded form displays in the browser when the cursor hovers over the abbreviation.
- **Acronym** inserts the <acronym> tag, which marks text as an acronym. You enter the full text of the acronym using the title attribute; the expanded form displays in the browser when the cursor hovers over the acronym.
- **Characters** inserts tags for special characters such as line breaks, quotation marks, currency symbols, and many more.

4. **In Design view, scroll down to the paragraph following the En Dash heading and select "not" in the second sentence.**

5. **Click the Bold button in the Properties Inspector.**

   There are no special attributes for the strong and em elements, so you can insert these elements with a single click.

Note:

The same Bold, Italic, Strong, and Emphasis options are also available in the Text>Style menu.

6. **With the text still selected, examine the Tag Selector.**

   The selected text is formatted with the <strong> tag, not the <b> tag.

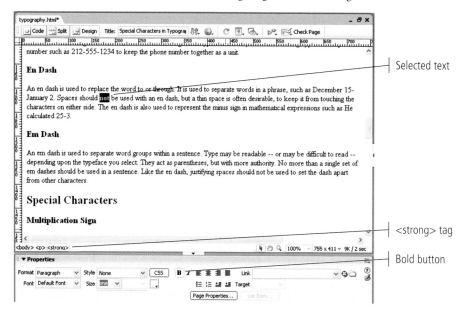

Selected text

<strong> tag

Bold button

7. **In the paragraph after the Multiplication Sign heading, select "never" near the end of the paragraph.**

8. **Apply the <strong> tag to the selected text by clicking the Bold button in the Text Insert bar.**

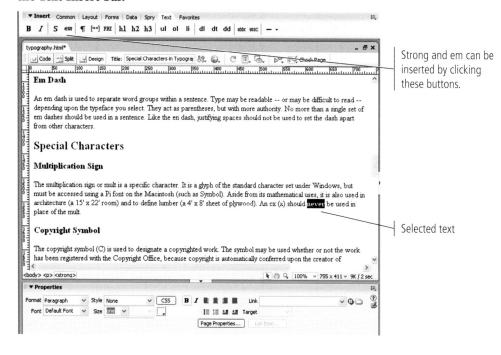

Strong and em can be inserted by clicking these buttons.

Selected text

9. **In the paragraph after the Em Dash heading, select "more authority" in the third sentence and click the Italic button in the Text Insert bar.**

An <em> tag is inserted in the document.

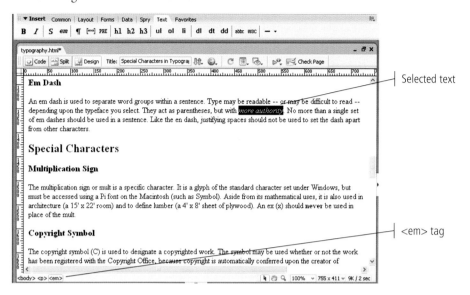

Selected text

<em> tag

10. **Save your changes and continue to the next stage of the project.**

Stage 3 Working with HTML Character Entities

HTML character entities are characters not directly available from your keyboard. HTML character entities can be specified in code using two methods: by name and by number. In both formats, the code begins with an ampersand (&) and ends with a semicolon (;). A **named character entity** uses a specific name for that character such as "©" for the © symbol and "™" for the ™ symbol. Alternatively, you can specify a character using its numeric code, such as "¢" for ¢. (When using the numeric code, be sure to insert a "#" between the & and the number.)

Some character names (such as "™") are not supported by all browsers; visitors see "™" in their browser window instead of the ™ symbol. However, all browsers support numeric codes for character entities.

Note:

The copyright, trademark, and registered trademark characters are among the more common HTML character entities that you will need to insert in your Web pages.

 INSERT SPECIAL CHARACTERS

In most cases, you don't need to worry about inserting the codes, named or numbered, for HTML character entities because you can select most characters from a list in the Text Insert bar and Dreamweaver inserts the code for you. However, only the more common characters exist in this list; less common characters must be entered manually.

1. **With typography.html open in Design view, select "(C)" in the paragraph following the Copyright Symbol heading.**

2. Click the arrow to the right of the last button on the Insert bar and choose Copyright from the list.

Your button icon might appear different than what you see in our screen shot, because the button reflects the last character inserted from this list. Simply clicking the button — not the arrow — inserts whatever character displays on the button.

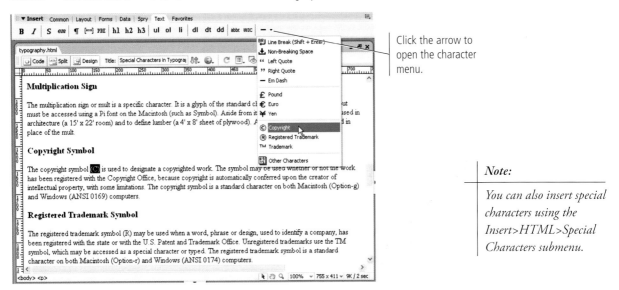

Click the arrow to open the character menu.

Note:

You can also insert special characters using the Insert>HTML>Special Characters submenu.

3. Change the document window to Split view and examine the code.

The copyright character code uses the name format (©) rather than the numeric format.

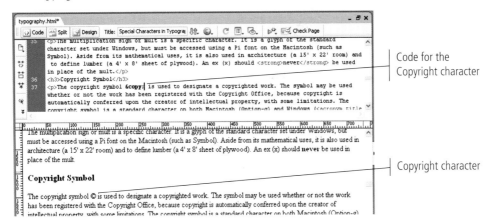

Code for the Copyright character

Copyright character

4. In the Design pane, select "(R)" in the next paragraph and replace it with the Registered Trademark character from the Character list in the Text Insert bar.

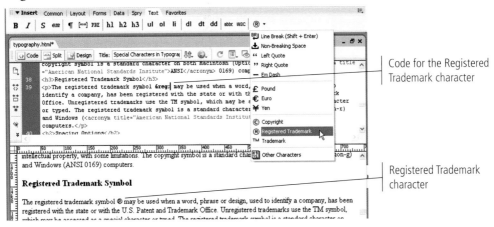

Code for the Registered Trademark character

Registered Trademark character

5. **Select "TM" later in the same paragraph and replace it with the Trademark character from the Characters menu in the Text Insert bar.**

In the Code pane, you can see that Dreamweaver creates this character using the numeric code rather than the name because some browsers do not support the name for this character.

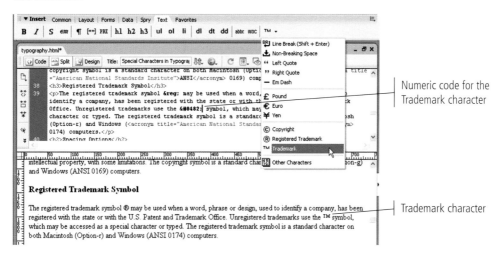

Numeric code for the Trademark character

Trademark character

6. **Save your changes and continue to the next exercise.**

INSERT EM DASHES AND NON-BREAKING SPACES

The em dash is as wide as an uppercase M. This dash can be used to separate part of a sentence — an aside — from the rest of a sentence. Unless the author of the document knows how to insert an em dash into the text, he or she might use a regular hyphen or a pair of hyphens. As there are strict grammatical rules about when to use a hyphen, an en dash, and an em dash, you should consult a professional copy editor for the proper application of these characters.

1. **With typography.html open in Split view, scroll to the paragraph below the Em Dash heading.**

2. **Select the first pair of hyphens in the first line of the paragraph.**

3. **Use the Characters menu on the Text Insert bar to insert an Em Dash.**

Remember, the Characters button defaults to the last-used option. You'll probably have to click the arrow part of the button so you can choose Em Dash from the list.

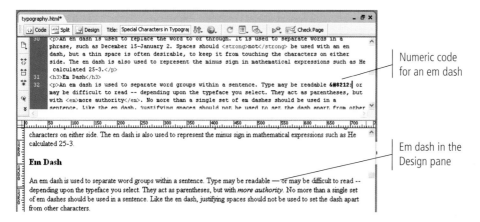

Numeric code for an em dash

Em dash in the Design pane

4. **Select the second pair of hyphens in the same sentence and click the Text Insert bar Characters button.**

   This time you don't need to access the list; you can simply click the button to insert the last-used character — the em dash.

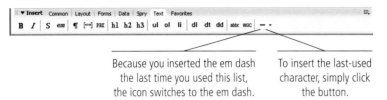

Because you inserted the em dash the last time you used this list, the icon switches to the em dash.

To insert the last-used character, simply click the button.

5. **In the paragraph below the Special Characters In Typography heading, replace the double hyphen with an em dash.**

6. **In the paragraph below the Spacing Options heading, replace the double hyphen with an em dash.**

7. **Scroll to the paragraph following the Non-Breaking Space heading and select the space between "St." and "Louis".**

   A non-breaking space character is used when you don't want words to split up if they don't fit on the same line, such as the space between the area code and telephone exchange in a phone number — as in (705) 555-1234. This character can be inserted from the Characters list.

8. **Using the Characters menu on the Text Insert bar, replace the selected space character with a non-breaking space.**

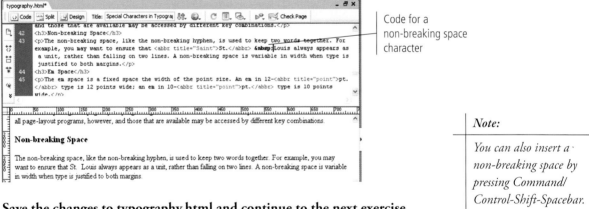

Code for a non-breaking space character

Note:

You can also insert a non-breaking space by pressing Command/Control-Shift-Spacebar.

9. **Save the changes to typography.html and continue to the next exercise.**

INSERT LESS COMMON CHARACTERS

En dashes are about as wide as an uppercase N. As you might have read in the text of this project page, en dashes are used to replace the word "to" or "through" as in "I worked in a retail store during the years 1999–2004." Again, unless authors know how to insert an en dash into the text, they commonly use a single hyphen. To ensure proper application of en dashes in your Web pages, consult a copy editor for assistance.

1. **With typography.html open in Design view, select the hyphen between "December 15" and "January 2" in the paragraph below the En Dash heading.**

2. **Open the Characters menu on the Text Insert bar and choose Other Characters at the bottom of the list.**

   Unlike em dashes, en dashes are not found in the main characters list. Instead, you have to access this character in the Other Characters dialog box. (Presumably, this character is used less than the em dash, so an extra step is required to insert the en dash.)

   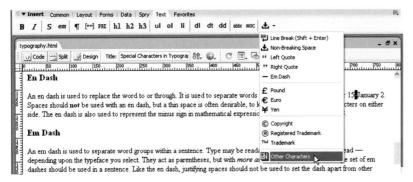

3. **In the Insert Other Character dialog box, click the en dash character in the bottom row of characters, and then click OK to insert the character.**

   The Insert field at the top of the dialog box shows the numeric code for the en dash.

   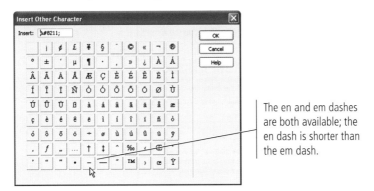

   The en and em dashes are both available; the en dash is shorter than the em dash.

4. **Select the hyphen between "25" and "3" at the end of the same paragraph.**

5. **Click the Characters (Other Characters) button to open the Insert Other Character dialog box.**

   When the last-used character is from the Insert Other Character dialog box, clicking the button in the Text Insert bar reopens the Insert Other Character dialog box; it does not automatically insert the last-used other character.

6. Choose the en dash in the dialog box and click OK.

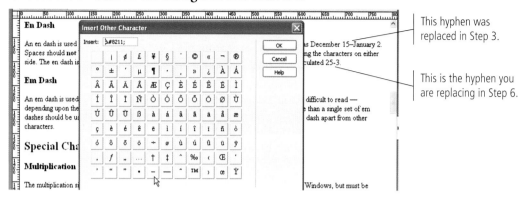

This hyphen was replaced in Step 3.

This is the hyphen you are replacing in Step 6.

7. Save the changes to typography.html and continue to the next exercise.

Insert Special Characters Manually

The multiplication sign is a seldom-used character, and it doesn't even appear in the Insert Other Character dialog box. You have to insert this character by typing in the Code window, or you can use the Insert field in the Insert Other Character dialog box.

There are many lists of HTML character entities on the Internet. Use your favorite search engine to search for "HTML characters." Some Web pages have more characters than others; for very unusual characters, you might need to check a few sites for the character code you need. Also, make note of both the name and the numeric code because some browsers support one but not the other (test both in your browsers).

1. With typography.html open in Split view, use the Design pane to scroll to the paragraph following the Multiplication Sign heading.

2. Select the letter "x" between 15′ and 22′.

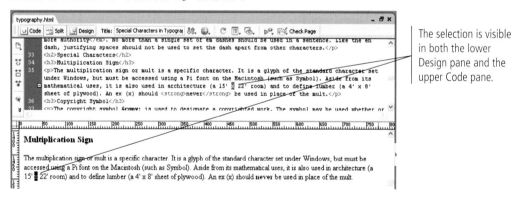

The selection is visible in both the lower Design pane and the upper Code pane.

3. Click the Code pane to bring it into focus, and then delete the selected x.

4. Type "&tim" and press Return/Enter to choose "×".

The code hints help you insert named character entities, but not numbered character codes.

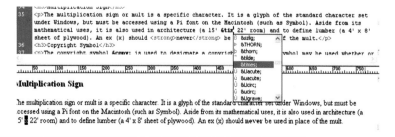

5. **In the Properties Inspector, click the Refresh button.**

6. **In the Design pane, compare the appearance of the mult (multiply) character and the letter x.**

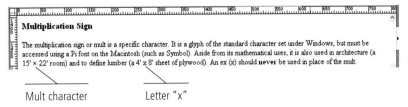

Mult character   Letter "x"

7. **Switch to Design view.**

8. **Select the letter "x" between 4′ and 8′ in the same sentence.**

9. **Click the Character (Other Characters) button in the Text Insert bar.**

10. **In the Insert field, type "×" and click OK.**

    This is the numeric code for the mult character. Dreamweaver's code hints for character entities in Code view do not support numeric codes for characters. You could just as easily have typed this numeric code in the Code window (without the support from the code hints). This step shows that you can continue to work in Design view (rather than switching to Code view) to insert the numeric or named codes for uncommon character entities.

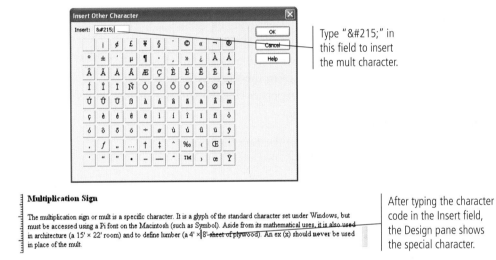

Type "×" in this field to insert the mult character.

After typing the character code in the Insert field, the Design pane shows the special character.

11. **Preview the page in your browser.**

    If you see "×" instead of the mult character, your browser doesn't support the named character code for the mult character. If this happens, return to Dreamweaver and change the code to "×" and preview again. If you see "&215;" instead of the mult character, you forgot to type the "#" between the "&" and "2"; remember that numeric character codes require the "#" before the number.

12. **Close your browser and return to Dreamweaver.**

13. **Continue to the next stage of the project.**

Stage 4 Creating Lists and Tables of Data

There are three common types of lists: ordered lists, unordered lists, and definition lists. (There are a couple of other types that are rarely used; they are marked for removal in the next version of XHTML). Ordered and unordered lists (numbered and bulleted, respectively) are very similar; these two types of lists are also found in word-processing software. Definition lists are different from the other two in structure, and there is no equivalent in word-processing software.

CREATE AN ORDERED LIST OF WEB RESOURCES

Ordered lists are commonly called numbered lists, although they are not always numbered. You can change the style to Roman numerals (i, ii, iii or I, II, III) or to the alphabet (a, b, c or A, B, C).

In code, an ordered list uses two tags: the <ol> tag and the <li> tag. The <ol> and </ol> tags surround the entire ordered list, identifying where the list starts and ends. Each list item within the list is surrounded by the <li> and </li> tags. In most cases, list items are relatively short, but it is perfectly valid to include multiple paragraphs within a list item. Dreamweaver doesn't support the principle of paragraphs within list items, however, so you would have to mark up the paragraph code manually.

One of the presentation properties of an ordered list is that each list item is automatically numbered; you don't need to type the number at the beginning of each list item. If you receive content from an outside source, the ordered lists might have the number already typed at the beginning of each list item. In this case, you should remove the number from each list item text (you don't want two numbers for each item).

Another presentation property of ordered lists is the white space around the list and between the list items. The list as a whole is indented from the left edge of the page, and the space between list items is reduced. These properties clearly identify that the text is part of a list, and not part of a regular paragraph.

> **Note:**
>
> *The purpose of ordered lists is to show a sequence of steps or an order of importance. If these purposes do not apply to the content of the list, use an unordered (bulleted) list instead.*

1. **With typography.html open in Design view, select the two numbered paragraphs at the bottom of the page.**

2. **Click the Ordered List button in the Properties Inspector.**

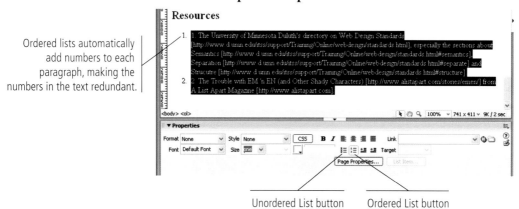

Ordered lists automatically add numbers to each paragraph, making the numbers in the text redundant.

Unordered List button   Ordered List button

3. **Click away from the selected text to deselect it, and then delete the extra typed numbers from the beginning of each of the list items.**

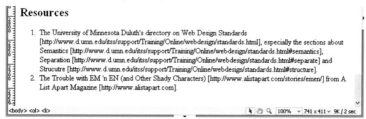

4. **Click at the end of the text in the second list item and press Return/Enter.**

Dreamweaver automatically creates a new numbered list item for you.

5. **Type "HTML 4.0 Entities from HTMLHelp.com" as the new list item, but do not press Return/Enter.**

6. **In the first list item, select the URL in the square brackets and cut it to the clipboard (Edit>Cut or Command/Control-X).**

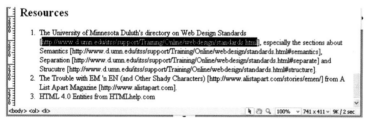

7. **Delete the two square brackets and the space before them.**

8. **Select "Web Design Standards", click in the Link field of the Properties Inspector, paste the copied URL, and press Return/Enter.**

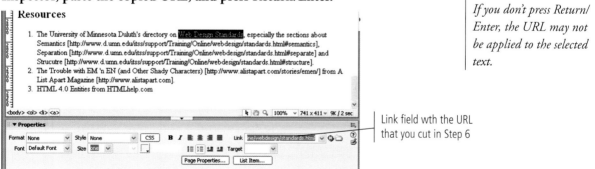

Link field wth the URL that you cut in Step 6

Note:

If you don't press Return/Enter, the URL may not be applied to the selected text.

9. Using the same basic procedure as in Steps 6–8, create links from the following words, using the URLs immediately following each word as the links:

>Semantics — in the first list item

>Separation — in the first list item

>Structure — in the first list item

>The Trouble with EM 'n EN (and Other Shady Characters) — in the second list item

>A List Apart Magazine — in the second list item

10. In the last list item, make "HTML 4.0 Entities" a link to "http://www.htmlhelp.com/reference/html40/entities/" and make "HTMLHelp.com" a link to "http://www.htmlhelp.com".

> **Resources**
>
> 1. The University of Minnesota Duluth's directory on Web Design Standards, especially the sections about Semantics, Separation and Strucutre.
> 2. The Trouble with EM 'n EN (and Other Shady Characters) from A List Apart Magazine.
> 3. HTML 4.0 Entities from HTMLhelp.com

11. Preview the page in your browser and test the links.

12. Close your browser, return to Dreamweaver, and continue to the next exercise.

CREATE A DEFINITION LIST

Definition lists are designed to match a term with its definition or description. The definition or description doesn't necessarily need to come from a dictionary or thesaurus; it might simply be an explanation of the term.

Three tags are part of a definition list. Similar to the <ol> tag that defines the beginning and end of an ordered list, the <dl> tag serves the same purpose. The <dt> and <dd> tags within the dl element wrap the term and description respectively.

1. With typography.html open in Design view, scroll to the Glossary heading near the bottom of the page.

2. Drag to select the four lines of terms and descriptions in the Glossary section.

3. In the Text Insert bar, click the dl button to wrap the selected text in a <dl> tag.

   The second and fourth lines are now indented.

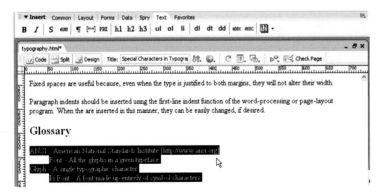

Note:

You can also create lists by choosing from the Text>List submenu.

4. **Click in the word "ANSI" (in the first line of the selection) to place the insertion point, and then look at the Tag Selector.**

   The first line is enclosed within the <dl> tag, meaning it is within the definition list. It is also within the <dt> tag, indicating that the first line is automatically marked up as a definition term.

   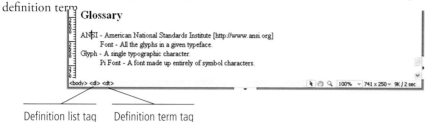

   Definition list tag   Definition term tag

5. **Move the insertion point to the second line.**

   The Tag Selector indicates that the indented line is within the <dd> tag, meaning it is marked as a definition description.

   Definition description tag

6. **Move the insertion point to the left of "American" in the first line. Press the Backspace key until the spaces and hyphen between "American" and "ANSI" have been deleted, and then press Return/Enter.**

   The description is now formatted as a definition description; however, the "Font" term is indented at the same level as the ANSI definition.

   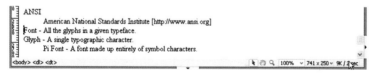

7. **Move the insertion point to the left of "Font", press Backspace, and then press Return/Enter.**

   The line beginning with Font is now formatted as a definition term.

8. **Repeat Steps 6 and 7 for the rest of the terms and descriptions.**

9. **Make "American National Standards Institute" a link to "http://www.ansi.org".**

   Glossary

   ANSI
        American National Standards Institute
   Font
        All the glyphs in a given typeface.
   Glyph
        A single typographic character.
   Pi Font
        A font made up entirely of symbol characters.

10. **Save the changes to typography.html and continue to the next exercise.**

CREATE A TABLE OF QUOTATION CHARACTERS

Tables, when used for tabular data only, are easy to work with. Common HTML tables consist of only three components: a caption, table header cells, and table data cells. However, when tables are used for the layout of the components of a Web page, they can be very complicated in structure, with tables within table cells (**nested tables**) and cells that have been merged with other cells.

A caption can be used to briefly describe the contents or purpose of the table. It generally appears at the top of the table. (There are CSS properties that position the caption at the left, right, or bottom of the table. Unfortunately, current browsers don't offer good support for these properties.)

Note:

You will learn how to use tables for layout in Project 4.

Table header cells appear at the top or left (or both) of the table to label the contents in the cells below or to the right. Think about a table consisting of the days of the week across the top and the working hours of the day down the left. If the cell at the intersection of the second row and second column contained the text "Staff Meeting," you would know that the staff meeting was scheduled for Tuesday at 10:00 a.m. by moving your eyes up to the top header cell and left to the left header cell. Even if these cells were not marked up as table header cells, you would still know when the staff meeting was scheduled.

Table header cells use the <th> tag, and they are very important for accessibility. People using screen-reader software depends on the table header cell markup; when they reach the staff meeting cell, they can prompt the software to read the headers associated with the cell; the screen-reader software would report "Tuesday" and "10:00 a.m." If the headers were not marked up, the software could not report the day and time of the meeting.

Table data cells make up the majority of the cells in a table. The <td> tag is used to mark up the table data cells.

Note:

There are also table row (<tr>) tags, which you rarely work with directly, and column tags (<col> and <colgroup>) but there isn't a great deal of support for them in current browsers.

1. **With typography.html open in Design view, place the insertion point at the end of the paragraph after the Inch and Foot Marks heading.**

2. **Switch to the Layout Insert bar by clicking the Layout tab.**

3. **Click the Table button in the Layout Insert bar.**

   The Common Insert bar also contains the same Table button (although in a different position), but you will use another feature later that is found only on the Layout bar.

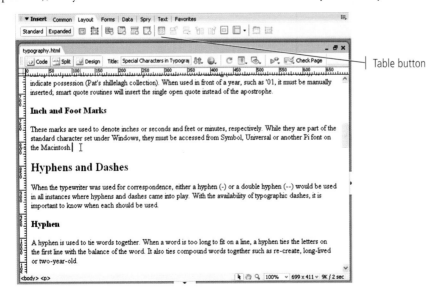

Table button

4. **In the Table dialog box, set both the number of rows and number of columns to "2". Leave the Table Width, Border Thickness, Cell Padding, and Cell Spacing fields empty. Choose the Top Header option. Type "Quotation Characters" in the Caption field.**

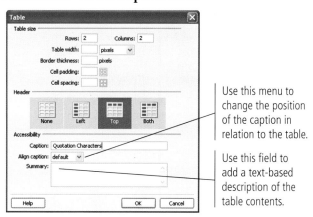

Use this menu to change the position of the caption in relation to the table.

Use this field to add a text-based description of the table contents.

Note:

You can also add a table to the page by choosing Insert>Table.

5. **Click OK to create the table.**

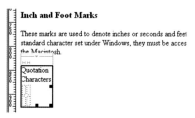

6. **Click the Expanded button in the Layout Insert bar.**

The four table cells are small and difficult to work with when empty. The Expanded Tables mode enlarges the cells so they are easier to work with. This is a temporary change that Dreamweaver provides to help designers work with empty table cells; the expanded appearance is not carried to the Web page.

7. **Read the warning message and click OK.**

If you are sharing your computer with other users, someone might have checked the Don't Show Me This Message Again option, so you might not see this warning. In addition, this message appears only the first time you choose Expanded Tables mode; if you shut down and restart Dreamweaver, this message will appear again the first time you choose Expanded Tables mode.

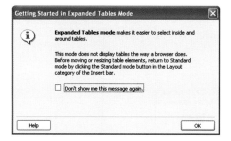

8. Examine the page while Expanded Tables mode is active.

Notice the enlarged cells in the table, and the blue Exit link at the top of the document window. You can click that link to exit or disable Expanded Tables mode.

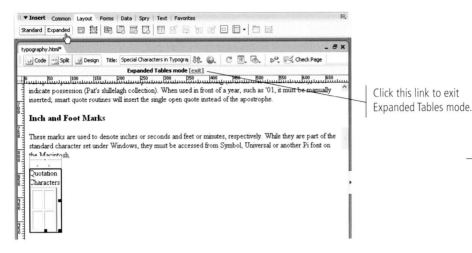

Click this link to exit Expanded Tables mode.

Note:

Expanded Tables mode is only necessary when a table is completely empty; once content has been entered in at least one cell per column, you can exit Expanded Tables mode.

9. Type "Character Description" in the top-left cell. Press Tab and type "Character" in the top-right cell.

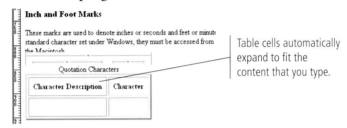

Table cells automatically expand to fit the content that you type.

10. Click the link at the top of the document window to exit Expanded Tables mode.

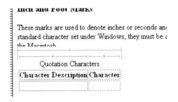

11. Click in the lower-left empty cell and type "Double Right Curly Quotation Mark".

12. Press Tab to move to the right cell and choose Right Quote from the Characters menu in the Text Insert bar.

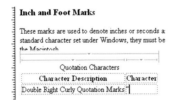

13. Press Tab to insert a new table row. In the left cell, type "Double Left Curly Quotation Mark". In the right cell, insert the Left Quote character from the Characters menu of the Text Insert bar.

14. **Press Tab to insert another table row. In the left cell, type "Single Right Curly Quotation Mark". In the right cell, insert the appropriate character from the Insert Other Character dialog box.**

15. **Press Tab to insert another table row. Type "Single Left Curly Quotation Mark" in the left cell and insert the appropriate character (from the Insert Other Character dialog box) in the right cell.**

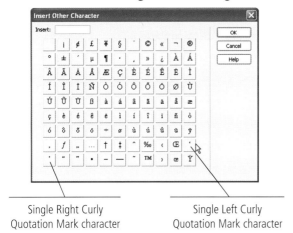

Single Right Curly
Quotation Mark character

Single Left Curly
Quotation Mark character

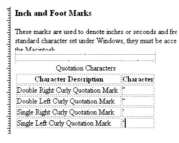

16. **Save the changes and continue to the next exercise.**

CREATE ADDITIONAL TABLES OF SPECIAL CHARACTERS

This page requires two additional tables: one to show the hyphen and dash characters, and one to show other special characters. You will use the same techniques from the previous exercise to create these elements.

1. **In the open file (typography.html), place the insertion point at the end of the paragraph after the Em Dash heading.**

2. **Insert a 2 × 2 table (2 rows, 2 columns) with a top heading, using "Hyphen and Dash Characters" as the caption.**

3. **Switch to Expanded Tables mode. In the top row, type "Character Description" in the left cell and type "Character" in the right cell.**

4. **Exit Expanded Tables mode and complete the table with the following three lines of information.**

Hyphen	-
En Dash	–
Em Dash	—

> **Note:**
>
> *Type the hyphen, but insert the en and em dashes from the Insert Other Character dialog box.*

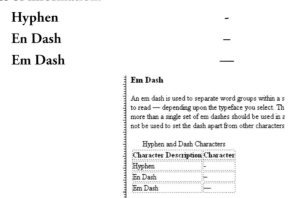

5. Place the insertion point at the end of the first paragraph after the Registered Trademark Symbol heading.

6. Insert a 2 × 2 table (2 rows, 2 columns) with a top heading and "Special Characters" as the caption.

7. Switch to Expanded Tables mode. In the top row, type "Character Description" in the left cell and type "Character" in the right cell.

8. Exit Expanded Tables mode and complete the table with the following rows.

   For now, type an "x" as a placeholder for the mult character; insert the rest of the characters from the Characters list in the Text Insert bar.

Multiplication Sign	x
Copyright Symbol	©
Registered Trademark Symbol	®
Trademark Symbol	™

9. Select the "x" placeholder character for the multiplication sign and change to Split view.

10. In the Code pane, replace the selected "x" by typing "×".

11. Return to Design view, save your changes, and continue to the next stage of the project.

Stage 5 Fitting a Page into an Existing Site

For all intents and purposes, the content of the Web page is complete. The text is finished and the markup is in place. However, this page does not look like the rest of the pages on the company's site, nor can you link to any other pages on the site (the only links in this page are to external sites).

You need to add a few more components before the page is ready to upload to the ATC site. Every page on the site contains a top header that states the name of the site and its purpose. Every page also contains a footer with the mailing address and an email link to ATC. Finally, every page includes two navigation bars, each with links to other parts of the ATC Web site.

ADD THE HEADER PARAGRAPH

The header paragraph is a basic paragraph with one distinction: To separate it from the main content, you add an id attribute with the attribute value of "header." The id does not change the structure of this paragraph, but simply identifies it for the purposes of CSS styling.

1. **With typography.html open in Design view, place the insertion point to the left of "You" at the beginning of the block quote text. Press Return/Enter to add a new paragraph before the block quote.**

2. **Move the insertion point up to the new empty paragraph and click the Text Outdent button in the Properties Inspector.**

   The Text Outdent button removes the <blockquote> tag from the current paragraph.

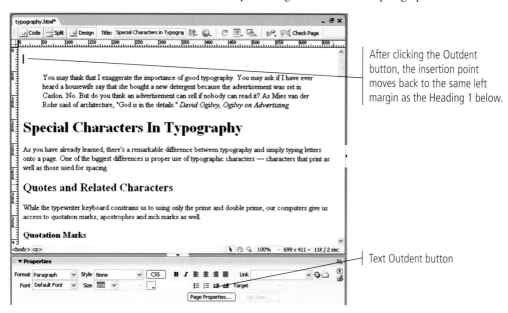

After clicking the Outdent button, the insertion point moves back to the same left margin as the Heading 1 below.

Text Outdent button

3. **In the empty paragraph, type "Against The Clock, Mastering Graphics Technology".**

4. **Control/right-click the <p> tag in the Tag Selector and choose Quick Tag Editor from the contextual menu.**

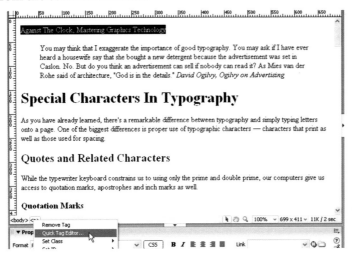

5. **Press the Spacebar and type "i".**

   By clicking the tag in the Tag Selector, you can use the Quick Tag Editor to edit existing tags.

6. **Press Return/Enter to accept the id attribute, type "header" between the quotation marks, and press Return/Enter.**

   The id you are assigning (header) has defined formatting in the CSS for this site. When you later attach the CSS file to this page, the appropriate header formats will be applied to page content that is identified (through the id attribute) as a header.

7. **Examine the text in the header paragraph.**

   The text appears no different than text in any other paragraph in the document. However, the id attribute will set it apart from the other paragraphs after CSS styling has been applied.

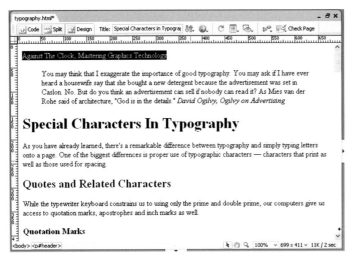

8. **Save the changes and continue to the next exercise.**

ADD THE FOOTER PARAGRAPH

The CSS for this site has a footer id attribute to separate and format the footer content apart from the rest of the paragraphs in this page. (The footer content in this page also has two abbreviations and an e-mail link, requiring a bit more effort to mark up.)

1. **In the open file (typography.html), place the insertion point at the end of the last item in the ordered list at the bottom of the page.**

2. **Press Return/Enter twice.**

   Pressing Return/Enter once creates the next list item — in this case, #4. If you don't type anything (including a space) and press Return/Enter again, Dreamweaver recognizes that you want to escape from the ordered list, deletes the last empty list item, and moves the insertion point into an empty paragraph below the ordered list.

3. **Type "Against The Clock, Inc. | PO Box 260092 | Tampa, Florida 33685 | 800-256-4282 | information@AgainstTheClock.com" in the empty paragraph.**

4. **Select "Information@AgainstTheClock.com" and type "mailto:information@againsttheclock.com" in the Link field of the Properties Inspector.**

5. **Click anywhere in the footer paragraph and, using the method described in Steps 4–6 of the previous exercise, assign the id of "footer" to the footer paragraph.**

   - **Select the footer content, then control/right-click the <p> tag in the Tag Selector and choose Quick Tag Editor from the contextual menu.**

   - **Press the Spacebar and type "i". Press Return/Enter to accept the id attribute, type "footer" between the quotation marks, and press Return/Enter.**

6. **Save the changes to typography.html and continue to the next exercise.**

CREATE A LIST OF LINKS

A navigation bar is simply a list of links. It is common practice among Web professionals to mark up a navigation bar as a list of links; after CSS has been applied, however, it takes on a much different appearance. The unordered list format is sufficient for creating a navigation bar.

1. **With typography.html open in Design view, place the insertion point at the end of the last list item in the Resources section and press Return/Enter twice.**

2. **Click the Unordered List button in the Properties Inspector.**

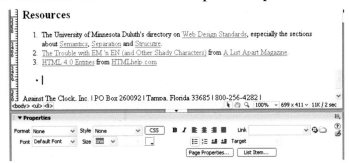

3. **Add five list items: Home, About Us, Links, Custom Services, and Downloads. Press Return/Enter between each one.**

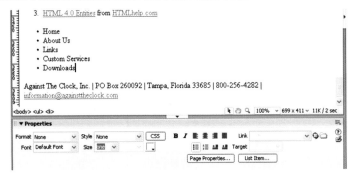

4. **Select the word "Home" and type "default.asp" in the Link field of the Properties Inspector.**

5. **Create the following links using the same method as in Step 4.**

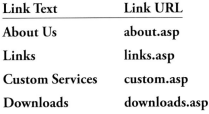

Link Text	Link URL
About Us	about.asp
Links	links.asp
Custom Services	custom.asp
Downloads	downloads.asp

6. **With the insertion point at the end of the Downloads list item, press Return/Enter twice to exit the unordered list.**

7. **Click the Unordered List button to create a new list.**

   Despite exiting the previous list, Dreamweaver assumes that you want to add another list item to the existing list, rather than create a new unordered list.

8. **Press Delete/Backspace to remove the extra (empty) list item.**

9. **Press Return/Enter three times to exit the list again, and then create an empty paragraph below the unordered list.**

10. **Click the Unordered List button to change the active (empty) paragraph into the first list item in a new unordered list.**

11. **Create an unordered list of links using the following text and URLs.**

List item and Link text	URL
Search the Site	**search.asp**
Use the Site Map	**browse.asp**
Hands-on Training Books	**hands_on.asp**
QuarkXPress Certification	**quark_certify.asp**
QuarkXPress Training Books	**quark_training.asp**
Companion Books	**companion.asp**

    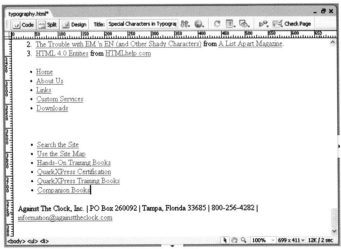

12. **Click in the empty paragraph between the two unordered lists, Control/ right-click the <p> tag in the Tag Selector, and choose Remove Tag from the contextual menu.**

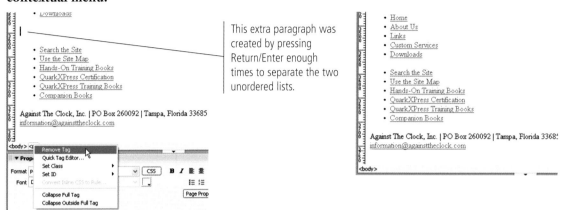

This extra paragraph was created by pressing Return/Enter enough times to separate the two unordered lists.

13. **Save the changes to typography.html and continue to the next exercise.**

 ## PREPARE THE UNORDERED LISTS FOR CSS

The two unordered lists are the navigation bars for the site. Although there are no other unordered lists on this page, other pages might have unordered lists. To be sure the CSS styling applies to these unordered lists only, you need to apply ids to these two lists. Each list item in the first navigation bar (unordered list) will have a different CSS treatment than the others in the list. In addition, each list item will have a different id.

As you saw with the header and footer paragraphs, adding an id to a paragraph does not change its structure; by applying CSS, which you will do when you attach an existing CSS file to this page, you can create different appearances that separate the lists from one another and from other paragraphs in the page.

1. **With typography.html open in Design view, click within the first unordered list.**

2. **Control/right-click the <ul> tag in the Tag Selector and choose Quick Tag Editor from the contextual menu.**

3. **To set the id, press the Spacebar, type "i", press Return/Enter, type "topnav", and press Return/Enter.**

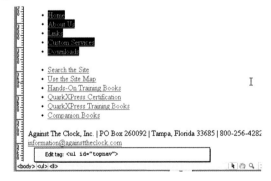

4. **Click in the second unordered list. Using the same method from Steps 2 and 3, set the id of the <ul> tag to "sidenav".**

5. **Click within the Home link of the first unordered list.**

6. **Control/right-click the <li> tag in the Tag Selector and set the id to "home".**

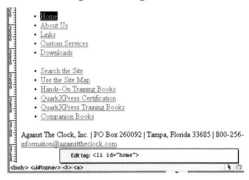

7. **Repeat Step 6 above for the following list items.**

List Item Text	ID of <li> Tag
About Us	about
Links	links
Custom Services	custom
Downloads	downloads

8. **Save the changes to typography.html and continue to the next exercise.**

 WRAP THE CONTENT IN A <DIV> TAG

For the purposes of CSS, it is sometimes necessary to wrap a block of content within a <div> tag. A div element has no structural meaning other than it forms a division and separates one block of content from another. In some pages, there might be multiple div elements, such as for the header (if there were multiple paragraphs), footer (same reasoning), content, advertising block, and others.

For this page, only one div element is required. The div element will enclose all of the content between the header and the first navigation bar — in other words, the unique content for this page. To ensure that this div element is unique, you assign a unique id to the element.

1. **With typography.html open in Design view, click to the left of "You" at the beginning of the block quote.**

2. **Scroll down to the bottom of the page and Shift-click to the right of the last item in the Resources ordered list.**

   All text between the word "You" at the beginning of the quote and the last Resources list item should be selected.

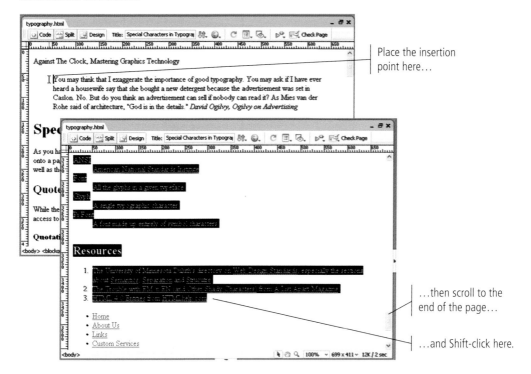

Place the insertion point here…

…then scroll to the end of the page…

…and Shift-click here.

3. **Switch to the Layout Insert bar and click the Insert Div Tag button.**

4. **Make sure the Insert field is set to Wrap Around Selection, type "content" in the ID field, and click OK.**

   When you attach the CSS file, text elements in the content div can be formatted apart from text elements with the same structure but which are outside the div.

5. **Examine the page.**

   The dashed border around the div element is a Dreamweaver feature; it is not the default appearance of a div element.

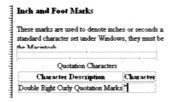

6. **Save the changes to typography.html and continue to the next exercise.**

Attach the CSS File

To make this page more visually pleasing to ATC's visitors — and to be consistent with the rest of the ATC site — you need to attach the CSS file that is already used for other pages in the client's existing site.

The CSS file, which is a file of instructions on how to display the Web page, is separate from the HTML document. When a browser downloads an HTML file, it examines the code for external files that are required to display it, such as images and CSS files. The browser then downloads the external files and merges them into the display of the Web page. In the case of a CSS file, the browser reads the instructions, and then applies the styles to the page.

After attaching the style sheet to the page, and depending on what the CSS file defines, you might see a dramatic difference in the appearance of the page. Not only will text styling change, but so will the layout — even to the point of moving some components of the page to locations far away from where they appear in the code. It can be difficult to work with a styled page, especially since Dreamweaver doesn't support some components of CSS, and therefore doesn't properly display the page.

1. **With typography.html open, click CSS at the top of the panel groups to open the CSS Styles panel.**

2. **Click the Attach Style Sheet button at the bottom of the panel.**

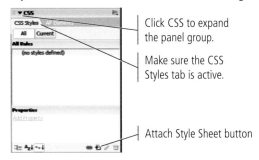

Click CSS to expand the panel group.

Make sure the CSS Styles tab is active.

Attach Style Sheet button

The Role of Div Tags for CSS

Although it might be a bit early to discuss the details of CSS, it will help to explain why **<div>** tags are used to wrap blocks of content.

On a page in which one unordered list (<ul>) is used for the list of navigation links and another unordered list is used within the content to list some information, how does the browser know to apply one style to the navigation list and another style to the information list? The answer is specificity — meaning that something within the code separates one unordered list from the other.

In the previous exercise, a <div> tag was wrapped around the main content of the page but not around the navigation unordered list. An unordered list in the main content appears in the Tag Selector as <body> <div> <ul>;

the navigation unordered list appears as <body> <ul>. This form of specificity is also referred to as the **DOM** (Document Object Model), a tree-like representation of the hierarchy of tags in a Web page.

To change the color of text in the two unordered lists, for example, the CSS code would be:

body div ul {color: blue;}

to color the text in the unordered list in the content (within the defined div). The CSS code

body ul {color: red;}

would color the text in the navigation unordered list (which is outside of the defined div).

DREAMWEAVER FOUNDATIONS

3. **In the Attach External Style Sheet dialog box, click the Browse button.**

4. **Navigate to styles.css in the root folder of the ATC site (WIP>ATC) and click Choose/OK.**

5. **When you return to the Attach External Style Sheet dialog box, click OK.**

6. **Examine the page in Dreamweaver.**

   The topnav unordered list appears at the top of the page instead of below the content, although it seems to be misaligned. Other elements might also appear misaligned or out of place, such as the navigation bars (as shown in our screen shot).

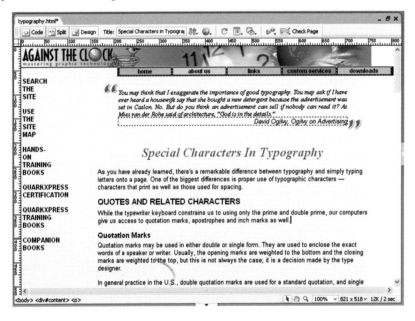

Note:

Dreamweaver is not a browser. It does not display active effects such as animated images or JavaScript. It adds visual features that are useful to the designer but do not represent the true display in a browser. The dashed outline of a div element is an example of this.

Dreamweaver also doesn't support CSS as well as browsers. This means that if some advanced CSS exists in the style sheet file, Dreamweaver might not display it as well as a browser. Don't depend solely on the Design view when you design pages, and don't depend on a single browser to test your pages. Every browser has its own bugs and weaknesses; you should test your pages in multiple browsers.

7. Preview the page in your browser.

The page looks much better. There are also graphic images that were not evident in the HTML page; these background images were inserted using CSS.

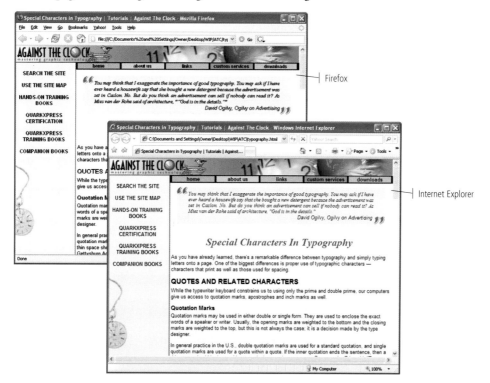

8. Close your browser and return to Dreamweaver.

Until you assigned ids to the header and footer paragraphs, you were simply creating a properly structured document. As much as the style of the page adds to the pleasure of exploring the site and reading the content, even without the CSS, the content was very readable. The page is also readable by all users (sighted or otherwise) because it is properly structured. This page would rank well in a search engine's results pages, too.

9. Close typography.html.

Summary

In this project, you learned how to use HTML tags and elements to structure and mark up a document so all visitors can successfully access and use a Web site. You learned that no matter how you receive content for a Web page, you need to correct the formatting with the appropriate HTML tags. You also learned that by applying id attributes and a <div> tag, you can turn a plain HTML document into something much different (and nicer).

Web pages you create for clients will seldom be as text-intensive as this page. But now that you have a solid understanding of how to work with HTML structures, both from Design view and Code view, you are ready to format content you receive from your clients — regardless of its condition.

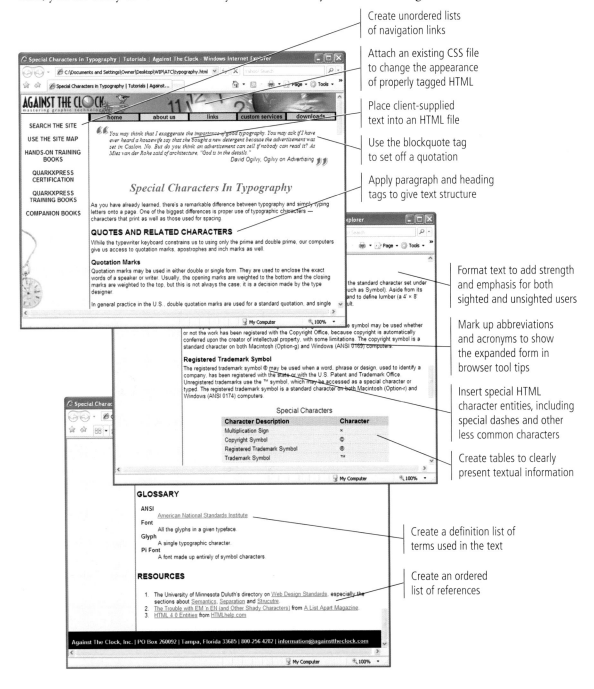

Create unordered lists of navigation links

Attach an existing CSS file to change the appearance of properly tagged HTML

Place client-supplied text into an HTML file

Use the blockquote tag to set off a quotation

Apply paragraph and heading tags to give text structure

Format text to add strength and emphasis for both sighted and unsighted users

Mark up abbreviations and acronyms to show the expanded form in browser tool tips

Insert special HTML character entities, including special dashes and other less common characters

Create tables to clearly present textual information

Create a definition list of terms used in the text

Create an ordered list of references

Portfolio Builder Project 2

The owner of Against The Clock has received a number of positive comments — and new sales — because of the *Typography Companion* sample chapter that you created for her to post on her Web site. She would like to add another page with a sample from the *Color Companion* from the same series.

To complete this project, you should:

❏ Use the ATC site folder that you already created for the new page.

❏ Create a new page and copy the text from ColorCh3.txt (RF_Builders>ATC) into the file.

❏ Mark up the page text with proper structural tags.

❏ Create header and footer elements, and attach the same CSS file that you used in the type chapter.

"We've had such a positive response from the type chapter that we also want to include a sample from the Color Companion. If we get the same increase in sales leads from this chapter, we'll probably go ahead and do online samples for all of our books.

"In addition to the text file for the Color Companion chapter, we've sent you a PDF file of the printed chapter so you can more easily see the different text elements — headings, lists, italics, special characters, and so on. You can just ignore the images and sidebars in the printed chapter; we don't need those in the online sample. There is, however, a table near the end of the file that we would like you to include in the online version.

"At the end of the text file, we added in the glossary terms that we think are important for this chapter. There aren't any resources, so you can leave out that section."

Biltmore Web Site

The Biltmore Village Inn has spent a lot of time and money redecorating, updating the living room, dining room, and many suites. They would like to showcase these improvements on their Web site, using photos taken by a professional photographer. You have been hired to create photo galleries that will allow potential guests to explore the inn, the suites, and the surrounding property.

This project incorporates the following skills:

❏ Using various methods to incorporate static images into a Web page

❏ Creating image links in a navigation bar and page header

❏ Assigning alt tags to images for improved usability

❏ Defining background colors and images

❏ Manipulating images in a Web page

❏ Working with multimedia files

Our inn has been a landmark for several decades, and we just spent a huge amount of money refurbishing and renovating the entire property to meet the needs of business and pleasure travelers. We want our Web site to reflect those efforts, which is why we had the photos taken by a professional. We hope you can use these photos within our existing site.

We'd also like to see some multimedia elements added to our site, since people seem to expect action of some kind on a Web page. We thought a photo slideshow might be a nice touch, and we also have some video clips that we want to incorporate.

One other thing: we've heard from a lot of people that the navigation list on the left side of our pages doesn't line up correctly. It looks fine on our computer, but many people have complained. Is there any way you can fix that?

I'm primarily concerned about the text elements that "don't line up." I don't think the client understands the issue of fonts on different systems, and that people can change the text size for their individual browsers. The only way to make sure the buttons always look the same and line up properly on any computer is to use graphic text instead of regular text.

Placing the room photos will be easy, but you will have to adjust some of them to fit the pages, and adjust others to fit into the script we use for slideshows. You might also have to make some minor sharpening adjustments after you resize the photos to make sure they look as good as possible.

Your last task is to develop the multimedia elements for the site. This is a very common request: "make something that blinks." I think we can give them what they want and still keep it tasteful.

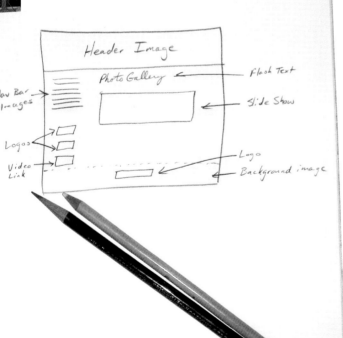

To complete this project, you will:

- ❏ Use multiple techniques to add images in Web pages

- ❏ Create a navigation bar from graphic text

- ❏ Control background colors, images, and repeat properties

- ❏ Use Dreamweaver tools to resize and sharpen images

- ❏ Set index transparency to blend images into backgrounds

- ❏ Resample images to reduce download time

- ❏ Create Flash text

- ❏ Insert a Flash animation file, a slideshow, a video file, and a favicon

Stage 1 Working with Static Images

Images serve two primary purposes in Web pages: informative and decorative. Examples of informative images include an illustration of how to put on a seat belt and a graphic of text such as links in a navigation bar. Decorative images are supporting images that could be removed from the site without affecting its content or message, such as a photo of the CEO beside the text of a speech, and the textured background behind the content of a page.

Images can be placed in the foreground or background, depending on the purpose of the image. Informative images must be placed in the foreground because they provide content. Decorative images can be placed in the foreground (such as the photo of the CEO) or the background.

The Alt Attribute

In Project 2 you learned about attributes, or components of HTML tags that provide additional information. For example, the title attribute of the <abbr> and <acronym> tags provides the long form of the abbreviation or acronym.

Most attributes are optional but some are required, such as the alt attribute of the <img> (image) tag. The purpose of the alt attribute is to provide a text alternative to the image (including graphic text) so visitors who use screen readers (or who have disabled image display in their browsers) will be able to access the content of the image. The alt text is also indexed by search engines, which allows them to show your site's images in the search engine image gallery and make a more qualified determination of your site's rank.

The alt attribute is also used when creating an image map to describe hotspots, such as "Home" or "Services." These hotspots provide navigation within the image map. If the image is simply decorative and does not provide alternate text, you use an empty alt tag (alt=""), which satisfies the requirement for the alt attribute. (Using alt="" is considered better than alt=" " because some screen readers pronounce the space.) Background images do not have the alt attribute option, so you should not put an informative image in the background.

> *Note:*
>
> *The alt attribute is commonly misnamed the alt tag; it is not an HTML tag but an attribute of a tag.*

DEFINE THE BILTMORE SITE

As in the previous project, the first step to working in Dreamweaver is to prepare the workspace and site definition. To keep the list of sites in the Files panel at a manageable number, you should get into the habit of removing the sites you are no longer working with (as you did in Project 2).

To ensure that links between documents and paths to images are created properly, the Biltmore site must be defined in Dreamweaver. The procedure for defining the site is essentially the same for the Biltmore site as for the sites you created in Projects 1 and 2 (except for the path, which is unique in every project). If necessary, refer to the first exercises in Project 1 for more detailed instructions.

1. **Copy the entire RF_Dreamweaver>Biltmore folder into your WIP folder.**

   As you complete the exercises in this project, work with the files in your WIP>Biltmore folder where you can save changes.

2. **In Dreamweaver, choose Manage Sites from the bottom of the Directory menu in the Files panel.**

3. **In the Manage Sites dialog box, choose the ATC site name, and then click the Export button.**

4. **Navigate to your WIP>ATC folder and click Save.**

5. In the Manage Sites dialog box, remove the ATC site from the list.

6. Click the New button and choose Site from the pop-up list.

7. In the Site name field, type "Biltmore".

8. Click the folder icon to the right of the Local Root Folder field, navigate to the WIP>Biltmore folder, and click Select/Choose.

9. Click OK to accept the Site Definition settings.

10. In the Manage Sites dialog box, make sure the Biltmore site appears in the list of sites and then click Done.

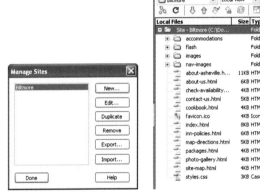

11. Continue to the next exercise.

 ## INSERT GRAPHIC TEXT USING THE COMMON INSERT BAR

Graphic text is text that has been typed and styled in a graphics application such as Adobe Illustrator or Photoshop, and saved in an image format that can be displayed in a browser. A graphic image is inserted into a Web page to replace typed text.

1. With the Biltmore site open in the Files panel, double-click index.html in the accommodations folder to open the file.

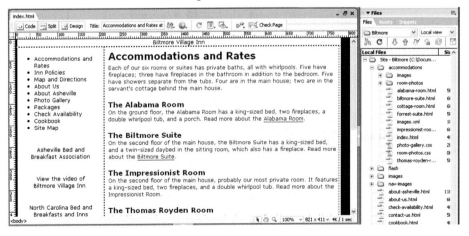

Note:

Although it has been done, it is inappropriate to create an image of all of the text on a Web page.

2. **In Design view, select the heading "Accommodations and Rates".**

3. **Delete the text.**

   An empty space remains. (In the code, this space is the now-empty <h1< tag.)

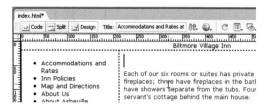

4. **Click the Images button on the Common Insert bar.**

   If the Images button does not appear as shown below (and the tool tip does not say "Images : Image"), click the arrow to the right of the button and choose the Image option from the top of the list.

   Inserting an image from the Common Insert bar is as simple as clicking the Images button, selecting the image from the appropriate folder, and then typing the alt text.

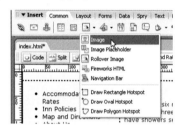

Note:

Dreamweaver provides a variety of ways to insert images, including clicking the Images button on the Common Insert bar, dragging an image from the Files panel, and selecting the Images option in the Insert menu.

5. **In the Select Image Source dialog box, open the accommodations>images folder, select the accommodations-rates.gif file, and click Choose/OK.**

   The image preview on the right side of the dialog box shows a small version of the image, the dimensions of the image, the file size of the image, and the download time (based on the connection speed settings in the Preferences dialog box).

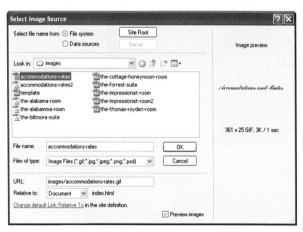

Note:

You could accomplish the same result by choosing Insert>Image.

6. **In the resulting dialog box, type "Accommodations and Rates" in the Alternate Text field and click OK.**

The alternate text of this image should be the equivalent to plain text so screen readers will find this heading, people with images disabled in their browser will see "Accommodations and Rates" in plain text, and search engines will treat the alternate text with the same degree of significance as plain text. Creating an image for each heading is fine as long as you supply the appropriate alt text for each image. (However, you might want to consider the extra weight added to the page each time you substitute a graphic text image for plain text.)

Note:

The Long Description field completes the longdesc attribute of an image. Its purpose is to allow the designer to offer a link to a longer description of an image on a separate Web page. None of the current browsers support this attribute, so you won't complete this field.

7. **Click the image in the window to make sure it's selected, and then examine the Tag Selector.**

In the Tag Selector, Dreamweaver shows the HTML form (<img>) instead of the XHTML form (<img />). This tag appears to the right of the <h1> tag, indicating that the image is enclosed within heading level 1 tags.

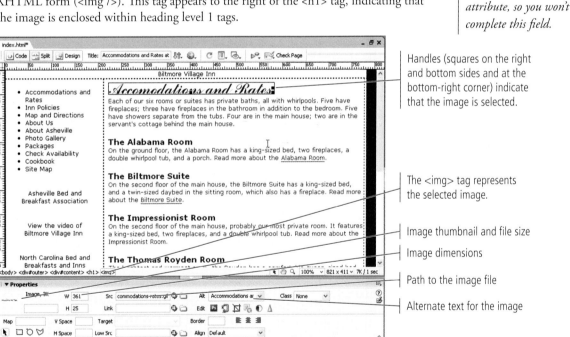

Handles (squares on the right and bottom sides and at the bottom-right corner) indicate that the image is selected.

The <img> tag represents the selected image.

Image thumbnail and file size

Image dimensions

Path to the image file

Alternate text for the image

8. **Click away from the image to deselect it.**

After you click off the image, you no longer see the handles.

9. **Save the changes to index.html and continue to the next exercise.**

The Image Properties Inspector

When an image is selected in the document window, the Properties Inspector not only displays properties (attributes) of the image, but also provides access to a number of image-related functions.

In the top-left corner, a thumbnail of the image displays, as well as the file size. The empty field below the image file size allows you to assign an ID to the image for CSS or JavaScript applications.

- The **W** (width) and **H** (height) fields are automatically populated based on the dimensions of the image file. These attributes are beneficial because browsers reserve the specified space for the image and wrap the text around the space while the image downloads; without these attributes, the browser reshuffles the text as more of the image downloads.

- The **Src** field is also automatically populated with the path to the image. As with links to pages, you can use relative or absolute paths. (If you preview your page locally on your computer, absolute paths to images will not work and the images will not be visible.)

- The **Link** field allows you to create an image link by typing the URL in the field or by using the Point to File or Browse for File buttons to select a link destination.

- The **Alt** field shows the alternate text assigned to the image (you can use this field to edit the text).

- A series of **Edit** options is available below the Alt field. Most of these allow you to do some basic image editing within Dreamweaver without having to open an image-editing application (although the first button opens the image into Fireworks). The other image-editing options are (left to right) Optimize, Crop, Resample, Brightness/Contrast, and Sharpness.

- The **Class** drop-down list allows you to create or select a class for the image for CSS or JavaScript applications.

In the lower half of the Properties Inspector, the left side includes tools for creating an **image map** and naming the related **hotspots** (in the Map field). The three shape tools allow you to create rectangular (or square), circular, or polygonal (multi-sided) hotspots respectively; the arrow tool allows you to select an existing hotspot to either edit or delete (you used these tools in Project 1).

- The **V Space** and **H Space** fields set vertical and horizontal margins around an image. (The CSS margin property is more flexible because you can specify a different margin width for each side of the image.)

- The **Target** field is only active when the image is a link; you can use this field to specify that the link should open in a new window or new frame (when working in a frameset).

- The **Low Src** field allows you to specify a low-quality (and smaller file size) image to display while the main image downloads. The purpose of the Low Src image is to support slow-speed connections, but this attribute is only supported by older Netscape and IE browsers.

- The **Border** option allows you to specify the width of the border around an image. (CSS is a better choice for this option since you can specify the width, color, and style — single, double, dashed and others — for all four sides or each side independently.)

- The three buttons in the right side of the Properties Inspector represent left, center, and right alignment. However, these attributes apply to the paragraph in which an image is placed, rather than directly to the image; you should not use these buttons.

- The **Align** menu provides proper image alignment options. Although there are several alignment options, only two (left and right) are commonly used.

Replace One Image with Another

While it's relatively easy to correct a spelling error in regular text, it's much more difficult to correct an error in a graphic text image. If graphic text has a spelling error, you have to recreate the graphic file and then replace the original image file in Dreamweaver.

1. **With index.html (from the accommodations folder) open in Design view, scroll to the heading image with the text "Accomodations and Rates."**

   In this graphic, the word "accommodations" is misspelled (one "m" is missing). Mistakes such as this are common; it's good practice to have someone else review your pages for spelling mistakes before uploading the pages to a Web server.

2. **Double-click the image.**

   Double-clicking opens a navigation dialog box, defaulting to the folder in which the image is located. If the accommodations/images folder does not open, navigate to that folder.

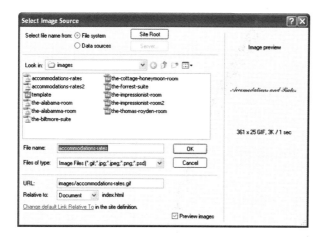

3. **Select the accommodations-rates2.gif image file and click Choose/OK.**

   Because the original image was assigned alternate text, the alternate text is applied to the replacement image, as well. Dreamweaver automatically adjusts the <img> tag for the width of the new image (as shown in the Properties Inspector); the original image was 361 pixels wide, and this image is 387 pixels wide.

4. **Save the changes to the file and continue to the next exercise.**

INSERT AN IMAGE FROM THE FILES PANEL

Dreamweaver provides many ways to insert images into Web pages, one of which is using the Images button on the Common Insert bar. Another way is to drag a file from the Files panel and place it onto a Web page. A third way is to use the Assets panel, which is part of the Files panel group. The Assets panel lists the image files located within the site's folders; you can drag an image from the Assets panel and place it onto a Web page. The Assets panel displays a thumbnail of the selected image at the top of the panel. (This helpful feature is not found in the Files panel. You'll learn more about the Assets panel in Project 4.)

1. **With accommodations/index.html open, select the text "Biltmore Village Inn" at the bottom of the page.**

2. **Choose Edit>Cut (Command/Control-X) to cut the selected text from the page.**

3. **In the Files panel, expand the main images folder (at the root of the Biltmore site).**

4. **From the Files panel, drag bvi_logo.jpg to the bottom of the page (the same location as the Biltmore Village Inn text that you just cut in Step 2).**

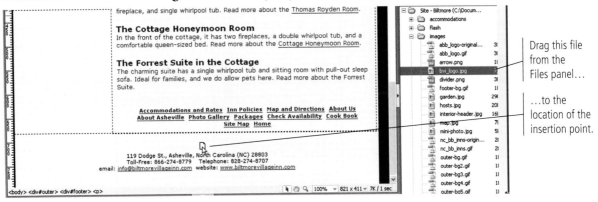

5. **Review the fields in the Image Tag Accessibility Attributes dialog box, then click the Cancel button.**

   You can click OK instead of Cancel, and the result will be the same; either way, no accessibility attributes will be added to the image.

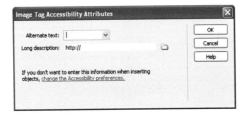

Note:

Do not double-click the image to insert it. Double-clicking an image in the Files panel prompts Dreamweaver to open the file in an image-editing application.

6. **With the image selected, click in the Alt field of the Properties Inspector and paste (Edit>Paste or Command/Control-V) the text you cut in Step 2, or type "Biltmore Village Inn". Press Return/Enter to save the alt text in the Alt field.**

Although it would have been easier to insert the alt text using the Image Tag Accessibility Attributes dialog box, we wanted to show you that you can also apply alt text via the Properties Inspector.

Image that you dragged into the page in Step 4

Alt text that you cut in Step 2

7. **Save the changes to index.html and keep it open for the next exercise.**

 EXPLORE FILE FORMATS FOR GRAPHIC TEXT

Graphic text tends to have few colors — perhaps only the text color and the background color. Graphics applications do use a gradient of intermediate colors to smooth out text edges against the background color, so graphic text should use the same color background that will appear in the surrounding portion of the Web page. However, some browsers display image colors differently than page colors, so even using consistent background colors might result in a discernible rectangle around the graphic text image. To solve this problem, you can use Dreamweaver to make the background color transparent in graphic text images.

Two Web-ready image formats are particularly well suited for graphic text: **GIF** (Graphics Interchange Format) and **PNG** (Portable Network Graphics). Both image formats employ lossless compression to reduce file size and download time, while ensuring that no information is lost during the compression.

Both GIF and PNG formats support **index transparency**, in which a specific color (generally the background color) is set to transparent. You can set the index transparency color in the graphics application, or you can use Dreamweaver's Optimize

Color Depth and Image Format

The GIF format supports only 256 colors; JPEG supports 16.7 million colors. These levels of support are often referred to as 8-bit and 24-bit color depths, respectively. A **bit** is a single unit of computer information that is either on or off (represented as 1 and 0). One bit has two states, two bits have four states (2×2=4), 8 bits have 256 states (2×2×2×2×2×2×2×2=256), and 24 bits has 16,777,216 (16.7 million) states.

Because of the color depth supported by the JPEG format, it is generally recommended that photographs be saved in JPEG format. While JPEG is the only acceptable format for medium- to large-size photographic images, you can use the GIF format for smaller files with no worry of degradation (loss of quality).

The PNG format has two color depth options: 8-bit and 24-bit. The lossless compression routine in the PNG format is generally better than the lossless compression used in GIF images, so you might achieve a slightly smaller file size if you use the 8-bit PNG format. Although 24-bit PNG is capable of displaying as many colors as 24-bit JPEG, PNG uses a lossless compression routine (unlike the lossy compression routine of the JPEG format). As a result, PNG doesn't compress 24-bit images as small as JPEG format.

Follow these general rules for optimal results: for Web-based files that contain only a few colors, use the GIF or PNG format; for Web-based files with many colors, use the JPEG format because it produces the smaller file size, even though the 24-bit PNG format produces the best image.

Image function to set the index transparency color. The PNG format also supports **alpha transparency**, which is a form of transparency in which each pixel has an alpha channel (0–255) that specifies the degree of transparency for that pixel.

When you create an index-transparent image, such as red text on a blue background where blue is set to transparent, a gradient of colors from red to blue exists at the edge of the text. If you design a Web page with the same blue-colored background, the results will look fine. But if the background of the Web page is changed to another color, such as yellow, then a noticeable blue halo will appear around the edge of the image. When you use alpha transparency — where the gradient at the edge of the text moves from the text color to transparent — the halo problem does not exist.

Note:

Internet Explorer 6 does not support alpha transparency; Internet Explorer 7 does.

No transparency   Index transparency   Alpha transparency

Yellow halo around image with index transparency.   No halo around image with alpha transparency.

Index transparency (enlarged)   Alpha transparency (enlarged)

JPEG is another common image format, used primarily for images with many colors (such as photographs). However, JPEG is not the best choice for images that have areas of flat color (such as text images) because JPEG uses a lossy compression method — pixels are discarded to achieve a smaller file size. When areas of flat color are over-compressed, speckles of other colors often appear, which negatively impacts the quality of the design.

Scalable Vector Graphics (SVG)

DREAMWEAVER FOUNDATIONS

Scalable Vector Graphics (SVG) is another up-and-coming Web graphics format. Images saved in this format consist of lines and shapes with fills, called **vectors**. Unlike **raster** images, which are made up of tiny dots called pixels, vector graphics are completely **scalable**; you can increase or decrease their size without affecting their quality.

SVG is a form of XML code, and SVG-based shapes are drawn using that code. The code for a basic circle, shown to the right, is quite simple; as the image complexity increases, however, so does the complexity of the code.

Although the specifications for SVG have been around for quite a while, browser adoption of the format has been slow; Firefox, Safari, and Opera support SVG natively within the browser, but IE depends on a plug-in from Adobe to view SVG images.

This circle was created by the code to the right.

Although the rest of the code is necessary in an SVG document, these two lines are responsible for creating the circle.

This turkey dinner clipart image requires over 500 lines of SVG code.

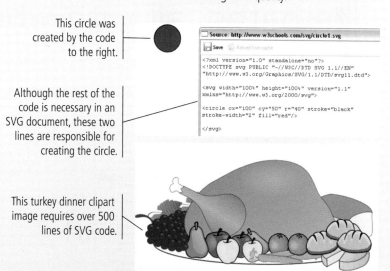

```
Source: http://www.w3schools.com/svg/circle1.svg

Save    Reload from cache

<?xml version="1.0" standalone="no"?>
<!DOCTYPE svg PUBLIC "-//W3C//DTD SVG 1.1//EN"
"http://www.w3.org/Graphics/SVG/1.1/DTD/svg11.dtd">

<svg width="100%" height="100%" version="1.1"
xmlns="http://www.w3.org/2000/svg">

<circle cx="100" cy="50" r="40" stroke="black"
stroke-width="2" fill="red"/>

</svg>
```

1. **With index.html open from the accommodations folder of the Biltmore site, click the Zoom tool on the right side of the status bar.**

2. **Drag a rectangle around the word "Rates" in the graphic text heading image.**

   Drawing a marquee with the Zoom tool zooms the page into the area that you surround with the marquee.

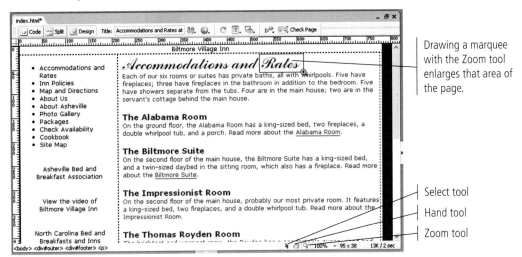

Drawing a marquee with the Zoom tool enlarges that area of the page.

Select tool

Hand tool

Zoom tool

Only two colors were used to create this GIF image (the background and text colors), but there are other colors at the edges of the letters that help to smooth the curves in the text. Note also that the background color is solid. In fact, the background color in the image has been set to transparent (using index transparency) so the light brown color is actually the background color of the page.

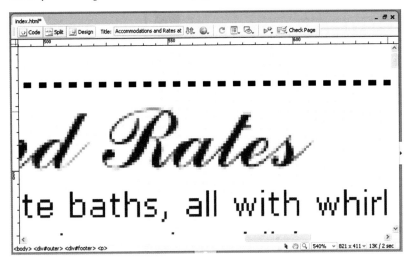

3. **Using the Magnification menu in the status bar, return the view percentage to 100%.**

4. Using the Zoom tool, zoom in on the word "Village" in the graphic text footer image.

5. Examine the image and compare its quality with the other graphic text image.

The designer used multiple colors in this JPEG image: the dark brown-red of the text, the sand-brown of the background, the beige "B" watermark behind the text, and the medium red-brown of the shape underlining the text. You can see more colors than these where the text meets the background. And if you look closely, you will also see light greens, yellows, and reds; these are artifacts caused by too much JPEG compression.

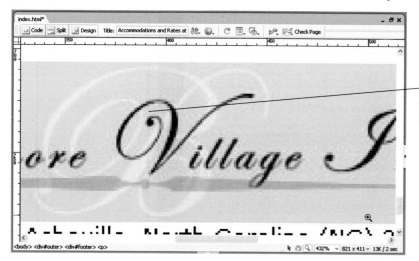

Notice the speckled appearance of the background — an artifact of too much JPEG compression.

6. Return the magnification to 100% and switch to the Select tool.

7. Continue to the next stage of the project.

Stage 2 Creating Image Links

Navigation bars are critical elements of every page on a Web site. Designers take great care when planning and developing navigation bars, ensuring they fit the form and function of the site. In designing the links on navigation bars, many designers prefer to use graphic text images rather than regular text. (If the site design requires an image for each heading, a new heading must be created as each new page is developed.)

 USE IMAGE LINKS IN A NAVIGATION BAR

When creating an image link, you can use the same methods you learned in Project 1 to create a text link. You can use the Browse for File method, the Point to File method, or type the URL in the Link field. Alt text for an image link does not need to indicate that the image is a link; screen-reader software provides that information to the user.

1. **With index.html open from the accommodations folder of the Biltmore site, select the text of the first list item in the top-left part of the page.**

Select the text in this list item.

2. **Delete the selected text, but leave the empty bullet point.**

   If you accidentally delete the empty bullet point, click to the left of the "I" in "Inn Policies," press Return/Enter, and then move the insertion point up to the empty bullet point.

3. **Click the Image button on the Common Insert bar.**

The insertion point should be flashing in the empty bullet item.

4. **In the Select Image Source dialog box, navigate to the nav-images folder (in the site root folder), select the accommodations_and_rates.gif image, and click Choose/OK.**

   The URL field in the lower section begins with two leading dots (..) because Dreamweaver is using a relative path from the location of the currently open page (accommodations/index.html) to the location of this image.

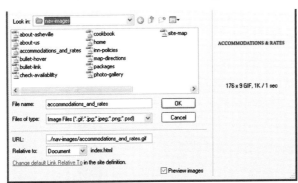

Note:

If the URL does not begin with ".." and the Relative To setting below it is set to Site Root instead of Document, click the Change Default Link Relative To link. In the Site Definition dialog box, change the setting of Links Relative To from Site Root to Document and click OK.

5. Type "Accommodations and Rates" in the Alternate Text field of the Image Tag Accessibility Attributes dialog box and click OK.

6. Using whatever method you prefer, link the graphic text image to the index.html file in the accommodations folder of the site.

You can type in the Link field of the Properties Inspector, use the Browse for File method, or use the Point to File method.

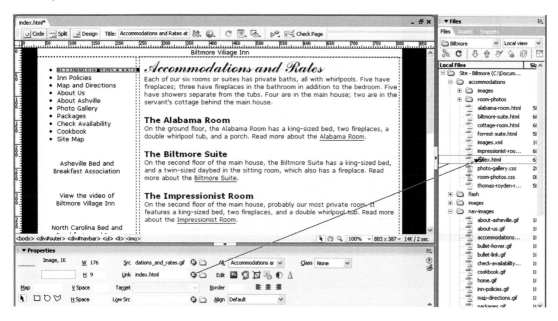

7. Click away from the placed image to deselect it.

By default, links in this unordered list are outlined or underlined with blue to indicate that they are links. In a later exercise, you will assign an identity to this navigation list and apply CSS to remove the blue outline (and the bullets, which will allow each navigation item to align properly.)

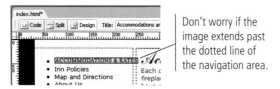

Don't worry if the image extends past the dotted line of the navigation area.

8. Repeat this process to replace the text list items with graphic text images, each with the appropriate alt text and links to pages (in the root folder) listed below.

Text	Image File	Alternate Text	Linked Page
Inn Policies	inn-policies.gif	Inn Policies	inn-policies.html
Map and Directions	map-directions.gif	Map and Directions	map-directions.html
About Us	about-us.gif	About Us	about-us.html
About Asheville	about-asheville.gif	About Asheville	about-asheville.html
Photo Gallery	photo-gallery.gif	Photo Gallery	photo-gallery.html
Packages	packages.gif	Packages	packages.html
Check Availability	check-availability.gif	Check Availability	check-availability.html
Cookbook	cookbook.gif	Cookbook	cookbook.html
Site Map	site-map.gif	Site Map	site-map.html

9. **Save the changes to index.html and continue to the next exercise.**

Normally you would copy these image links to each new page in the site; but in this project, the rest of the links have been completed.

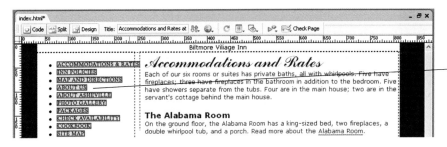

Later in this project, you will use CSS to remove the blue border around the image links.

 CREATE A HEADER IMAGE LINK

Rather than including a link in the navigation bar that points to the site home page, many designers prefer to use the logo at the top of the page instead. In this situation, the alt text can't be an exact translation of the text in the image because you want to make it clear that the image (of text or a logo) is a link to the home page. You might want to add the words "Home Page" to the alt text so that it reads "ABC Company Home Page." Screen readers will identify that the image is a link, so you don't need to add the word "link" to the alt text.

1. **In the open file (accommodations/index.html), place the insertion point to the right of "Biltmore Village Inn" at the top of the page.**

2. **Insert the file named interior-header.jpg from the images folder in the root folder of the Biltmore site. Use "Biltmore Village Inn Home Page" as the alternate text.**

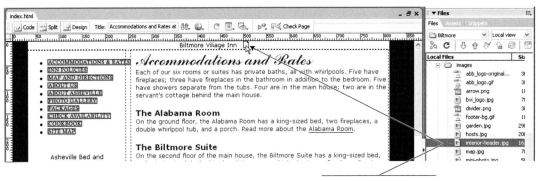

Drag this image to the right of the existing text in the header area.

3. **Delete the "Biltmore Village Inn" text from above the image.**

If you deleted this text before adding the image, the header area would have collapsed, making it very difficult to work with.

4. **Using any method available in the Properties Inspector, create a link from this image to index.html in the root folder of the Biltmore site.**

5. Click away from the image to deselect it.

Because you linked this image to the main site home page, it has a heavy blue border around it. You will not use CSS to format this section of the page, so you can simply remove the border from the image.

6. Click to select the header image. In the Properties Inspector, change the Border field to 0.

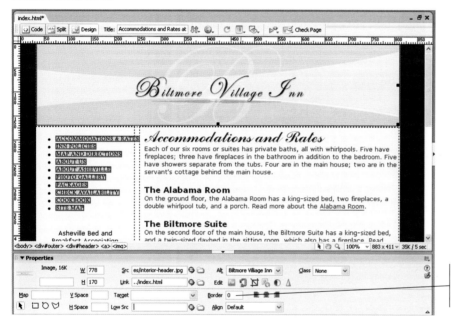

Set the border for the linked header image to 0.

7. Save the changes to index.html and continue to the next exercise.

 CREATE TITLE ATTRIBUTE TEXT

The **title** attribute can be used in any HTML tag to provide additional information; it acts as a tool tip pop-up when the user moves the mouse over an object — including images. (You used the title attribute in the <abbr> and <acronym> tags in Project 2.)

1. In the open file (accommodations/index.html), select the text "Asheville Bed and Breakfast Association" below the list of navigation links.

2. **Cut the text to the clipboard (choose Edit>Cut or press Command/ Control-X).**

3. **Insert the abb_logo.gif image from the images folder, using the text you cut as the alternate text.**

4. **Link the image by typing "http://www.ashevillebba.com/" in the Link field of the Properties Inspector.**

Despite being an image link, this image isn't surrounded by a border; CSS was used to remove the border.

5. **With the image still selected, Control/right-click the <img> tag in the Tag Selector and choose Quick Tag Editor from the list.**

6. **Click to the right of the closing quotation mark after height="52" and press the Spacebar. Type "t" and choose title from the code hints list.**

Alt Text, Title Text, and Tool Tips

Internet Explorer displays alt text as a tool tip when you hover your mouse cursor over any image with alt text. However, the W3C specification for alt text states that it should not display as a tool tip. In addition, developers might choose to use alternate text as a means to instruct the user, such as including "Click here to see our hockey skates"; this text is better suited for the title attribute than the alt attribute.

The title attribute is optional; title text is not required to make sense of the information in the tag to which the title attribute has been applied. Consider the use of title text in abbreviations; if you know what "SVG" means, for example, you don't need the title attribute information. On the other hand, alt text should contain information that describes the image; screen readers always read alt text, but they might not read title text (a verbosity setting in screen-reader software enables the user to control this behavior).

Alt text is the text equivalent of the image. Alt text should not appear as a tool tip (sighted users can see that a particular image is a photo of George Washington; they don't need a tool tip to tell them that). Alt text is only visible if image display is disabled in the browser; if alt text contains extra information that all users need, sighted users who have images enabled in their browsers might not have access to the alt text. To provide extra information that's required for all users, it must be placed in the title attribute.

Some developers prevent IE from displaying alt text in a tool tip by adding an empty title attribute (title=" "). When an <img> tag has both an alt attribute and a title attribute, the title text displays as a tool tip instead of the alt text; an empty title attribute has nothing to display, so IE displays no tool tip at all.

7. Type "Asheville Bed and Breakfast Association" and press Return/Enter.

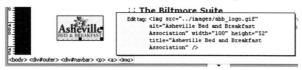

8. Save the changes. Preview the page in a browser and hover your mouse cursor over the image.

The title attribute is displayed as a tool tip.

> **Note:**
>
> *In IE it is difficult to determine whether the tool tip was generated by the alt text or the title text. In other browsers that do not display alt text as a tool tip, the text that appears in a tool tip must come from the title attribute.*

9. Return to Dreamweaver and select "North Carolina Bed and Breakfasts and Inns" at the bottom of the left column. Cut the text and insert the nc_bb_inns.gif image with the cut text as the alternate text.

10. Link the image by typing "http://www.ncbbi.org/" in the Link field of the Properties Inspector.

11. With the image still selected, repeat Steps 5–6 to insert a title attribute for the image, with "North Carolina Bed and Breakfasts and Inns" as the title text.

12. Save your changes to index.html and continue to the next exercise.

INSERT AN IMAGE WITH AN EMPTY ALT ATTRIBUTE

An image that is simply decorative can be given an empty alt. This doesn't mean there is no alt attribute assigned to the <img> tag; it means there is no content between the quotation marks of the attribute (i.e., alt="").

1. In the open file (accommodations/index.html), click to the left of the word "View" in the middle paragraph and press Shift-Return/Enter to insert a line break.

2. Move the insertion point to the new empty line, and then insert the mini-photo.jpg image from the images folder.

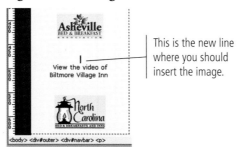

This is the new line where you should insert the image.

3. **In the Image Tag Accessibility Attributes dialog box, open the Alternate Text menu, choose <empty>, and then click OK.**

   Leaving the Alternate Text field empty is not the same as creating an **empty alt attribute**. If you enter nothing in the Alternate Text field and you don't choose <empty> from the pop-up menu, Dreamweaver creates no alt attribute. To insert an empty alt attribute, you must choose <empty> from the Alternate Text menu.

Click here to open the menu.

Note:

WebAIM (Web Accessibility In Mind, http://webaim.org/) is an organization that promotes Web accessibility and offers instructions and tutorials on how to meet accessibility guidelines.

4. **In the document window, select the image and the text below it.**

5. **Link the selected image and text to the file video.html in the flash folder (at the root of the Biltmore site).**

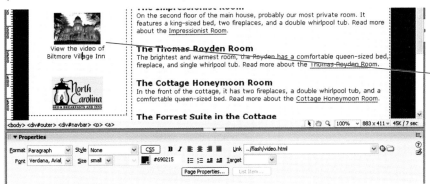

This text and the image above it should be linked to video.html in the flash folder of the Biltmore site.

6. **Save the changes to index.html and continue to the next stage of the project.**

Stage 3 Controlling Backgrounds with CSS

Knowing how to use and apply CSS is especially helpful when you need to work with background images. Without CSS, a background image can be placed behind the whole page or behind a table. With CSS, a background image can be placed behind any HTML element, it can repeat, it can scroll with the element or remain locked in position, and it can be positioned anywhere within the element.

The most common application of a background image is to allow it to repeat until it fills the browser window. In this situation, be sure the color of the background image contrasts with the color of the text (such as dark text on a light-colored background); otherwise, the text will blend into the background, making it difficult (or impossible) to read the text. We also recommend that you do not use animated background images.

The files in the Biltmore site have been create with a number of sections or divisions. Each division has been assigned a unique name (using the <div> tag) so that different CSS styles can be applied to different sections of the page, thus applying different backgrounds and formatting options for elements within each division.

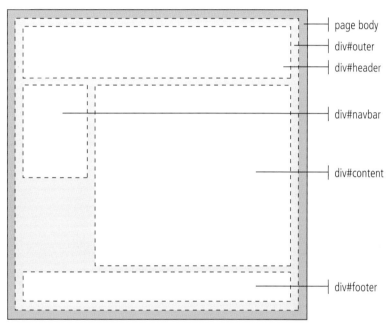

INSERT A BACKGROUND IMAGE IN THE FOOTER

Unless you specify otherwise, a background image will repeat across and down until the background of the element has been completely filled with the background image. If the width of the image is the same or larger than the width of the element, it will only repeat down; if the height of the image is the same or larger than the height of the element, it will only repeat across.

1. **In the open file (accommodations/index.html), click once on the Biltmore Village Inn image in the page footer.**

   In the Design window, divisions are identified by dotted lines. Division names are listed in the Tag Selector, so you can quickly identify which div contains a specific element.

The Tag Selector shows that this element is in the footer div, which is itself inside the outer div.

2. **Expand the CSS panel group, then display the CSS Styles panel in the group.**

3. **In the CSS Styles panel, click the All button.**

Click this arrow to expand the CSS panel group.

Make sure the CSS Styles tab is selected.

The All button shows all styles in the CSS style sheet.

The Current button shows only the styles that apply to the currently selected element.

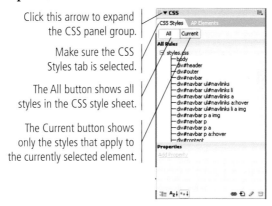

4. **Using the scrollbar on the right side of the CSS Styles panel, scroll down until you see div#footer, and then click once on div#footer to select it.**

5. **Control/right-click div#footer and choose Edit from the contextual menu.**

   The proper name of div#footer, in the context of CSS, is a selector.

Note:

To edit a CSS selector, Control/right-click the selector in the CSS Styles panel and choose Edit.

6. **In the CSS Rule Definition dialog box, display the Background category options.**

Choose a category of options from this list.

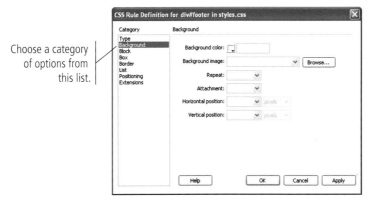

7. **To the right of the Background Image field, click the Browse button.**

8. **Navigate to the images folder in the root folder of the Biltmore site, select footer-bg.gif, and click Choose/OK.**

Below the image preview in the Select Image Source dialog box, you see that the image is 7 pixels wide and 600 pixels high. The narrow width means this image will repeat across the width of the footer; but because the footer is less than 600 pixels in height (about 250 pixels), the background image will not repeat down.

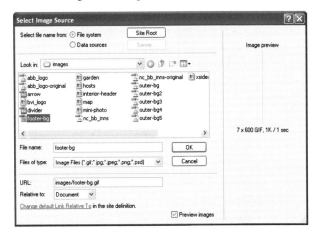

Note:

Occasionally, you might see a "_notes" folder within a site folder. Dreamweaver creates "_notes" folders to store notes or comments about files. You can create your own notes or edit existing notes by Control/ right-clicking a file and selecting Design Notes from the contextual menu, or by choosing File>Design Notes. These "_notes" folders (and the files within them) are never loaded to the Web server; they remain on your local computer.

9. **Click OK to close the CSS Rule Definition dialog box and apply the background image to the footer.**

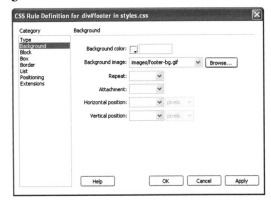

10. **Examine the footer on the page.**

This background image consists of only the medium brown color with a 1-pixel line at the top. As the image repeats across the width of the footer, the footer fills with this background color and a burgundy line stretches across the top of the footer.

The dashed lines that identify the footer div make it difficult to see the solid burgundy line across the top of the footer.

11. **Continue to the next exercise.**

There is no need to save because the CSS rules are stored in an external CSS style sheet file (not in the HTML file). When you click OK at the end of the process of creating or modifying a CSS rule, the changes are automatically written to the style sheet file.

SET THE BACKGROUND COLOR OF THE NAVIGATION BAR

Many Web pages use a different background color to separate the navigation bar from the main body of the page. However, if the height of the navigation bar area is shorter than the body of the page, the navigation background color stops at the bottom of the navigation bar. In some cases, however, you might want to use the same color for the entire left region of the page instead of stopping at the bottom of the navigation bar.

As you saw at the beginning of the last exercise, the navigation bar division is surrounded by another division (div#outer). By placing a background image for the surrounding division, the image will repeat over the full height of the outer division, regardless of whether the navigation bar division extends the full height of the page.

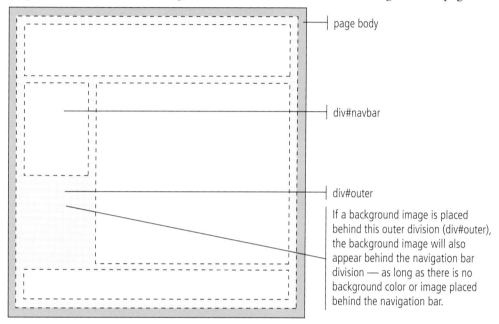

page body

div#navbar

div#outer

If a background image is placed behind this outer division (div#outer), the background image will also appear behind the navigation bar division — as long as there is no background color or image placed behind the navigation bar.

1. **In the open file (accommodations/index.html), click anywhere within the navigation bar on the left.**

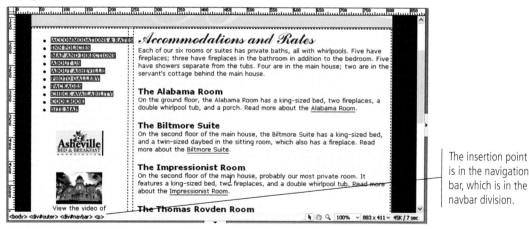

The insertion point is in the navigation bar, which is in the navbar division.

2. In the CSS Styles panel, scroll up to locate div#navbar. Control/right-click div#navbar and choose Edit.

3. In the CSS Rule Definition dialog box, select the Background category. Type "#E6CE9E" in the Background Color field and click OK.

The code #E6CE9E is a hexadecimal code for the medium brown color. There are various means of representing color using CSS; hexadecimal code is the most common.

Note:

Don't forget to type the "#." If you do, Dreamweaver will not interpret the code correctly.

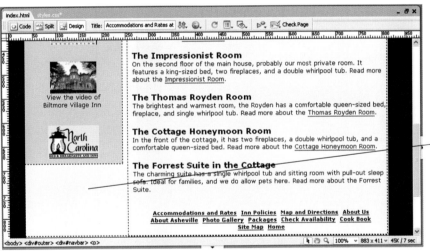

Because the navigation bar is shorter than the main content area, the background color on the left stops before the bottom of the page.

Hexadecimal Color Codes

The RGB color model describes colors using values for red, green, and blue respectively. Each color can be assigned a value from 0 (none of that color) to 255 (full strength of that color), for a range of 256 values.

Black has zero values for all three colors, so it is represented as 0, 0, 0. White has full values for all three colors, so it is represented as 255, 255, 255. The hexadecimal system is a numeric system that uses 16 numerals from 0 – 9 plus A – F (11 is represented by A, 12 by B, up to 15 by F). Since 256 = 16 × 16, in hexadecimal, 256 = F × F.

The range of 256 values for each color is from 0 to FF (by convention, the first 16 values from 0 to F are given a leading zero: 00 to 0F). Since RGB requires a value for each of the three colors, you will see hexadecimal color values such as EE04F3, 40896C, and E843A0.

In Web design, the hexadecimal color code must be preceded by the "#" sign (called the hash, pound, or octothorpe character). By convention, the letters should be uppercase, but neither Dreamweaver nor browsers differentiate between #EE04F3, #ee04f3, or #eE04f3.

DREAMWEAVER FOUNDATIONS

4. **Edit the div#navbar CSS definition again. Delete the background color code and click OK.**

5. **Edit the div#outer CSS definition (immediately above div#navbar in the list).**

6. **In the Background category, define outer-bg.gif (in the main images folder) as the background image.**

Note:

Although Dreamweaver offers Undo and Redo functions, they don't apply to changes to CSS unless you are working directly on the code of the CSS file (in Code view). If you make a change to the CSS that you want to undo, you must recreate the code.

7. **In the CSS Rule Definition dialog box, click OK to apply the image to the background of div#outer.**

8. **Save the file and then preview the page in your browser.**

As the background image repeats down, it creates a tan-brown area on the left side and a sand-brown area on the right side; a burgundy line (part of the image) divides the two areas. Also note that the color continues below the navigation bar content, which did not occur when you applied a background color to only the navigation bar.

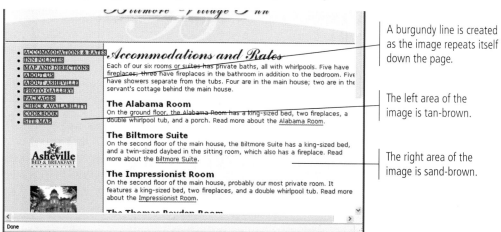

A burgundy line is created as the image repeats itself down the page.

The left area of the image is tan-brown.

The right area of the image is sand-brown.

9. **Return to Dreamweaver, then continue to the next exercise.**

USE REPEAT AND POSITION BACKGROUND PROPERTIES

The **background-repeat** property of CSS has four options: repeat (the default), repeat-x (horizontally only), repeat-y (vertically only), and no-repeat (the background image appears only once in the top-left corner of the element).

The **background-position** property requires two values: horizontal positioning (left, right, or center) and vertical positioning (top, bottom, or center). You can also use measurements such as "5 pixels" to position the background image.

You will also use two additional components in this exercise — padding and the :hover pseudo-class. In CSS, **padding** is the extra space around an element. Background colors and images can extend into the padding. You can also place a background image in the padding region of an element, but not behind the content of that element.

The **:hover** pseudo-class is also a common component of CSS. In many Web sites, when the mouse cursor is over a link (hovering), the text color changes, the background color changes, and/or the underline disappears. These changes are commonly created using the :hover pseudo-class.

1. **In the open file (accommodations/index.html), click any of the graphic-text images in the navigation bar bulleted list.**

2. **Control/right-click the <ul> tag in the Tag Selector and choose Set ID>navlinks.**

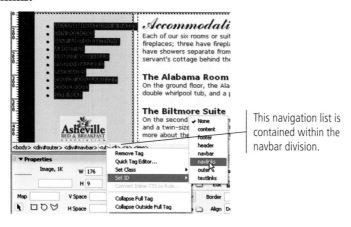

This navigation list is contained within the navbar division.

3. **In the document window, click outside the navigation bar to deselect it.**

The navigation bar is an unordered list with a unique style. No other unordered lists on this or other pages will have the same style as the one applied to the navigation bar. To ensure that it's different, the navigation bar is assigned a unique ID. The CSS rules use this ID to apply the navigation bar styles to this unordered list and only this unordered list. Without an ID, all unordered lists in this site would have the same style.

4. **In the CSS Styles panel, locate div#navbar ul#navlinks a and click to select it.**

The selector looks similar to the one following it, which uses the :hover pseudo-class; make sure you chose the correct one.

5. **Control/right-click the selector and choose Edit from the contextual menu. In the Background category, define bullet-link.gif (from the nav-images folder) as the background image.**

6. **Click Apply (don't click OK).**

    The Apply button allows you to view the changes without exiting the dialog box.

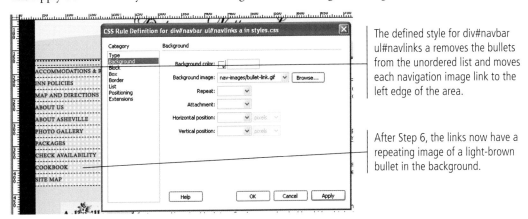

The defined style for div#navbar ul#navlinks a removes the bullets from the unordered list and moves each navigation image link to the left edge of the area.

After Step 6, the links now have a repeating image of a light-brown bullet in the background.

7. **Choose no-repeat in the Repeat menu and click Apply.**

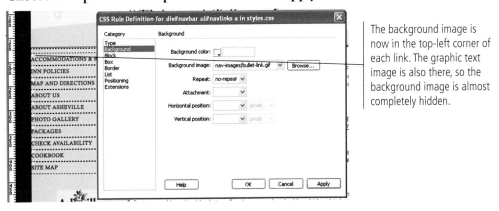

The background image is now in the top-left corner of each link. The graphic text image is also there, so the background image is almost completely hidden.

8. **Switch to the Box category on the left. Type "15" in the Left Padding field and click Apply.**

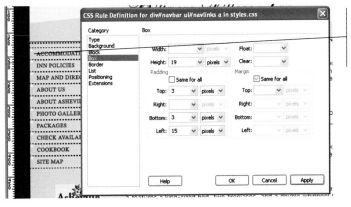

Left padding creates space between the left edge of the area and the left edge of the links.

9. **Switch to the Background category. Type "3" in the Horizontal Position field (pixels will be selected automatically as the unit). Choose center from the Vertical Position menu and click Apply.**

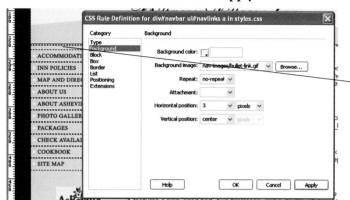

The horizontal position of 3 pixels moves the background image 3 pixels to the right. The vertical position centers the image vertically, making the image look like a bullet.

10. **Click OK to close the CSS Rule Definition dialog box.**

11. **Control/right-click the div#navbar ul#navlinks a:hover selector in the CSS Styles panel and choose Edit from the contextual menu.**

    The "hover" selector defines the mouseover state, or what happens when the user moves the mouse cursor over the navigation link.

12. **In the Background category, browse to select bullet-hover.gif from the nav-images folder. Set the Repeat menu to no-repeat and set the Horizontal field to 3 pixels. Make sure Center is selected in the Vertical Position field and Click OK.**

    The :hover pseudo-class only applies when the mouse cursor hovers over a link; it does not apply when the mouse cursor is away from the link. The :hover pseudo-class is a dynamic effect that Dreamweaver cannot display.

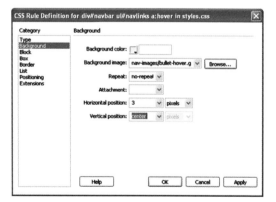

13. **Preview the page in your browser and move your mouse over the links. If you see a message asking if you want to save related files, click Yes.**

    As you move your mouse cursor over a link, the :hover pseudo-class is activated and swaps the light-colored bullet image with the dark one.

Note:

On some browsers, you might have to refresh your browser window to see the changes. If your bullets don't seem to be changing, click your browser's Refresh button and try again.

14. **Return to Dreamweaver.**

15. **Edit the style rule for div#navbar ul#navlinks a and switch to the Background category. Change the Repeat option to repeat-x. Change the Horizontal Position to left and the Vertical Position to bottom. Click OK.**

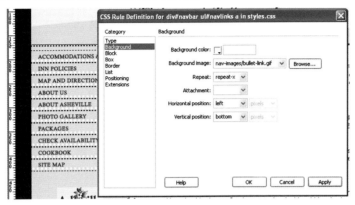

16. **Apply the same settings to the div#navbar ul#navlinks a:hover selector.**

17. **Preview the page in your browser and move your mouse cursor over the links.**

    Notice that the background images line up along the bottom of the link and switch with the dark image when you hover the mouse cursor over a link.

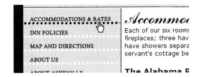

18. **Return to Dreamweaver and close index.html.**

19. **Close styles.css.**

    When you change the CSS style settings, Dreamweaver automatically opens the CSS file behind the current HTML document; your dialog-box based changes are automatically written to the CSS file. You do, however, have to manually close the CSS file when you are done with it.

Note:

When you continually preview the same page in the same browser, you might have to click the browser's Refresh button to see the effects of your changes.

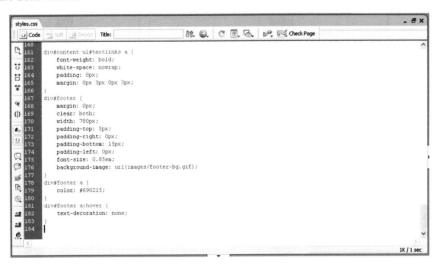

20. **Continue to the next stage of the project.**

Stage 4   Editing Images in Dreamweaver

Dreamweaver is not an image-editing application, but you can use it to perform some basic image-editing functions such as resizing an image, resampling a resized image, increasing sharpness, cropping, adjusting brightness and contrast, and setting image transparency. These tools cannot replace Adobe Photoshop or Fireworks (or other image-editing applications), but they are well suited for making quick adjustments to an image from directly within the Dreamweaver application.

A common mistake made by novice Web designers is to insert a large image into a Web page, and then resize the image so that it requires less space on the page. The problem with simple resizing — for example, adjusting the width and height from 3,000 × 1,500 pixels to 300 × 150 — is that while the image may appear smaller on the screen, the size/weight of the file remains the same. Your visitors will be forced to wait a considerable length of time to download such a large file. Rather, you should resize the image to the dimensions you want and then resample the image. **Resampling** discards pixels (when downsizing) so the specified dimensions of the image are the actual dimensions of the image. This reduces the weight of the image, which reduces the download time for your visitors.

When you resize and resample an image, the process can soften the image (especially after upsizing). You might want to use the Sharpening tool to restore some of the image's original sharpness. Be careful with the Sharpening tool, however, because too much sharpening will damage the image.

Dreamweaver's Crop tool is also very useful. **Cropping** is the process of cutting out/off portions of an image. Resampling is not necessary when you crop because the information in the remaining portion of the image is unchanged. You can also combine cropping, resizing, and resampling techniques.

CROP AN IMAGE

Photo galleries and product shots in online stores typically show a collection of smaller images (thumbnails) on one page, with each thumbnail containing a link to a larger version of the image. Using a gallery page, visitors can browse the entire collection of products and choose which products they want to see in more detail. Clicking the thumbnail image typically results in an enlarged image in a pop-up window, an enlarged image in a new page with additional information about the product, or an enlarged image without a background page. (An added benefit of thumbnail-size images is that they keep download times to a minimum.)

1. **With the Biltmore site open in the Files panel, open alabama-room.html from the accommodations folder.**

2. **In Design view, drag the file alabama-1-sm.jpg (from the accommodations/ room-photos/ folder) from the Files panel to the empty paragraph below the Photo Gallery text.**

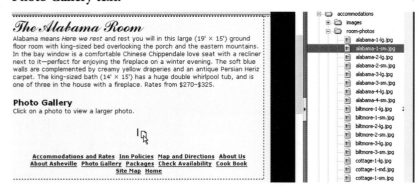

> *Note:*
>
> *You can use the resize and resample technique to increase the size of an image, but be careful if you do. The resampling tool must add pixels to the image to make it larger, and the results are often poor. You will almost always get better results from downsizing, so try to start with a larger image.*

> *Note:*
>
> *All of the Dreamweaver image-editing tools permanently modify the edited file. Always keep a backup image so if you over-edit, you can copy the backup image and start over.*

> *Note:*
>
> *When users click a photo gallery image or a link to an enlarged image, they expect the image to be significantly larger than the thumbnail; the goal of the enlarged image is to provide details that the thumbnail cannot offer.*

3. **In the Image Tag Accessibility Attributes dialog box, type "View of room entrance and fireplace" in the Alternate Text field, and then click OK.**

4. **In the Properties Inspector, click the Crop button.**

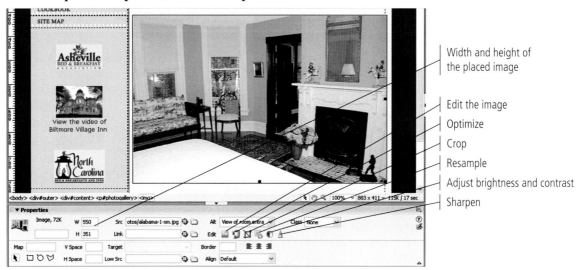

Width and height of the placed image

Edit the image

Optimize

Crop

Resample

Adjust brightness and contrast

Sharpen

5. **Read the warning dialog box and click OK.**

   When you apply any of the image-editing functions to an image, the selected image is permanently altered.

Note:

If another user clicked the "Don't show me this message again" option, you won't see this warning.

6. **Click in the lighter area of the image and drag it to the bottom-right corner of the photo.**

   This lighter area shows the portion of the image that will remain after cropping. When the cursor is inside the area, it changes to the Move cursor (a hand on Macintosh or a four-headed arrow on Windows), allowing you to move the area around the image.

The lighter area shows the portion of the image that will remain after the crop has been applied.

7. **Move the mouse pointer over the middle-left handle and drag it right so the picture on the wall remains inside the crop area.**

   When the mouse hovers over any of the eight handles (the black squares around the light region), the mouse cursor changes to a double-pointed arrow. You can drag the side handles up, down, right, or left; the corner handles allow you to change two dimensions (height and width) of the light area at the same time.

Keep this picture inside the crop area.

You can drag any of the eight handles to resize the crop area.

8. **Drag the top-center handle up over the picture above the mantle.**

9. **Double-click within the light area to finalize the crop.**

10. **Examine the Properties Inspector. Compare the current image's dimensions and file size with the original dimensions and size.**

    Don't worry if your dimensions are slightly different than the ones shown here.

The original image was 72 KB; it's now 34 KB.

The thumbnail shows the cropped image.

The original dimensions were 550 × 351; now the dimensions are 297 × 341.

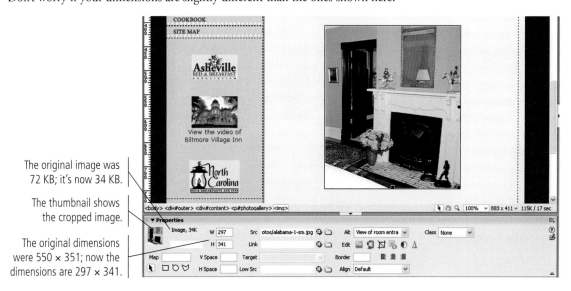

11. **Save the changes to alabama-room.html and continue to the next exercise.**

You can resize an image proportionately or disproportionately. Proportionate resizing means the ratio of width to height is maintained; disproportionate resizing changes the width-to-height ratio. In most cases, you will want to resize proportionately. For example, if your image is 3,000 × 1,500 pixels (width by height) and you want to change the height to be 150 pixels, then the proportionate width must be 300. This is a very simple mathematical calculation that you can probably do in your head and then enter the new values in the Properties Inspector.

If your image is 897 × 445 pixels, however, determining the correct width of the image when you change the height to 150 pixels isn't such an easy calculation. Fortunately, Dreamweaver can help — it's as easy as holding down the Shift key while you drag a corner handle to resize the image. When you do so, Dreamweaver automatically constrains the resizing proportionately.

After resizing, you can resample the image to change it permanently and, if necessary, sharpen the image to remove some of the softening created by the resampling process.

Note:

You can access all of the built-in image adjustments in the Modify>Image submenu. If you have Photoshop or Fireworks installed, you can use this menu to open the selected image directly in one of those applications.

1. **In the open file (accommodations/alabama-room.html), click once on the photo of the room.**

2. **Move the mouse pointer to the bottom-right handle. When the cursor changes to the double-headed arrow, click and drag the handle to the left.**

3. **Release the mouse button.**

   The image is obviously not proportionately resized.

4. **Examine the Properties Inspector. Note that the dimensions are bold and the Reset Image to Original Size button is visible.**

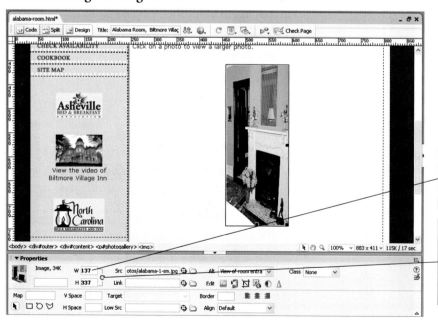

When the dimensions (one or both) appear in bold, it means the image has been resized in one or both dimensions.

The Reset Image to Original Size button appears only when the image has been resized. If you click this button, the image will be resized to its original (actual) dimensions.

5. **Click the Reset Image to Original Size button to undo the resizing.**

6. **Drag the bottom-right handle again, but hold down the Shift key while you drag.**

The Shift key constrains the resizing to proportional dimensions.

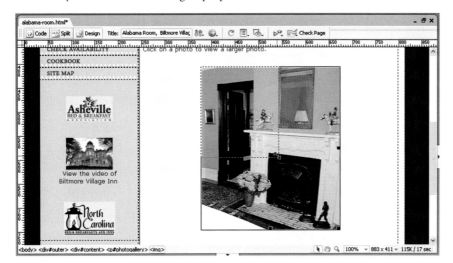

Note:

As you Shift-drag, both the Width and Height values change in proportion.

7. **Shift-drag until the Height value in the Properties Inspector reaches 90, and then release the mouse button.**

If your starting dimensions and proportions are different than ours (from the previous cropping exercise), your width might be slightly different than ours when you set the height to 90. For the purposes of this exercise, the intent is to set the height of each thumbnail image to 90 and allow the width to be proportionate to the original dimensions.

If the Height value skips from 91 to 89 and doesn't stop at 90, set the Height value to either 91 or 89, and then type "90" in the Height field. Doing so will create a minor distortion because the new size might be slightly disproportional — so slight, in fact, that it will be unnoticeable.

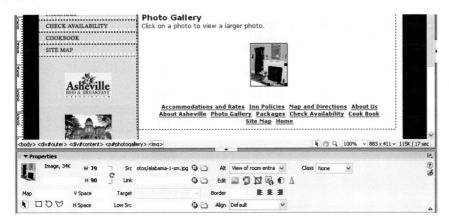

8. **In the Properties Inspector, click the Resample button.**

9. **Click OK to acknowledge the warning.**

As with the rest of the image-editing operations available in Dreamweaver, resampling permanently changes the image file; the resized dimensions become its (new) actual size.

The numbers in the Width and Height fields are no longer bold, and the Reset Image to Original Size button is no longer visible. These visual clues tell you the dimensions in the Properties Inspector are the image's actual dimensions.

Also note the file size of the resampled image; it was originally 72 KB, after cropping it was 34 KB, and now (after resizing) it's 4 KB.

After resampling, the Reset Image to Original Size button no longer displays in the Properties Inspector.

10. **Click the Sharpen button in the Properties Inspector.**

11. **Click OK to acknowledge the warning.**

On your own computer, you can check the Don't Show Me This Message Again option; but on a shared computer, we recommend you leave the option unchecked so other people using the computer can see these messages.

Note:

As with cropping and resampling, sharpening an image changes it permanently.

12. **In the Sharpen dialog box, make sure the Preview option is checked and then type "1" in the Sharpen field. Note the change in the image, and then click OK.**

In most cases, we find the Sharpen setting of 1 is sufficient.

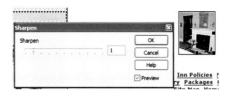

13. **With the image still selected, create a link from this image to the file alabama-1-lg.jpg in the accommodations/room-photos folder.**

You can use either the Point to File or Browse for File method to create this link.

14. **Save the changes to alabama-room.html and continue to the next exercise.**

 FINISH THE PHOTO GALLERY FOR THE ALABAMA ROOM

In this exercise, you practice the techniques you learned in the previous exercise by adding three more images to the photo gallery. You crop, resize, resample, and sharpen the images, and then configure them as links to the larger versions of the images.

1. **In the open file (alabama-room.html), click to the right of the existing thumbnail image to place the insertion point.**

2. **Insert the image alabama-2-sm.jpg from the accommodations/room-photos folder, using "View of the 2-person bath" as the Alternate text.**

When you first place Alabama-2-sm.jpg, the image is too large to fit into the space to the right of the navigation bar; the paragraph where the image is placed moves down the page below the navigation bar division.

You might have to scroll down the page to find the placed image; after you crop and/or resize it, the thumbnail paragraph will move back into the proper place to the right of the navigation bar.

3. **Crop the image to keep the bath and the painting above it.**

4. **Proportionately resize the image so its height is 90.**

5. **Resample and, if necessary, sharpen the image.**

6. **Link the image to alabama-2-lg.jpg in the accommodations/room-photos folder.**

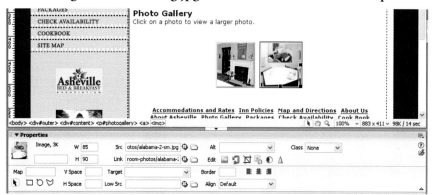

7. **Repeat Steps 1–6 for the following images.**

Image File Name	Alternate Text	Crop Image to show	Link Image to
alabama-3-sm.jpg	View of the king-size bed	bed	alabama-3-lg.jpg
alabama-4-sm.jpg	View of the bathroom fireplace	fireplace and towels on side of bath	alabama-4-lg.jpg

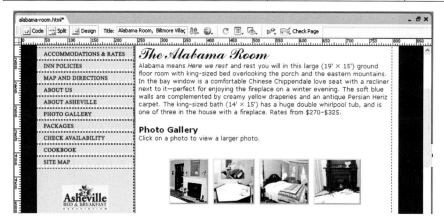

8. **Preview the page in your browser and click the links to test them.**

   Each thumbnail should open the larger image file in the primary browser window.

9. **Return to Dreamweaver and close alabama-room.html.**

 SET IMAGE TRANSPARENCY

When you create an image, you usually use the same color for both the background of the image and the background of the Web page itself. But as we have already explained (when we discussed graphic text images), this does not always ensure that the images will blend seamlessly into the background color. To eliminate the visible background color in an image, you should (as a general rule) set the background color of the image to transparent.

Dreamweaver's Image Optimization features are perfectly suitable for setting index transparency. To take full advantage of the features of alpha transparency, however, you should use an image-editing application such as Photoshop.

1. **Open biltmore-suite.html from the accommodations folder of the Biltmore site.**

2. **Click to select the Asheville Bed and Breakfast Association image below the navigation bar on the left.**

   The background color of this image is slightly different than the color behind it. (Changing the background color in any Web site can easily create this situation.)

3. **Click the Optimize button in the Properties Inspector.**

   In order to optimize an image, it must be selected in the document window.

4. **Set type of transparency to Index Transparency.**

   GIF images support index transparency only. To apply alpha transparency, you must set the Format menu to PNG.

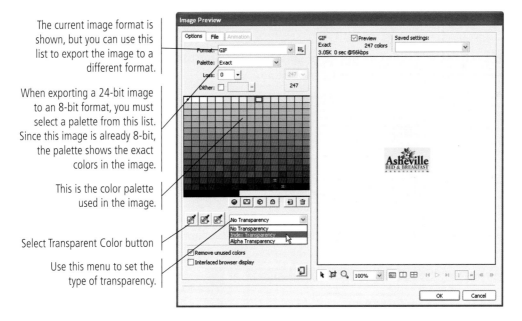

The current image format is shown, but you can use this list to export the image to a different format.

When exporting a 24-bit image to an 8-bit format, you must select a palette from this list. Since this image is already 8-bit, the palette shows the exact colors in the image.

This is the color palette used in the image.

Select Transparent Color button

Use this menu to set the type of transparency.

5. **Click the Select Transparent Color button (to the left of the transparency type menu).**

   The two other options are Add Color to Transparency and Remove Color from Transparency. For the purpose of index transparency, you can use either of the buttons on the left to select one color.

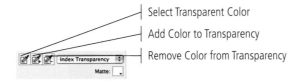

Select Transparent Color

Add Color to Transparency

Remove Color from Transparency

6. **Move the Eyedropper over the light-brown background of the image and click.**

   When a color is set to transparent, a checkerboard pattern appears.

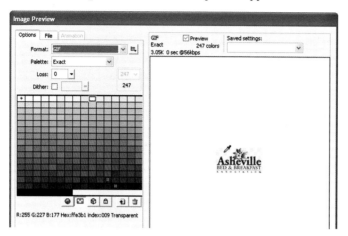

Note:

Alpha transparency allows you to select multiple colors; you must choose the Add Color to Transparency button to select additional colors after defining the primary transparent color. The Remove Color from Transparency button removes transparency values from a color.

7. **Click OK to apply the change and return to the document window.**

   The light-brown background of the image is no longer visible in the document window.

8. **Command/right-click the North Carolina Bed and Breakfast and Inns image and choose Optimize from the contextual menu.**

   This is another way to access the Optimize Image function.

9. **Using the same procedures in Steps 4–7, set the light-brown background as the indexed transparent color.**

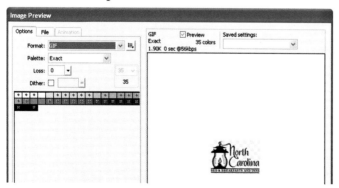

10. **Save the changes to biltmore-suite.html, and then close the file.**

11. **Continue to the next stage of the project.**

Stage 5 Working with Flash Objects

In addition to static images such as photos, logos, and graphic text, two other forms of images are commonly used — Flash animations and video files, collectively known as **multimedia**.

Depending on the configuration of the Web page, video and audio files might need to completely download to the user's computer before playing, or they might be embedded within a Web page and play as they download — known as **streaming**. The purpose of streaming is to allow the video or audio to play before the entire file has been downloaded; streaming can also provide some copyright protection because the video and audio files aren't stored on the user's computer.

Adobe Flash can be used to create simple animations such as moving text, as well as more complex animations that react to a user's actions (such as online games, animated buttons, and hotel reservation forms). Flash can also be used to display and control video. One of the advantages of Flash-based video is that most Internet-enabled computers have the Flash Player plug-in installed; other formats (QuickTime, WMV) might be available only to certain operating systems, or they might require a less common plug-in (for example, RealPlayer).

 INSERT A FLASH ANIMATION

Many Web sites contain Flash animations to add visual interest to a site. Because both Dreamweaver and Flash are developed by the same company, and because Flash animations appear in so many Web pages, Dreamweaver provides the option of viewing Flash animations from directly within the Dreamweaver interface.

Inserting Flash objects into a Web page requires a complicated mix of HTML tags, including the **<object>** and **<param>** tags. Furthermore, to comply with an ongoing patent dispute regarding the embedding of plug-ins within a Web page, Flash objects (among others) must be loaded into a browser using JavaScript. Fortunately, Dreamweaver embeds Flash objects within Web pages and properly writes the <object> and <param> tags for you, surrounding them with the appropriate JavaScript code to comply with the patent.

1. **Open index.html from the root folder of the Biltmore site.**

2. **In Design view, click to the right of the word "Flash" at the top of the page.**

    Without content in a <div> tag, the element in the document window collapses on itself. Although the <div> code still exists, it becomes virtually impossible to position the insertion point in the empty element in Design view. For that reason, we inserted dummy text to keep the <div> element open; you'll delete this dummy text later.

3. **In the Common Insert bar, click the arrow to the right of the Media button and choose Flash.**

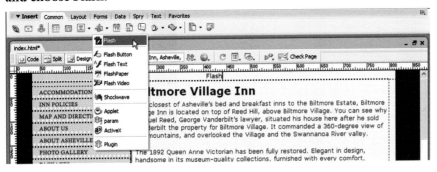

Note:

Video can be converted to Web-enabled formats such as QuickTime, Windows Media Video (WMV), or Progressive Networks' RealPlayer format.

Note:

Dreamweaver provides some basic Flash functionality, such as buttons, but Dreamweaver is not a Flash development application.

*For more sophisticated Flash animations, you need Flash Professional; we recommend the book **Adobe Flash CS3: The Professional Portfolio** from Against The Clock.*

Note:

To view Flash objects in your browser, the Flash plug-in must be installed on your computer. In the past, you had to manually download and install the plug-in; but today, most browsers have the Flash plug-in installed, or it is automatically installed the first time you need the plug-in to view a Flash movie.

4. **Open the flash folder in the root of the Biltmore site, select home.swf, and click Choose/OK.**

5. **Type "Biltmore Village Inn" in the Title field of the Object Tag Accessibility Attributes dialog box, and then click OK.**

   The title attribute provides some measure of accessibility to Flash objects. This animation is simple, containing the text "Biltmore Village Inn," as well as some photos of the inn. In this case, the text of the animation is sufficient for accessibility purposes. Interactive Flash objects that change with user interaction and include a large amount of text require accessibility to be built into the Flash object.

Note:

SWF is the final, compressed, uneditable format of Flash files. The FLA format is the editable format.

6. **With the Flash object selected in the Design window, examine the Properties Inspector.**

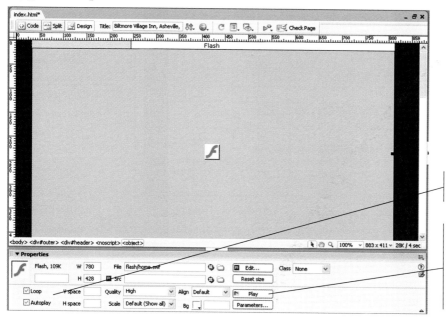

These options control the playback of the animation.

Although Dreamweaver cannot display JavaScript and animated GIF images, Dreamweaver does provide the option to play Flash animations directly in the document window.

7. **Click the Play button and watch the animation. When you're finished, click the Stop button.**

   The Play button changes to the Stop button after the animation has started to play.

When the animation is playing, the Properties Inspector includes a Stop button to control the preview.

8. Delete the word "Flash" above the Flash object.

9. **Save the file. Click OK in the warning message that the page now uses an object or behavior that requires supporting files.**

    The necessary files — in this case, a script named AC_RunActiveContent.js — is automatically added to a Scripts folder in your site folder. For the Flash movie file to work properly, this file should be uploaded along with the rest of your site files.

10. **Close index.html, then continue to the next exercise.**

Insert Flash Text

Flash text is one form of Flash that Dreamweaver can create without requiring the full Flash application. You can use Flash text to create static text such as a heading, or to create a graphic text link. You can even create a simple animation by configuring the text to change color when the mouse rolls over it.

There are a few advantages to using Flash text:

*   You can create it in Dreamweaver.

*   It embeds the shape of the font within the image, so it doesn't matter if your visitors have that font installed on their computers.

*   It is easily editable, in case you need to change a color or correct a mistake.

There are also disadvantages to using Flash text:

*   It is not as accessible as standard image formats.

*   It does not support transparency, so you can't use it against a textured background.

*   Flash text, similar to all Flash objects, requires the Flash plug-in.

1. **From the accommodations folder of the Biltmore site, open impressionist-room.html.**

2. **Click to the right of the Photo Gallery heading.**

3. **In the Common Insert bar, click the arrow to the right of the Flash button and choose Flash Text from the menu.**

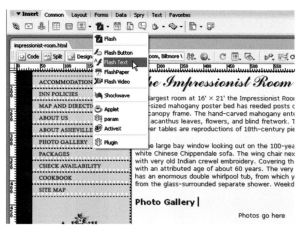

Note:

You also can insert Flash objects, Flash text, and other multimedia elements using the options in the Insert>Media submenu.

4. **Type "Photo Gallery" in the Text field. From the Font list, search for a script font, and then type "25" in the Size field.**

If you don't have Vivaldi, which we used here, select any script font you prefer. If you don't like the way it looks in the Text field, select a different font.

Select a font from this list of the fonts installed on your system.

Set the text color using the Color box.

Type the text here, and then view the font changes.

Ensure that the Show Font option is checked so you can view the changes to the font.

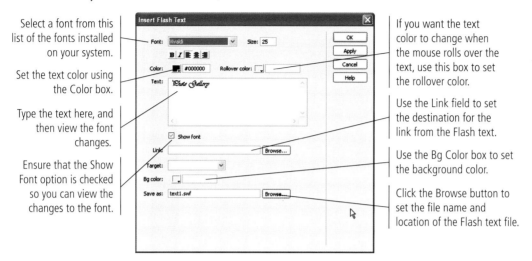

If you want the text color to change when the mouse rolls over the text, use this box to set the rollover color.

Use the Link field to set the destination for the link from the Flash text.

Use the Bg Color box to set the background color.

Click the Browse button to set the file name and location of the Flash text file.

5. **Click the Color swatch. Move the Eyedropper tool onto the page over the burgundy of the Photo Gallery text until the color code at the top of the Color Swatch dialog box displays #690215. Click to select that color.**

The Eyedropper can pick up colors from anywhere in the document window; you don't have to click one of the swatches to select a color.

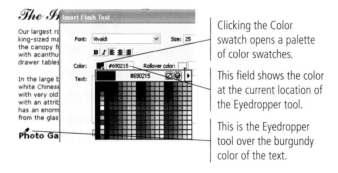

Clicking the Color swatch opens a palette of color swatches.

This field shows the color at the current location of the Eyedropper tool.

This is the Eyedropper tool over the burgundy color of the text.

6. **Click the Rollover Color swatch and choose a dark blue color from the swatch palette.**

7. **Click the Bg Color swatch. Move the Eyedropper tool over the light-brown background color until the color code shows #FBEFDC. Click to select the color.**

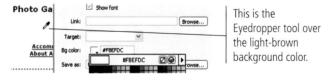

This is the Eyedropper tool over the light-brown background color.

8. Click the Browse button to the right of the Save As field. Navigate to the accommodations/images folder in the Biltmore site, type "photo-gallery.swf" in the File Name field, and click Save.

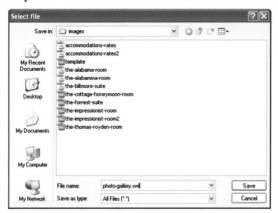

9. Click OK in the Insert Flash Text dialog box.

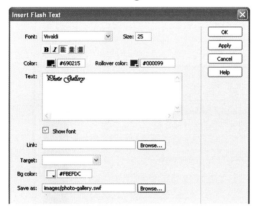

10. Type "Photo Gallery" in the Title field of the resulting Flash Accessibility Attributes dialog box, and then click OK.

Flash images do not support transparency, so the background color must be specified.

11. Delete the text "Photo Gallery" before the new text image.

12. Save the file, and then preview the page in your browser.

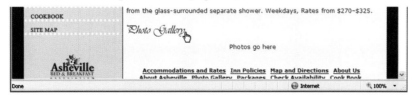

13. Return to Dreamweaver and continue to the next exercise.

Note:

It is very easy to edit Flash text. Simply double-click the text element in the document window and the Insert Flash Text dialog box opens with all of the settings for the selected text. You can edit the text, color, rollover color, and/or link destination, and then click OK to save the changes.

INSERT AND CONFIGURE A FLASH SLIDESHOW

The Flash animation that you added in the first part of this stage used images from the Biltmore Village Inn. To change the images, you would have to use Flash Pro to rebuild the animation.

Todd Dominey (www.whatdoiknow.org) created a Flash-based slideshow object that you can easily configure to use your own photos. The slideshow reads the content of an XML file called images.xml, which contains the file names (and paths if necessary) of the photos to be shown in the slideshow. By changing the file names, you can use the same Flash object to show different photos. You must save the images in JPEG format, and you must resize the images to fit within the dimensions of the Flash object. Once those tasks are done, you have access to an easily customizable slideshow animation — without using Flash Pro.

Note:

The slideshow used in this exercise is available at no cost. But for a small fee, you can purchase Todd Dominey's SlideShowPro (www.slideshowpro.net), which contains a wide range of features.

1. **In the open file (accommodations/impressionist-room.html), select the text "Photos go here" below the Flash text you created. Delete the text.**

2. **In the Common Insert bar, click the arrow to the right of the Flash Text button and choose Flash from the top of the menu.**

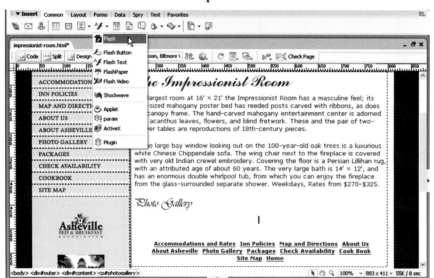

3. **Navigate to the flash folder in the Biltmore site, select slideshow.swf, and click Choose/OK.**

4. **In the Title field of the Object Tag Accessibility Attributes dialog box, type "Photos of the Impressionist Room", and then click OK.**

5. **With the Flash slideshow object selected, click the Play button in the Properties Inspector.**

   The slideshow is black because the images identified in the XML file don't exist in this site. You need to edit the images.xml file and replace the image file names with those found on this site.

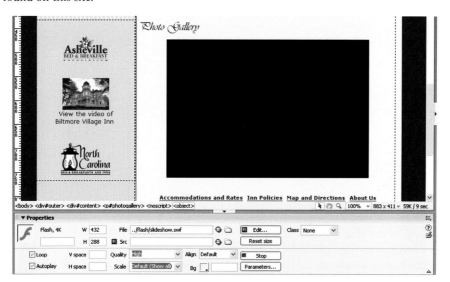

6. **Click the Stop button to stop the slideshow.**

7. **Using the Files panel, double-click images.xml in the accommodations folder to open the XML file.**

Some options for the slideshow are described in the comments at the top of the XML file; they are inserted as attributes of the opening <gallery> tag.

You can create a slideshow from as many images as you like by listing them here.

8. **Select and replace the image path for the first image (images/calliandra.jpg) with "room-photos/impressionist-1-ss.jpg".**

Note:

Dreamweaver is capable of editing XML files in Code view.

9. **Replace the image paths for the next three images with "room-photos/impressionist-2-ss.jpg", "room-photos/impressionist-3-ss.jpg", and "room-photos/impressionist-4-ss.jpg".**

10. **Delete the remaining four <image /> tag lines, but keep the closing </gallery> line.**

For this slideshow to work properly, the file slideshow.swf can be placed in any folder within your site but images.xml must be placed in the same folder as the page calling it. Because of code in the slideshow.swf file, images.xml cannot be renamed; if you want to use it for two different slideshows in the same folder, you must move one of the slideshows to another folder. Finally, the paths to the images must be relative to the location of the images.xml file. (You can also use absolute paths, but you won't be able to preview the slideshow from your local computer.)

```
8    -->
9    <gallery timer="5" order="sequential" fadetime="2" looping="yes" xpos="0" ypos="0">
10   <image path="room-photos/impressionist-1-ss.jpg" />
11   <image path="room-photos/impressionist-2-ss.jpg" />
12   <image path="room-photos/impressionist-3-ss.jpg" />
13   <image path="room-photos/impressionist-4-ss.jpg" />
14   </gallery>
```

11. **Save the changes to images.xml and close the file.**

12. **With the Flash slideshow object selected in the impressioninst-room.html file, click Play in the Properties Inspector.**

In the Properties Inspector, you can see that the dimensions of the Flash object are 432 × 288 pixels. If the photos had been larger than the slideshow dimensions, they would have been cropped by the slideshow; if the photos had been smaller than the slideshow dimensions, they would have appeared in the top-left corner against a black canvas.

13. **Stop the Flash animation, save the file and close it, and then continue to the next exercise.**

INSERT A FLASH VIDEO

A variety of video formats are available on the Web, including QuickTime (from Apple), Windows Media Video (from Microsoft), and Flash Video (from Adobe). Although the QuickTime plug-in is available for Macintosh and Windows computers, Windows Media Video can be played on Windows computers only. Flash Video can be played on Windows, Macintosh, and Linux computers because the Flash plug-in is available for all three operating systems.

Using Flash CS3, you can import videos in a variety of formats and save them in the Flash video format (.flv). You can wrap video inside a Flash video player and then use Dreamweaver to embed it in a Web page. This way, your visitors can view the video from directly within the Web page.

1. **Open video.html from the flash folder of the Biltmore site.**

2. **Select the text "Insert video here" and delete it.**

3. **In the Common Insert bar, click the arrow to the right of the Flash button and choose Flash Video from the menu.**

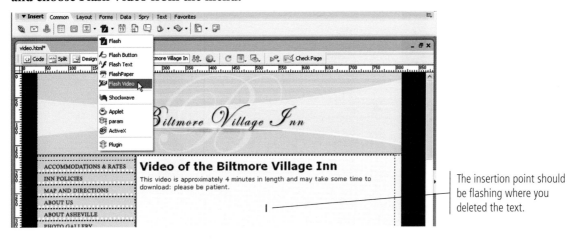

The insertion point should be flashing where you deleted the text.

4. **In the resulting Insert Flash Video dialog box, set the Video Type menu to Progressive Download Video.**

   The other option, Streaming Video, is used when the video is very large, the copyright owner doesn't want visitors to have a copy of the video on their systems, or there is a continuous feed from the source.

5. **Click the Browse button to the right of the URL field. In the resulting navigation dialog box, choose biltmore-village-inn.flv from the flash folder and click Choose/OK.**

6. **In the Insert Flash Video dialog box, click the Detect Size button.**

   The width and height of the video are detected and the fields are filled. The benefit to this step is that the dimensions of the video affect the skin options.

7. **Click the arrow on the Skin menu to view the options.**

   There are three basic skin appearances — Clear, Corona, and Halo. Each skin appearance has three Width options. The Width options affect the number and appearance of video controls. Video controls include play, pause, stop, skip to anywhere within the video, mute the sound, and increase/decrease the volume. A narrow-width video has less room for video controls. This video is wider than any of the minimum widths, so any Skin option will work.

8. **Select Clear Skin 3 and check the Auto Play option below the Height field.**

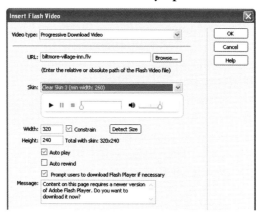

9. **Click OK to insert the video into the open HTML file.**

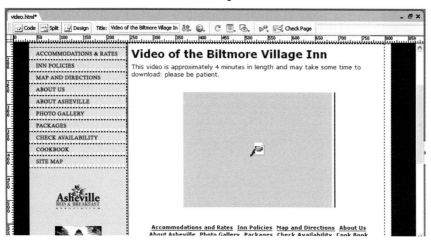

10. **Save the file and then preview the page in your browser.**

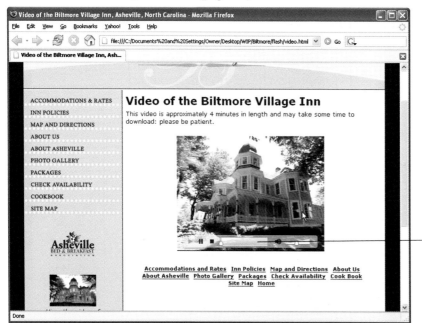

After the video starts playing, the controls fade out. If you move your mouse over the video, the controls will reappear.

11. **Close your browser, return to Dreamweaver, and close video.html.**

12. **Continue to the final exercise.**

ADD A FAVICON

Favicon is a word created by combining "favorite" and "icon." It refers to the icon that represents a site in your favorites or bookmarks list (beside the site name). A favicon is not randomly generated; it is downloaded from the bookmarked site. In addition to the favorites or bookmarks list, the favicon also appears at the left end of the browser's address bar or tab (if your browser supports tabs).

The site's favicon appears at the left of the address bar in all browsers, and on the tab in all but Safari.

A favicon is an image in the icon format. The icon format supports a limited number of colors, and it is generally restricted to 16×16 and 32×32 pixels. (The format supports both resolutions within the same file, which is one reason why it is unique.)

Although many applications can create icons, some graphic and Web design applications (such as Corel Photo Paint, Paint Shop Pro, and Adobe Fireworks) do not support the icon format. The icon format is not a Web-ready format — icon images cannot be viewed within a browser — which explains why the common graphics applications do not support this format.

If you want to convert a particular image to an icon (as long as it is in GIF, PNG, JPEG, or BMP format and square in shape), you can go to http://www.html-kit.com/favicon/ and create the icon at no cost. Ideally, you should create the image beforehand at 16×16 pixels so you can see and edit the file before converting it to the icon format.

Because the icon is commonly used as a representation of an entire Web site, the favicon.ico file is commonly stored in the root folder of the Web site. The file must be named "favicon.ico."

Dreamweaver does not provide code hints for most of the attribute values of the <link /> tag, so it is easiest to simply type the code in the appropriate location. The following code block is supported by most browsers:

```
<link rel="shortcut icon" type="image/x-icon" href="favicon.ico" />
```

1. **Open index.html from the root folder of the Biltmore site.**

2. **Click the Code button to switch to Code view.**

3. **Click to the left of the closing </head> tag on line 8, press Return/Enter, and move the insertion point into the empty line.**

   In general, the <link /> tag should be used to insert the favicon as the last tag in the head section of the document.

Note:

In an actual site, you would likely use an absolute path to the favicon file (such as ../favicon.ico) so the browser will always look for the favicon.ico file in the root folder of the Web site. Since you can't use absolute paths when previewing pages on your local computer, however, you must use a relative path.

4. **Type the code required to insert the favicon:**

   <link rel="shortcut icon" type="image/x-icon" href="favicon.ico" />

```
5  <title>Biltmore Village Inn, Asheville, North Carolina</title>
6  <link href="styles.css" rel="stylesheet" type="text/css" />
7  <script src="Scripts/AC_RunActiveContent.js" type="text/javascript"></script>
8  <link rel="shortcut icon" type="image/x-icon" href="favicon.ico" />
9  </head>
```

As you type, code hints will appear when Dreamweaver recognizes a specific tag. In this case, it is easier to simply ignore these hints and type the required code.

5. **Save the file, and then preview the page in your browser.**

   If possible, preview in a browser other than Safari or IE; these browsers require the site to be online, not local.

File:///C:/Documents%20and%20Settings/Owner/Desktop/WIP/Biltmore/index.html   Go

CHECK AVAILABILITY

There's the favicon in Firefox.

6. **Return to Dreamweaver and close index.html.**

Summary

In this project, you learned the importance of images in the design and appearance of a Web site. You learned that when you prepare the design for a site, you need to determine which images will carry content (they must be placed in the foreground using the <img> tag), and which images will appear in the background. You also learned that appropriate alt text is required for all foreground images. Alt text enables visually impaired visitors, users who have disabled the display of images, and search engines to use the content of your pages.

You also explored the use of CSS for adding background images to your pages. By combining different images and various CSS properties, you found that you have virtually unlimited options for background images.

You discovered that Dreamweaver provides image-editing tools enabling you to crop, resize, resample, and sharpen images. Although these tools do not replace full-featured image-editing applications such as Photoshop, the Dreamweaver tools enable you to complete simple editing tasks quickly and easily, without requiring another application.

And finally, you learned that Flash objects can provide both content and design elements to your sites. Although Dreamweaver isn't a Flash design or development application, it allows you to create Flash text and insert Flash objects such as animations and videos.

Use various methods to place graphics into a page

Replace plain text with graphic text

Use Dreamweaver to define transparency in placed images

Resize and resample images to meet layout requirements

Create a photo gallery slideshow

Place a Flash movie into a Web page

Use CSS to define background colors and images

Use CSS to format graphic text images as a navigation bar

Portfolio Builder Project 3

Everything Green Flowers wants to include a digital portfolio in the company's new Web site. As part of the team that is building the new site, your job is to create and implement pages for a Flash version and an HTML version of the portfolio.

To complete this project, you should:

❑ Create a new site in Dreamweaver using the files that have already been created (in the RF_Builders> Flowers folder).

❑ Create a single HTML page that supports the main-gallery SWF file in the portfolio folder.

❑ Create thumbnails for the different portfolio images, and link each thumbnail to the HTML page containing the larger image.

"The basic page layouts are already done; they're in the portfolio folder.

"The Flash version is easy because the SWF files have already been created — you only need to put them into place. The Main Gallery SWF file should appear first. That file has links to the other three SWF files in the folder, so make sure you leave those four files in the same location.

"Use the portfolio_html.html file as the basis of the HTML portfolio. You'll need to create enough pages from that file to show the larger version of each image. Because there are eighteen images, you'll end up with 18 total pages. The primary HTML portfolio page can simply be the first page of the Reception portfolio.

"You need to create thumbnails for each image in the three portfolio folders. The thumbnails have to fit in the table on the right side of the page, but you can crop the thumbnails to show only a small part of the overall images.

"You also need to create image map links from the three phrases on the left (Reception Flowers, Ceremony Flowers, and Personal) to the first page for each portfolio category."

Apple Homes Site Layout

Your client, Apple Homes of Florida, has hired you to build a Web site for their home-building company. This family-owned and -operated business specializes in model home communities. Since Apple Home sells ready-built houses, the company requires a fairly simple Web site to showcase some of the homes they've built and a sample of their floor plans. The focus of the Web site will be graphical, requiring minimal written content.

This project incorporates the following skills:

❑ Defining page properties in new HTML pages

❑ Using tables to manage page layout

❑ Inserting rollover images

❑ Defining a Dreamweaver template

❑ Creating pages from a template file

❑ Creating and applying snippets

❑ Creating links using the Site Map

Our primary audience is potential first-time home buyers. We've heard complaints from some people that too many sites don't work on their browsers, but they're saving money to buy a home instead of buying a new computer. Our site needs to be very simple, and it needs to work on every browser that people are still using — including the older ones.

There are five primary areas of the site — the home page, a page with information about our different models, a page with general information about our company, a page with contact information, and a links page.

We've provided you with a number of images, including navigation rollover images that my brother created in Photoshop. We want the top of all the pages to be the same, basically reassembling the image (and rollovers) into something that looks like a single seamless image.

When you build a new site, you should start by thinking about the different elements that will be involved in different pages. This site is going to have a consistent layout for all pages except the home page — although the home page will also have most of the same elements as the secondary pages.

Because you have a consistent layout, the best thing to do is design everything that stays the same, then save a template so you can easily add the page-specific content without needing to re-design the common elements (or even copying and pasting from one page to another). When you've finished building the secondary pages from the template, you can make whatever modifications are necessary for the home page in the file that you used to create the original template.

While you're building the template, I'm going to have your assistant build the content for the secondary pages. Depending on timing, at least some of those pages will be ready to merge into the template that you define.

To complete this project, you will:

- ❏ Create a new page and define its properties
- ❏ Create and format tables and nested tables
- ❏ Define rollover images and navigation links
- ❏ Create a Dreamweaver template
- ❏ Create a new page from a template file
- ❏ Attach a template file to existing pages
- ❏ Modify a template to modify related pages
- ❏ Create a snippet for common content
- ❏ Create navigation links using the Site Map

Stage 1   Planning a Web Site

When you plan a Web site, your first task is to identify all of the content that is likely to be used in the site. Doing so helps you define the overall structure of the Web site. You must also keep in mind that the site's content is likely to change over time. Regardless of whether you can identify all of the content before beginning the project, it's best to design a page that can lend uniformity to the appearance of the site while being able to accommodate new and differently structured content.

Positioning Elements on Web Pages

A first-time visitor to a Web site quickly builds certain expectations in terms of navigation and location of information — being able to predict where links will be placed on any page of the Web site, how information will be organized, etc. To meet these expectations, every page of your Web site must include certain common elements. To ensure your sites are easy to use, remember these important pointers when designing a Web site:

- Place links in the same location on every page.

- Position the company logo in the same location on every page.

- Use common page properties such as colors, margins, and images to "train" a visitor to easily locate and identify content.

A typical Web page consists of four parts (five, if you count each sidebar individually). These parts are not standard elements of an HTML page, so the names cannot be assigned to parts of the page. However, a working knowledge of these parts can help you understand the structure of Web pages:

- **Top Banner (Header).** Usually contains the logo of the site and the navigation bar.

- **Sidebars.** Navigation bars on the left (and sometimes right) that often contain additional sets of links or other information.

- **Body.** Part of the Web page that holds the actual content of the page; while the other parts usually remain constant with regard to appearance and content, this part of the page changes considerably throughout the Web site.

- **Footer.** Often contains copyright information and a set of links, including a contact link.

DEFINE THE APPLE HOMES SITE

As in previous projects, the first step to creating a Web site is to prepare the workspace and create the site definition. To keep the list of sites in the Files panel to a manageable number, you should export and remove the sites you are no longer using.

To ensure that links between documents and paths to images are created properly, the Apple Homes site must be defined in Dreamweaver. The procedure for defining the site is basically the same for the Apple Homes site as it was for sites in previous projects.

1. **Copy the RF_Dreamweaver>Realty folder into the WIP folder where you are saving your work.**

   As you complete this project, you will work with the files in your WIP folder so you can make changes and save frequently.

2. **In Dreamweaver, export the Biltmore site (from Project 3) as a site definition file in your WIP>Biltmore folder.**

3. **After you have exported the site definition, remove the Biltmore site from the Manage Sites dialog box. (Click Yes, when asked to confirm the removal.)**

4. **In the Manage Sites dialog box, click the New button and choose Site from the menu.**

5. **In the Site Name field, type "Apple Homes".**

6. **Click the folder icon to the right of the Local Root Folder field, navigate to the WIP>Realty folder, and click Choose/Select.**

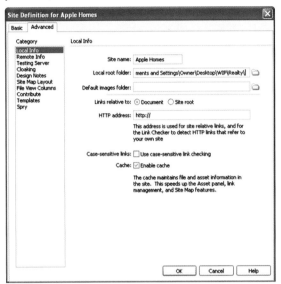

7. **Click OK to accept the Site Definition settings. Click Done to close the Manage Sites dialog box and create the new site.**

8. **Continue to the next exercise.**

 CREATE A WEB PAGE

The next step is to create the basic layout structure that will hold the content of different pages in the site. You are going to use Dreamweaver tables to assemble page elements — including navigation links — that have been created and sliced in an image-editing application.

All of the pages you create for this site will have the same basic layout structure, which aids users by creating an expectation for how to navigate through the site from one page to the next. Because each page has the same basic structure, you will assemble the common layout elements first, and then save a template that can be used to create each of the site's pages.

To begin, you create an HTML page and define some basic page properties. Even though you start by working on an HTML page, remember that you are also forming the basis for a template. The properties used for this page will apply to all other pages you create from the template.

Note:

The home page content has a slightly different structure than the second-level pages in the site. However, the header and footer content is the same on all pages. You'll address differences in the home page structure in the final stage of this project.

1. **Choose File>New and create a new HTML file based on the None layout.**

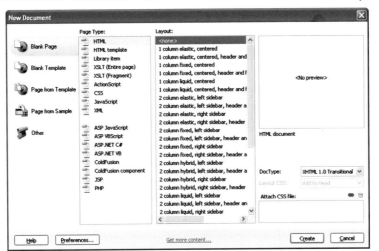

Note:

If the Welcome Screen is visible, simply click HTML in the Create New column to create a new HTML file.

2. **Choose Modify>Page Properties to view the properties of the blank page.**

3. **Display the Appearance options by clicking Appearance in the Category list on the left.**

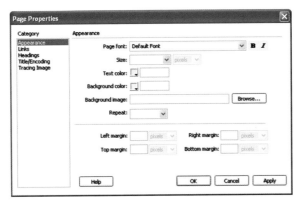

4. **Choose the Verdana, Arial, Helvetica, sans-serif combination in the Page Font menu.**

This font option includes more than one font because you can't be sure what fonts will be available on your site visitors' computers. This list creates an order of priority for displaying the site text. In other words, the list you just selected tells the browser to:

"Display this text in Verdana if possible.

"If Verdana is not available, use Arial.

"If neither Verdana nor Arial are available, use Helvetica.

"If none of these fonts is available, use whatever font the user defined as the default sans-serif font."

5. **Choose 10 in the Size menu and make sure pixels is selected as the unit of measurement in the adjacent menu.**

6. Type "#000000" in the Text Color field, and type "#D3BE96" in the Background Color field.

#000000 is the hexadecimal code for black, which will be the default text color. The other code results in a light brown color, which will be the page background color.

Note:

You can also select a color by clicking the color swatch to open the Color Picker, which displays a color palette from which you can select a color.

Another alternative is to select a color on the screen — even if from an element outside Dreamweaver — using the palette's eyedropper.

7. Type "0" in all four Margin fields.

Margin values of zero ensure that the page content area will be equal to the browser window area. If you want to design pages that show space between the edges of the browser window and the content area of the page, then you would define a margin value greater than zero.

8. Click Links in the Category pane to display the Links options.

9. Change the Link Color and Visited Links fields to #000000; leave the other two color fields empty. In the Underline Style menu, choose Show Underline Only On Rollover.

Using these settings, the links on this page will appear in black, they will not change color even if clicked, and they will be underlined only when the user places the cursor over the link text.

10. Click Title/Encoding in the Category pane. In the Title field, type "Custom Home Builder Tampa Bay : Apple Homes".

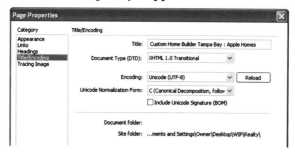

DREAMWEAVER FOUNDATIONS

Appearance Category

Page Font, Size, and Text Color. The font combination, size, and color you select will be used as the default font for the page. Select a font combination, or add a new one by clicking Edit Font List in the menu. For the default text color, either select a color or type its code in the field adjacent to the Color Picker; you can use the Color Picker's eyedropper to select a color from any element on the screen.

Background Color and Background Image. The background color covers the entire area of the page. You can also select a background image by clicking the Browse button. The **Repeat** menu controls how many times the image appears. For the image to appear only once, select No-Repeat. If you select Repeat, the image tiles horizontally and vertically until it covers the entire page. If you select Repeat-X, the image repeats horizontally until it covers the width of the page. If you select Repeat-Y, the image tiles vertically and covers the height of the page.

Margins. Margins determine the space between the main body of the page and the borders of the browser window. You can specify margins for all four edges using one of the nine units supported by Dreamweaver.

Links Category

Link Font and Size. You can decide to use a different combination of fonts for the links on the page, or you can use the same font combination as the rest of the page. You can also use a different font size even if you use the same font as the rest of the page.

Link Colors. You can select colors for links in four different states: default (unvisited), rollover (when the mouse cursor is over the link text), visited (links that have been clicked), and active (the link that is currently clicked). You can also determine when the links appear underlined by choosing one of the four options in the Underline Style menu.

Headings Category

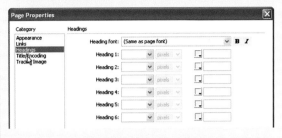

These options allow you to set the combination of font, size, and color to be used for the heading styles. You can specify a single combination for all heading styles, or you can specify a different combination for each heading style.

Title/Encoding Category

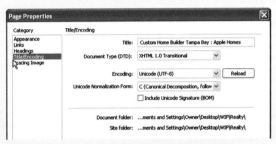

Title. This value is the title of the page, which appears in the title bar of the browser. An appropriate title helps search engines gauge the relevance of the page to search queries.

Document Type. This value indicates the version of HTML or XHTML used by the page.

Encoding. This value is the character set used by the page. Unicode UTF (8) is recommended for multi-language sites; Western European is adequate for sites in English.

Unicode Normalization Form. This option determines how Unicode is converted into binary format; it is available only if Unicode is selected from the Encoding list.

Include Unicode Signature. If this check box is selected, a byte order mark is included in the file.

Document Folder and Site Folder. These options define the locations of the page and the site to which it belongs.

Tracing Image Category

Some designers prefer to create a Web page design in an image for reference. This **tracing image** can be imported into the HTML page for easier reference. The image never displays in a browser, but it displays when the page opens in Dreamweaver.

11. Click OK.

The rest of the page properties for this site can remain at the default values.

12. Choose File>Save As and save this document as "index.html" in the root of the Apple Homes site folder (WIP>Realty).

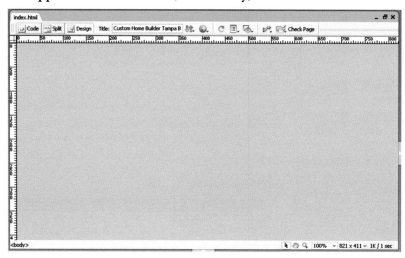

13. Continue to the next exercise.

Tables vs. CSS

When HTML tables were first conceived, they were intended to allow Web content developers to more easily and clearly present tabular text — primarily charts of data — in a Web page. It didn't take long, however, before visually oriented designers figured out that the structure provided by HTML table elements could also be used to assemble visual elements and give designers better ability to include decorative and presentational elements. In essence, tables gave visual designers a way to combine graphic elements in a way more similar to what they did for print design. As the Web — and Web design — evolved, a significant number of Web pages were designed with tables.

One problem with table-based design, however, is that HTML tables were never intended as a graphic design tool. The overall page code that results is extremely long and complex, which results in longer download times (still a significant problem for users with slow dial-up connections). The complexity of table-based page code also makes it more time consuming to make changes, especially when the same change needs to be made on multiple pages.

Another problem with table-based design is that the resulting code mixes content in with purely presentational elements. This makes it very difficult (if not impossible) for screen-reader and other accessibility software to separate the content from the structure. Search engines have a similar problem sifting the content from the presentation, which means that table-based pages might not rank as high as a similar page that is designed without tables.

To solve the inherent problems with table-based page design, cascading style sheets (CSS) provide a way to separate content from presentation. CSS-based layout is now the recommended and preferred method of Web standards organizations such as the World Wide Web Consortium (W3C, www.w3c.org) because the separate content is more readily accessible to all users.

In Project 2 you applied appropriate HTML tags to text content, which correctly defined the *structure* of the content to be usable by both search engines and accessibility software. The basic structural elements (h1, strong, etc.) provide some visual differentiation for types of the content; but you also saw that attaching a CSS file could change the appearance of different content elements.

The primary argument against CSS-based design is that visually oriented designers have a more difficult time relating CSS code to what they see (or want to see) in their pages. However, Dreamweaver makes CSS-based design fairly easy using a dialog-box interface to create the code for CSS rules behind the scenes.

As CSS gains popularity in the design community and continuing support from standards organizations, you will at some point undoubtedly have to *disassemble* a table-based layout — and deconstruction is far easier when you understand the original construction process.

We use table-based design in this project because you should understand how this type of page is created so you will be able to work with these pages when necessary. In Project 5 you will use CSS to create an entire page structure.

INSERT TABLES IN A WEB PAGE

Using tables to control Web page layout is fairly common practice, partly because older versions of various browsers did not interpret cascading style sheets (CSS) uniformly. Instead of applying CSS, tables were used to ensure consistent appearance of a Web site across different browsers.

The current versions of most browsers interpret CSS according to the World Wide Web Consortium (W3C) standards, which makes the use of tables to design HTML pages a bit redundant. However, tables still provide an effective layout option. (You will learn how to use CSS for designing page layout in Project 5.)

1. **With index.html open (from your Apple Homes site), switch to Design view and choose Insert>Table.**

2. **In the Table dialog box, define a table with 6 rows and 1 column. Type "100" in the Table Width field and choose Percent in the related menu.**

   Table width specified in pixels is better for precise layout of text and images; it remains constant regardless of the width of the browser window. Table width specified in percentage allows the table (and thus, the page content) to expand or contract based on the available browser window width.

3. **Make sure the border thickness, cell padding, and cell spacing values are set to zero.**

   If these fields are left blank, most browsers display tables with border thickness and cell padding of 2 pixels and cell spacing of 1 pixel. By setting the fields to 0 instead of leaving them blank, you override the default behavior of browsers and allow the page content to occupy the entire browser space. Otherwise, you would see gaps created by the default browser settings.

4. **Choose the None option in the Header section and click OK.**

   Because you are using this table for layout purposes, it doesn't need a header row.

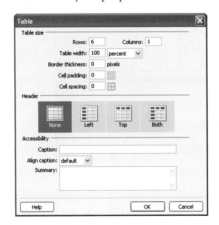

Note:

When you don't explicitly assign values for border thickness, cell spacing, and cell padding, most browsers display a 1-pixel table border thickness and cell padding and a 2-pixel cell spacing. To ensure that browsers display the table with no border, padding, or spacing, set cell padding and cell spacing to 0.

Note:

The Header area of the Table dialog box determines which cells (if any) are marked up as table header cells.

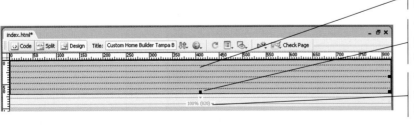

The new table has six rows and one column.

The button closer to the table is used to access specific columns in the table.

These indicators show the width properties of the selected table.

5. **Click the green arrow button that shows the table dimensions to open the table-specific menu.**

6. **In the menu, choose Select Table to select the entire table.**

   When you work with tables, these arrow buttons provide access to options relative to the entire table and to individual columns within the table. (Handles indicate that the table is selected.)

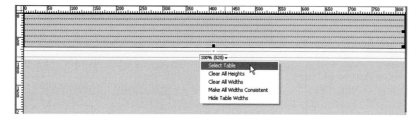

Note:

If you don't see the green-arrow table indicators, choose View>Visual Aids>Widths. These are only visible when a table (or a cell in a table) is selected.

7. **In the Properties Inspector (with the table selected), choose Center in the Align menu.**

   Table alignment refers to how the table is positioned relative to the other elements that surround it. For example, if you select left alignment and there is text on the page, the table moves to the left of the page and the text appears to its right.

Note:

The number in parenthesis shows the width of the table in pixels. Because you set the table to be 100% of the available window, this number on your screen might be different than what you see in our screen shots.

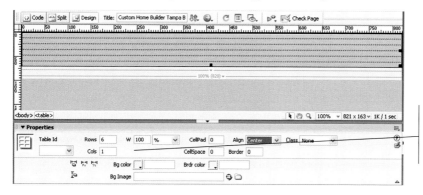

When the table is selected, the Properties Inspector shows options relative to the entire table.

8. **Click the second row of the table to place the insertion point.**

9. **In the Properties Inspector, type "#C16648" in the Background Color field.**

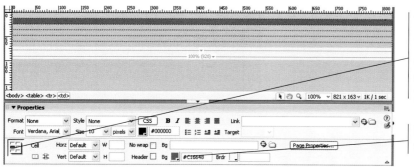

When the insertion point is placed in a cell (or one or more cells are selected), the Properties Inspector shows options relative to the active cell(s).

Use this field to define the cell's background color.

10. **Repeat Steps 8–9 for the fourth row of the table.**

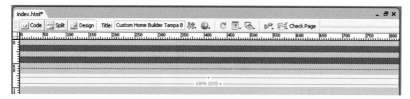

11. **Save the file and continue to the next exercise.**

CREATE A NESTED TABLE

In this exercise, you create a new table within the first row of the existing table, which will contain all the pieces of the header area (graphics and navigation buttons that were created in an image-editing application). This method of placing one table in a cell of an existing table is called **nesting** tables.

1. **With index.html open in Design view, click in the first row of the table to place the insertion point.**

2. **Choose Insert>Table.**

3. **Insert a new table with 2 rows and 7 columns, using 800 pixels as the table width. Make sure the border thickness, cell padding, and cell spacing values are set to 0, and then click OK to create the table.**

   Border thickness, cell padding, and cell spacing must be set to 0 because the elements in the header must have no space between them. This gives the header section a seamless appearance in the final Web page; it must appear as a single element, even though it is comprised of multiple images (as you will see in the next exercise).

Note:

The table and column arrow buttons typically appear above the active table unless the active table is the first object on the page. If there is no room above the table in the Design window, then the arrow buttons appear below the active table.

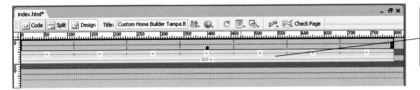

This nested table with seven columns has seven buttons to access column-specific controls.

The Modify>Table Menu in Depth

Most common features associated with tables are grouped in the Modify>Table menu. Some of these options, such as the Select and Delete commands, are self-explanatory. Others require a bit of explanation.

- **Merge Cells** combines selected adjacent cells so they are treated as a single cell.

- **Split Cells** allows you to create multiple cells (by rows or columns) within a single cell, without affecting other cells in the same row or column.

- **Insert Row** adds a new row of cells above the current selection.

- **Insert Column** adds a new column of cells to the left of the current selection.

- **Insert Rows or Columns** opens a dialog box where you can add a specific number of rows or columns. You can also choose where to add the new cells (to the left or right for columns, or above or below for rows) relative to the current selection.

- **Increase Row Span** merges the current cell with the cell below it.

- **Increase Column Span** merges the current cell with the cell next to it on the right side.

- **Decrease Row Span** splits two or more previously merged or spanned cells into two cells from the bottom.

- **Decrease Column Span** splits previously merged or spanned cells into two cells from the right side.

- **Table Widths** displays the width of the selected table.

- **Clear Cell Heights** removes all defined numeric row height values from the selected table.

- **Clear Cell Widths** removes all defined numeric column width values from the selected table.

- **Convert Widths to Pixels** and **Convert Widths to Percent** allow you to change defined widths from a percentage of the available browser space to a specific number of pixels, and vice versa.

- **Convert Heights to Pixels** and **Convert Heights to Percent** allow you to change defined heights from a percentage of the available browser space to a specific number of pixels, and vice versa.

4. Command/Control-click the top-left cell of the table to select that cell.

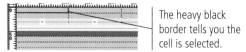

The heavy black border tells you the cell is selected.

5. Shift-click the bottom-left cell to select the entire column of cells.

Pressing Shift and clicking selects all cells between the one already selected and the one you click.

Note:

You can also place the cursor above a column or to the left of a row and click to select the entire column or row.

6. With both cells in the first column selected, click the Merge Cells button in the Properties Inspector.

By merging adjacent cells in a table, the two cells in this first column now function as a single table cell. This technique allows you to avoid multiple levels of nested tables in a single row of the main table (which could be very confusing).

Some of the remaining rows in the main table will require multiple nested tables; but in this case, the header area can be more easily created using merged table cells.

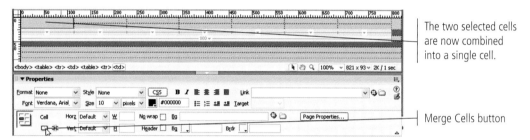

The two selected cells are now combined into a single cell.

Merge Cells button

7. Click the green arrow button at the bottom of the right column and choose Select Column from the pop-up menu.

Note:

The number next to the column or table arrow button indicates the size of the table or column. If no number appears, then you know no defined width has been assigned to that column or row.

8. Using the Properties Inspector, merge the selected cells into a single cell.

9. Click the first unmerged cell in the top row, hold down the mouse button, and drag to the rightmost unmerged cell in the row.

You can select a range of cells by simply clicking and dragging.

These five cells should now be selected.

These two cells were merged in Step 8.

10. Merge the selected cells into a single cell.

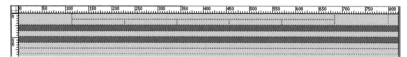

11. Save the file and continue to the next exercise.

INSERT IMAGES INTO TABLES

The header section of this Web site is comprised of multiple images that began as a single image, which was cut (sliced) in an image-editing application. In this exercise, you use the nested table (with cell padding, spacing, and borders of 0) to reassemble the image slices into what appears as a single unit in the final Web page.

Note:

It isn't necessary to select the table before dragging an image into a cell. We do this primarily for the sake of identification.

1. **With index.html (from your Apple Homes site) open in Design view, click in the first (merged) column of the nested table to place the insertion point.**

2. **Drag the file header_left.jpg from the images folder in the Files panel into the merged cell.**

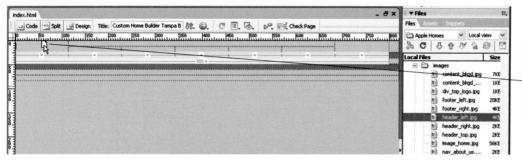

Drag the file header_left.jpg from the Files panel into this cell.

3. **In the Image Tag Accessibility Attributes dialog box, type "header" in the Alternate Text field and click OK.**

The cell width automatically expands after you place the image.

The table width remains unaffected because you defined the table width as a specific number of pixels.

4. **Drag the file header_top.jpg from the same images folder to the merged cell above the second through sixth columns of the nested table.**

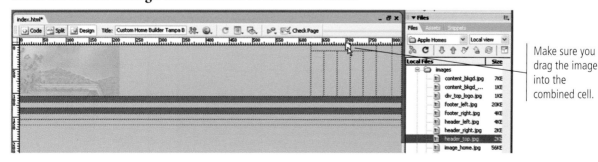

Make sure you drag the image into the combined cell.

5. **In the Image Tag Accessibility Attributes dialog box, type "header" in the Alternate Text field and click OK.**

   Because these images are actually slices of a single header image, it is acceptable to use the same alternate text for all the pieces.

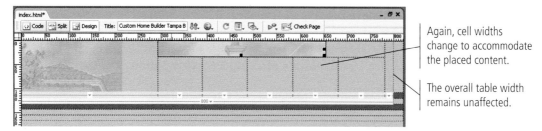

Again, cell widths change to accommodate the placed content.

The overall table width remains unaffected.

6. **Drag the file header_right.jpg into the merged cell in the right column of the nested table. Assign "header" as the alternate text.**

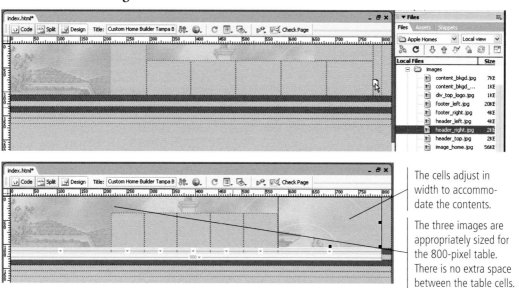

The cells adjust in width to accommodate the contents.

The three images are appropriately sized for the 800-pixel table. There is no extra space between the table cells.

7. **Insert the file spacer.gif into the fourth row of the main table. Assign "spacer" as the alternate text.**

   From this point on, assign appropriate alternate text whenever asked. We will not repeat this instruction or provide specific alternate text unless it is critical to the exercise working properly.

8. **Double-click the bottom cell border of the cell where you just placed the spacer image.**

   Double-clicking a cell border forces the cell to snap to the height of the placed image.

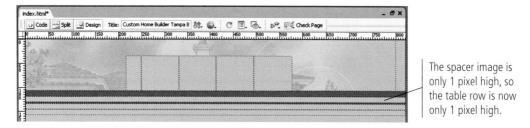

The spacer image is only 1 pixel high, so the table row is now only 1 pixel high.

9. **Save the file and continue to the next exercise.**

INSERT ROLLOVER IMAGES

Rather than simple text-based navigation buttons, your client wants image-based navigation buttons that change appearance when the mouse hovers over them. You create this effect using **rollover images**, where a different image appears in place of the original (default state) image when the mouse cursor hovers over the image area.

There are five navigation buttons for this site, which will occupy the five remaining cells in the header area (the nested table).

1. **With index.html open, place the insertion point in the first empty cell of the nested table in row 1 of the main table.**

2. **Choose Insert>Image Objects>Rollover Image.**

Note:

You can also choose Rollover Image (under the Image button) in the Common Insert bar.

3. **In the Insert Rollover Image dialog box, type "nav_home" in the Image Name field.**

4. **Click the Browse button adjacent to the Original Image field, navigate to the images folder in the Apple Homes site root folder (WIP>Realty>images), and double-click nav_home.jpg.**

5. **Click the Browse button adjacent to the Rollover Image field, navigate to the same images folder as in Step 4, and double-click nav_home_rollover.jpg.**

6. **Make sure the Preload Rollover Image box is checked.**

   When this option is checked, the rollover image automatically downloads to the cache of the user's browser; this prevents any delay in the appearance of the rollover image when the user moves the cursor over the original image.

7. **Type "Apple Homes home page" in the Alternate Text field.**

8. **Type "index.html" in the When Clicked, Go to URL field.**

   This rollover image is a link to the site home page.

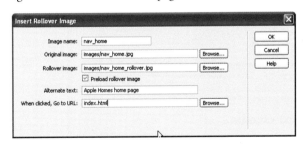

Note:

You can click the Browse button to select a file to which you want to link.

9. **Click OK to create the rollover image.**

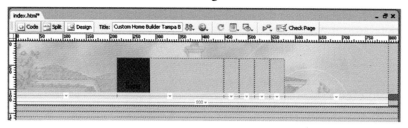

10. **Applying the same basic process, add the remaining four navigation rollover images, using the following specifications.**

Place the images from left to right in the remaining empty cells of the nested table.
All files are in the site's images folder.

Image name	Original image	Rollover image	Alternate Text	Go to URL
nav_models	nav_models.jpg	nav_models_rollover.jpg	Apple Homes model information	models/index.html
nav_about_us	nav_about_us.jpg	nav_about_us_rollover.jpg	Apple Homes company information	about_us/index.html
nav_links	nav_links.jpg	nav_links_rollover.jpg	Apple Homes links of interest	links/index.html
nav_contact	nav_contact.jpg	nav_contact_rollover.jpg	Apple Homes contact information	contact/index.html

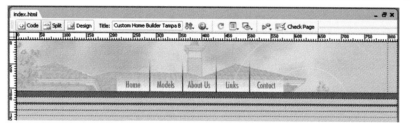

Make sure you place the insertion point in the appropriate table cell before you insert each rollover image. If you forget to place the insertion point in a different cell, then each new rollover image you place will overwrite the existing image.

Note:

The index.html file in the Links folder does not yet exist; you will create this file later. You can still define the link path now, but be aware that testing the link will result in a "page does not exist" warning.

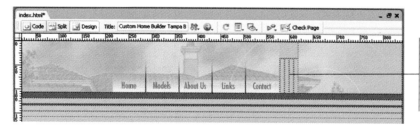

If you forget to place the insertion point, then you'll end up with blank cells and the images will align improperly.

11. **Save the file and continue to the next exercise.**

CREATE THE REMAINING NESTED TABLE STRUCTURE

The remaining layout structure requires a number of additional tables and images. When you have finished creating the basic structure, you will save the page as a template so you can reuse the structure to create the individual pages of the site.

1. **With index.html open, insert the image div_top_logo.jpg in the second row of the main table.**

   This image is a narrow slice of the logo that will be placed in the third row of the table. Note the width of the placed image; you will use this image width to define the width of the cell that will hold the rest of the logo.

2. **Double-click the lower border of the second row to snap the cell height to the image height.**

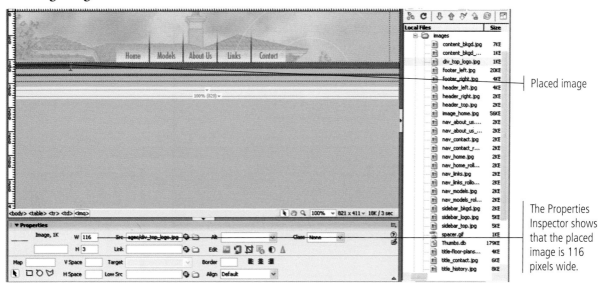

Placed image

The Properties Inspector shows that the placed image is 116 pixels wide.

3. **In the third row of the main table, insert a new table (Insert>Table) using the following specifications:**

   - 1 row and 3 columns
   - 800-pixel table width
   - 0 border thickness, cell padding, and cell spacing

   The first column of this table will contain a sidebar, the second column will have page-specific content, and the third column will contain an image that will appear to extend the background of the second column.

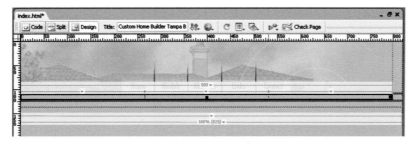

4. **Click to place the insertion point in the first column of the new nested table.**

5. **In the Properties Inspector, type "116" in the W (width) field.**

   By setting a specific width for this column, you can prevent the column from extending beyond a certain point (regardless of the content you place in the cell). One hundred sixteen pixels is the width of the image you placed in Step 1 (the top slice of the logo), so the first cell of this table, which will contain the rest of the logo, should also be set to 116 pixels.

6. **Choose Top in the Vert (vertical alignment) menu and choose Left in the Horz (horizontal alignment) menu.**

   The horizontal and vertical cell alignment affects how elements are positioned within the cell (the elements will be aligned to the top left of this cell).

7. **In the Properties Inspector, use the BG [image] option to define sidebar_bkgd.jpg (in the images folder) as the background of this cell.**

   When the insertion point is placed in the cell, you can use the Point to File method to define the cell's background image.

When you define a specific column width, that width displays in the column indicator.

Changing the column width does not affect the overall table width.

Each of the two remaining columns is half of the remaining table width.

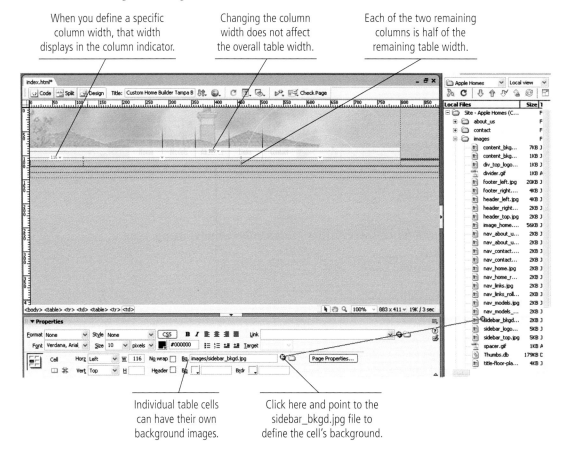

Individual table cells can have their own background images.

Click here and point to the sidebar_bkgd.jpg file to define the cell's background.

8. **Drag the file sidebar_logo.jpg (from the site images folder) into the left cell of the nested table.**

   This table cell now has a background image, and it contains a foreground image, as well. You can't see the background image at this point because the row is only as high as the placed logo image.

9. **Place the insertion point in the third column of the nested table. Using the Properties Inspector, define content_bkgd_right.jpg as the background image for the selected cell.**

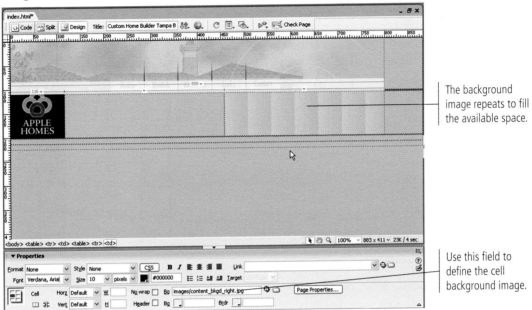

The background image repeats to fill the available space.

Use this field to define the cell background image.

10. **In the Properties Inspector, change the selected cell width to 50 pixels.**

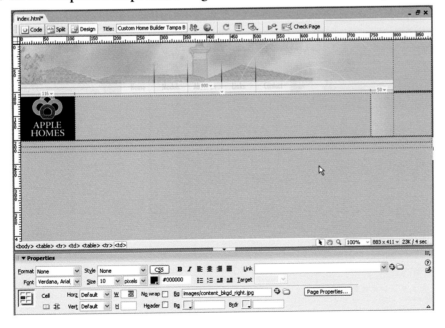

Note:

In this nested table, the left column is 116 pixels and the right column is 50 pixels (116 + 50 = 166). The entire width of Nested Table 2 is 800 pixels, which means the middle column is 634 pixels wide (800 − 166 = 634).

11. Place the insertion point in the second column of the nested table. Change the cell width to 634 pixels and the cell height to 200 pixels.

This cell will contain the section-specific content for each page in the site.

Although the cell is already 634 pixels wide, manually defining the width can prevent problems later.

After resizing the row height, you can now see the background image in place behind the logo (in the left column of the nested table).

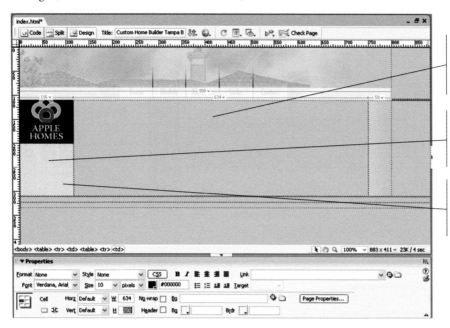

Adjusting the row height in the nested table expands the height of the containing cell as necessary.

Adjusting the row height in the center of the nested table affects all other cells in the same row.

The background image of this cell is now visible behind the image that is the cell content.

12. With the insertion point in the middle column of the nested table, change the vertical cell alignment to Top and define content_bkgd.jpg as the background image for the cell.

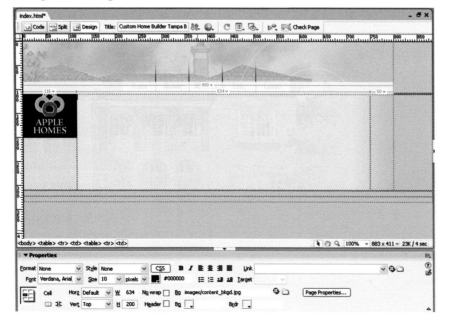

Note:

If an entire table is selected in the design window, you can use the Properties Inspector to define a background image for an entire table instead of a selected cell.

13. **In the fifth row of the main table, insert a new table using the following specifications:**

    - 1 row and 2 columns
    - 800-pixel table width
    - 0 border thickness, cell padding, and cell spacing

    This table will contain an image and contact information.

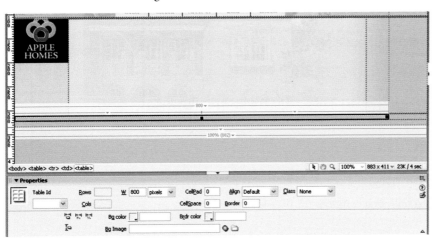

14. **In the first column of the new nested table, insert footer_left.jpg.**

    Insert the image by dragging it from the Files panel. Don't define the image as a background image for the cell.

15. **Click the right edge of the table cell with the footer image, and drag the edge left as far as possible.**

    By dragging the cell edge, you dynamically define the cell width. Because the cell must be large enough for the contained image, you can't drag the cell edge past the image edge.

16. **Using the Files panel, open footer.txt from the text_files folder, copy its contents, and then close the file.**

17. **Place the insertion point in the right cell of the nested table and paste the contents you copied in Step 16.**

18. **Select all of the pasted text and apply centered paragraph alignment. Set the vertical cell alignment to Middle.**

19. **Select applehms@aol.com. In the Link field of the Properties inspector, type mailto:applehms@aol.com to define an email link.**

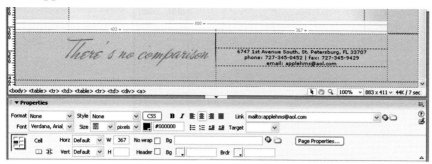

20. **In the last row of the main table, insert a new table using the following specifications:**

    - 1 row and 1 column
    - 800-pixel table width
    - 0 border thickness, cell padding, and cell spacing

    This table will contain the text links that comprise the page footer.

21. **Click to place the insertion point in the single cell of the new nested table. In the Properties Inspector, change the horizontal alignment for the cell to Center.**

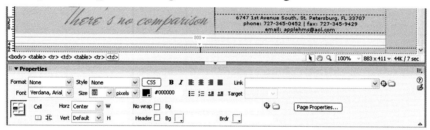

    The four nested tables — which define the width of rows 1, 3, 5, and 6 in the main table — have the same width of 800 pixels. Rows 2 and 4 of the main table, which do not have nested tables, extend the entire width of the main table — 100% of the browser window width.

    You might recall that you set the page margins to zero, which allows the main table to cover the entire width of the browser window instead of leaving blank space at the edge. This arrangement of fixed table widths in certain rows creates the impression of a margin on the right side of the page, without defining an actual page margin.

22. **Save the file and continue to the next stage of the project.**

    This is the final layout for the pages you will design for the Apple Homes Web site. Before you begin creating the specific pages, however, you should save this page as a template to make it easier to maintain consistency from one page to another.

Stage 2 Working with Template Files

HTML pages can be accessed over the Web; Web designers use templates — with the ".dwt" extension in Dreamweaver — to create HTML pages. The primary benefit of using templates is that you create common page elements only once, rather than recreating them every time you add a new page to your site. A template can contain everything an HTML page requires, including text, graphics, and hyperlinks.

When you create a template, you indicate which elements of a page should remain constant (non-editable; locked) in pages based on that template, and which elements can be changed. While the non-editable regions appear exactly the same from one page to the next, the editable regions enable you to add unique content to each new page.

You can modify a template even after you have created pages based on it. When you modify a template, the locked (non-editable) regions in pages based on the template automatically update to match the changes to the template.

CREATE A TEMPLATE

To create a template, you can modify an existing HTML document to suit your immediate needs, or you can create a template from scratch, i.e., start with a blank HTML document. Dreamweaver saves template files (with the ".dwt" extension) in a templates folder in your site's local root folder. If the templates folder does not already exist, Dreamweaver automatically creates the folder when you save a new template.

1. **With index.html (from the Apple Homes site root folder) open in Design view, choose File>Save As Template.**

2. **In the Save As Template dialog box, make sure Apple Homes is selected in the Site menu.**

3. **In the Description field, type "Apple Homes secondary pages".**

   This template will work for all but the site home page, which has a slightly different layout to accommodate the main content.

4. **In the Save As field, type "ah_template" and click Save.**

   The extension ".dwt" is automatically added on both Macintosh and Windows computers.

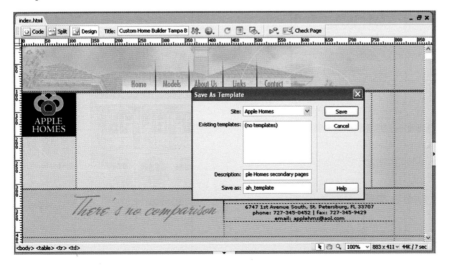

Note:

*If you open a template file, you can edit everything in it, whether it is marked as editable or locked. If you open a document based on a template file, you can edit only the regions marked as editable. The terms **editable** and **locked** refer to whether a region is editable in a document based on a template, not to whether the region is editable in the template file itself.*

Note:

Do not move your templates out of the templates folder or save any non-template files in the templates folder. Also, do not move the templates folder out of your local root folder. Doing so causes errors in paths in the templates.

Note:

This description is only relevant in Dreamweaver; it will not appear in any page based on the template. You can also modify the template description by choosing Modify>Template>Description.

5. Click Yes in the resulting dialog box.

The template is saved in a templates folder in the local root folder of the Apple Homes Web site, which Dreamweaver automatically creates for you when saving the template. To be sure that all images and links function properly, you should allow Dreamweaver to update the link information as necessary.

Your template contains the layout structure you created in the first stage of this project, but when converted into a template, all parts of the page became non-editable. Until you define an editable region, you won't be able to add page-specific content to any pages based on this template.

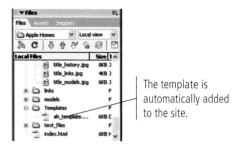

The template is automatically added to the site.

6. Place the insertion point in the center column of the nested table in row three of the main table.

7. Choose Insert>Template Objects>Editable Region.

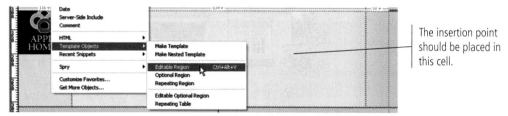

The insertion point should be placed in this cell.

8. In the New Editable Region dialog box, type "Page Content" in the Name field and click OK.

When pages are created from this template, this editable region will be the only area that can be modified (e.g., adding content or including additional nested tables).

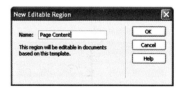

The single editable region is the only area that will change from one page to the next within the site — with the sole exception of the Home page, which you will create using the original index.html file you created earlier.

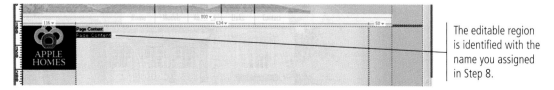

The editable region is identified with the name you assigned in Step 8.

9. Save the file, close it, and continue to the next exercise.

Unlike other applications, you do not have to use the Save As command to rewrite a Dreamweaver template. You can simply choose File>Save or press Command/Control-S.

The Insert>Template Objects Menu in Depth

Template objects consist primarily of different types of regions.

- **Make Template.** The Make Template option enables you to convert an HTML file into a template. This option automatically prompts you to save the HTML file as a template. If a template is edited, the HTML files created from that template will be updated accordingly.

- **Make Nested Template.** The Make Nested Template option enables you to insert a template in a page created from an existing template. The template from which a nested template is created must contain at least one editable region. The editable region in the nested template will display in green, while the editable region in the original page displays in yellow.

- **Editable Region.** Editable regions are the areas of a template that are modifiable. You don't edit the regions in the template itself; you modify the pages created from the template. By default, editable regions are highlighted in blue, and locked regions are highlighted in yellow. (You can change the highlight colors in the Highlighting pane of the Preferences dialog box.)

- **Optional Region.** The Optional Region option is used to define a section of the page that will either be shown or hidden, depending on the content you are presenting. Optional Region is controlled by a conditional "if" statement in code view. That is, you can show or hide certain areas of the page conditionally.

- **Repeating Region.** The Repeating Region option enables you to control the layout of sections of the template that need to be repeated. A repeating region is a section of template content that you can easily duplicate. Although you can apply repeating regions to many elements, they are primarily used in tables.

- **Editable Optional Region.** If an optional region is created in a template with editable attributes, then the region becomes an Editable Optional Region. An Editable Optional Region of a template combines elements of both editable and optional tags. It works as an editable region when made visible on a page.

- **Repeating Table.** Repeating regions are commonly used in tables. Dreamweaver includes a tool that creates both a table and repeating regions simultaneously. Selecting a repeating table object opens the standard table dialog box for defining rows within a repeating region. When inserted, the repeating region contains a separate editable region in each cell.

CREATE A PAGE FROM A TEMPLATE

In this exercise, you create a page for the Apple Homes Web site based on the template you created in the previous exercise. You use the editable region to include content specific to the page. The non-editable regions ensure that all the pages of the site are consistent and provide the predictability users expect from a professionally designed Web page.

1. **With the Apple Home site open in the Files panel, display the Assets panel in the Panel dock by clicking the Assets tab (in the same group as the Files panel).**

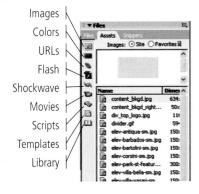

2. **In the left side of the panel, click the Templates button to show the templates used to create this site.**

   Only one template — the one you just created — is currently used on this site.

   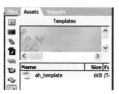

3. **Control/right-click the ah_template option and choose New from Template in the contextual menu.**

The Modify>Templates Menu in Depth

DREAMWEAVER FOUNDATIONS

The commands on the Modify>Templates menu are useful when you want to make changes to a template or to pages based on a template.

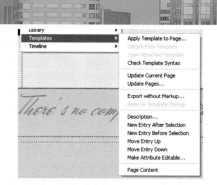

- **Apply Template to Page.** This option applies a template to the current HTML page.

- **Detach from Template.** If you do not want a page to be based on a template, this option separates the page from the template. Non-editable regions from the template become editable, but changes in the template will not reflect in the page.

- **Open Attached Template.** This option opens the template attached to a page.

- **Check Template Syntax.** If code is written directly in the code area, there is a chance that the code might contain some errors. This option enables Dreamweaver to automatically check the code syntax in the template.

- **Update Current Page.** This option updates a page if the template on which it is based is modified. Before closing the file, Dreamweaver prompts you to update the page; a dialog box appears, asking if you want to save the changed document.

- **Update Pages.** If you update only the template and not the pages derived from the template, you can use this option to update all pages based on the template.

- **Export without Markup.** This option exports an entire site to a different location by detaching all pages from the templates on which they are based. You can also save the template information in XML by selecting Keep Template Data Files after you choose this command from the menu. If you exported the site earlier, then you can choose to extract only the modified files.

- **Remove Template Markup.** You can use this option to convert an editable region in a template-based page to a non-editable region.

- **New Entry Before or After Selection.** In template working areas, repeating regions include more than one editable region, which enables you to add repeated page elements such as rows of a table. (When you click the "+" button on the right side of the Repeat region's tab, it enables you to add a new entry in the region.)

- **Move Entry Up or Down.** You can use this option to move a repeating element up or down, or add or delete a repeating region.

- **Make Attribute Editable.** You can use this option to make an attribute editable in a template. For example, you can create a template with a background color, while making it possible for users to modify the background color when they create a page from the template.

A new HTML page is created, containing the same elements you placed in the template. If you move the cursor over a part of the page other than the editable region, an icon indicates that you can't select or modify that area. You can modify the editable region only.

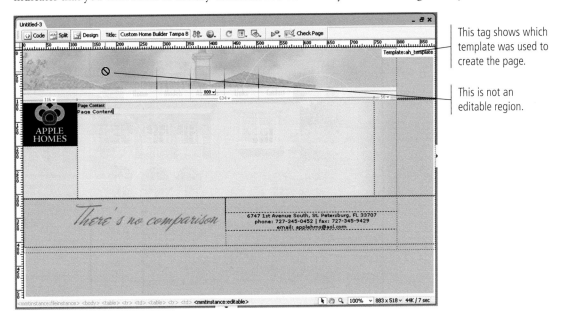

This tag shows which template was used to create the page.

This is not an editable region.

4. **Choose File>Save As. In the Save As dialog box, navigate to the links folder in the Apple Homes site root folder. Name the page "index.html" and click Save.**

This will be the Links page of the Web site. This page should contain a description of, and a link to, the mortgage center.

Note:

Remember, index.html is recognized as the default page of the containing folder. You are creating the default page for the Links section of the site, so the name index.html is appropriate.

5. In the Title field of the document toolbar, add the text "Links : " to the beginning of the existing document title.

Even though it is not part of an editable region in the document window, the page title can always be modified in a page created from a template.

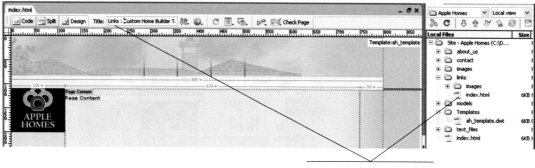

You are working on the index page in the links folder.

6. Select and delete the words "Page content" from the editable region.

Because you defined a table cell as the editable region, Dreamweaver adds these words as placeholders to keep the editable region open for you to add content.

7. Insert a new nested table in the editable region, using the following specifications:

- 2 rows and 2 columns
- 634-pixel table width
- 0 border thickness and cell padding, and 10 cell spacing

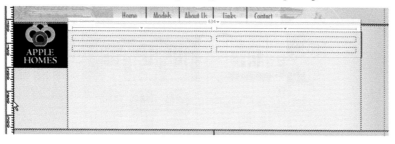

8. Select and merge both cells in the first row, and then insert the file title_ links.jpg (from the main images folder) into the merged cell.

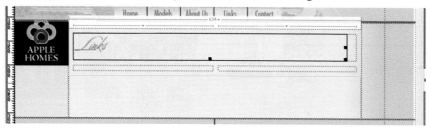

9. Insert logo-mortgage-ctr.gif (from the links/images folder) into the left cell of the second row.

10. **Drag the right cell edge until it snaps to the right side of the inserted image.**

11. **Open links.txt from the text_files folder, copy the contents, and close the file.**

12. **Paste the copied content into the second column of the nested table in the editable region.**

13. **Place the insertion point before the words "visit site" in the pasted text and press Shift-Return/Enter to move the link text to a new line.**

14. **Select the words "visit site >" in the pasted text. Using the Properties Inspector, create a link to "http://www.the-mortgage-corner.com/".**

    Remember, you defined the template page properties to underline links only when the mouse hovers over the link text.

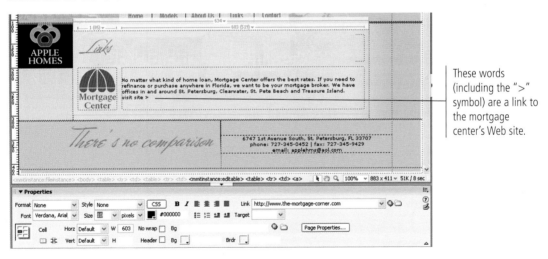

These words (including the ">" symbol) are a link to the mortgage center's Web site.

15. **Save the file, close it, and continue to the next exercise.**

APPLY A TEMPLATE TO EXISTING PAGES

Templates can also be applied to existing pages, basically "re-designing" those pages with a few clicks. You can simply map existing page content to editable regions in the template, while adding the non-editable regions to the page design.

1. **Open the file index.html from the about_us folder in the Apple Homes site.**

   This page contains the content that should be included in the final page, but none of the navigation structure is included. Rather than re-do the work you already completed, you can simply attach the ah_template file to this page.

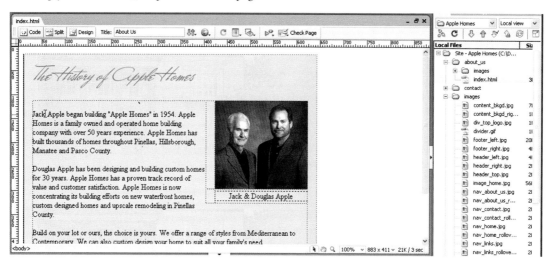

2. **Choose Modify>Templates>Apply Template to Page.**

3. **In the Select Template dialog box, make sure Apple Homes is selected in the Site menu.**

   Since this is the active site, the menu should default to the correct choice.

4. **Click ah_template in the Templates list to select it, and make sure the Update Page box is checked.**

5. **Click Select to apply the template to the open page.**

   In the Inconsistent Region Names dialog box that appears, you have to determine where to place the editable regions of the open file, relative to the editable regions in the template you selected. Although the template for this site has only one editable region, other options allow you to access the head and title information in the HTML code. You can also choose Nowhere to include no page content in the newly "templated" page.

6. **In the Name column, click the Document Body item to select it. In the Move Content to New Region menu, choose Page Content.**

   Remember, "Page Content" is the name you assigned to the template's editable region. The page body (named "Document body" by default) will be placed into the "Page Content" editable region when the template is applied to the page.

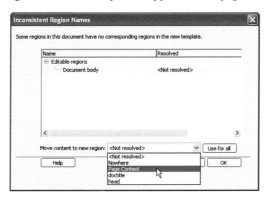

7. **Click OK to finalize the process.**

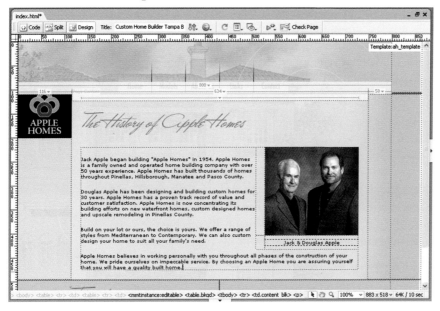

8. **In the Document Title field of the toolbar, add "About Us : " to the beginning of the existing page title.**

9. **Save the file and close it.**

10. **Repeat the same general procedure from Steps 1–9 for the index.html files in the Contact and Models folders of the Apple Homes site. For the document titles, use "Contact : " and "Models : ".**

    For the Models page, assign the Document head information from the existing file to the head region of the template file.

11. **Continue to the next stage of the project.**

Note:

Although not specifically defined as an editable region in the Design window, header information in the HTML code is always editable when you work with Dreamweaver template files.

Stage 3 Working with Snippets and Libraries

You have seen how templates enable efficient and consistent Web design. Templates are most effective when you want an almost identical visual appearance across multiple pages. However, there are times when you need to use some design elements on many — but not all — pages. This means that you cannot include those elements in a template.

Fortunately, Dreamweaver organizes files in such a way that it makes it easy to locate and reuse elements. For example, the Assets panel conveniently sorts all elements in your site according to type. You can also store "favorite" elements so they always remain available, regardless of which site you are currently building.

Snippets and libraries are two additional options for storing elements so they are readily available when you need or want them. **Libraries** can include any element that can be stored directly and used across pages. You do not need to know a programming language to create libraries. **Snippets** are basically chunks of code that can be stored and used on any page in Dreamweaver.

It might seem daunting to work with snippets if you don't know how to write programming code, but Dreamweaver has a large collection of pre-defined code snippets, arranged by type. You can use snippets as they are, or with even basic knowledge of code, you can make small changes to better suit them for your needs.

Both snippets and libraries make it convenient to reuse design elements. When you use snippets and libraries, however, remember this: when you edit a library, the associated design element can be updated across all pages that use that library; once you edit a snippet, however, it cannot be updated in the actual pages.

> **Note:**
>
> *A **library** is a file in Dreamweaver where a collection of items — images, text, or any other element — is stored. Dreamweaver stores all library items in a library folder, which in turn is stored in the root folder of that site.*

> **Note:**
>
> *Library items are accessed in the Assets panel. You can drag an existing library item from the Assets panel to the page. If a library item is edited, placed instances of that item will reflect the same changes.*

Create a Snippet

The template you created needs another set of links at the bottom of the page, making the links easily accessible when a user scrolls down. In this exercise, you create and insert a snippet in the template to add a missing structural element. By placing the snippet in the template file, the change also appears in the rest of the pages associated with that template.

1. **Open footer_links.txt from text_files folder. Select its contents, copy them, and then close the file.**

2. **Display the Snippets panel.**

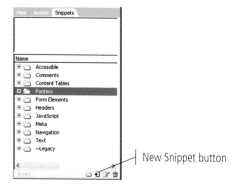

New Snippet button

3. **Click the Footers folder to select it, and then click the New Snippet button at the bottom of the panel.**

   The Footers folder automatically opens; the as-yet-unnamed snippet appears in the selected folder.

4. **In the Name field of the Snippet dialog box, type "AH Footer Links". In the Description field, type "Insert text links for Apple Homes site".**

   Snippets are not specific to the active site, so it's a good idea to include something about the project or client in the snippet name and/or description.

5. **Click the Insert Block radio button.**

   The Insert Block option inserts code as a single unit at the location of the insertion point. If you select Wrap Selection, you can define different blocks of code to insert before and/or after the active selection.

6. **Click in the Insert Code field. Press Command/Control-V to paste the contents that you copied from footer_links.txt in Step 1.**

7. **Click the Preview Type>Design radio button.**

   This selection controls what displays in the preview area of the Snippets panel. You can preview a snippet by code or design, just as you can preview a page by code or design.

Note:

Choosing Modify> Templates>Open Attached Template allows you to access the template file used for a specific page.

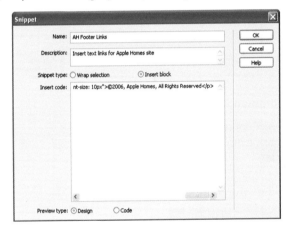

Note:

If you use the Wrap Selection option, you need to type separate code to insert before and/or after the selection.

8. **Click OK to create the snippet.**

   The snippet is added to the Footers folder.

9. **Continue to the next exercise.**

MODIFY THE TEMPLATE FILE

Site development is rarely final. Changes are often required not only to correct mistakes, but also to make enhancements to the existing content. Making even small changes can be quite time-consuming, however, especially when a change affects multiple pages. In addition, it can become difficult to keep track of the pages you modified. Templates effectively solve these problems by enabling you to make a single change in the template that is automatically applied to all pages based on that template.

1. **Double-click ah_template in the Files panel (in the Templates folder) to open the template file.**

2. **Place the insertion point in the empty nested table in the bottom row of the main table.**

3. **Double-click AH Footer Links in the Snippets panel to insert the snippet at the location of the insertion point.**

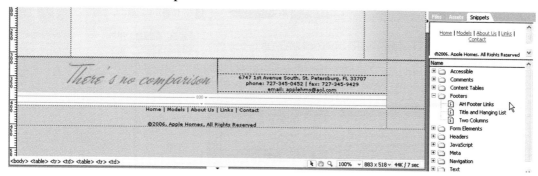

4. **Save the template file by pressing Command/Control-S.**

    Unlike other applications, Dreamweaver does not require you to use the Save As function to re-write an existing Dreamweaver template file. You can simply use the Save command to save changes to the ".dwt" file.

5. **Click Update when prompted to update the files based on the template.**

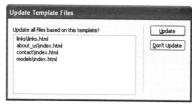

6. **Once the update is complete, click Close.**

    This dialog box shows the status of the update process. Because this is a small site, the Status bar should almost immediately show Done.

7. **Close the template file, and then open index.html from the links folder of the Apple Homes site.**

The links from the snippet appear in the links/index.html page because this page is based on the template in which you placed the snippet. The same links should also appear on the about_us/index.html, contact/index.html, and models/index.html pages.

The links from the modified template also appear in files based on the template.

8. **Close the open file, and then continue to the next exercise.**

COMPLETE THE HOME PAGE DESIGN

In this exercise, you return to the page you created at the beginning of the project and convert it into a template. This HTML page — not the ".dwt" file — will be the home page of the Web site. Its layout structure is slightly different from the rest of the pages in the site, so it cannot be based on the existing template. The home page design is very similar, however, so you can take advantage of work you have already completed: you modify the original index.html page to suit the specific requirements of the home page.

1. **Open index.html from the root folder of the Apple Homes site.**

2. **Replace the narrow image in the second row of the table with the file spacer.gif from the main images folder.**

You might need to zoom in to select the narrow image so you can replace it with the spacer.gif file.

The image that was in this cell has been replaced with the spacer.gif file, which is one pixel by one pixel.

3. **Delete the logo from the left cell of the table, and then insert the file sidebar_top.jpg in place of the logo.**

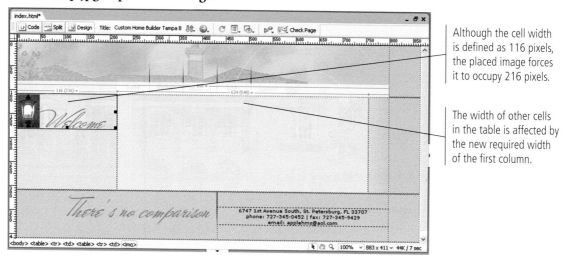

Although the cell width is defined as 116 pixels, the placed image forces it to occupy 216 pixels.

The width of other cells in the table is affected by the new required width of the first column.

4. **Place the insertion point in the third column of the nested table in row 3 of the main table.**

5. **Choose Modify>Table>Delete Column.**

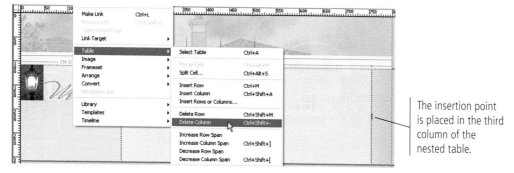

The insertion point is placed in the third column of the nested table.

This table does not need the third column. You can easily delete entire rows and columns using the commands in the Modify>Table menu.

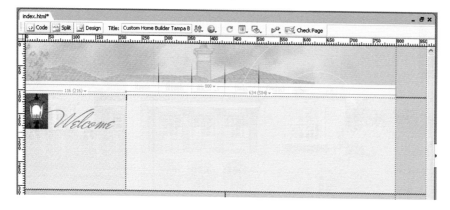

6. **Command/Control-click the left cell in the table to select it, and then click the Split Cell button in the Properties Inspector.**

7. In the Split Cell dialog box, divide the cell into three rows, and then click OK.

You are going to paste a block of text into a cell below the "Welcome" image. You are splitting the cell into three rows so there will be an empty row between the image cell and the text cell.

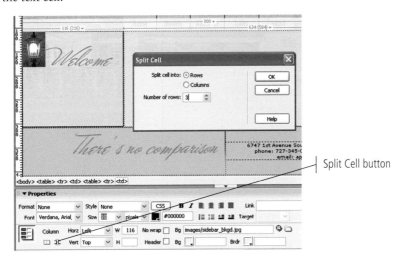

Split Cell button

8. Select only the third cell in the first column and click the Split Cell button. Divide this cell into two columns.

This third row will contain the home page text. You are splitting it into two columns to create a false left margin and move the text away from the browser edge.

This is the selected cell.

9. Using the Files panel, open homepage_content.txt from the text_files folder. Copy its contents, close the file, and then paste the copied contents into the bottom-right cell below the "Welcome" image.

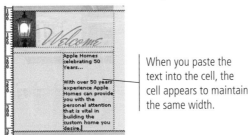

When you paste the text into the cell, the cell appears to maintain the same width.

10. Place the file image_home.jpg into the right cell (the right column of the table).

After clicking away from the text cell, the cell expands to fill as much space as possible.

The empty cells collapse to the smallest possible size.

11. Preview the file in your browser.

The empty table cell collapses to the smallest possible space, which is smaller than what you see in Dreamweaver.

The text runs directly to the edge of the placed picture.

12. Return to Dreamweaver and select the cell with the home page text.

13. Click the Split Cell button in the Properties Inspector and divide the cell into two columns.

When you split a cell with existing content, the content remains in the originally selected cell.

The new empty table cell provides some space between the text and the image to the right.

14. Save the file, and then preview the file in your default broswer.

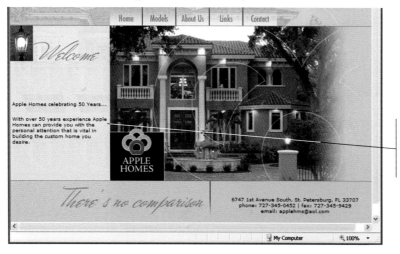

The empty table cell creates a slight space between the text and the image to the right.

15. Return to Dreamweaver, close the open HTML file, and continue to the next exercise.

CREATE LINKS USING THE SITE MAP VIEW

The home page design is almost complete. You only need to add links and a copyright notice in the footer. You could use the Footer Links snippet you already created, but there is another way to create links in Dreamweaver. A **site map** is a graphic representation of how pages in a site are linked to one another. The Site Map view, which is available in the expanded Files panel, can be used to easily create links from one page to another within a site.

1. **In the Files panel, click the Expand button.**

2. **On the toolbar of the expanded Files panel, click the Site Map button and choose Map and Files from the menu.**

   The Site Map view shows an illustration of how the pages are linked to one another. The home page displays as the root page; the links from it are illustrated with arrows.

   Each page that contains links shows a "+" sign, which you can click to see the pages, Web sites, and email IDs to which it is linked. External links, including links to other Web sites and email links, display in blue.

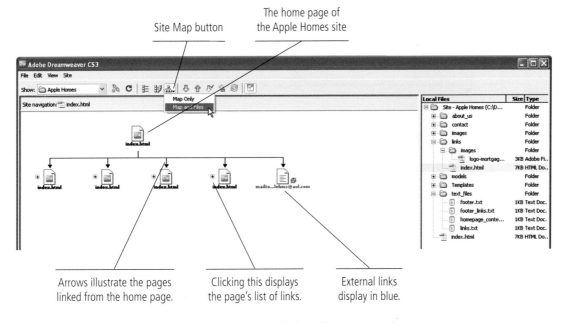

   By default, all files are listed in the Site Map view with their file names. In this project, they all appear as index.html because they are all default pages of the main folders/categories in the site. Such a naming structure can be difficult to work with; fortunately, you can change the settings to list files with their page titles.

3. Macintosh users: Open the Files panel options menu and choose View>Site Map Options>Show Page Titles.

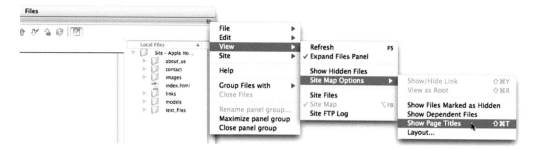

Windows users: Choose View>Site Map Options>Show Page Titles.

The site map now appears with page titles instead of file names, which makes it easier to identify the files.

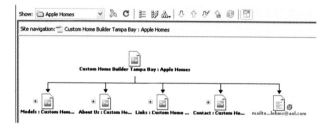

4. Control/Right-click the home page in the site map and choose Link to Existing File. Navigate to the index.html file in the root of the Apple Homes site and click OK.

A link to this file appears at the bottom of the page (links from a file to itself do not display in the site map).

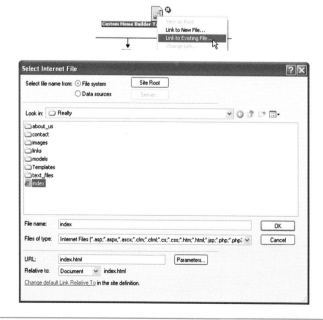

5. **Click the Point to File icon of the site home page icon, and then drag to the Models page icon to create another link.**

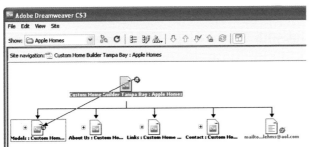

Note:

You can use the Point to File method to create a link to any page in the right pane of the expanded Files panel, or you can drag to an existing thumbnail in the site map pane.

6. **Repeat Step 5 to add links to the remaining pages in the site map, adding the links from left to right (as they appear in the site map).**

7. **Double-click the home page file icon to open it in Design view, and then scroll to the bottom of the page.**

   Five links appear, all of them using the word "index." Links created using the site map are automatically based on the file names to which you link. Because all of these files are named "index.html," all five links use the word "index" as the link text. You need to select each link and change the text to something more appropriate.

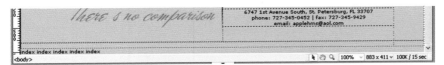

8. **Select all the links and cut them to the clipboard (Command/Control-X).**

9. **Place the cursor in the empty nested table in the bottom row of the main table, and then paste the links you cut in Step 8.**

10. **Select each link individually and change the text to the appropriate page titles. From the left, change the links to:**

    Home **Models** **About Us** **Links** **Contact**

11. Place the cursor at the end of the "Home" link in the first line and press the Spacebar. Press Shift-\ to insert the pipe character (|), and then press the Spacebar again.

12. Repeat Step 11 to separate each link with the space-pipe-space sequence.

13. Place the cursor at the end of the line and press Return/Enter.

14. Switch to the Text Insert bar and use the Special Characters menu to insert the Copyright character.

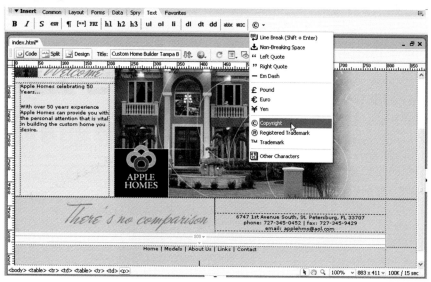

15. Type "2006, Apple Homes, All Rights Reserved".

16. Save the file and close it.

Summary

To complete this project, you learned how to create a new page from scatch — defining page properties to control the default appearance of different elements and assign a title to the basic page.

Although standards-compliant sites use CSS to assemble different pieces and create Web page structure, you used HTML tables to compose the different elements of this site. The table-based method was extremely common several years ago, and still persists in a number of sites today despite the increased emphasis on and support for CSS. You will undoubtedly run into a table-based site at some point in your career as a Web designer, so you need to understand how tables work to be better able to take them apart and replace them with a standards-compliant CSS-based layout.

You also learned the advantage to using template files to create multiple pages with a cohesive, consistent appearance. By placing common elements in a template file, you can easily create new pages from the template or attach the template to existing pages to quickly unify the entire site design.

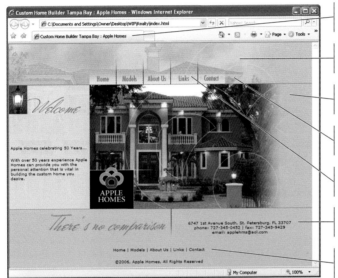

Define page properties for a new blank page

Use an HTML table to define Web site structure

Control table and cell properties (including background images)

Use a nested table to reassemble a sliced image

Define rollover images as navigation tools

Save a template file with common design elements

Create links with the Site Map view

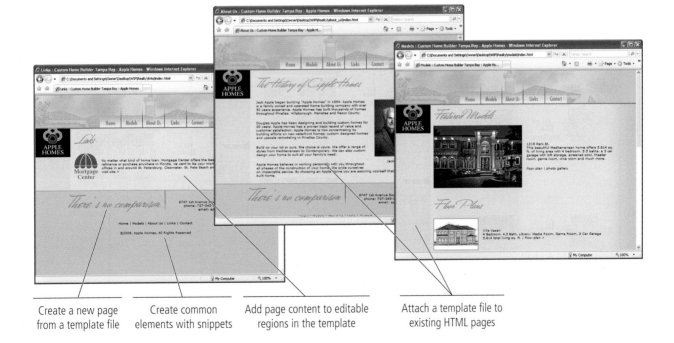

Create a new page from a template file

Create common elements with snippets

Add page content to editable regions in the template

Attach a template file to existing HTML pages

Portfolio Builder Project 4

As a member of the development team at a regional design agency, you are responsible for creating the overall site structure for your agency's clients' Web sites. You work in tandem with a graphic designer who designs the look and feel of the site, then slices it apart and hands you the pieces to reassemble in Dreamweaver.

To complete this project, you should:

❏ Create a new site in Dreamweaver to manage the various files that will make up the site.

❏ Use a table to reassemble the site image that was sliced apart in Photoshop after the design was approved.

❏ Save a template that can be used to design all the different pages of the site.

"The site will start out very basic, with only five main pages: Home, About Us, About Our Boards, Shop Online, and Contact Us.

"The interface layout has been approved based on the Photoshop file, and the designer sent you a CD with all the necessary slices. They're in the RF_Builder>Klaus folder. The navigation buttons on the left are rollover buttons; you'll find both 'states' of the button files in the Klaus folder. The designer also sent a flattened JPEG of the final design that you can use for reference when you're reassembling the pieces.

"Because all the pages are going have a consistent layout, you should create a template with as much of the common content as possible. Once the template is created, create placeholder files for each of the five pages. Then we can simply feed in the relevant content as soon as we get it from the client.

"We already have the home page content, which is just a small blurb of text for the box above the navigation buttons; the text is in the same folder with the sample JPEG file. The heading for that page should be 'Life is better when you surf!', and the content for the home page is just an image (the one you see in the sample JPEG file)."

Showcolate CSS Layout

Showcolate USA has hired you to build a Web site to promote its franchising business. Although you're building the site, Showcolate wants complete control over the layout and design. The company wants a Web site that can be quickly and easily updated and modified. In addition, the site should project a consistent look and style across all pages. To fulfill these requirements, you will create and apply a cascading style sheet (CSS) for the Web site.

This project incorporates the following skills:

❏ Working with tracing images to replicate a site designed in an image-editing application

❏ Creating and linking an external CSS file

❏ Creating ID selectors

❏ Creating a layout with div elements

❏ Editing CSS rules to adjust the layout

❏ Using the float property to control nested divs

❏ Using margins and padding to affect element placement

❏ Defining HTML tag selectors and descendent tag selectors

❏ Creating pseudo-class selectors

❏ Adding and modifying selectors to meet specific design requirements

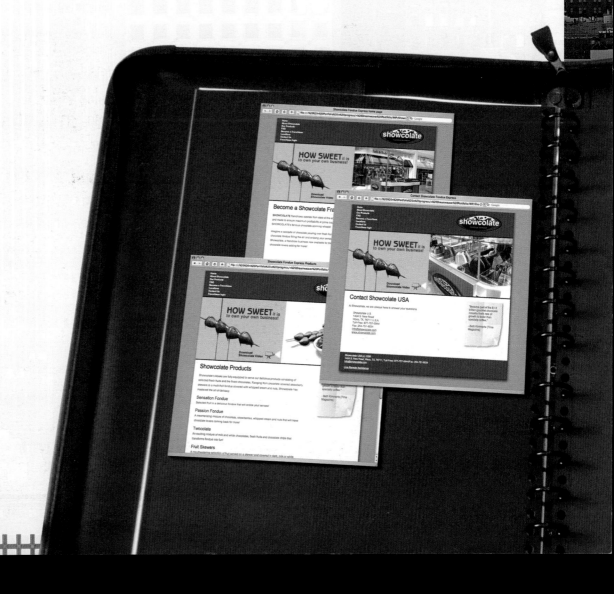

Client Comments

We have been getting a lot of inquiries about our franchise business, and we would like to create a new Web site to help answer some of the preliminary questions so our administrative time can focus on those who express a serious interest.

We have an existing site, but we can't really figure out how it was built so it is extremely difficult to change even a comma. In fact, we called the old designer and he said it would take a week for him to have time to make the changes. This is simply not acceptable.

The new site should be very easy to manage and, more importantly, easy to change — whether it's a comma or the entire site layout.

The other problem we have is that the site doesn't appear very high on search engine rankings. The old designer said this is because we insisted on controlling the appearance of the page text. He said it would take several weeks — and a lot of money — to redesign the site for search engine compatibility.

Art Director Comments

I've had the graphic designer put together the look and feel of the new site. She's created a comp image that shows the overall layout, which you should review carefully to see what elements you need to implement the new site in Dreamweaver.

The client wants to be able to make his own changes to the actual page content, but we don't want him to be able to destroy the integrity of the page layout. Cascading style sheets are the best way to accomplish this goal because the actual HTML pages will be almost entirely text. The layout will be defined in the CSS file so he can edit the text all he wants without touching the layout.

CSS separates the page content from the presentational issues like containers and backgrounds, so search engines can more easily scan and rank the actual page content. Although this won't get around the issue of companies that pay for higher rankings, the Showcolate site should appear much higher on the list than the old site that was designed entirely using images of the page text.

Project Objectives

To complete this proect, you will:

❑ Define a tracing image

❑ Create and link an external CSS file

❑ Create ID selectors

❑ Understand the CSS box model

❑ Create a layout with div elements

❑ Edit CSS rules to adjust the layout

❑ Use the float property to control nested divs

❑ Use margins and padding to affect element placement

❑ Define properties for the body tag

❑ Define HTML tag selectors

❑ Create descendent tag selectors

❑ Create pseudo-class selectors

❑ Create a template file

❑ Add and modify selectors to meet design requirements

Stage 1 Creating Layouts with Style Sheets

A cascading style sheet (CSS) is a collection of formatting rules that control the appearance of different elements in a Web page. By attaching a style sheet to an HTML page and applying the styles to the content of the page, you can control every aspect of the page layout.

A CSS file includes formatting instructions in **rules**. A rule consists of a **selector** (basically, selecting which element will be formatted) and attributes (such as font, color, width, height, etc.) that will be applied to the element.

A style sheet offers a great deal of flexibility in applying styles. You can apply one style to a single element of a page or to multiple elements at once. You can first create the complete style sheet and then apply styles to the Web page, or you can simultaneously create styles while building the Web page.

Using a style sheet, you don't need to modify individual elements of a Web page. Changing the style applied to a group of elements effectively changes the appearance of all elements in the group. This method not only makes your work easier, but it also adds a consistent look and style to the Web page — as well as to all pages that use the same style sheet.

Note:

You can apply similar styles to multiple pages in a Web site, or you can apply different styles to different pages.

 DEFINE A TRACING IMAGE

Before creating CSS rules, you should have a clear idea about how the page or site should look. Understanding the appearance (and other requirements) of your site helps you determine what rules you need to create.

In many workflows, the look and feel of a site is first designed in a graphics application such as Adobe Photoshop. In this case, you can import the final image file into Dreamweaver and use it as a map when defining CSS rules to replicate the image as an HTML page. Using Dreamweaver's **Tracing Image** feature, the image you select appears in the background in Design view; you can change the opacity and position of the image as necessary. When you have finished the layout design, you can hide or remove the tracing image.

Note:

A tracing image can be a JPEG, GIF, BMP, or PNG file.

1. Copy the Showcolate folder from the RF_Dreamweaver folder to the WIP folder where you are saving your work.

2. Choose Manage Sites in the Files panel.

3. If the Realty site is still available, export the site definition into your WIP>Realty folder, and then remove the Realty site from the Manage Sites dialog box.

4. Click New>Site in the Manage Sites dialog box.

5. Create a new site named "Candy" and choose the WIP>Showcolate folder as the site root folder.

6. Click OK to close the Site Definition dialog box, and then click Done to return to Dreamweaver.

7. **With the Candy site open in the Files panel, choose File>New.**

8. **Using the New Document dialog box, create a new, blank HTML page.**

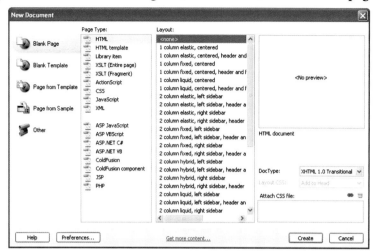

9. **Choose File>Save. Save the new page as an HTML file named "design.html" in the root folder of the Candy site (WIP>Showcolate).**

10. **With design.html open in Design view, choose View>Tracing Image>Load.**

11. **In the Select Image Source dialog box, navigate to the file Showcolate.jpg in the site images folder and click Choose/OK.**

When you load a tracing image, the Page Properties dialog box automatically appears. You can use the Tracing Image options to change the transparency of the tracing image, or to browse to select a different image.

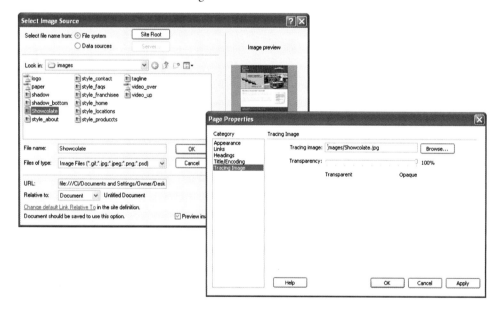

12. Click OK to close the Page Properties dialog box.

The tracing image Showcolate.jpg appears in design.html. If you have a small screen, you might be unable to see the entire image at 100% magnification.

Note:

Show or hide the tracing image using the Show/ Hide toggle control in the View>Tracing Image menu.

You can't scroll to see the rest of the tracing image.

13. Choose View>Tracing Image>Reset Position.

This command moves the tracing image to the actual document edges.

Note:

When rulers are visible, you can click the zero point crosshairs (in the top-left corner) and drag to reposition the rulers' zero point. Doing so can make it easier to measure elements in the tracing image.

14. Change your view percentage as necessary so you can see the entire tracing image.

15. Analyze the image to determine what you need to do to create this site layout.

- The primary layout is 800 pixels wide.
- The primary layout appears to be centered in the horizontal space.
- The layout is broken into four primary rows.
- The first three rows each have two elements/pieces of content.
- The entire 800-pixel layout has a drop shadow.

16. Consider and take note of the following information, which was provided by the designer who developed the look of the site:

- A sans-serif font should be applied to all text in the site.
- There are eight total pages in the site.
- Each page will have the same layout; only the image in the second row and the main text in the third row will be different from page to page.
- The client wants to use gray text instead of plain black text.
- First-level headings should be the darkest brown color from the chocolate strawberry image.
- Second-level headings should be a bit smaller than first-level headings, and they should be the same color as the background of the header area.
- Links should be underlined in the main text and the footer, but not underlined in the primary navigation text links.
- All text links should switch to a light orange/red (from the strawberry image) when the mouse rolls over the links.

17. Save the file and continue to the next exercise.

CREATE AN EXTERNAL CSS FILE

Dreamweaver supports three types of styles: external, embedded, and inline. To make the best use of styles, you should have a clear understanding of these different types — including when each is best suited to your specific goal. (All three types of styles can be applied to the same HTML page at the same time.)

An **external style sheet** is a separate file containing CSS rules. This file can be attached to multiple HTML pages at one time, applying the same rules to similar elements in the different pages. Because an external style sheet can format many pages at once, this method can be used to format an entire site quickly and easily.

An external style sheet is saved as a CSS file (with the extension ".css"), which is uploaded to the Web server along with the Web pages to which the file is attached. If you change the CSS rules, you need only replace the CSS file on the server to affect the pages in the site. (When you use embedded or inline styles, you need to re-upload all pages affected by the modified rules.)

When a user calls a specific page URL, the Web browser reads the HTML, finds the directions to the attached CSS file, and reads the rules in the CSS file to present the HTML content exactly as you intended.

An **embedded style** is added directly in an HTML page, within style tags (<style>...</style>); this type of style affects only the particular HTML page in which it is placed.

The following code for an embedded style defines the font of H1 elements and the text color of paragraph elements:

```
<style type="text/css">
<!--
h1 {
    font-family: Arial, Helvetica, sans-serif;
    font-size: 24px;
    font-weight: bold;
}
p {
    font-family: Arial, Helvetica, sans-serif;
    font-size: 12px;
    color: #0000CC;
}
-->
</style>
```

The set of "<!--" and "-->" tags prevents a few older browsers from displaying the style rules. Although most Web designers prefer to use an embedded style within header tags, an embedded style can be placed anywhere in a page.

An **inline style** applies directly and instantly to an individual element within a tag, affecting only that single element of the HTML page. For example, if you apply a font size and color to a paragraph, the inline style looks like this:

```
<p style="font-size: 10pt; color: blue">Paragraph content goes here.</p>
```

The CSS Styles panel plays a significant role in creating and modifying styles. CSS styles display in two modes — **All** and **Current**. All mode displays external and embedded styles. Current mode displays the style of the current selection (external, embedded, and inline).

- In **All mode** the top half of the panel shows a list of styles. The lower half shows the properties associated with the selected option in the list of styles.

- In **Current mode**, the Summary for Selection pane shows the properties and values applied to a selection. The top pane shows rules attributed to the selection or information of the selected property in the Summary for Selection pane (the two buttons at the top of the Rules pane help you switch between these two options.) The Properties pane shows the properties of the selected rule.

When you select a rule, the properties and values of the rule display in the Properties pane. You can use the Properties pane to add new properties or modify the values for existing properties.

You can view the properties and values in the Properties pane in Show Category view, Show List view, or Show Only Set Properties (the default view).

- **Show Category view** shows properties and values, categorized in nine groups (the same groups that are available in the CSS Rule Definition dialog box). Every available property is listed; properties with defined values are shown in blue. You can add new properties by clicking the white space to the right of a property and typing a new value or choosing from a menu (if one becomes available).

- **Show List view** lists all the CSS properties in alphabetical order. Properties that already have defined values appear in blue.

- **Show Only Set Properties** displays only the list of properties for which you have already defined values. You can add new properties to the rule by clicking the Add Property link at the bottom of the list.

Four buttons in the bottom right corner of the CSS Style panel provide additional functionality:

- The **Attach Style Sheet** button attaches an external style sheet to the active HTML page. You can browse and attach the saved style sheet to the HTML page by using the import or link method.

- The **New CSS Rule** button creates a new CSS rule for class selectors, tag selectors, and ID/pseudo-class selectors.

- The **Edit Style** button opens the CSS Rule Definition dialog box for the selected style (in the list at the top of the panel).

- The **Delete CSS Rule (or Property)** button deletes the selected style (selected in the top half of the panel) or property (selected in the bottom half of the panel).

1. **With design.html open, choose File>New.**

2. **In the New Document dialog box, choose Blank Page in the left column.**

3. **Choose CSS from the Page Type list and click Create.**

   A new cascading style sheet is created.

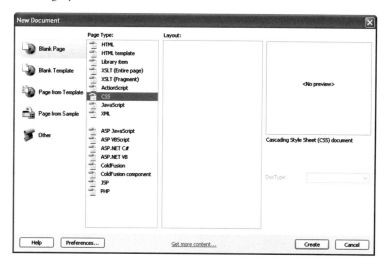

4. **Choose File>Save.**

   Macintosh users: In the Save As dialog box, navigate to the WIP>Showcolate>css folder. Name the file "master.css", and then click Save.

   Windows users: In the Save As dialog box, navigate to the WIP>Showcolate>css folder and name the file "master.css". Choose Style Sheets (*.css) in the Save As Type menu, and then click Save.

   This file will contain all the selectors you define to format the Showcolate Web site.

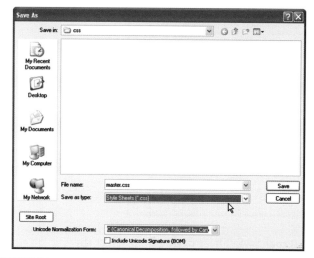

Master.css is open in a separate file. It is not yet related to design.html.

5. **Choose Window>CSS Styles or click CSS in the panel dock to expand the CSS Styles panel.**

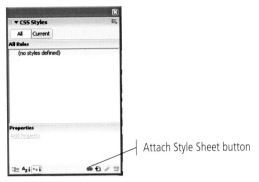

Attach Style Sheet button

6. **Click the design.html tab to make that file active, and then click the Attach Style Sheet button at the bottom of the CSS panel.**

   The resulting dialog box allows you to select an external style sheet to use for the active HTML file.

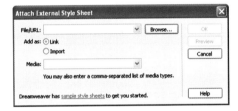

7. **Click the Browse button to the right of the File/URL field.**

8. **Navigate to the master.css file that you saved in Step 4 and click Choose/OK.**

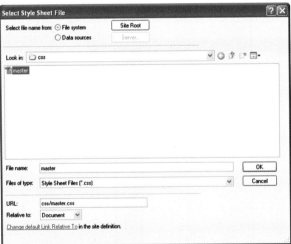

9. **When you return to the Attach External Style Sheet dialog box, select the Link option in the Add As area.**

   External style sheets can be attached using either the link method or the import method. The link method is better supported by most browsers, and it is the default option in Dreamweaver.

10. Select Screen from the Media menu.

Each page can have different style sheets to define the appearance of different types of devices and applications. The Screen option controls the appearance of a page as it displays in a Web browser (on screen).

11. Click OK to attach the style sheet file to design.html.

The file master.css now appears in the CSS Styles panel for the design.html file.

12. Save the file and continue to the next exercise.

 CREATE ID SELECTORS

Using the information you received from the tracing image and the graphic designer, you can now begin to build the overall site layout. Because all eight pages in the site have the same basic layout, you are going to build all the common elements and save them as a template; this workflow makes it much faster and easier to create a site.

To build a layout with CSS, you first need to understand the concept of the div HTML element. A <div> tag marks a division (or section) of a page. A style sheet can define a large number of properties for each div, including height, width, background color, margins, and more.

Note:

If you completed Project 3, you already know a bit about div tags. This project looks deeper into div tags, showing you how to create and control your own divs.

Each div on a page has a different identity (defined using the id attribute), which allows you to define different properties for different areas of the page, as in:

```
#header {
    background-color: #999999;
}
#footer {
    background-color: #00CCCC;
}
```

Note:

Properties and values for the selector are contained within curly brackets; each property is separated by a semicolon.

Using the code shown above, the header div will have a gray background and the footer div will have a light aqua background.

You can define ID selectors in a style sheet to control the appearance of HTML div elements. When you insert a div element into a page, you choose a defined ID for that div element; the properties defined in the ID selector (in the style sheet) are then used to format the div in the page.

1. **With design.html open, click the New CSS Rule button at the bottom of the CSS Styles panel.**

New CSS Rule button

In the New CSS Rule dialog box, you can define the type and name of a selector, as well as where to create the rule (in the attached external CSS file or embedded in the active HTML file).

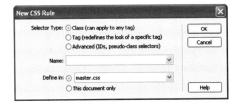

2. Click the Advanced radio button in the Selector Type area.

As the parenthetical notation suggests, the Advanced option controls the properties of IDs and pseudo-classes (variations of tags, such as a:hover to define a link appearance when the mouse hovers over the link text).

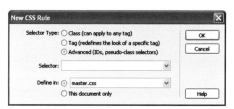

Note:

CSS rules are created using selectors — you select which element (tag, div ID, etc.) you are formatting with a specific rule.

3. In the Selector field, type "#wrapper" (without the quotation marks).

This ID will be the outermost container for the page layout. Although you know that the primary content is 800 pixels wide, the only way to accomplish the drop shadow effect is to place an image behind the divs that contain the page content. This #wrapper div will contain the shadow image, and it will also contain the remaining divs that will hold the 800-pixel divs for the primary page elements.

Note:

All ID selector names must begin with the "#" character.

4. In the Define In area, make sure the first radio button is selected and master.css is showing in the related menu.

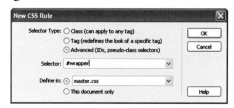

Note:

The header of the dialog box includes the name of the selector currently being edited. For the sake of brevity, we exclude this distinction when we refer to the dialog box.

5. Click OK to open the CSS Rule Definition dialog box.

This dialog box includes eight categories of options. All the properties that can be saved in a CSS rule are available in the different panes of this dialog box.

6. Click Background in the list of categories.

7. Click Browse to the right of the Background Image field.

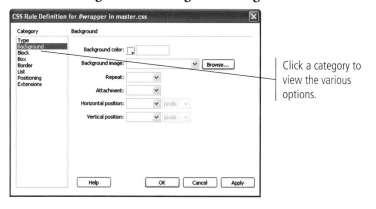

Click a category to view the various options.

Note:

Choosing Fixed in the Attachment menu causes a background image to remain in place while the rest of the document scrolls over it. Choosing Scroll allows the background image to scroll along with the page, maintaining the same position relative to the page content.

The CSS Rule Definition Dialog Box in Depth

The CSS Rule Definition dialog box is the primary tool for defining CSS rules. When you create a new selector, the CSS Rule Definition dialog box for that selector opens so you can set the selector's properties and values.

Type options control the appearance of the text.

- Font defines the font sequence for the text (e.g., Arial, Helvetica, sans-serif); you can also edit the available list.
- Size sets the size of the font in a variety of measurement units (using pixels can prevent text distortion).
- Style specifies the font style (normal, italic, or oblique).
- Line height determines the height of the line.
- Decoration sets a predefined style (underline, overline, line-through, blink, or none). This is particularly useful for removing the default underline of hyperlink text.
- Weight affects the apparent boldness of the text (normal, bold, bolder, lighter, or specific values).
- Variant sets the text as normal or small-caps.
- Case controls the capitalization of the text (capitalize changes the first letter of the each word, uppercase shows all letters as capitals, and lowercase shows all letters as lowercase).

Background options control the background color and images.

- Background color can be set by typing a hexadecimal color code in the field, by clicking the color swatch and choosing a color from the color picker, or by clicking the color swatch and using the eyedropper cursor to sample a color from anywhere on your screen.
- Background images can be set by typing the path or by clicking the Browse button and navigating to the image.
- Repeat determines how background images fill the available space.
  - No-repeat places the image once in the top-left corner of the page.
  - Repeat tiles the image horizontally and vertically.
  - Repeat-x tiles the image only horizontally.
  - Repeat-y tiles the image vertically.
- Attachment controls how a background image moves in relation to the page.
  - Fixed keeps the image in place if the page scrolls.
  - Scroll allows the background image to stay in the same position relative to the page; the image will scroll along with the page.
- Horizontal position allows the image to be set to the left, center, or right.
- Vertical position sets the image to the top, center, or bottom of the page.

Block options define spacing and alignment settings for content within a container.

- Word spacing controls the spacing between words.
- Letter spacing controls the spacing between individual characters.
- Vertical alignment aligns the selected element vertically.
- Text align aligns text to the left, right, or center, or justifies (stretches) the text the entire width of the container.
- Text indent specifies where text begins on a line.
- Whitespace manages extra spaces and tabs.
  - Normal collapses all whitespace (ignoring double spaces and tabs).
  - Pre retains all whitespace.
  - Nowrap prevents lines of text from wrapping (unless a <br> tag is used).
- Display controls the visibility of an element.

Box options control the element dimensions.

- Width and Height control the element size.

- Float determines where an element will be placed in relation to its containing element. Other content in the same element will float around the affected element on the opposite side.

- Clear enables a layer to disappear on the selected side of an element — left, right, or both.

- Padding is the amount of space that separates the element border and the content in the element.

- Margin is the amount of space that separates the element border and surrounding elements.

Border options control the style, width, and color for element edges. You can specify values individually (top, right, bottom, left) or select the Same for All check box to apply the same border attributes to all four sides of an element.

List options control the appearance and style of lists.

- Type specifies the type of a list identifier to use.

- Bullet Image defines a custom image to use as a bullet character.

- Position defines the list position as inside or outside (the list wraps indented from the bullet character or to the left margin).

Positioning options control the position of the elements.

- Type determines the position of the element.
  - Absolute enables the element to remain stable, regardless of the position of the other elements.
  - Fixed position is based on window size.
  - Relative position is based on the position of other elements.
  - Static positions the element as it appears in an HTML page.

- Width and Height determine the dimensions of the element. These options are the same as the same-named options in the Box category; values entered in one category automatically reflect in the other.

- Visibility determines whether the element is shown in the page. If no visibility property is selected, the element inherits its visibility from the containing element parent. Visible displays the element. Hidden hides the element.

- Z-index shows the depth of an element in the layer stacking order. Elements with higher z-index values appear above elements with lower z-index values.

- Overflow determines how the element should appear when the element exceeds the allotted space.
  - Auto inserts a scrollbar (horizontal, vertical, or both).
  - Visible enables the block to expand to view content.
  - Hidden only shows content that fits in the block; the remaining content is clipped and not hidden.

- Placement specifies where elements can be positioned.

- Clip specifies the visible parts of an element.

Extensions options create breaks and apply visual effects.

- Page break sets a page break for printing.

- Cursor specifies the pointer style when you place the mouse cursor over the element.

- Filter adds artistic effects to change element appearance.

8. **Navigate to shadow.jpg in the site images folder and click Choose/OK.**

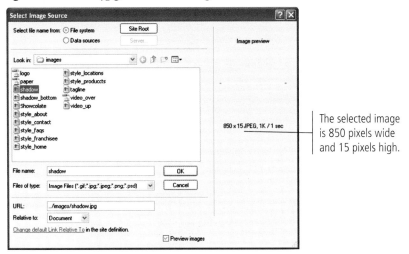

The selected image is 850 pixels wide and 15 pixels high.

Note:

On Windows, you might not see the file extensions in the Select Image Source dialog box.

9. **Choose repeat in the Repeat menu.**

This image is only 15 pixels high. By allowing it to repeat, it will occupy the entire height of the div element when content in the element expands beyond the #wrapper div.

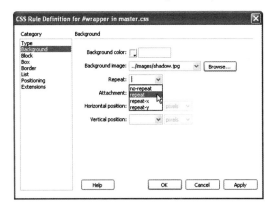

Note:

Repeat *repeats the image vertically and horizontally.*

No-repeat *prevents the image from repeating.*

Repeat-x *repeats the image horizontally.*

Repeat-y *repeats the image vertically.*

10. **Click Box in the list of categories.**

11. **Change the Width to 850 pixels. Make sure the Same For All check boxes are both selected, and change the Top Padding and Top Margin fields to 0.**

As you saw earlier, the shadow image is 850 pixels wide; because it is placed as a background image, however, the size of the image does not affect the size of the div. To make the div show the entire width of the shadow image, you have to manually define the width of the #wrapper selector.

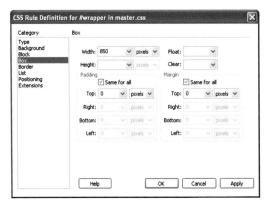

12. **Click OK to add the rule to the master.css file.**

In the design window, the design.html file is not affected because the #wrapper div has not yet been placed in the file. The new rule appears only in the CSS Styles panel; specific properties of the rule are listed in the lower half of the panel.

This area shows the properties you just defined for this ID selector.

13. **Click the master.css tab at the top of the document window.**

You can now see the code for the rule you just defined.

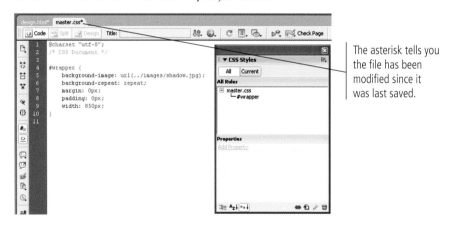

The asterisk tells you the file has been modified since it was last saved.

14. **Click the design.html tab to make that file active.**

15. Using the same basic process as outlined for the #wrapper selector, create six additional ID selectors using the following information:

If an option isn't listed here, leave it at the default setting (in most cases, blank).

Selector Name	Purpose	Category	Settings to Apply
#wrapperInside	*This will be placed within the #wrapper div; it will contain additional divs for the four rows of the page layout.*	Box	Width: 800 pixels Padding: 0 pixels on all four sides Margins: 0 pixels on all four sides
#header	*This will be placed in the #wrapperInside div; it will contain the navigation links and the logo.*	Background	Background color: Click the color swatch and then sample the orange color at the top of the tracing image.
		Box	Width: 800 pixels
#Row2Wrap	*This will be placed in the #wrapperInside div; it will contain the chocolate strawberry image and a different image on each page.*	Box	Width: 800 pixels
		Border	Top: 3-pixel width, solid style, using a dark brown color from the tracing image as the border color. Bottom: 3-pixel width, solid style, using a dark brown color from the tracing image as the border color.
#Row3Wrap	*This will be placed in the #wrapperInside div; it will contain the main text for each page and a quote over the wrinkled-paper image.*	Background	Background color: #FFFFFF
		Box	Width: 800 pixels
#footer	*This will be placed in the #wrapperInside div; it will contain the company contact information at the bottom of the page.*	Background	Background color: Sample the same color you used for the header background color.
		Box	Width: 800 pixels
#bottomShadow	*This will be placed outside the #wrapper div; it will contain an image that will create the bottom of the drop shadow.*	Background	Background image: shadow_bottom.jpg
		Box	Repeat: no-repeat Width: 850 pixels

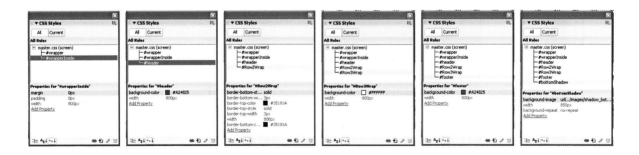

16. **Click the master.css tab.**

Appropriate code for all selectors has been added to the file.

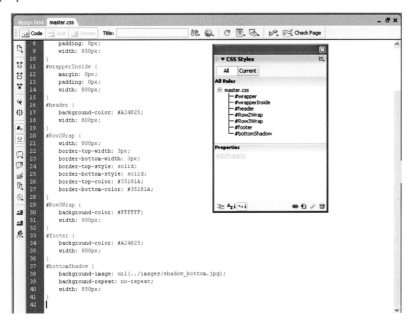

17. **Save the master.css file.**

18. **Click the design.html tab to make that file active.**

19. **Save the HTML file and continue to the next exercise.**

Understanding the CSS Box Model

When you design layouts using CSS, think of any specific element as a box. In the context of this discussion, any box is made up of four parts: margin, border, padding, and content. (Padding, border, and margin must be added to the content to calculate the total space occupied by the box.)

```
1
2    <HTML>
3    <HEAD>
4    <style type="text/css">
5    #box {
6        width: 200px;
7        border: 10px solid #009933;
8        padding: 20px;
9        margin: 20px;
10       margin-left: 100px;
11       padding-right: 100px;
12   }
13   </style>
14   <BODY>
15
16   ▼ <div id="box">This illustrates the box model.</div>
17   </BODY>
18   </HTML>
19
```

This illustrates the box model.

- 100-pixel left margin is added outside the box edge.
- 10-pixel border is on all four sides of the box.
- 100-pixel right padding is added inside the box edge.
- 20-pixel padding is applied to the other three edges (the padding-left value overrides the padding value for only the left edge).

20-pixel margins are applied to the other three edges (the margin-left value overrides the margin value for only the left edge).

- The **margin** is outside the box edges; it is invisible and has no background color. Margin does not affect content within the element.

- The **border** is the edge of the element (whether visible or not), based on the specified dimensions. When working with block-type elements such as paragraphs, the border is implied by the amount of content in the element (rather than specified with actual width and height values).

- The **padding** lies inside the edge of the element, forming a cushion between the box edge and the box content. If you are familiar with print design applications such as Adobe InDesign, think of padding as text inset.

- The **content** lies inside the padding. When you define a width and height for your box using CSS, you are defining the content area.

CREATE A LAYOUT WITH DIV ELEMENTS

You now have six different IDs defined in the external style sheet file. As you completed the previous exercise, however, you might have noticed that the design.html file was not affected by the new IDs. This is because you have to create div elements in the file, which you can then associate with specific ID selectors to create the page layout.

1. **With design.html open, choose View>Tracing Image>Show.**

   Toggling this option makes the tracing image disappear. It is still defined in the file, but you can no longer see it.

   If you close the file and reopen it, the tracing image will again be visible; you can simply hide it again as necessary.

2. **Choose Insert>Layout Objects>Div Tag.**

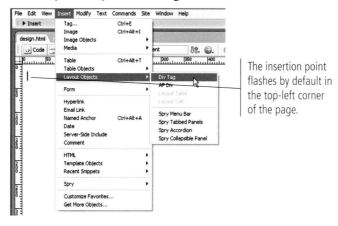

The insertion point flashes by default in the top-left corner of the page.

3. **In the Insert Div Tag dialog box, leave the Insert menu set to At Insertion Point.**

   The div you insert will be placed at the current insertion point, which is by default in the top-left corner of the page. The insertion point is slightly indented because Dreamweaver automatically adds several pixels of padding around the content of a new page. (Some browsers do the same, so Dreamweaver tries to accurately show what you will see when you preview the page in a browser).

4. **Choose wrapper from the ID menu.**

   Remember, this is the outer-most container that will create the drop-shadow effect on the bottom, left, and right edges of the main page content.

Note:

Other options in the Insert menu will be useful when you start to nest div elements inside one another.

5. Click OK to add the div tag to the page.

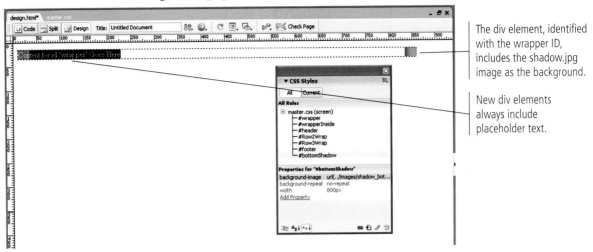

The div element, identified with the wrapper ID, includes the shadow.jpg image as the background.

New div elements always include placeholder text.

6. Show the page in Split view.

Because the placeholder text is highlighted in the Design pane, the corresponding text is also highlighted in the Code pane; this allows you to easily identify the code for the placed div element.

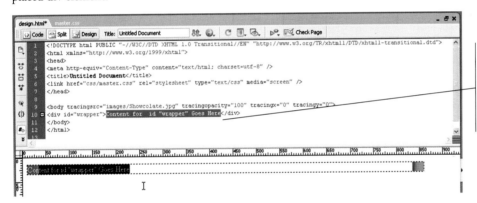

In the page code, the div element has no mention of the background image or div width. Those attributes are entirely controlled by the rule in the attached style sheet.

7. Press Delete to remove the highlighted placeholder text from the div element.

When you remove the div content, the div collapses to the smallest possible height. Because you did not define a specific height in the #wrapper selector rules, the div height will expand as necessary to accommodate whatever you place in the container.

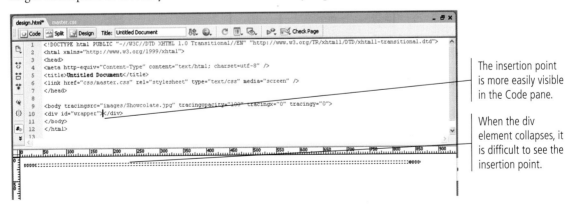

The insertion point is more easily visible in the Code pane.

When the div element collapses, it is difficult to see the insertion point.

8. Choose Insert>Layout Object>Div Tag.

9. **In the Insert Div Tag dialog box, choose wrapperInside from the ID menu.**

Remember, this ID will define the primary page width at 800 pixels, and it will contain the divs for the four rows of content.

The wrapper ID is not available. You can use an ID selector only once on any given page.

10. **Click OK to add the div element to the page.**

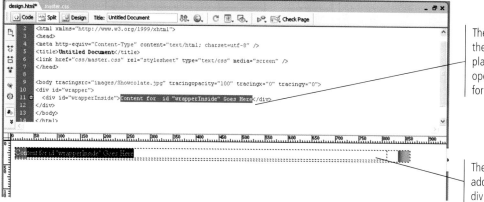

The entire line of code for the wrapperInside div is placed within the opening and closing tags for the wrapper div.

The wrapperInside div is added inside the wrapper div element.

11. **Delete the placeholder text from the wrapperInside div, and then use the same method from Steps 8–10 to place another div with the header ID inside the wrapperInside div.**

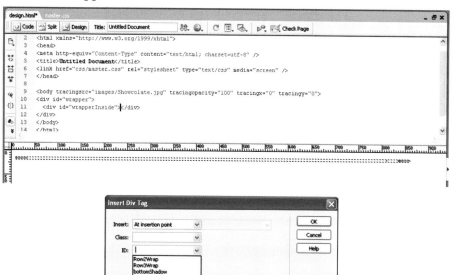

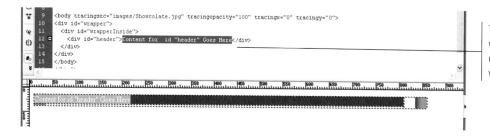

The header div is placed within the opening and closing tags of the wrapperInside div.

12. With the header div placeholder content selected, choose Insert>Layout Object>Div Tag.

13. In the Insert Div Tag dialog box, choose After Tag in the Insert menu.

Using the After Tag option, you can place a new div element after any existing div, regardless of the location of the insertion point.

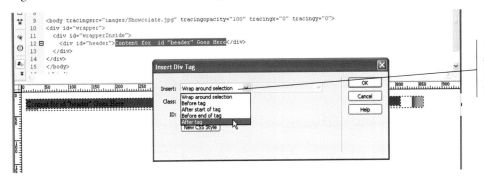

If anything is selected when you insert a div tag, the Insert menu defaults to Wrap Around Selection.

14. In the secondary menu, choose <div id "header">.

You want to place each additional row, one right after the other. Since the header div is already in place, you are adding the next div tag immediately after the existing one.

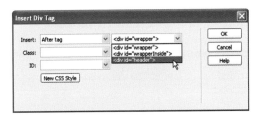

Note:

The Wrap Around Selection option is useful if you need to add a new div element around existing content. Because you are creating the layout from scratch, this option will not be useful for this exercise.

15. Choose Row2Wrap in the ID menu and click OK.

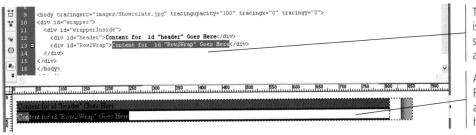

The Row2Wrap div is placed at the same nesting level as the header div.

As you specified, the Row2Wrap div is added after the header div.

16. Use the same process as in Steps 12–15 to add the Row3Wrap div after the Row2Wrap div.

17. Use the same process to add the footer div after the Row3Wrap div.

18. Use the same process to add the bottomShadow div after the wrapper div.

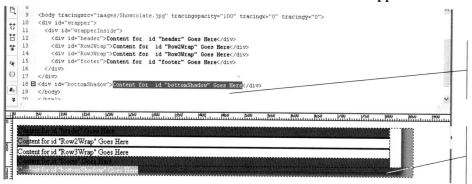

The Code pane shows that the bottomShadow div is placed after the closing tag of the original wrapper div.

The bottomShadow div is added immediately below the wrapper div.

19. Save the design.html file and continue to the next exercise.

Edit CSS Rules to Adjust the Layout

As you saw in the previous exercise, adding div elements adds to the page's HTML code. Those elements, however, are very short — basically identifying each div element and adding some placeholder content. In the page code, there is no mention of background images, colors, or other attributes that make up the page layout. Those attributes are controlled by editing the ID selectors applied to each div element.

1. With design.html open, review the current layout.

The original tracing image showed that the primary page layout was centered horizontally in the available space.

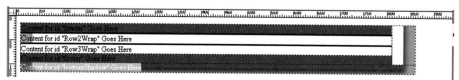

Comparing the <span> and <div> Tags

Both span and div tags are used to apply styles in portions of an HTML page. However, the two tags serve very different purposes. A **span tag** is used for "inline" content — within another piece of text such as a heading or paragraph. A span tag does not create a line break in the text; it applies styles to text (usually a small section) even in the middle of a sentence. For example:

A span tag can <span style="font:18pt times">change font</span> in the middle of a sentence.

results in:

A span tag can change font in the middle of a sentence.

A **div tag** is more commonly used to divide a page into different sections. If you apply a div tag in the middle of a sentence, a line break is automatically added before the div. For example:

Using div tags, you can divide a Web page <div style="text-align:center"> into different divisions. </div>

results in:

Using div tags, you can divide a Web page

into different divisions.

2. In the CSS Styles panel, click the #wrapper selector.

Because the wrapper div is the primary container for the page content, you have to center this element to center the page content.

3. Click the Edit Style button to open the CSS Rule Definition dialog box.

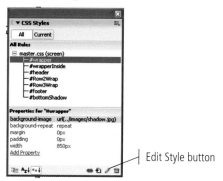

Edit Style button

4. In the Box category, deselect the Same For All option in the margin section. Change the Right and Left fields to auto.

Using the auto margin option, the available space outside the element width is equally split on the left and right sides — in other words, the element is centered horizontally.

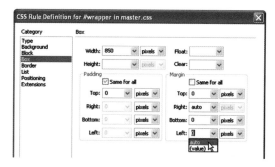

5. Click OK to add the new properties to the #wrapper selector.

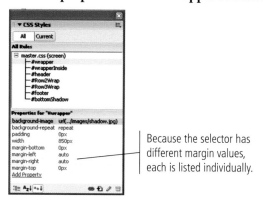

Because the selector has different margin values, each is listed individually.

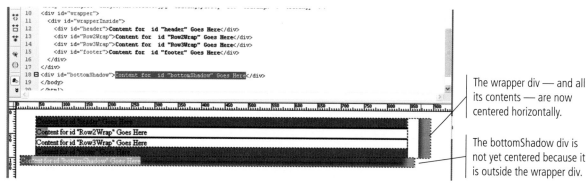

The wrapper div — and all its contents — are now centered horizontally.

The bottomShadow div is not yet centered because it is outside the wrapper div.

6. **Repeat Steps 2–5 to center the bottomShadow div.**

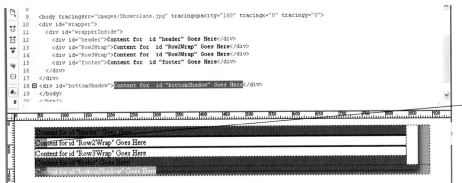

The wrapperInside div aligns by default to the left edge of the containing div.

7. **In the CSS Styles panel, select the #wrapperInside selector.**

8. **In the lower half of the panel, click Add Property.**

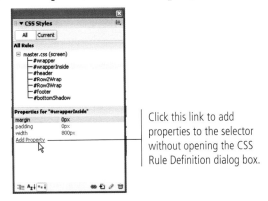

Click this link to add properties to the selector without opening the CSS Rule Definition dialog box.

9. **In the resulting menu, choose margin-left.**

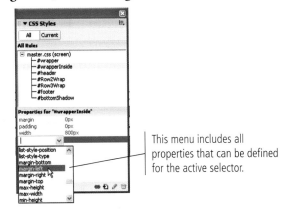

This menu includes all properties that can be defined for the active selector.

10. Highlight the field to the right of the new property and type "auto".

Note:

If you click away from the new property field before typing a value, the field seems to disappear. Just click again in the empty space to type the property value.

11. Click the empty area in the bottom of the panel to finalize the new property.

12. Repeat Steps 8–11 to add the margin-right property to the #wrapperInside selector with a value of auto.

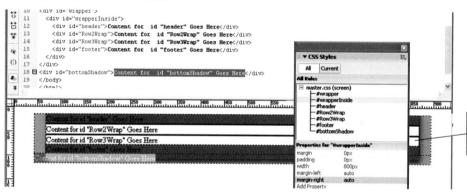

The wrapperInside div is now centered within the wrapper div.

13. In the design window, select and delete the placeholder text in the bottomShadow div element.

When you delete the placeholder content, the div collapses and the bottom shadow — which is a background image — disappears.

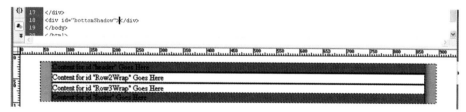

14. In the CSS Styles panel, select the #bottomShadow selector. Add the height property with a value of 30 pixels.

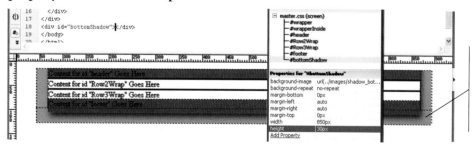

Because the ID selector now has a defined height value, the shadow is again visible, even though the div has no actual content.

15. Save the design.html file.

16. Click the master.css tab and save that file.

17. Continue to the next exercise.

USE THE FLOAT PROPERTY TO CONTROL NESTED DIVS

As you might have noticed, nested div elements automatically align based on the horizontal alignment properties of the containing element. If no specific alignment is defined, the nested div aligns to the left side of the container. The float property allows you to attach a nested div to the left or right edge of the containing element, which gives you greater flexibility when creating complex layouts such as the one in this project.

In the previous exercises, you created ID selectors and placed div elements using the selectors you had already defined. If you are experimenting with a layout, or you want to work from within the context of the existing layout, you can also insert div tags and create ID selectors at the same time.

1. **With the design.html page active, select and delete the placeholder content in the header div.**

   When you delete the placeholder content, the header div collapses to the smallest possible size. The insertion point remains in place within the div tag, as you can see in the Code pane.

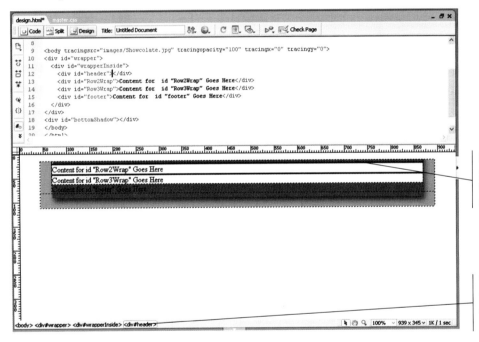

When you delete the placeholder content, the div collapses to the smallest possible size.

The tag selector shows that the insertion point is currently inside the header div.

2. **Choose Insert>Layout Objects>Div Tag.**

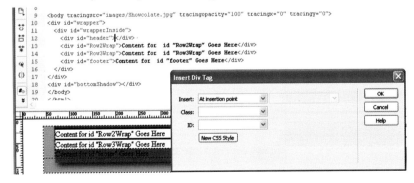

3. **In the Insert Div Tag dialog box, click the New CSS Style button.**

The Selector field automatically includes the full path of nested div IDs.

4. **Delete the contents of the Selector field and type "#navigation".**

It is not necessary to include the containing IDs in the selector name unless you want to use the same selector name for divs in different nested areas (for example, #header #navigation, and #footer #navigation).

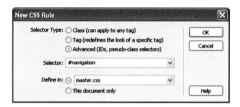

5. **Click OK to define the properties for the new selector.**

6. **In the Box options of the CSS Rule Definition dialog box, define the box width as 300 pixels.**

7. **Choose left in the Float menu.**

The float property forces a div to the right or left edge of the containing element. In this case, the navigation div will snap to the left edge of the header div.

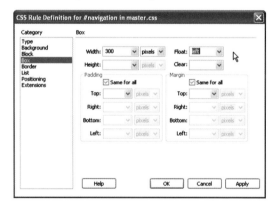

8. **Click OK to create the selector, and then click OK again to insert the div tag into the page.**

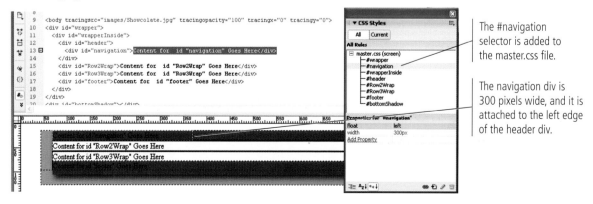

The #navigation selector is added to the master.css file.

The navigation div is 300 pixels wide, and it is attached to the left edge of the header div.

9. **Place the insertion point immediately to the right of the navigation div element (outside the navigation div element).**

    You can do this in either the Design pane or the Code pane. If you have difficulty seeing the insertion point in the Design pane, try the Code pane instead.

10. **Choose Insert>Layout Object>Div Tag and click New CSS Style in the Insert Div Tag dialog box.**

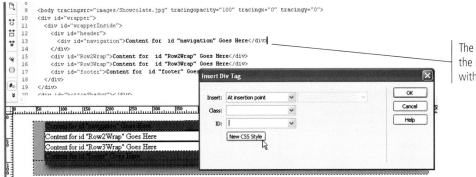

The insertion point is after the navigation div but within the header div.

11. **Name the new selector "#logo", and then click OK to define the rule properties.**

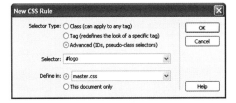

12. **In the Box category, define the box width as 330 pixels and set the float property to right.**

    This div will attach to the right edge of the containing element (the header div).

13. **Click OK twice to add the logo div to the page.**

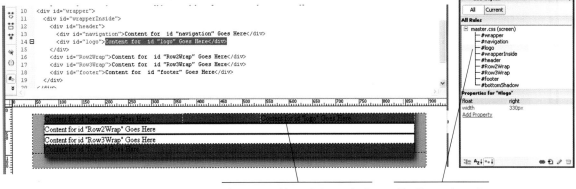

The 330-pixel logo div is attached to the right edge of the header div.

The #logo selector is automatically created.

14. **Delete the placeholder content from the Row2Wrap div. Use the same method from Steps 10–13 to add a new div inside the Row2Wrap div, creating an ID selector named "#taglineImage".**

- **In the Background options for the selector, define tagline.jpg as the background image for the #taglineImage selector.**

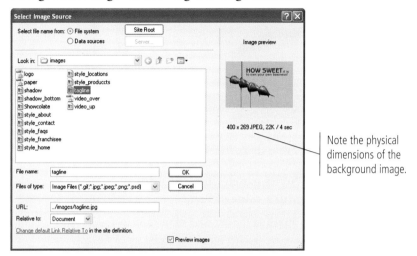

Note the physical dimensions of the background image.

- **In the Box options for the #taglineImage selector, define the box height and width to match the dimensions of the background image.**

- **Set the selector float value to Left to attach the taglineImage div to the left edge of the Row2Wrap div.**

When you work with nested div elements, strange and unexpected things can sometimes happen in the Design pane. In this case, the left edge of the Row2Wrap moves to the middle of the page (to the right of the navigation div in the header div). Interestingly, this page would display correctly in a browser. However, it makes your work in Dreamweaver much more difficult.

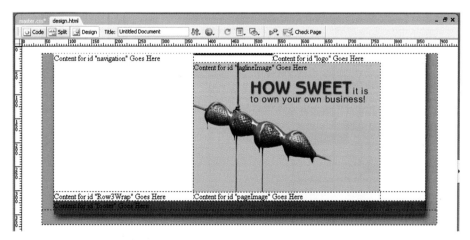

15. **In the Tag Selector, click div#Row2Wrap to select that entire element in the page.**

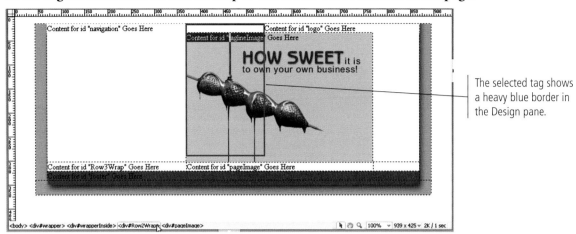

The selected tag shows a heavy blue border in the Design pane.

16. **Click the #Row2Wrap selector in the CSS Styles panel. Click the Add Property link, and add the float property with a value of Left.**

This command forces the Row2Wrap element to attach to the left edge of its container (#wrapperInside).

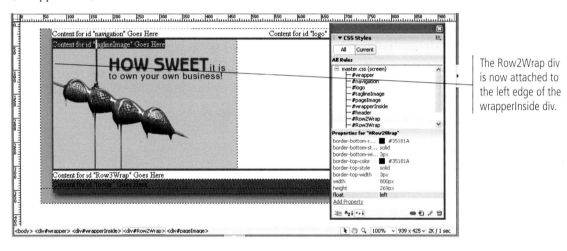

The Row2Wrap div is now attached to the left edge of the wrapperInside div.

17. **Repeat Step 16 to add the left float property to the #header and #Row3Wrap selectors.**

18. **Create another nested div named "#pageImage" inside the Row2Wrap div. For the pageImage div, define the box width as 400 pixels and set the float property to right.**

19. Delete the placeholder content from the Row3Wrap div.

20. Inside the Row3Wrap div, add a new div using a selector named "#contentMain". For the #contentMain selector, define a 530-pixel box width and use the left float property.

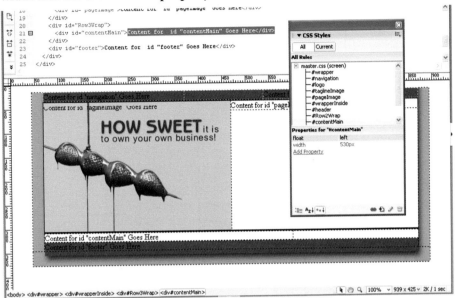

21. Save the HTML and CSS files, and continue to the next exercise.

Use Margins and Padding to Affect Element Placement

You have already defined most of the layout elements you need to create the Showcolate site pages. Two more divs are needed, but they require a bit of adjustment to place them correctly within the context of their containing elements.

1. With design.html open, place the insertion point after the contentMain div (inside the Row3Wrap div).

2. Add a new div with a selector named "#contentSidebar".

   • In the Background category, define paper.gif as the background image and set the Repeat property to no-repeat. Set the Horizontal Position to Left and the Vertical Position to Top.

   • In the Box category, define a 160-pixel width and a 205-pixel height. Set the float property to right to attach the div to the right edge of the Row3Wrap div.

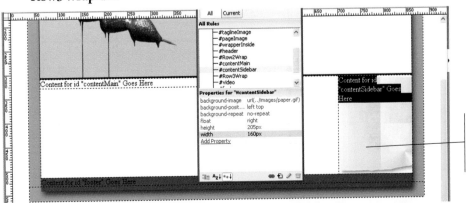

The background image doesn't entirely fit within the defined box dimensions.

3. Click the edge of the contentSidebar div to select it.

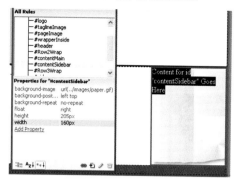

4. In the CSS Styles panel, select the #contentSidebar selector.

5. Click the Add Property link. Add the padding property with a 20-pixel value.

This adds 20 pixels of padding to all four sides of the div element. Because the element is selected in the layout, you can see the padding, as indicated by the thin diagonal lines within the element edges.

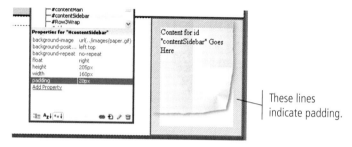

These lines indicate padding.

Note:

You have to type the "px" in the field when you add the padding property to the selector.

Note:

It is important to realize that padding is added inside the element — which affects the overall size of the element. The contentSidebar div is now 200 pixels wide (160 defined width + 20 left padding + 20 right padding). The clear area inside the element is still 160 pixels wide by 205 pixels high; content in this div is restricted to this area.

6. Click away from the div element to deselect it.

Padding affects the physical size of the element; the background image extends into the padding area because the padding area is part of the actual element area.

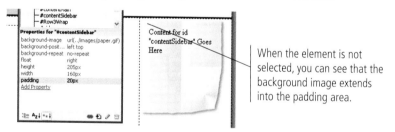

When the element is not selected, you can see that the background image extends into the padding area.

7. Click the element edge to select it again. With the #contentSidebar selector still selected in the CSS Styles panel, add the margin property with a 15-pixel value.

Because the element is selected in the page, you can see the margin area indicated by heavier diagonal lines (in the opposite direction from the padding indicators). Margin values are added *outside* or *around* the element, so they do not affect the physical dimensions of the element.

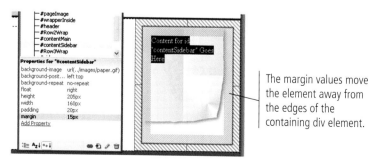

The margin values move the element away from the edges of the containing div element.

8. **Deselect the contentSidebar element in the page.**

   Because margin values are added outside the element area, the background image does not extend into the margin area.

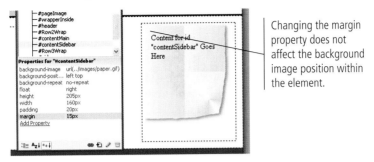

   Changing the margin property does not affect the background image position within the element.

9. **Delete the placeholder content from the taglineImage div.**

10. **Inside the taglineImage div, add a new div using a selector named "#video". For the #video selector, define a 200-pixel box width, use the right float property, and define a 215-pixel top margin value.**

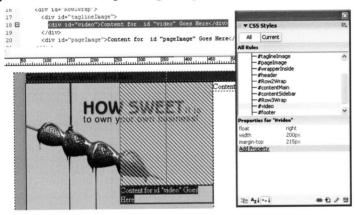

11. **Save both the HTML and CSS files, and then continue to the next stage of the project.**

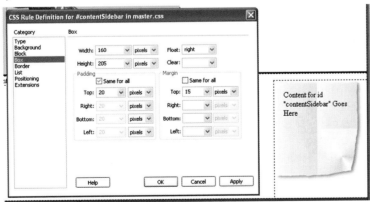

Stage 2 Using CSS to Control Content

The first stage of this project focused on building a layout structure with div tags and ID selectors. Although a significant part of designing pages, structure is only half the story — professional Web design also requires controlling the content in pages.

When you create a complex project such as a complete Web site, it is a good idea to have a solid plan for completing the required work. You have already completed the structure of this site, but that's the easy part because the tracing image showed exactly what you needed to do. When it comes to the content of the site, however, a single tracing image rarely shows each element that you need to create.

Consider what you know from the tracing image and from the art director's earlier comments:

A. All text in the site should use a sans-serif font.

B. Heading 1 in the main text area needs to be large, light, and colored dark brown.

C. Heading 2 should be slightly smaller than Heading 1, and it should use the same color as the background of the header area.

D. Paragraphs of copy in the main text need to be small and gray, with large spacing between lines in a single paragraph.

E. Navigation links in the header need to be bold white. The link text should not be underlined.

F. The sidebar text needs to be the same size and color as paragraphs in the main text area, but it should not have the large line spacing of paragraphs in the main text area.

G. Footer text should be white, and link text should be underlined.

H. Each text link should switch to a light orange/red (from the strawberry image) when the mouse rolls over the link.

In addition to this fairly lengthy list, the content for different pages will almost certainly have other requirements, which you will discover as you build those pages. The best way to proceed, then, is to create as much as you can with what you already know. When you have solved all of the known problems, you can then bring in the page-specific content and fill in whatever holes might exist.

In Project 4, you learned about using Dreamweaver templates to create elements common to multiple pages. For this site, that means all of the div elements that define the page structure. Other content elements are also used on each page of the site, so you should begin by adding those elements and creating a template. Once the template is saved, you will use it to build each page in the site.

As you build the individual pages, changes to the overall layout might become necessary, depending on the content placed into the pages. Because changes in a template file trickle down to the pages based on the template, changing the entire site at once makes the whole process much faster and easier.

Following the same logic, keep in mind that the master.css file is attached to the design.html file (which will become the template). Any pages created from the template file will also be attached to the master.css file, so changes in the master.css file will be applied in all pages created from the template.

DEFINE PROPERTIES FOR THE BODY TAG

As you learned in an earlier project, the <body> tag surrounds all content that is visible in a Web page. Similar to any other HTML tag, you can use a CSS rule to define properties for the body tag — which will affect the entire page behind any content.

1. **With design.html open, click the New CSS Rule button at the bottom of the CSS Styles panel.**

2. **In the New CSS Rule dialog box, click the Tag radio button.**

    <body> is an HTML tag, so you have to create a tag selector to define properties for the body element.

3. **Scroll through the Tag menu and click body in the list of options.**

   This menu lists all HTML tags that can be affected by CSS rules. You can either choose from the menu or simply type a tag name in the field.

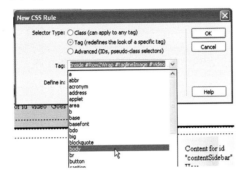

4. **Make sure master.css is targeted in the Define In options, and then click OK.**

5. **In the CSS Rule Definition dialog box, change the following settings:**

Type category	**Font: Arial, Helvetica, sans-serif**
	Color: #666666
Background category	**Color: #999999**
Box category	**Padding: 0 pixels for all four edges**
	Margin: 0 pixels for all four edges

Note:

For the background color, you can sample the gray color in the drop-shadow image to the left or right of the main page area.

6. **Click OK to add the body selector to the master.css file.**

   The new body selector is a tag selector, so it does not have the preceding # at the beginning of the selector name.

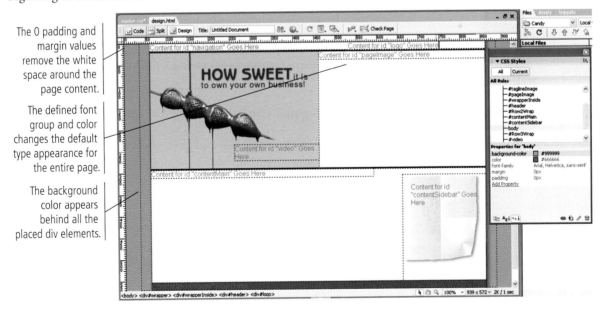

The 0 padding and margin values remove the white space around the page content.

The defined font group and color changes the default type appearance for the entire page.

The background color appears behind all the placed div elements.

7. **Save the CSS file, and then continue to the next exercise.**

DEFINE HTML TAG SELECTORS

In addition to the body tag that encloses the page content, properly structured pages use HTML tags to identify different types of content. CSS uses tag selectors to format HTML tags such as paragraphs (<p>), headings (<h1>, <h2>, etc.), ordered and unordered lists (<ol> and <ul>), and so on.

Based on your existing knowledge, you already know of several tag selectors that need to be defined:

A. All text in the site should use a sans-serif font.
This was accomplished when you defined the default font in the body selector.

B. Heading 1 needs to be large, light, and colored dark brown.

C. Heading 2 should be slightly smaller than Heading 1, and it should use the same color as the background of the header area.

D. Paragraphs of copy in the main text area need to be small and gray, with large spacing between lines in a single paragraph.

E. Navigation links in the header area need to be bold, white text. The link text should not be underlined.

F. The sidebar text needs to be the same size and color as paragraphs in the main text area, but it should not have the large line spacing of paragraphs in the main text area.

G. Footer text should be white, and link text should be underlined.

H. Each text link should switch to a light orange/red (from the strawberry image) when the mouse rolls over the link.

In this exercise, you will use tag selectors to complete items B, C, and D in the list.

1. **With design.html open, click the New CSS Rule button at the bottom of the CSS Styles panel.**

2. **In the New CSS Rule dialog box, click the Tag radio button.**

3. **Choose h1 in the menu or simply type "h1" in the Tag field, and then click OK to open the CSS Rule Definition dialog box.**

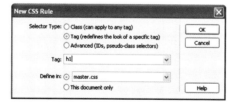

4. In the Type options, define the size as 26 pixels and choose Lighter in the Weight menu. Click the Color swatch and sample a dark brown color from the strawberry image in the second row of the layout.

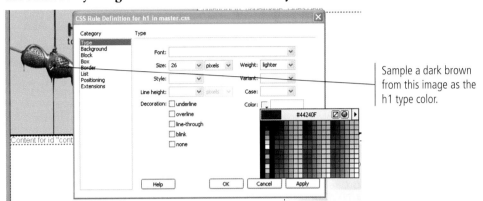

Sample a dark brown from this image as the h1 type color.

5. In the Box options, define 0 pixels for padding and margin values (using the Same For All option).

6. Click OK, and then click OK again to create the new selector.

Note:

If you're familiar with formatting text in print design applications, think of the top and margin options as space before and space after a paragraph. The left and right margins translate to the left and right indents.

7. Use the same process from Steps 1–6 to add the following tag selectors:

Selector Name	Category	Properties to Define
h2	Type	Font size: 18 pixels
		Weight: lighter
		Color: sample a medium orange from the strawberry image
	Box	Padding: 0 pixels
		Margins: 0 pixels
p	Type	Size: 12 pixels
		Line height: 20 pixels
	Box	Top margin: 13 pixels

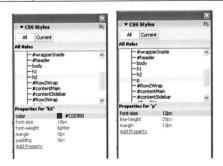

8. Save the CSS file and continue to the next exercise.

When two or more selectors have the same properties and values, they can be grouped to avoid repetition and save time. For example, you need four element selectors (h1, h2, h3, and h4) with the same margin and padding values:

```
h1 {
        margin: 0px;
        padding: 0px;
}
h2 {
        margin: 0px;
        padding: 0px;
}
h3 {
        margin: 0px;
        padding: 0px;
}
h4 {
        margin: 0px;
        padding: 0px;
}
```

Rather than defining separate selectors, you can group them by typing all four selector names, separated by commas:

```
h1, h2, h3, h4 {
        margin: 0px;
        padding: 0px;
}
```

PLACE COMMON PAGE CONTENT

The header, sidebar, and footer information is also common to every page in the site, so you can now add the actual content for these areas. When you define the descendent selectors in the next exercise, you will be able to see the results immediately.

1. **With design.html open, double-click common.txt (in the text folder) in the Files panel to open that file.**

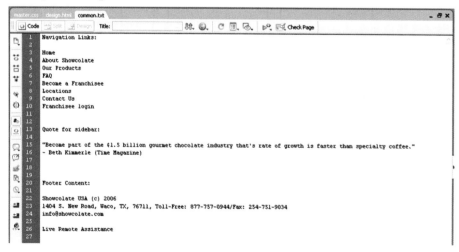

2. **Select the text on lines 3–10 in the text file and copy it to the clipboard.**

3. **Click the design.html tab to activate that file.**

4. **Select and delete the placeholder text in the navigation div, and then paste the copied text into the navigation div.**

5. **Select all the pasted text. Using the Text Insert bar, format the pasted text as an unordered list.**

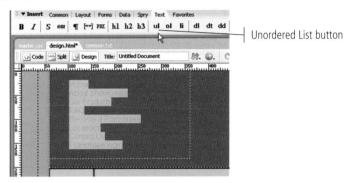

Unordered List button

Because of the nature of copying from text files, only the first item has a bullet. You need to manually separate each item in the list.

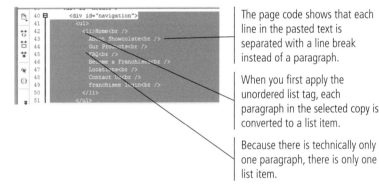

The page code shows that each line in the pasted text is separated with a line break instead of a paragraph.

When you first apply the unordered list tag, each paragraph in the selected copy is converted to a list item.

Because there is technically only one paragraph, there is only one list item.

6. **Place the insertion point at the beginning of the second line, press Delete/Backspace, and then immediately press Return/Enter.**

After separating the first and second lines, the second line is a distinct list item with its own bullet.

7. **Repeat Step 6 for each line in the list.**

You now have an unordered list of 8 items, each of which will become a link to the different pages in the site.

8. **Switch to the common.txt file and copy the text from lines 15 and 16.**

9. **Return to the design.html file. Delete the placeholder text from the contentSidebar div and paste the copied content into that element.**

10. **Select all the text in the sidebar and click the Paragraph button in the Text Insert bar.**

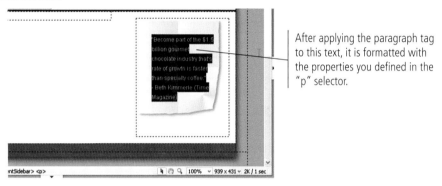

After applying the paragraph tag to this text, it is formatted with the properties you defined in the "p" selector.

As with the navigation link text, each line in this pasted text is separated with a line break but not a paragraph tag (as shown in the page code). You have to manually separate the two lines into individual paragraphs.

11. **Use the same method from Step 6 to separate the two lines of sidebar text into distinct paragraphs.**

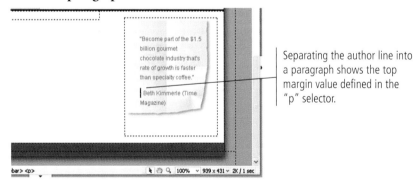

Separating the author line into a paragraph shows the top margin value defined in the "p" selector.

12. **Switch to the common.txt file and copy the text from lines 22–26.**

13. In design.html, paste the copied content in place of the placeholder text in the footer div.

14. Delete the placeholder content from the video div.

15. With the insertion point in the video div, choose Insert>Image Objects>Rollover Image.

16. Apply the following options in the Insert Rollover Image dialog box:

Image Name	VideoLink
Original Image	images/video_up.jpg
Rollover Image	images/video_over.jpg
Preload Rollover Image	Checked
Alternate Text	Link to Showcolate Video
When Clicked, Go to URL	flash/showcolate-flash.swf

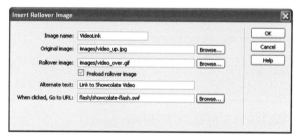

17. Click OK. With the rollover image object selected in the page, choose _blank from the Target menu in the Properties Inspector to cause the video to download in a new browser window.

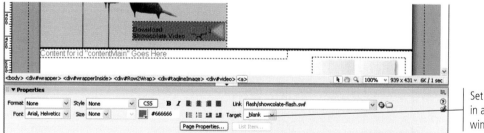

Set the link to open in a new browser window.

18. Delete the placeholder content from the logo div, and then place the file logo.gif into the div element. When asked, use "Showcolate logo" as the alternate text.

19. Save the HTML file and continue to the next exercise.

CREATE DESCENDENT TAG SELECTORS

Four items remain in the list of known formatting requirements:

    E. Navigation links in the header area need to be bold, white text. The link text should not be underlined.

    F. The sidebar text needs to be the same size and color as paragraphs in the main text area, but it should not have the large line spacing of paragraphs in the main text area.

    G. Footer text should be white, and link text should be underlined.

    H. Each text link should switch to a light orange/red (from the strawberry image) when the mouse rolls over the link.

    E, F, and G all refer to content in specific areas of the page. To meet these requirements without affecting similar tags in other areas, you will define descendent tag selectors to format elements within a specific div tag only (for example, ordered lists within the navigation div only).

Because you placed the content for these areas, you will see the results of your choices as soon as you make them.

1. **With design.html open, place the insertion point anywhere in the unordered list in the header area.**

   This list is placed in the navigation div. To modify the appearance of this list without affecting lists in other areas (in the main content area, for example), you will define a selector for unordered lists in the navigation div only — in other words, only this list of navigation links.

2. **Click the New CSS Rule button at the bottom of the CSS Styles panel.**

3. **In the New CSS Rule dialog box, select the Advanced option.**

   Although you are using this selector to format content in a specific tag (the <ul> or unordered list tag), you have to create an ID selector to first identify the div that contains the tag you want to format.

4. **In the Selector field, type "#navigation ul".**

   In plain English, this means you are formatting the unordered list in the navigation div.

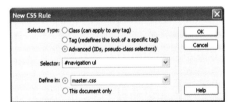

5. **Click OK to open the CSS Rule Definition dialog box.**

6. **In the Type category, define 10-pixel size, bold weight, and 10-pixel line height. Define white (#FFFFFF) as the type color.**

7. **Click Apply in the CSS Rule Definition dialog box.**

   Because you are working with actual content, the Apply button makes it very easy to experiment with different properties and options.

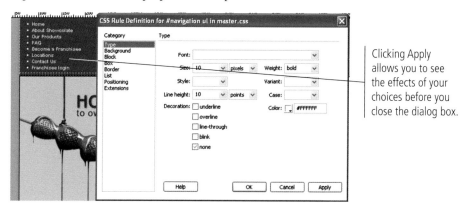

Clicking Apply allows you to see the effects of your choices before you close the dialog box.

8. **In the Box category, define 5-pixel top and bottom margins and define 25-pixel left padding.**

9. **In the List category, choose None in the Type menu to remove the bullet characters from the beginning of each list item.**

10. **Click OK to create the new selector.**

Note:

Experimentation is a very important part of creating a Web layout with CSS rules.

11. **Use the same basic process to create the following descendent selectors:**

Selector Name	Category	Properties to Define
#footer p (formats paragraph tags in the footer div)	Type	Font size: 11 pixels
		Line height: 13 pixels
		Color: White (#FFFFFF)
	Box	Margins: 0 pixels on all four sides
		Top padding: 12 pixels
		Right padding: 25 pixels
		Bottom padding: 0 pixels
		Left padding: 25 pixels

Selector Name	Category	Properties to Define
#contentSidebar p (formats paragraph tags in the contentSidebar div)	Type	Line height: 14 pixels
	Box	Margins: 0 pixels on all four sides
		Top padding: 0 pixels
		Right padding: 15 pixels
		Bottom padding: 15 pixels
		Left padding: 0 pixels

12. **Save the CSS file, and then continue to the next exercise.**

 CREATE PSEUDO-CLASS SELECTORS

Several items remain on your list of things to do:

   E. Navigation links in the header area need to be bold, white text. The link text should not be underlined.

   G. Footer text should be white, and link text should be underlined.

   H. Each text link should switch to a light orange/red (from the strawberry image) when the mouse rolls over the link.

Controlling the default appearance of link text is accomplished with the "a" tag selector (<a> is the HTML tag that creates a link). To affect the rollover behavior, you have to use a **pseudo-class** (variant) of the "a" selector.

1. **With design.html open, highlight the email address and create a link to "mailto:info@showcolate.com".**

2. **Highlight the words "Live Remote Assistance" and create a link to "www.gotoassist.com/ph/txwi" that opens in a new browser window.**

   By default, link text automatically appears in blue with an underline.

Note:

A class selector is used when the same style needs to be applied to more than one element in a page. Unlike an ID selector, which is used only once per page, a class selector is used to repeat the same style throughout the page.

3. **Click the New CSS Rule button in the CSS Styles panel and create a new descendent selector named "#footer a". In the Type category of the CSS Rule Definition dialog box, change the type color to white (#FFFFFF). Click OK to create and apply the selector.**

4. **Click the New CSS Rule button in the CSS Styles panel.**

5. **Make sure the Advanced radio button is selected.**

6. **Open the menu attached to the Selector field and choose a:hover.**

   This menu shows the four pseudo-classes that can be defined for the "a" tag. The hover pseudo-class determines what happens when the mouse cursor moves (hovers) over link text.

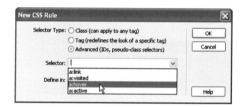

Note:

The four pseudo-class selectors are:

a:link — *Refers to a hyperlink that has not yet been visited*

a:visited — *Refers to a hyperlink that has been visited*

a:hover — *Refers to a hyperlink when the mouse pointer is hovering over the hyperlink*

a:active — *Refers to an active hyperlink*

7. **Type "#footer " (including the space character) before the a:hover entry and click OK.**

   By adding the ID selector to the pseudo-class, you are defining the behavior for links in the footer area only. You will have to create the same pseudo-class for other IDs that contain links. Unfortunately, this bit of redundancy is necessary because you have to create the pseudo-class inside every ID where you have defined a descendent selector for the "a" tag.

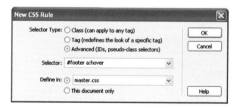

8. **In the Type category, use the Color sampler to find a light orange color in the strawberry image to use as the hover Color property.**

Sample a light orange color for the hover Color property.

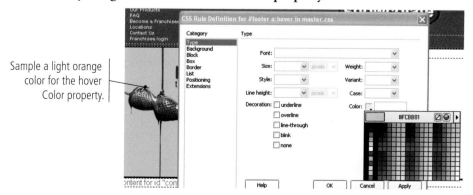

9. **Click OK to create the pseudo-class selector.**

10. **Save the HTML and CSS files, and then preview the HTML file in your default browser. Test the rollover property of the footer links.**

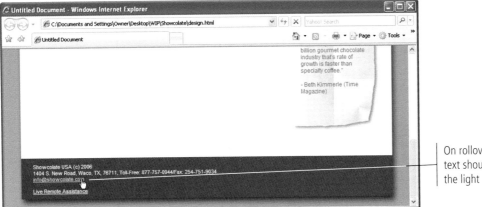

On rollover, the link text should switch to the light orange color.

11. **Close the browser window and return to Dreamweaver.**

12. **With design.html open in Dreamweaver, create additional link and hover pseudo-class selectors:**

Selector Name	Category	Properties to Define
#navigation a	Type	Color: White (#FFFFFF)
		Decoration: None
#navigation a:hover	Type	Color: Same color you used for the #footer a:hover selector

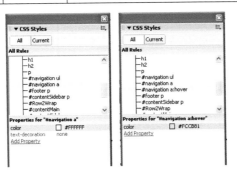

Note:

You can't test these links because they aren't defined as links.

13. **Select the #logo selector in the CSS Styles panel and click the Edit Style button.**

14. **In the Block options, choose Center in the Text Align field.**

Although you are centering an image, remember that an image in a Web page is treated as a character in the page, and it is aligned horizontally using the same tools you would use to align text.

15. In the Box options, define a 16-pixel top margin.

16. Click OK to apply your changes.

17. Save the CSS file and continue to the next exercise.

 CREATE A TEMPLATE FILE

The common elements in your HTML file are now in place, and much of the element formatting is complete. Remaining work will be more easily accomplished when you see the actual content that will be placed in the different site pages. To easily create and manage the different pages in the site, you will save your working HTML file as a template.

1. With design.html open, choose File>Save As Template.

2. Make sure Candy is selected in the Site menu, leave the remaining options at their default values, and click Save. Click Yes when asked if you want to update the links.

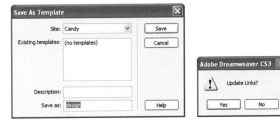

3. With the template file open, select the pageImage div element in the page.

4. Choose Insert>Template Objects>Editable Region.

5. Type "Image" in the Name field of the New Editable Region dialog box, and then click OK.

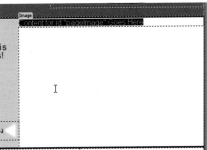

6. **Repeat Steps 3–5 to convert the contentMain div into an editable region named "Text".**

7. **Switch to Code view and locate the opening body tag on Line 37.**

8. **Select and delete the code related to the tracing image.**

The tracing image is no longer necessary, and it can actually cause problems when you create pages from the template. It is better to simply delete your tracing image when you no longer need it.

9. **Switch back to Design view, save the template file, and then close it.**

10. **In the Assets panel, Control/right-click the design template and choose New from Template from the contextual menu.**

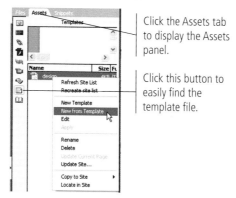

Click the Assets tab to display the Assets panel.

Click this button to easily find the template file.

Note:

If you try to Control/ right-click the template file in the Files panel, you will be working with the actual template file. You have to use the Assets panel to create a new HTML file based on an existing template.

11. **Immediately save the new file as "index.html" in the root folder of the Candy site (WIP>Showcolate).**

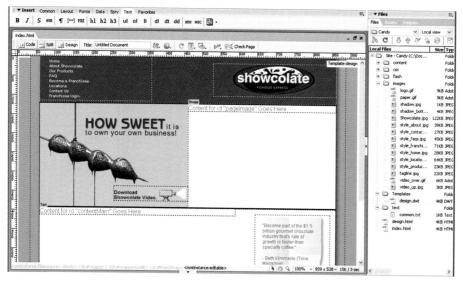

12. Close the index.html file.

13. Repeat Steps 10–12 to create the remaining pages in the site:

about.html   contact.html   faq.html   franchisee.html

locations.html   login.html   products.html

14. Continue to the next exercise.

 ADD AND MODIFY SELECTORS TO MEET DESIGN REQUIREMENTS

The final step in this project requires placing the individual page content. As you place content — for this or any other project — you will almost always find issues that need to be addressed, either by adding new CSS selectors or modifying existing ones.

1. With the Candy site open, open index.html from the site root folder, and then open index_content.html from the content folder.

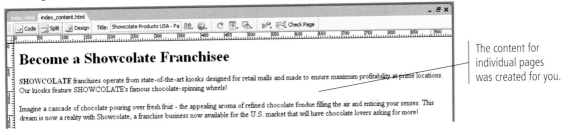

The content for individual pages was created for you.

2. Select all the content in the index_content file, copy it, and then close the file.

3. In index.html, paste the copied content into the Text editable region.

4. Replace the placeholder content in the Image editable region with the file style_home.jpg (from the site images folder). When asked, use "Showcolate kiosk" as the alternate text.

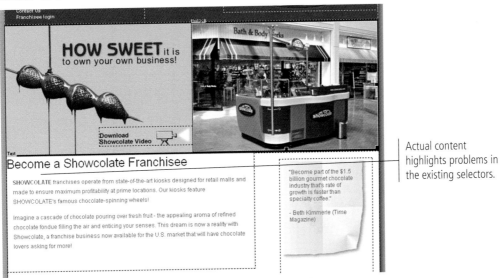

Actual content highlights problems in the existing selectors.

5. Edit the h1 selector to have a 25-pixel left margin and a 12-pixel top margin (leave the other two margins at 0 pixels).

6. Edit the "p" selector to have a 25-pixel left margin (leave the other side margins at 13-pixels).

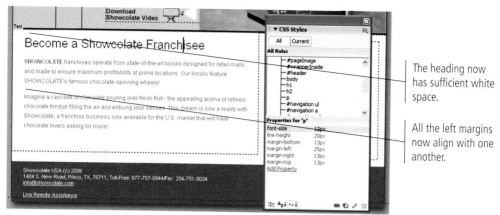

The heading now has sufficient white space.

All the left margins now align with one another.

7. Save the index.html file and close it.

8. Open about.html and about_content.html.

9. Copy the content from about_content.html, and then close the file.

10. Paste the copied content into the Text region of the about.html file.

11. Place the image file style_about.jpg into the Image editable region. When asked, use "Showcolate close-up" as the alternate text.

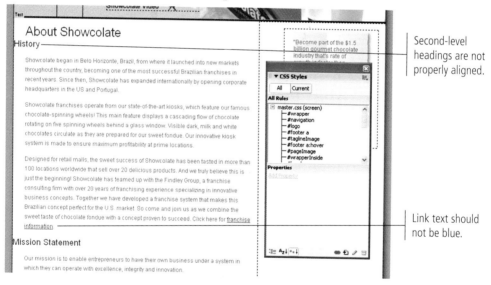

Second-level headings are not properly aligned.

Link text should not be blue.

12. Edit the h2 selector to have a 25-pixel left margin, 5-pixel top margin, and –12-pixel bottom margin.

13. Add a new selector named "#contentMain a" that formats link text as gray (#666666) with an underline decoration.

14. Add a new selector named "#contentMain a:hover" that formats link text as the same color you used for the navigation a:hover selector.

15. Save and close the about.html file.

16. Using the same basic process, place the page content in the remaining six pages:

Page	pageImage div	Alternate Text
Contact.html	style_contact.jpg	Showcolate offices
Faq.html	style_faqs.html	Showcolate employee 1
Franchisee.html	style_franchisee.html	Showcolate employee 2
Locations.html	style_locations.html	Showcolate outside
Login.html	style_home.html	Showcolate kiosk
Products.html	style_products.html	Showcolate products

17. As you create the remaining pages, create or modify CSS selectors as necessary, based on the content in the individual pages.

We found it necessary to create two additional selectors:

#contentMain ul   Formats unordered lists in the contentMain div

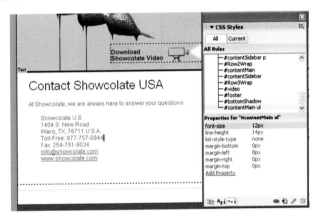

#contentMain ol   Formats ordered lists in the contentMain div

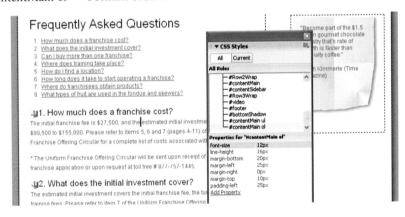

18. Save and close any open HTML files.

19. Save master.css, close the file, and then continue to the next exercise.

Note:

The login page is simply a placeholder because the form has not yet been created. For the sake of this project, simply use the placeholder text that exists on the provided HTML page (login_content.html).

The same is true of the content for the Franchisee page. The form has not been provided; using the methods from this project, you can easily add the completed form later.

CREATE THE NAVIGATION LINKS AND FINISH THE SITE

Now that all the site pages have been created, it is very simple to create the navigation links in the header area. By creating the links in the template file, the same changes will be reflected on all pages based on that template.

1. **With the Candy site open, open the design.dwt template file (from the Templates folder).**

2. **Highlight the word "Home" in the header and create a link to the index.html file in the Candy site.**

   Because you already defined the "a" and a:hover selectors for the navigation div, you won't see any visual difference after the link is created.

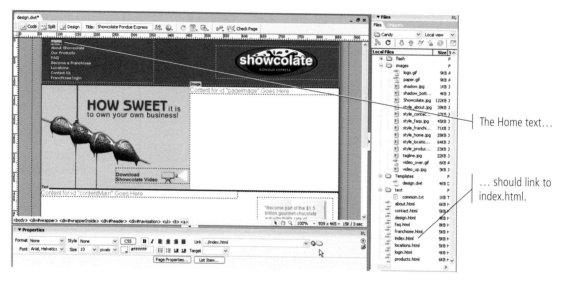

The Home text...

... should link to index.html.

3. **Create the remaining links in the navigation area:**

Text	Link to
About Showcolate	about.html
Our Products	products.html
FAQ	faq.html
Become a Franchisee	franchisee.html
Locations	locations.html
Contact Us	contact.html
Franchisee login	login.html

4. **Save the template file.**

5. **Click Update when asked if you want to update files based on the template.**

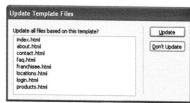

6. When the Update Pages dialog box shows the update process is done, click Close.

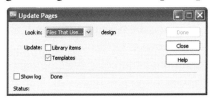

7. Open index.html and preview the page in your default browser.

The #navigation a:hover pseudo-class changes the color of the navigation links.

8. Close the browser window, return to Dreamweaver, and close the HTML file.

Device-Specific Cascading Style Sheets

Cascading style sheets are primarily used to design the layout of a Web page, but they have other uses as well. When you attach a style to HTML pages, you have the option to choose the media for which a specific style sheet will apply. In this project, you created a CSS file to control the appearance of the site on screen. You can create separate style sheets for print, projection systems, handheld devices, and a number of assistive devices, each of which has unique capabilities and goals.

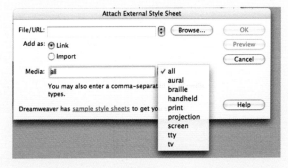

Print Styles

Aside from accessibility concerns, the Print option is particularly useful if you want to help users minimize waste by omitting unnecessary decorative elements from a printed version of the page. A separate print style sheet can be created to print only certain content and disable the rest. (The Display option in the Block categories of the CSS Rule Definition dialog box is used to hide specific elements.) Links such as "Printer-friendly version" or "Print this document" in Web sites typically have a print style sheet attached.

Design-Time Styles

Applying styles to a Web page is a matter of experimentation. While you design a Web page, you try a certain style and then you change it. You keep trying different options until you are satisfied with the appearance of the page.

As you experiment, you may want to try some styles that only appear in the Design pane. For these purposes, you can use a specific cascading style sheet called a design-time style sheet — a separate style sheet (in addition to the main cascading style sheet) that affects only the Design pane in Dreamweaver. To attach a design-time style sheet to an HTML page, choose Text>CSS Styles>Design-Time.

Summary

Cascading style sheets offer tremendous flexibility when you are designing the look and feel of a Web site. By linking multiple HTML files to a single external CSS file — with or without an HTML page template — you can experiment with options by altering the CSS selectors and immediately seeing the effect on all linked pages. In addition to this flexibility, CSS is also compliant with current Web design standards, which means pages designed with CSS are both search-engine and accessibility-software friendly.

By completing this project, you have worked with different types of selectors to control both the layout of an HTML page and the formatting attributes of different elements on different pages in the site. The site structure is entirely controlled by the selectors in the linked CSS file, so you could change the appearance of the entire site without ever touching the individual HTML pages. And the inverse is also true — you can change the content of individual pages without affecting the site structure.

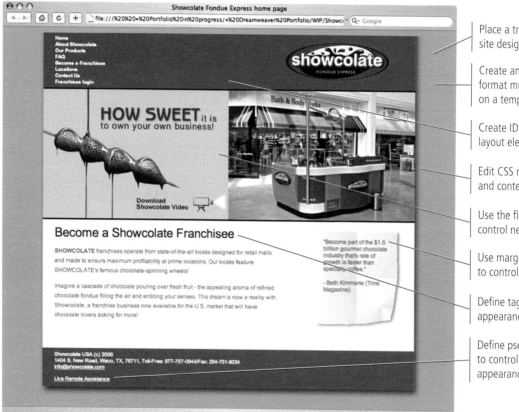

Place a tracing image to review site design requirements

Create an external CSS file to format multiple pages (based on a template file)

Create ID selectors to define layout elements (divs)

Edit CSS rules to adjust layout and content formatting

Use the float property to control nested div positioning

Use margin and padding options to control content positioning

Define tag selectors to control the appearance of specific HTML tags

Define pseudo-class selectors to control the alternate appearance of link text

Portfolio Builder Project 5

Al Fresca Café, a French patisserie, has hired you to design a Web site to help promote their new catering services. The café is very popular, but the catering service is new so they want the site to be very accessible and easy to find.

To complete this project, you should:

❏ Create a Web site using the client's provided text and logo (in the RF_Builders>Cafe) folder.

❏ Use the client's provided images, or find or create other images as necessary to enhance the different pages of the site.

❏ Use CSS to control the layout and the content formatting. Don't use graphic-text images anywhere in the site.

"Our primary target market for the catering business is other businesses, although we also hope to capture some of the social club functions that happen all over the peninsula. I don't want the site to be overcrowded with 'stuff', glaring colors, or anything flashing or blinking.

"Our site needs to have four main buttons: Home, Catering Menu, Testimonials, and The Café.

"I sent you the text for the Menu and Home and Menu pages, and I sent one quote that you can use to experiment with the design for the testimonials page. (Eventually there will be lots of quotes on this page, but I have to gather them all together.) The Café link should navigate to the restaurant's site at www.alFrescaMonterey.biz.

"I also sent you some photos that you can use, but don't have to. If you have some other decorative images we're open to suggestion; just keep in mind our goal of 'simple elegance'.

"Because of the local demographics, I need two versions of the site — one in English and one in Spanish. I haven't sent you the Spanish text yet, but I will as soon as I get it. Because we're going to maintain both language versions, I don't want to have to mess around with new images every time we make a change. Keep the entire site as text so I can make minor edits myself."

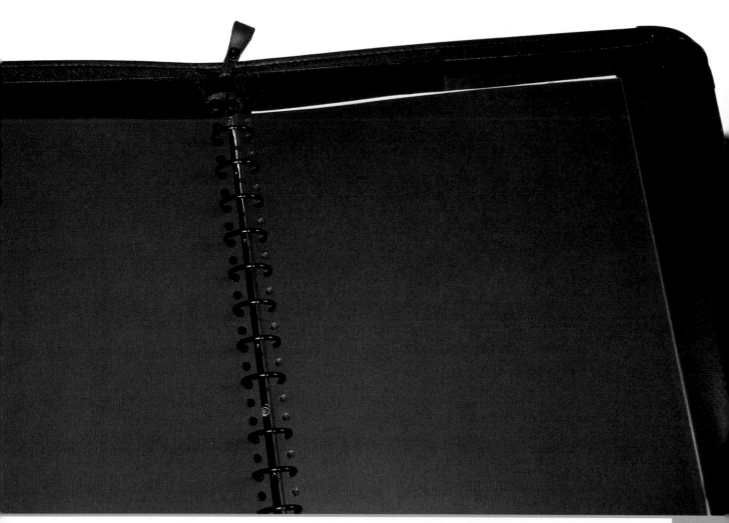

AppleOne Registration Form

AppleOne is organizing a trade show for members of the publishing and related industries. To facilitate registration for the show, AppleOne would like to include an online registration form. As a member of the team building the new Web site for the show, your job is to create the registration page, complete with all the necessary form elements.

This project incorporates the following skills:

❏ Creating a form object to gather user information

❏ Creating a variety of different form fields, including text fields, text areas, menus, lists, radio button groups, and check boxes

❏ Modifying form field properties to gather specific types of information

❏ Using label tags to identify form fields for users with accessibility software

❏ Adding submit and reset buttons to control form actions

❏ Formatting forms with CSS

❏ Using classes to format specific objects in a page

❏ Validating form entries with Spry widgets

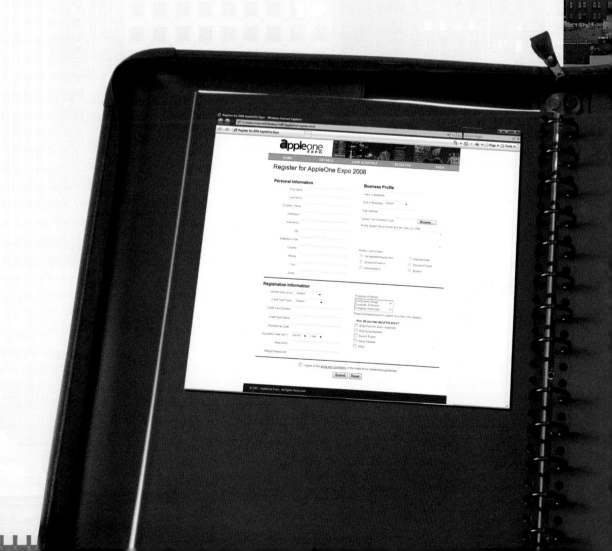

Client Comments

Our industry used to have several major trade shows, but over the years they have been absorbed by other shows in related industries like printing and computer software. That wasn't a problem in the beginning, but now the publishing aspect of those shows has been overpowered by non-related manufacturing and gaming. There isn't much of a venue for publishing-specific concerns anymore

We're launching our new trade show to make up for the lack. Of course, it's no small task to start a new trade show. One of the problems we're facing is the cost of print mailings, so we'd like as much information as possible to be available on our Web site.

Beyond merely providing information, we want to allow people to register online instead of worrying about the hassles of mailing or faxing a form. The form needs to let users submit all of the required information (including payment). We also want to gather a bit of preliminary demographic information so we can see the types of businesses that are interested in attending the show.

Art Director Comments

Creating an online form is not a particularly difficult job, especially considering the tools that Dreamweaver provides to create the different types of form fields.

Usability is a very important concern for online forms so making the form easy to read and fill out will be just as important as creating the different form fields. To make the form user-friendly, you should use CSS to format the different elements so they are both aesthetically pleasing and functionally correct.

To register for the show, certain information will be required — name, contact information, and payment information. Other user information — specifically, the demographic questions — is requested but not required. You need to build that functionality into the form. Dreamweaver includes a number of options for adding form-field validation, so this will be easier to add than manually coding the required fields.

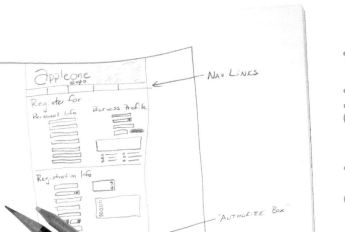

Project Objectives

To complete this project, you will:

- ❏ Create a form object to gather user information

- ❏ Create a variety of different form fields, including text fields, text areas, menus, lists, radio button groups, and check boxes

- ❏ Modify form field properties to gather specific types of information

- ❏ Use label tags to identify form fields for users with accessibility software

- ❏ Add submit and reset buttons to control form actions

- ❏ Format a form with CSS

- ❏ Use classes to format specific objects in a page

- ❏ Validate form entries with Spry widgets

Stage 1 Creating Online Forms

Online forms are used to collect user information, and then transfer that information to Web servers. Surveys, electronic commerce, guest books, polls, and membership applications all make use of online form technologies. While well-designed forms are easy to use, poorly designed forms prove troublesome for both users (who complete the forms) and Web server managers (who access user data). Fortunately, Dreamweaver makes it easy to create robust yet understandable forms — simplifying and streamlining the interaction between users and Web servers.

Web-based forms are composed of a series of **form objects** (also referred to as **form fields**). Different types of form objects have different purposes, and they gather different types of information. Basically, all form objects allow users to enter data; each object type facilitates a distinct format of data input. You can use Dreamweaver to create thirteen different form objects: text fields, text areas, radio buttons, radio groups, check boxes, lists/menus, jump menus, file fields, image fields, hidden fields, labels, fieldsets, and buttons.

 ## DEFINE THE APPLEONE SITE

As in the previous projects, the AppleOne site must first be defined in Dreamweaver so the links between documents and images are created properly. The procedure for defining the site is essentially the same for the AppleOne site as it was for the sites in the previous projects.

1. **Copy the RF_Dreamweaver>AppleOne folder into the WIP folder where you are saving your work.**

2. **Open the Manage Sites dialog box from the Directory menu in the Files panel.**

3. **If the Candy site is still available in the list of sites, export the site definition file into your WIP>Showcolate folder, and then remove the Candy site from the dialog box.**

4. **Choose New>Site.**

5. **Create a new site named "AppleOne", using the WIP>AppleOne folder as the site root folder.**

6. **Click OK, and then click Done to create the new site.**

7. **Continue to the next exercise.**

CREATE A FORM ELEMENT

A **form element** is a distinct element of a Web page; it is the container for all form objects. As a container, the form element ensures that different form fields are related to one another, which makes it possible to combine all of the form information as a single submission. A form's Submit button works by identifying all the related form elements and collecting their information in a single string.

1. **With the AppleOne site open in the Files panel, double-click register.html to open that file.**

   This page was created from the defined site template. You will create the form in the editable region of the page.

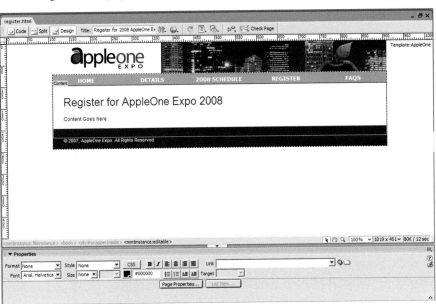

2. **In Design view, highlight and delete the placeholder paragraph text below the heading.**

The Forms Insert Bar

Although form objects can be added using the Insert>Form menu, the Forms Insert bar provides easy access to all of the form fields that can be added in Dreamweaver.

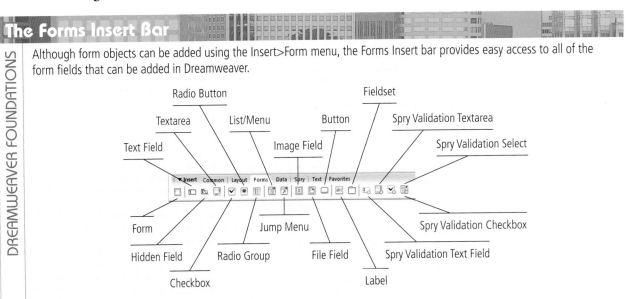

3. **With the insertion point in the now-empty paragraph, show the Forms Insert bar and click the Form button.**

A red dashed outline appears across the window, indicating the boundary of the newly inserted form.

Note:

If you don't see the red dashed outline, choose View>Visual Aids>Invisible Elements.

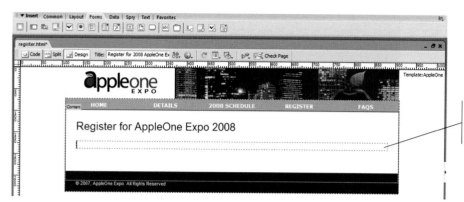

The dashed red outline shows the form object boundary.

4. **In the Properties Inspector, type "register" in the Form Name field and type "mailto:info@appleone.com" in the Action field. Leave the remaining fields at their default values.**

The form name identifies what information you are receiving from a browser. The email address (with the mailto: protocol) in the Action field causes the user-supplied data to be submitted in an email message.

Note:

The form name will also be useful later when you apply CSS to format the different form elements.

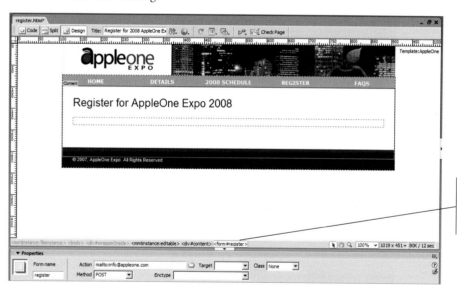

The form tag now includes the defined name "register", including the "#" sign that indicates an ID.

5. **Place the insertion point inside the form outline. Create a new table (Insert>Table) with 25 rows and 3 columns, 750 pixels wide. Assign 0 border thickness and cell padding, 10-pixel cell spacing, and no header row. Click OK to create the table.**

Although standards organizations do not recommended using tables for laying out Web pages, most experts still allow the use of tables for organizing form fields.

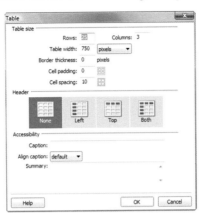

Note:

The editable region of the page allows a 750-pixel width for the content of each page, hence the 750-pixel table width.

The Form Properties Inspector

The Form Properties Inspector allows you to easily control the options related to a specific form area.

- **Form name** is a unique name that identifies the form. The form name enables you to reference a form using JavaScript or other scripting languages, as well as format the form using CSS. If you do not specify a name, Dreamweaver inserts a default name of "formN", where "N" is simply a sequential number representing the number of forms on the page.

- **Action** specifies the page or script that will process the form data, essentially determining what should be done with the form content. Generally, the action is set to a URL for running a specific Web application or for sending an email.

- **Target** defines the window or frame in which the server displays the action page's response (data) to the form. If the target is not specified, the response displays in the current page or window (i.e., the default target type is **_top**).

- **Class** allows you to apply a class selector (from a CSS style sheet) to the form.

- **Method** sets the method in which the browser and Web server present the form data to the application that processes the form (the action page). The three possible method choices are Default, GET, and POST.

  - **Default** uses the browser's default settings to send the form data to the server. According to W3C specifications, the default method for forms is GET.

  - **GET** attaches the form data to the URL of the action page (the page mentioned in the action field, which processes the form data). The GET method cannot be used to send long forms because it limits the amount and format of data that can be passed to the action page.

  - **POST** sends form data as a standard input to the action page. This method does not impose any limits on the passed data. The POST method is preferred for processing confidential data such as user names and passwords, credit card numbers, etc., but the data needs to be encrypted to ensure total security.

- **Enctype** (short for "encoding type") specifies the format in which the data will be sent to the server. This information enables the server software to interpret the input correctly. The default enctype is **application /x-www-form-urlencoded**, which encodes the form response with ampersands, equal signs, plus signs, and hexadecimal format. The **text/plain** enctype is used for email replies. When a file is being uploaded with the form, the **multipart/form-data** enctype must be used.

DREAMWEAVER FOUNDATIONS

6. **Using the Column menu for the right column in the table, select the entire right column.**

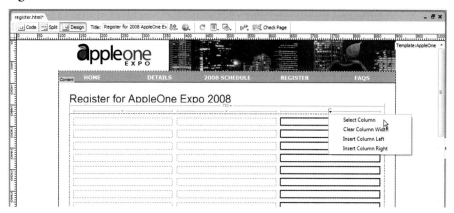

7. **In the Properties Inspector, change the column width to 360 pixels.**

The final table will ultimately appear to have two equal-width columns. (the two columns on the left will actually comprise the left half of the table).

To determine the appropriate column width for each half of the table, you have to subtract the defined cell spacing (30, including 10 pixels on the left and right side of the table, and 10 pixels in the middle of the table) from the total width of the table (750), and then divide by the number of columns (750 − 30 = 720 / 2 = 360 pixels for each column).

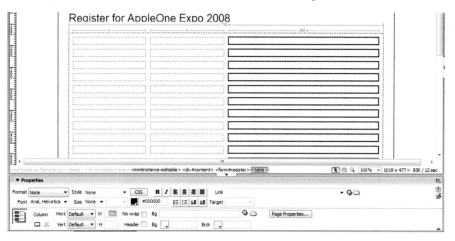

8. **Select the cells at the top of the first two columns and merge them into a single cell.**

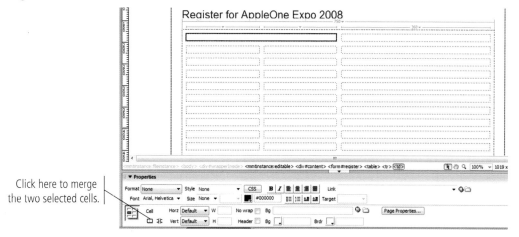

Click here to merge the two selected cells.

9. In the merged cell of the table, type "Personal Information".
   Choose Heading 2 in the Format menu of the Properties Inspector to
   change the text to a Level 2 heading.

10. In the top-right cell of the table, type "Business Profile".
    Choose Heading 2 in the Format menu of the Properties Inspector to
    change the text to a Level 2 heading.

Use the Format menu to define the text in the top cells as Heading 2.

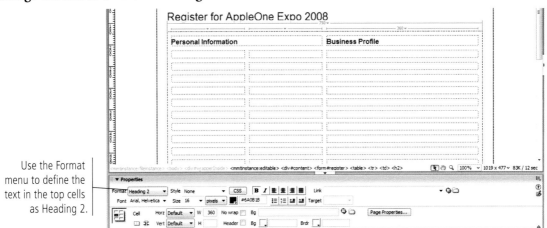

11. Select all three cells in row 13 and merge them into a single cell.

12. Change the merged cell background color to the same color used in the
    footer area of the page.

13. Drag the file spacer.gif into the merged cell (use "spacer" as the alternate
    text). With the placed image selected, use the Properties Inspector to change
    the image height to 2 pixels.

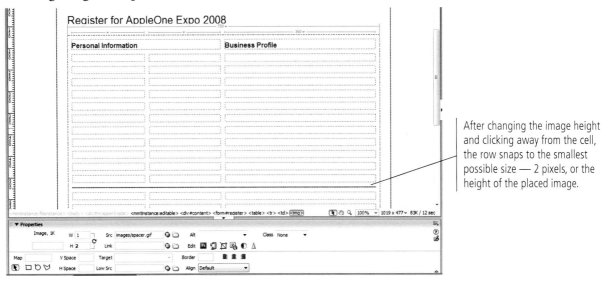

After changing the image height and clicking away from the cell, the row snaps to the smallest possible size — 2 pixels, or the height of the placed image.

14. Repeat Steps 11–13 for row 23 of the table (third from the bottom).

15. Merge the three cells in row 14 into a single cell.

16. Type "Registration Information" in the merged cell, and then format the text as a Level 2 heading.

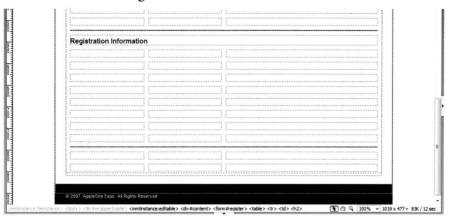

17. Save the file and continue to the next exercise.

Processing Form Data

DREAMWEAVER FOUNDATIONS

When it comes to collecting data from online users, creating a form is only half the job. Browsers alone cannot process the data in a form and send it you. You need to make some decisions, and then appropriately configure your form to ensure that the browser sends the data correctly. First you must decide where you want to receive the data. If you have a database, you can save user-supplied data directly to the database. You can also receive the data in an email message.

Scripts

You need to use a script to receive form data. These scripts contain instructions to identify the user's data, and then perform certain tasks based on that data. For example, a script can check whether the submitted data contains all the required information. It can also display relevant messages to form users.

Forms that access scripts using the Common Gateway Interface are referred to as CGI scripts. Most scripts that use CGI are written in the Perl scripting language. You can also use JavaScript to process form data, although some browsers do not support JavaScript, and some users turn off JavaScript support.

Most Web-hosting companies provide at least one processing script. The URL where the script is located on the server must be entered as the "Action" attribute of the form.

The mailto Protocol

One method of receiving data through email (without using a script) is using the mailto protocol. Here, you specify the email address in the "mailto:<email@Address>" format. This method causes the user's default email application to open and create a message with the form data. This is not a particularly reliable method of receiving form data, but it suits the purpose if you are gathering general information; however, it is not suitable for gathering sensitive information such as credit card numbers. (You use the mailto protocol in this exercise because we cannot be certain that everyone has access to the same script on a specific type of server.)

Methods

Methods are another way of determining how data is sent. The older method, GET, sends form data in a URL. This method limits the number of characters that can be sent to 255, and it is not a secure method of information transfer. The POST method, on the other hand, posts data to the Web server; this method can be used to securely transfer information.

Data Format

When data is sent through a form, the Name attribute of each form element is used with an equals sign (=) to include the data provided for that element. Each form element is separated by an ampersand (&), and spaces are indicated by a plus sign (+), as in the following example:

    Firstname=Sarah&lastname=Jacob&address=
    6740+Winston+Park+Oakville

Non-alphanumeric characters such as the exclamation mark are replaced by their hexadecimal values.

CREATE TEXT FIELDS

Text fields are the fundamental building blocks of almost all online forms; in fact, some forms use *only* text fields to gather user information.

Text fields accept alphanumeric characters — that is, letters and numbers. They can be set as single-line, multi-line, or password fields. (When a text field is designated as a password field, the user-entered text appears as asterisks or dots.) You can also alter the settings of single-line text fields and password fields to prevent users from entering more than a specified number of characters (such as no more than 16 characters for a credit card number).

A text area is similar to a standard text field, but intended for larger amounts of text, such as multiple sentences or paragraphs. Unlike single-line text fields, you cannot limit the number of characters entered in a text area.

1. **With register.html open in Design view, click the second cell in the second row of the table.**

2. **In the Forms Insert bar, click the Text Field button.**

Text Field button |

The insertion point is in this cell. |

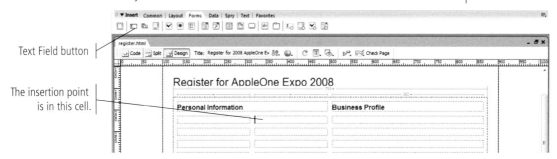

3. **Enter the following information in the Input Tag Accessibility Attributes dialog box**:

ID:	**Type "firstname"**
Label:	**Type "First Name:"**
Style:	**Select the Attach Label Tag Using 'for' Attribute option**
Position:	**Select the Before option**
Access Key:	**Leave blank**
Tab Index:	**Type "1"**

Note:

All of the different form objects can also be created using the Insert>Form menu.

Note:

If the accessibility for form objects is enabled, the Input Tag Accessibility Attributes dialog box displays. If the dialog box does not appear, choose Edit> Preferences>Accessibility, select the Form Objects check box, and click OK to enable accessibility for form objects.

Note:

***Tab index** determines the order in which fields will be selected when the user presses Tab sequentially.*

4. Click OK to create the text field.

The firstname text field appears in the table cell with the text label "First Name:" before the field (as you defined). The field ID identifies the user's entry when the form data is submitted; this ID can also be used to apply CSS to the named field.

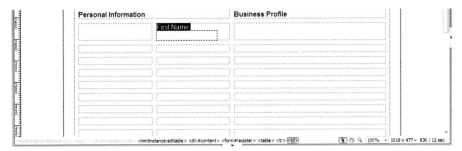

After clicking away from the table cell, the cell dimensions change based on the cell content. The right table column does not change because you already defined a specific width for that column.

The Input Tag Accessibility Attributes Dialog Box

The Input Tag Accessibility Attributes dialog box allows you to set up accessibility aids for form objects so they are more usable to visitors with visual, auditory, motor, or other impairments.

If this dialog box fails to appear when you insert a form field, open the Accessibility pane of the Preferences dialog box and make sure the Form Objects option is checked. Once you enable accessibility, the Input Tag Accessibility Attributes dialog box opens every time you insert certain types of form objects. Some form objects (such as radio groups, hidden fields, jump menus, labels, and fieldsets) do not need accessibility information, so the dialog box does not appear for those objects.

The ID is the identity of the form object. The server identifies the form object with the value typed in the ID box when the form is submitted to the server. The ID can also be used in JavaScript to refer to the form object.

The Label is the text that identifies the form object in the page. While ID identifies the form object to the server, Label identifies the form object to users and screen readers.

The Style area determines how the Label tag will be attached to the field.

- **Wrap with Label Tag.** As the name suggests, the <label> </label> tag pair entirely wraps/encloses the code of the form object. Use this style when you want the form object and its label next to each other.

- **Attach Label Tag Using 'for' Attribute.** A 'for' attribute matches the ID of the form object to the <label> tag. Use this style when you want to place the form object and its label in separate columns of a table (as you are doing in this project).

- **No Label Tag.** The <label> </label> tag pair is not attached to the form object. Instead of using label tags to name a form object, you can visually achieve the same effect by simply typing the text in the Web page. (This method does not support accessibility such as screen readers, which read label text for a form object.)

The Position area determines the positioning of label text in relation to the form object.

- **Before Form Item.** The label text is placed before the form object.

- **After Form Item.** The label text is placed after the form object.

Access Key allows you to define a letter that, when typed with the Control (Macintosh) or Alt (Windows) key, brings the selected form object into focus. For example, if you type "V" in the Access Key field, users can select the form object by pressing Control-V (Macintosh) or Alt-V (Windows).

Tab Index defines the order in which form objects are selected by pressing the Tab key. When a user presses the Tab key, the next field in the sequential tab order is selected. By defining specific tab index values for different fields, you can control users' movement through the fields in the form.

5. Repeat Steps 2–4 to insert text fields in the form, using the following information. For each text field, use the Attach Label Tag Using 'for' Attribute style option and the Before position option. Leave the Tab Index field empty.

Cell (Column, Row)	ID	Text Field Label
2, 3	lastname	Last Name
2, 4	companyname	Company Name
2, 5	address1	Address 1
2, 6	address2	Address 2
2, 7	city	City
2, 8	state	State/Zip Code
2, 9	country	Country
2, 10	phone	Phone
2, 11	fax	Fax
2, 12	email	Email
2, 17	ccnumber	Credit Card Number
2, 18	ccname	Credit Card Name
2, 19	discount	Promotional Code
2, 21	password1	Password
2, 22	password2	Retype Password
3, 2	yearsexperience	Years in Business
3, 4	url	Web Address
3, 6	designtypes	Briefly explain the products and services you offer.

Note:

You are going to add a separate field in row 8 for the user's zip code, but you are using a single label for both fields.

6. Highlight the First Name label in the design window, and then click the Split button at the top of the document window.

To align the different elements of the form, you are going to move the field labels to the first column in the table. In the code window, you can see that highlighting the label in the page layout does not automatically highlight the code that designates the text as a label.

Because you are going to use CSS later to add styles to your table, you need to make sure the label code moves with the label text.

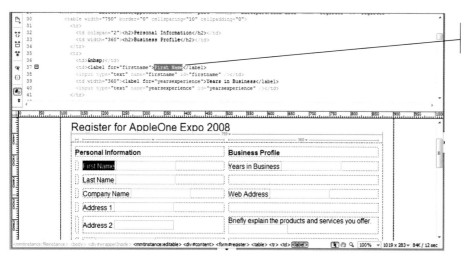

This is the code related to the field label.

7. **Click the label tag in the Tag Selector.**

In the code window, you can see that the entire label — including the appropriate code — is now selected.

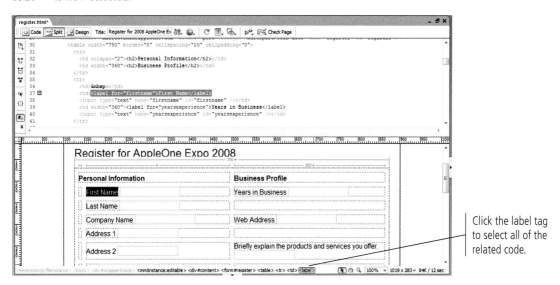

Click the label tag to select all of the related code.

8. **In the design window, drag the selected text to the first cell in the row.**

The code window shows that all of the appropriate code has been moved to the first cell.

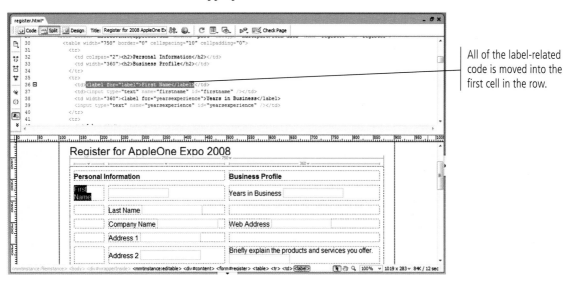

All of the label-related code is moved into the first cell in the row.

9. **Repeat this process to move all of the field labels in the left half of the form into the first column of the table.**

For now, don't worry about the appearance of the text. You will define the appearance of the entire form later in this project.

Note:

It is common (although improper) practice to simply type field label text in front of the input field; however, this method adds HTML text outside the label tag. When the field label is properly created inside the label tag, you can use CSS to format the field label text.

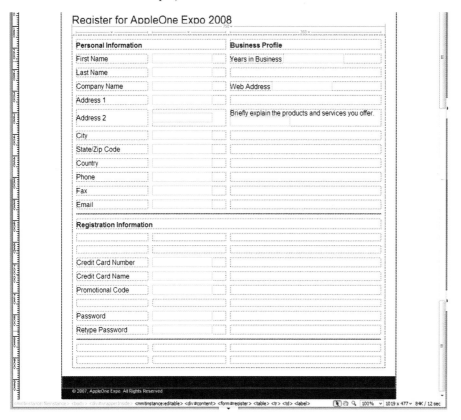

10. **Return to Design view.**

11. **Save the file and continue to the next exercise.**

 ## Modify Text Field Properties

Basic text fields are very simple to create — which is convenient because they make up the majority of form fields. Once you have created the fields, however, you can change the attributes of individual text fields to allow different amounts and kinds of information to be entered.

1. **With register.html open, click the State/Zip Code text field to select it.**

2. **In the Properties Inspector, type "8" in the Char Width field. Press Return/Enter to apply the change.**

Notice the reduced width of the field. Users will be able to type more than 8 characters, but only 8 will be visible at one time. In this case, you are reducing the field width to make room for the separate Zip Code field that needs to be included on this line.

Note:

You could also create a menu with all 50 states, forcing users to select from the list of options. The advantage to this technique is that you can force users to submit the correct state postal abbreviation (Minnesota = MN, Pennsylvania = PA, etc.) by defining the appropriate code as the value for each list item.

3. **Click to the right of the state text field to place the insertion point, and then click the Text Field button in the Forms Insert bar to add another text field after the existing state field.**

4. **In the Input Tag Accessibility Attributes dialog box, type "zip" in the ID field. Leave the Label field blank and select No Label Tag in the Style options. Click OK.**

   Another text field appears below the first text field. Because the label for the state field includes text explaining both fields, the new zip field does not need its own label.

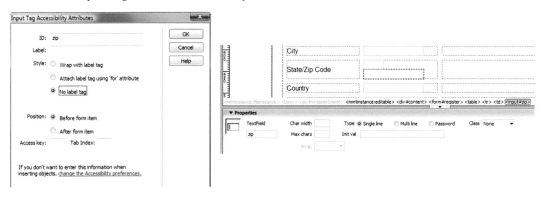

The Text Field Properties Inspector

DREAMWEAVER FOUNDATIONS

The Properties Inspector for a text field provides access to the attributes of a text field form object. You can enter attributes directly in the Properties Inspector to define a newly inserted text field, or you can edit values for an existing text field.

Text Field shows the name of the text field.

Char Width defines the maximum number of characters that can display in the text field. (This value also refers to the visible width of the text field.) Users can type more than the defined character width, but the excess characters will not be visible in the form page. By default, Dreamweaver inserts a text field that is approximately 20 characters wide (this default character width might vary, depending on the browser that displays the page).

Max Chars defines the maximum number of characters that can be entered in a single-line text field. If a user tries to input more characters than the defined value, the form produces an alert sound.

Init Val defines text that displays in the text field when the form loads in the Web page (before a user enters data). This is generally used to include examples or notes.

Class attaches a class selector (from a CSS style sheet) to the field.

Type defines a text field as a single-line, multiple-line, or password field.

- **Single-line** creates a field that is a single line.
- **Multi-line** creates a field with multiple lines (also called a textarea field). For this type of field, you can also define the number of visible lines (**Num Lines**), and the way lengthy entries wrap in the field (**Wrap**).
  - **Default** leaves the wrapping at the default settings of browsers.
  - **Off** turns off text wrapping. Extra text entered in the type area keeps scrolling to the right until the user presses Return/Enter, which moves the insertion point to the next line in the type area.
  - **Virtual** causes the displayed text to wrap after it reaches the right edge of the type area, but sends the text as a single long string to the server. In other words, the word wrap is applied to the displayed text, but not to the text submitted to the server.
  - **Physical** wraps both the displayed text and the text submitted to the server.
- **Password** creates a field in which text appears as asterisks or bullets (dots) to prevent others from observing the text being typed.

5. Select the new zip field and set the Char Width to 10 in the Properties Inspector.

6. With the zip field still selected, type "6" in the Max Chars field.

Using this option, users can type no more 6 characters in this field. (Although U.S. zip codes have only 5 digits, many foreign countries have 6-character zip codes.)

7. Click the Password field, and then click the Password radio button in the Type area of the Properties Inspector.

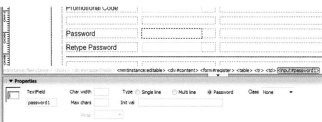

Note:

Text typed in this field will display as asterisks (*) or dots (•).

Password: ▓▓▓▓▓

8. Repeat Step 7 to apply the Password type to the password2 field.

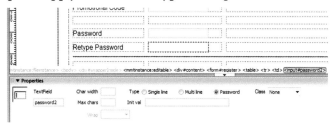

9. Click the text field in row 6 of the right column.

10. In the Properties Inspector, select the Multi Line option to change this field to a text area.

You can create a new text area by clicking the button in the Insert bar, or you can change an existing text field to a multi-line text area.

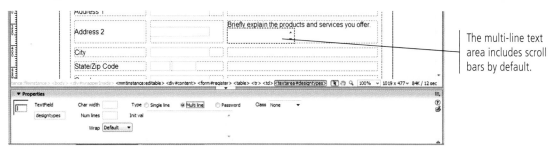

The multi-line text area includes scroll bars by default.

11. **Type "40" in the Char Width field and type "4" in the Num Lines field.**

The Char Width field is the same for a text area as it is for a single-line text field; it simply defines the width of the field that users see in their browsers. The Num Line option determines how many lines of the user's input will be visible at one time.

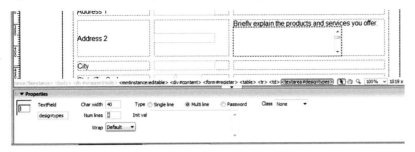

12. **Select the table cell containing the text area, Shift-click to add the two cells directly below to the selection, and then merge the three selected cells.**

Together, the three cells will be high enough to accommodate the label and four-line text area.

Merging the three cells allows three fields in the left half of the form to appear in the same vertical space as the text area.

13. **Save the file and continue to the next exercise.**

 CREATE A FILE FIELD

A file field is simply a text field with a Browse button. A file field allows users to select a file and upload it to your server. Users can either manually type a file path in the text field or click the Browse button to search for the file they want to upload. (The selected file uploads to the server using the POST method.)

1. **With register.html open, click in the fifth cell in the right column.**

2. **Click the File Field button in the Forms Insert bar.**

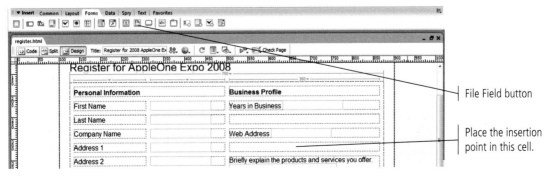

File Field button

Place the insertion point in this cell.

3. **In the Input Tag Accessibility Attributes dialog box, do the following:**

- **Type "logo" in the ID field.**
- **Type "Upload Your Company Logo" in the Label field.**
- **Select the Attach Label Tag Using 'for' Attribute style option.**
- **Select the Before position option.**

4. **Click OK to insert the file field.**

5. **Click the text field portion of the file field object. In the Properties Inspector, change the Char Width field to 10.**

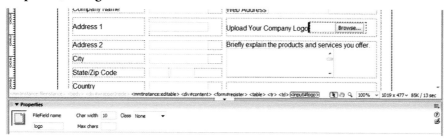

6. **Save the file and continue to the next exercise.**

The File Field Properties Inspector

The Properties Inspector for a file field provides access to the attributes of a file field form object. You can enter attributes directly in the Properties Inspector to define a newly inserted file field, or you can edit the values of an existing field.

FileField Name shows the ID/name of the file field (the two values are the same for a file field).

Char Width defines the maximum number of characters that can display in the text field of the file field form object. (This value also refers to the visible width of the text field.) Users can type more than the defined character width, but the excess characters will not display in the form page.

Max Chars defines the maximum number of characters that can be entered in the text field of a file field form object. If a user tries to input more characters than the defined value, the form produces an alert sound.

Class attaches a class selector (from a CSS style sheet) to the field.

CREATE MENU FIELDS

Menus and lists display a set of options, from which users can select one or more responses. These two types of form fields have the same basic underlying structure, but with different appearances and purposes.

A basic menu shows a single option; when a user clicks the menu, the menu opens (drops down) and more options appear. With a standard menu field, users can choose only a single response from the available options. The menu closes when the user chooses a response, displaying only the selected option.

Note:

If a drop-down menu is close to the bottom of the screen, the list of other options pops up instead of dropping down.

DREAMWEAVER FOUNDATIONS

The List/Menu Properties Inspector

The Properties Inspector for a list/menu field provides access to the attributes of a list/menu form object. You can enter attributes in the Properties Inspector to define a newly inserted list/menu field, or you can edit values of an existing field.

List/Menu shows the ID/name of the list/menu (the ID and name of a list/menu field are the same).

Type determines whether the selected form object will function as a scrolling list or as a drop-down menu. (The number of characters in the longest label determines the width of scrolling lists and drop-down menus.)

Height, only available for list type fields, defines the number of options that will be visible in the list at one time. The default/minimum height of a list is 1; a scrolling list appears as a drop-down menu if its height is set to 1 — although users can still choose multiple options.

Allow Multiple Selections is also restricted to list objects. When checked, users can choose more than one list option.

Initially Selected determines which item appears by default in a menu object, or which item(s) are already selected in a list object.

Clicking the **List Values** button opens the List Values dialog box, where you can create and edit the labels and values of individual items in the list for a specific form object. The order of list items in the form is the same as that in the List Values dialog box; the first item on the list is the default selection. Use the Up and Down Arrow buttons to rearrange list items.

Class attaches a class selector (from a CSS style sheet) to the field.

1. **With register.html open, click in the second column of row 15 to place the insertion point.**

2. **In the Forms Insert bar, click the List/Menu button.**

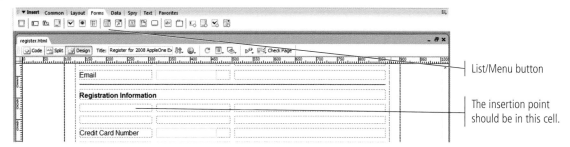

List/Menu button

The insertion point should be in this cell.

3. **In the Input Tag Accessibility Attributes dialog box, do the following:**
   - **Type "level" in the ID field.**
   - **Type "Membership Level" in the Label field.**
   - **Select the Attach Label Tag Using 'for' Attribute style option.**
   - **Select the Before position option.**

4. **Click OK to create the menu field.**

5. **Click the List/Menu field and choose the Menu radio button in the Type area of the Properties Inspector.**

The field will now function as a drop-down menu. Notice that the Height and Selections options have been disabled; these properties do not apply to drop-down menus.

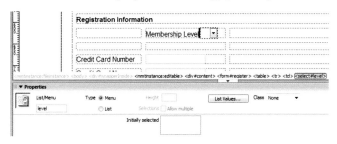

6. **Click the List Values button in the Properties Inspector to define the selections that will appear in the menu.**

The cursor automatically appears in the first Item Label field in the List Values dialog box.

7. **Type "Platinum ($1499)" as the first item label. Press Tab to move to the Value column and type "platinum".**

Note:

It's a good idea to include prices in the label so users can clearly see the information. It usually isn't necessary to include that information in the submitted data because the site owner presumably knows how much each item costs.

8. **Press Tab again to move to the Item Label field in the second line.**

Each line in the dialog box represents a new list/menu option. When the insertion point is within the last item value, pressing Tab adds a new list item. Alternatively, you can simply click the Plus button above the Item Label column to add a new list item (or click the minus button to remove the currently selected list item).

9. **Type "Gold ($999)" as the item label, press tab, and type "gold" as the item value.**

10. Repeat Steps 8–9 to add two more list items:

Label	Value
Silver ($599)	silver
Bronze ($299)	bronze

11. After typing the bronze value, press Tab to add a final list item.

12. Type "-Select-" (including the opening and closing hyphens) as the Item Label and leave the value field blank.

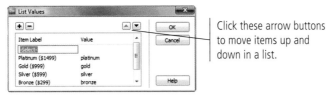

13. Click the Up Arrow button (above the value column) until the -Select- option appears at the top of the list.

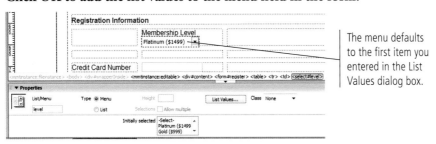

Click these arrow buttons to move items up and down in a list.

14. Click OK to add the list values to the menu field in the form.

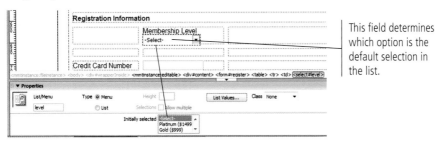

The menu defaults to the first item you entered in the List Values dialog box.

Note:

Although you moved the Select option to the top of the list, the menu defaults to the Platinum option because you created that item first.

15. In the Properties Inspector, make sure -Select- is highlighted in the Initially Selected list.

In the design window, the width of the placed menu expands to accommodate the longest option in the list.

This field determines which option is the default selection in the list.

16. **Place the insertion point within the label text, click the label tag in the Tag Selector, and drag the selected label to the first column of the row.**

The label (including the relevant code) is moved to the first column of the table.

17. **Using the same basic process, add four more menus to the form using the following information.**

For fields in the left half of the form, don't forget to move the field label (including the label code) to the first column in the table.

Position (Column, Row)	ID	Label	Item Labels	Item Values
2, 16	cctype	Credit Card Type	-Select-	
			Visa	visa
			Master Card	mc
			American Express	amex
			Discover	discover
2, 20	month	Expiration Date (M/Y)	-Month-	
			01	01
			02	02
			03	03
			04	04
			05	05
			06	06
			07	07
			08	08
			09	09
			10	10
			11	11
			12	12
2, 20	year	[None]	-Year-	
			2007	2007
			2008	2008
			2009	2009
			2010	2010
			2011	2011
			2012	2012
3, 3	businesstype	Type of Business	-Select-	
			Advertising	advertising
			Graphic Design	graphics
			Printing	printing
			Publishing	publishing
			Web Design	web

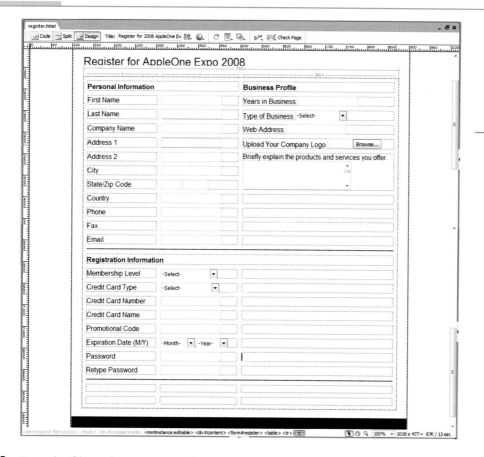

Note:

The two menus of the expiration date area have a single label. For the month and year menus, you are using the first menu item to identify the individual fields rather than using the basic Select option that you defined for the Membership Level menu.

18. **Save the file and continue to the next exercise.**

 CREATE A LIST MENU FIELD

A list menu is very similar to a regular drop-down menu, but a list menu can show more than one available option at a time. The height of the field can be adjusted, and a scroll bar on the list field allows users to view options outside the original dimensions of the field. Using a list field, you can enable users to choose multiple responses from the available list.

1. **With register.html open, click in row 15 of the third column.**

2. **Click the List/Menu button in the Forms Insert bar.**

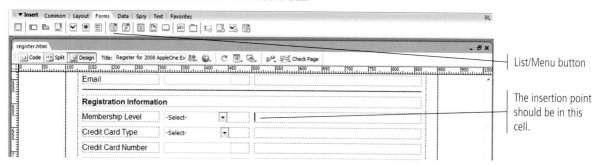

List/Menu button

The insertion point should be in this cell.

3. **In the Input Tag Accessibility Attributes dialog box, do the following:**
   - **Type "products" in the ID field.**
   - **Type "Products of Interest" in the Label field.**
   - **Select the Attach Label Tag Using 'for' Attribute style option.**
   - **Select the Before position option.**

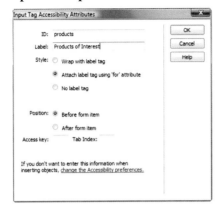

4. **Click OK to create the menu field, and then click the list box in the layout to select the form object.**

5. **In the Properties Inspector, select the List option.**

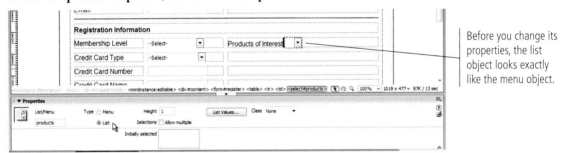

Before you change its properties, the list object looks exactly like the menu object.

6. **Click the List Values button. Create the following list items, and then click OK:**

Item Label	Item Value
Art/Graphic Design	design
Computer Software	software
Computer Hardware	hardware
Supplies and Consumables	supplies
Printing Equipment	print
Bindery Equipment	bindery
General Office	office

The list object still looks exactly like a menu object.

7. **In the Properties Inspector, type "3" in the Height field.**

   The list field object now functions as a scrolling list.

8. **Check the Allow Multiple option so users can express interest in more than one product category.**

   The modified height allows more than one item to appear in the form object.

   Checking this option allows users to choose multiple items in the list.

9. **Select the table cell with the Products list, Shift-click to add the two cells directly below to the selection, and merge the selected cells into a single cell.**

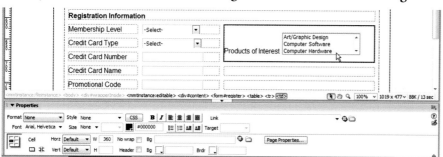

   Note:

   If the height of a scrolling list is set to 1, it appears with a single Down Arrow key to its right; however, users can still make multiple selections in the menu.

10. **Place the insertion point before the list object in the design window and press Return/Enter.**

    The form object moves to a new paragraph, rather than appearing immediately after the field label.

    By default, form objects are not structurally tagged as paragraphs or headings. When you press Return/Enter in the design window, the list field and the line you type in Step 12 adopt the paragraph tag, but the label line does not. Because the label is properly structured with the label tag, the paragraph tag should not wrap around the label text.

11. **Place the insertion point after the list object and press Return/Enter.**

12. **Type "Press Command/Control to select more than one category."**

    This bit of information is commonly added near a list menu to tell users they are allowed more than one selection in the list.

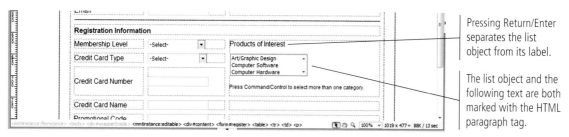

    Pressing Return/Enter separates the list object from its label.

    The list object and the following text are both marked with the HTML paragraph tag.

13. **Save the file and continue to the next exercise.**

CREATE RADIO BUTTONS IN A RADIO GROUP

Radio buttons are useful tools for allowing users to select from a list of predetermined options. In Dreamweaver you can insert a single radio button, or you can insert multiple radio buttons at once using the Radio Group option. A **radio group** is simply a group of radio buttons with the same name. Only one option in a group can be selected; selecting a different radio button in the same group automatically deselects the previous choice. (Individual radio buttons can be made to function as a radio group by assigning a common name to all buttons.)

1. **In register.html, click in the empty cell below the text area field in the right column of the table.**

2. **Click the Radio Group button in the Forms Insert bar.**

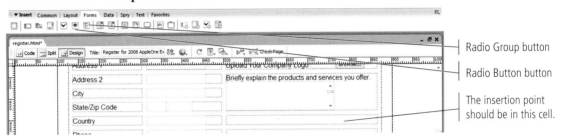

Radio Group button

Radio Button button

The insertion point should be in this cell.

3. **In the Radio Group dialog box, type "job" in the Name field.**

   To be treated as a group, all radio buttons in the group must have the same name attribute.

Note:

The Input Tag Accessibility Attributes dialog box does not appear when inserting a radio group; however, the dialog box does appear when you insert an individual radio button.

4. **Click the first label to select it, and then type "Management/Supervisor". Press Tab and type "management" as the value.**

5. **Press Tab to highlight the second label, and then type "Designer/Creative". Press Tab and type "design" as the value.**

6. **Click the "+" button (above the Label list) four times to add four more radio buttons to the list.**

   Unlike the List Item dialog box, pressing Tab after the last value does not add a new radio button. You have to click the "+" button to add a radio button to the group.

7. **Highlight the third label and type "Administrative". Press Tab to highlight the value and type "admin".**

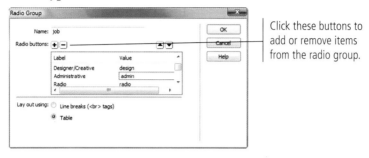

Click these buttons to add or remove items from the radio group.

8. **Pressing Tab to move through the labels and values, define the three remaining radio buttons as follows:**

Label	Value
Editorial/Media	press
Educator/Trainer	education
Student	student

9. **At the bottom of the dialog box, select the Lay Out Using Table option.**

   This option creates a new table with one cell per radio button, arranged in a single column. The Line Breaks option places each radio button in a separate line, without the table structure.

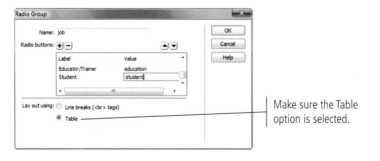

Make sure the Table option is selected.

10. **Click OK to create the radio button group.**

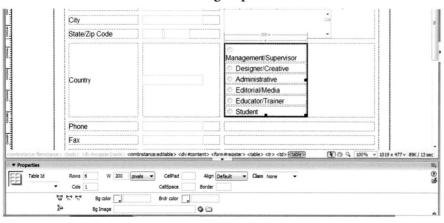

Note:

Notice that the first column of the radio button is titled "Label." When you created text fields and lists, the label appeared outside the actual field. For radio buttons and check boxes, however, the labels are the actual text associated with the individual buttons. If you want to add a text label for the group, you have to do it manually in the page code.

11. **From the menu for the table column, choose Insert Column Right.**

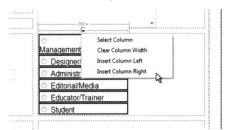

12. **Place the insertion point anywhere in the Editorial/Media label, and then click the label tag in the Tag Selector to select the entire radio button and label (including the appropriate code).**

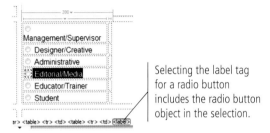

Selecting the label tag for a radio button includes the radio button object in the selection.

13. **Drag the selection into the top-right cell of the table.**

14. **Repeat Steps 12–13 to move the Educator/Trainer radio button into the second cell of the second column, and move the Student radio button into the third cell of the second column.**

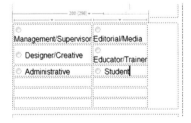

15. **Define the width of the table as 350 pixels, and then delete the three empty rows from the bottom of the table (Modify>Table>Delete Row).**

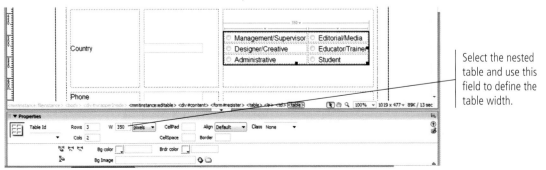

Select the nested table and use this field to define the table width.

16. **Place the insertion point before the nested table that contains the radio buttons, and then click the code window to activate that pane.**

    If necessary, use the Code window to place the insertion point, then click back on the Design window to bring it back into focus.

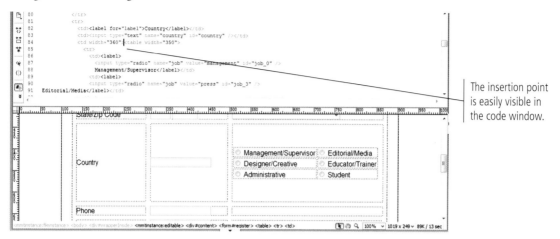

The insertion point is easily visible in the code window.

17. **Press Return/Enter to move the nested table tag to a new line in the code.**

    This action has no effect on the appearance of the page; you are simply moving the table to its own code line for the sake of clarity.

18. **Move the insertion point after the table cell tag (<td>) that contains the nested table and type:**

    <label for="job">Primary Job Function</label>

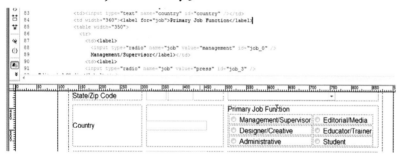

19. **Click Refresh in the Properties Inspector.**

The label for the radio button group appears above the nested table.

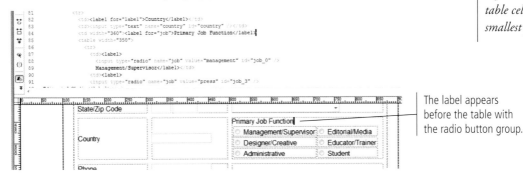

Note:

Refreshing also causes the table cell to collapse to its smallest possible height.

The label appears before the table with the radio button group.

20. **In the design window, merge the cell with the radio button group with the three cells directly below.**

21. **Save the file and continue to the next exercise.**

 CREATE CHECK BOXES

Like radio buttons, check boxes allow users to select from a group of predetermined options. Unlike radio buttons, however, users can select more than one check box because each check box has a different name and value. Check boxes cannot be grouped, and they must be created one at a time.

1. **With register.html open, click in the empty cell below the Products of Interest list.**

2. **Click the Checkbox button in the Forms Insert bar.**

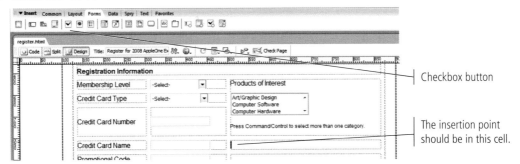

Checkbox button

The insertion point should be in this cell.

3. In the Input Tag Accessibility Attributes dialog box, do the following:

- Type "eblast" in the ID field.
- Type "Email from the show organizer" in the Label field.
- Select the Attach Label Tag Using 'for' Attribute style option.
- Select the After position option.

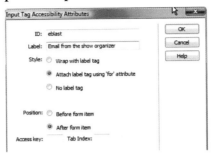

Note:

You already have a field with the ID "email" in the left half of the form. If you try to assign "email" as the ID for this check box, Dreamweaver would automatically change the ID to "email2" because you can't have two input fields, regardless of type, with the same ID.

4. Click OK to create the check box.

5. Click at the end of the check box label to place the insertion point, and then press Shift-Return/Enter to add a line break.

On Macintosh, you won't see the new line until after you add the next check box. If you look at the code, however, you will see the <br /> tag added after the first check box

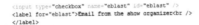

Note:

You can determine whether the check box appears selected when the form loads by using the Initial State option of the Properties Inspector.

6. Repeat Steps 2–5 to insert four more check boxes in the same table cell, using the following values:

ID	Label
advertisement	Print Advertisement
searchengine	Search Engine
pressrelease	Press Release
other	Other

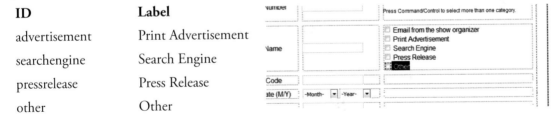

7. Select the table cell containing the check boxes, Shift-click to add the four cells directly below to the selection, and merge the selected cells.

8. Merge the three empty cells in the row below the second solid line.

9. Click in the merged cell and add another check box with "terms" as the ID. For the label, type "I agree to the terms and conditions of the trade show membership guidelines."

10. Highlight the words "terms and conditions" in the check box label. Create a link from the selected text to the file terms.html (in the site root folder) that opens in a new browser window.

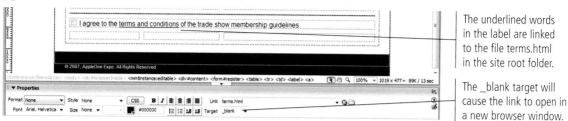

The underlined words in the label are linked to the file terms.html in the site root folder.

The _blank target will cause the link to open in a new browser window.

11. Save the file and continue to the next exercise.

 CREATE A FIELDSET

Fieldsets are used to combine multiple form fields into a group. This method allows you to define a legend for the grouped form objects (similar to a label for individual fields), as well as define CSS rules that affect only objects in a particular fieldset.

1. With register.html open, select the five check boxes (and their labels) in the right column of the table.

2. Click the Fieldset button in the Forms Insert bar.

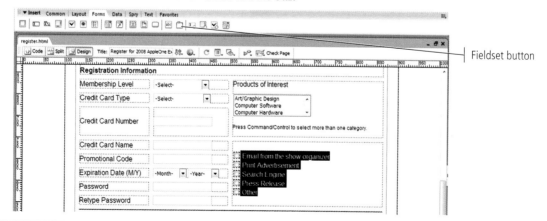

Fieldset button

3. Type "How did you hear about this show?" in the Legend field of the Fieldset dialog box and click OK.

The fieldset legend appears above the selected check boxes. Because each check box has its own label — and because check boxes cannot be grouped — this is the easiest way to attach a properly structured heading to a group of related check boxes.

This line, surrounding the selected fields, indicates the boundaries of the fieldset.

4. Save the file and continue to the next exercise.

ADD SUBMIT AND RESET BUTTONS

Buttons perform an assigned task when clicked. The **Submit** button is crucial to any form user's data, ensuring the data is not sent to the server until the user clicks Submit. The **Reset** button clears all entries in form objects and restores the form to its original, unfilled state.

By default, buttons in Dreamweaver are set to Submit, although you can easily alter the settings to make them function as Reset buttons. You can even use JavaScript or other programming languages to customize a button to perform a specific task (these customized buttons are called Command buttons in HTML).

1. With register.html open, merge the three cells in the bottom row of the table.

2. With the insertion point in the newly merged cell, click the Button button in the Forms Insert bar.

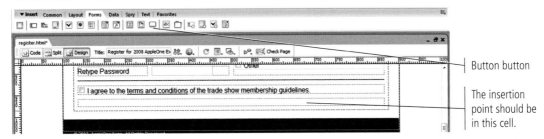

Button button

The insertion point should be in this cell.

3. In the Input Tag Accessibility Attributes dialog box, do the following:
   - Type "Submit" in the ID field.
   - Select the No Label Tag style option.

4. Click OK to create the button.

The Submit button appears in the column.

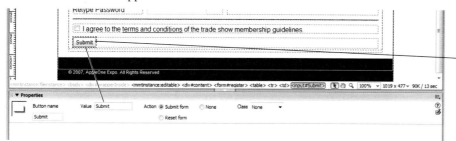

The text on a button is defined by the button value, not by the label tag.

5. Place the insertion point to the right of the existing button.

6. Repeat Steps 2–4 to add a second button, using "Reset" as the ID.

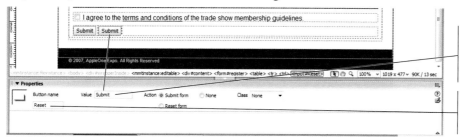

The second button defaults to the Submit action even though you defined "Reset" as the button ID.

The ID is just a name; it does not control the button's behavior.

7. Select the button in the design window. In the Properties Inspector, select the Reset Form option.

Since Submit is the default button in Dreamweaver, every button is initially inserted with the name "Submit." After you select the Reset Form option in the Properties Inspector, the button value and the text on the button automatically change to Reset.

Choosing the Reset action automatically changes the button value, which automatically changes the text on the button.

The Button Properties Inspector

The Properties Inspector for a button provides access to the attributes of a Button form object. You can enter attributes directly in the Properties Inspector to define a newly inserted button, or you can edit values for an existing button.

Button shows the ID/name of the button object (the two values are the same for a button).

Value assigns a value for the button; this value also defines the text that appears on the button object in the form. (The default value for a Submit button is "Submit," and the default value for a Reset button is "Reset.")

Action determines what happens when a button is clicked:

- **Submit Form** submits the form data to the server.
- **Reset Form** clears the user's entered data.
- **None** specifies an action other than Submit or Reset. For example, you can add a JavaScript behavior to open another page when the user clicks the button.

Class attaches a class selector (from a CSS style sheet) to the button.

8. Save the file and continue to the next stage of the project.

Stage 2 Formatting Forms with CSS

For all intents and purposes, the AppleOne registration form is complete. All of the form fields are in place, and they will gather the necessary information. However, professional Web design means not only controlling the content of a page, but also making it look as good as possible. In Project 5 you learned how to use CSS to apply styles to the content of a Web site. In this stage of this project, you use the same concepts to format the different elements of the registration form.

Based on what you have already created, you need to apply the following options to different parts of the form:

A. All text in the form should be the same size, smaller than the heading text.

B. Form labels in the left column should align with the right edge of their cells.

C. Text fields in the left half of the table should be consistently sized (excluding the state and zip fields), and they should occupy the entire available space.

D. The bottom two cells (the terms check box and the buttons) should be centered.

If you look at the page code, you will see several HTML tags are used for most objects in the form:

- The <form> tag encloses the entire form (including the table in which the form objects were organized).

- The <input> tag identifies each form object that allows user input. Different types of form objects are identified with the type attribute, such as **<input name="last" type="text" id="last" />** or **<input type="reset" name="reset" id="reset" value="Reset" />**.

- The <select> tag creates drop-down menus and selection lists.

- The <label> tag creates the text that identifies individual form fields, including the text of individual radio buttons and check boxes.

- The <legend> tag adds the heading text for the fieldset that encompasses the five check boxes.

- The <p> tag adds the instructions text below the selection list in the right column.

As with any project, there are a number of ways you can accomplish the same task. Before you define CSS selectors, you should — as always — evaluate your options.

A. *All text in the form should be the same size, smaller than the heading text.*
Because all of the text is contained within the <form> tag, you will create a selector to adjust all type styles contained within the <form> tag.

B. *Form labels in the left column should align with the right edge of their cells.*
Because you want to affect only some labels, you will use a class selector that can be applied to specific labels.

C. *Text fields in the left half of the table should be consistently sized (excluding the state and zip fields), and should occupy the entire available space.*
Because you don't want to affect all text fields in the form (i.e., not the ones in the right half of the form), you will create a class selector that can be applied to only specific field objects.

D. *The bottom two cells (the terms check box and the buttons) should be centered.*
Although you could simply apply center alignment to the table cells, it is more appropriate to create a class selector that applies center alignment to specific areas.

APPLY STYLE TO THE FORM TAG

According to the list of goals, all text in the form should be the same size. Because all of the text is contained within the <form> tag, you will start by creating a selector to adjust all type within the <form> tag.

You could define a tag selector for the form tag to accomplish this task, but a tag selector applies to all tags to which the same CSS file is attached. In other words, defining a tag selector for the <form> tag would affect all forms in the site — which might not be what you want.

To apply style to only the form you are building, you will use the defined ID of the registration form to create an ID selector that affects only this single form.

1. **With register.html open, click anywhere in the form to place the insertion point.**

The Tag Selector shows the form tag, including the name (ID) of the selected form.

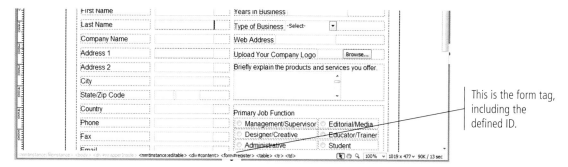

This is the form tag, including the defined ID.

2. **Open the CSS Styles panel if it is not already visible.**

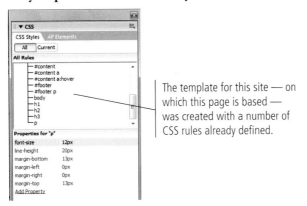

The template for this site — on which this page is based — was created with a number of CSS rules already defined.

3. **Click the New CSS Rule button at the bottom of the CSS Styles panel.**

4. **In the New CSS Rule dialog box, choose the Advanced Selector Type option.**

5. **Change the name field to "#register".**

   Remember, "register" is the name you assigned when you defined the original form object at the beginning of the project.

6. **Make sure the master.css option is selected in the Define In options, and then click OK.**

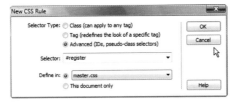

7. **In the Type category of the CSS Rule Definition dialog box, change the type size to 11 pixels. Click the Color swatch and choose the medium gray option (#666666) for the type color.**

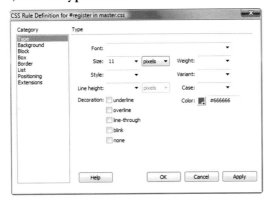

8. Click OK to define the rule.

Most of the text within the form tag adjusts, based on the new definition. Several elements (including menu and list text and the text below the list object) remain unchanged; you will address this issue in the next exercise.

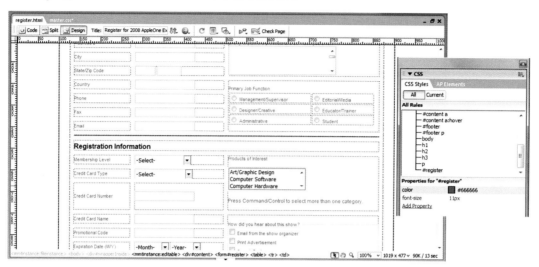

9. Save the CSS file, and then continue to the next exercise.

 ## USE SELECTORS TO CONTROL SPECIFIC FORM OBJECTS

Most of the text within the form tag has been adjusted, based on the defined #register selector. Several elements, however, remain unchanged:

- Type within the menus and list still uses larger, black letters.

- The paragraph text (below the list object in the right half of the form) is still larger than the rest of the text in the form.

To change these elements, you must define additional selectors that change those specific elements.

1. With register.html open, click any of the menu form objects.

The Tag Selector shows that these objects are created with the <select> tag.

This menu is selected.

This is the associated tag.

Defining a tag selector would affect all menus in all pages attached to the master.css file. Instead, you will use an ID selector to style <select> tags within this specific form only.

2. Click the New CSS Rule button at the bottom of the CSS Styles panel.

3. **In the New CSS Rule dialog box, choose the Advanced option and change the Name field to "#register select".**

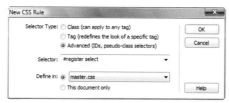

4. **Click OK to open the CSS Rule Definition dialog box.**

5. **In the Type options, change the size to 11 pixels and change the color to #666666.**

6. **Click OK to apply the new style.**

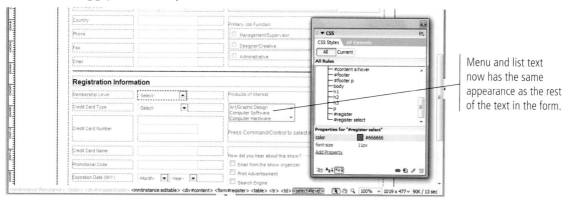

Menu and list text now has the same appearance as the rest of the text in the form.

7. **Create another new CSS ID selector named "#register p" using the following settings:**

   • **In the Type options, define the size as 11 pixels and define the color as #666666.**

   • **In the Box options, apply a 2-pixel top margin and a 0-pixel bottom margin.**

   The box options override the margin settings defined for the "p" tag selector that applies to the entire site.

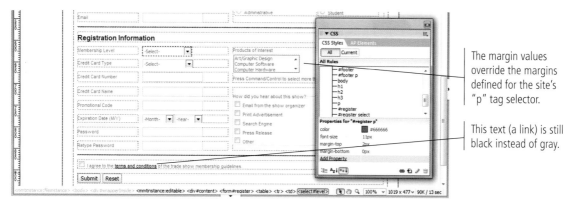

The margin values override the margins defined for the site's "p" tag selector.

This text (a link) is still black instead of gray.

8. Create another new CSS ID selector named "#register a" using the following settings:

- In the Type options, make sure the Underline Decoration option is selected, and change the color to #666666.

All the text in the form is now the same size and color.

9. Save the CSS file, and then continue to the next exercise.

 ## USE CLASS SELECTORS TO CONTROL ALIGNMENT

Because different parts of the form require different alignment, you can't simply define "a" tag selectors. If you defined a label tag selector to apply right alignment, for example, all labels — including the labels next to the radio buttons and the check boxes — would become right-aligned. To affect only certain elements of the form, you need to use class selectors.

1. With register.html open, click the New CSS Rule button at the bottom of the CSS Styles panel.

2. In the New CSS Rule dialog box, choose the Class selector type.

3. In the name field, type ".alignRight".

Note:

If you forget to include the beginning period in the name of a class selector, Dreamweaver will add it for you. It's a good idea, however, to get into the habit of typing the period yourself.

4. Click OK to open the CSS Rule Definition dialog box.

5. In the Block options, choose Right from the Text Align menu.

6. Click OK to create the class selector.

Nothing in the form changes because you haven't yet assigned the class to specific elements.

7. **Place the insertion point in the First Name label.**

8. **In the Tag Selector, Control/right-click the label tag and choose Set Class>alignRight from the contextual menu.**

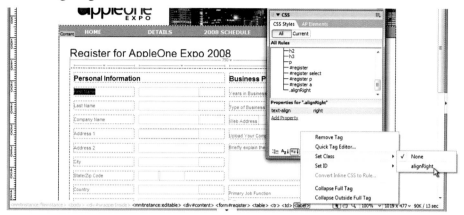

Again, nothing happens. The Block options of a CSS rule control the position of content within a container. Instead of applying the class to the content, you need to apply it to the container of the content.

Nothing happens because the class is applied to the label instead of the container.

9. **Press Command/Control-Z to undo Step 8 (where you applied the class to the label tag).**

10. **Control/right-click the <td> tag in the Tag Selector and choose Set Class>alignRight from the contextual menu.**

The cell is selected because you clicked the <td> tag in the tag selector.

The <td> tag identifies a table cell. By applying the class to the <td> tag, the text within the container (the table cell) properly aligns to the right side of the cell.

11. **Repeat Step 10 for all cells containing field labels in the left column of the table.**

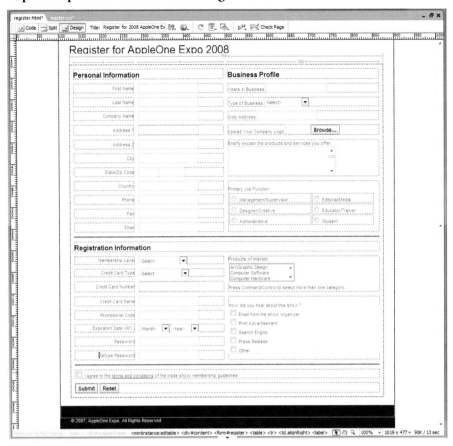

12. **Using the same basic method, create another class selector named ".alignCenter" that changes the Text Align property (in the Block options) to Center.**

13. **Apply the alignCenter class selector to the two table cells at the bottom of the form.**

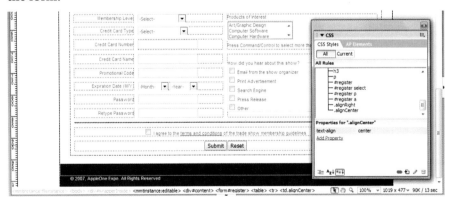

14. **Create another class selector named ".alignTop" that changes the Vertical Alignment property (in the Block options) to Top.**

15. **Apply the alignTop class selector to the four cells in the right half of the form, where multiple table cells have been merged to span more than one table row.**

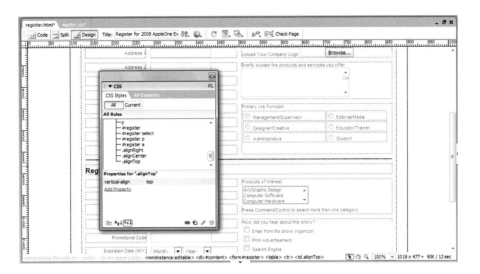

16. **Save the HTML and CSS files, and then continue to the next exercise.**

USE A CLASS SELECTOR TO CONTROL INPUT FIELD WIDTH

The final bit of fine-tuning requires you to adjust the width of the text fields in the left half of the form. Although the Char Width property can be used to adjust the field width, the property is a rather ambiguous function of the defined character width. The CSS Box Width property gives you more precise control over the field width because you can use different (and known) units of measurement that remain unaffected by users' browser display settings.

1. **With register.html open, click the New CSS Rule button at the bottom of the CSS Styles panel.**

2. **Select the Class selector type option and type ".textFieldWidth" in the Name field.**

3. **Click OK to open the CSS Rule Definition dialog box.**

4. **In the Box options, type "2" in the Width field and choose In from the attached menu.**

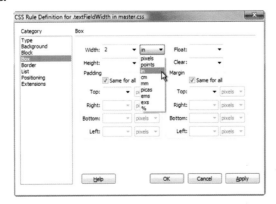

5. **Click OK to create the class selector.**

6. **Click the First Name field in the form to select it.**

7. **In the Properties Inspector, choose textFieldWidth in the Class menu.**

The field is now 2 inches wide.

The tag selector shows the name of the applied class.

8. **Repeat Steps 6–7 for all text fields in the left half of the form except the fields for the state and zip code.**

9. **Save the HTML and CSS files.**

10. **Preview the HTML file in your browser.**

11. **Return to Dreamweaver, and then continue to the final stage of the project.**

Stage 3 Validating Forms

The information collected through forms plays an increasingly important role in corporate marketing efforts. Not only is there a need to collect information, but also to ensure that the information received is correct. To address this business need, forms must including built-in validation that screens user-entered data to ensure that all the required information is provided in the correct format.

AppleOne needs to ensure that registrants complete all fields in the Personal Profile section of the form (except Address 2 and Fax fields) and all fields in the left side of the Registration Information area. Users also must agree to the terms of the show by clicking the Terms check box.

Validation can be added to a form by designing scripts. This is called **server-side validation** because the form data is submitted to the server, and then a script on the server verifies the data and sends the results to the browser. Some validation must be done by scripts on the server because the server must compare the new form data with the data it already has. For example, a Web site that allows users to create accounts must compare each new ID with IDs already in the database; this validation process ensures that each user ID is unique.

The other type of validation is called **client-side validation**. In this case, scripts are attached to the actual form elements, and the validation is performed before the data reaches the server. This type of validation can reduce the time it takes to verify the data because the action is performed in the browser (the client). In fact, validation can be performed even before the user clicks the Submit button, such as when the user exits a field without providing the required information or if the required information is in an incorrect format.

Note:

It can be helpful to draw attention to required fields by adding an asterisk next to the field and using a legend to explain that such fields must be filled for the form to be accepted.

Note:

The Validate Form behavior (in the Behaviors panel) can be used to make form fields required, as well as to restrict the type of input. However, the Validate Form behavior does not provide the option of displaying warning messages if users complete the form incorrectly.

Dreamweaver's Validation Widgets

DREAMWEAVER FOUNDATIONS

Dreamweaver's validation widgets were designed using Adobe's Spry framework, which in turn uses AJAX (Asynchronous JavaScript and XML), a technology used to design interactive Web pages. Spry is also used to provide other functionality in Dreamweaver.

Dreamweaver CS3 includes validation widgets for four types of form elements: text fields, text areas, lists/menus, and check boxes; there is no validation widget for radio buttons. These widgets can be accessed from the Insert>Form or Insert>Spry menus, the Forms Insert bar, or the Spry Insert bar. We use the Forms Insert bar in this project because that option also contains all of the Form objects — providing a single source for all of the tools you need to build the form.

Validation widgets display messages (alongside the related fields) to draw attention to improper or omitted information. You can use the widgets to control when these messages display, as well as the specific message that appears. By default, messages display after the user clicks the Submit button, but you can also choose to display the messages when a user exits a field without typing the required information or if the information is in an incorrect format.

To insert a Spry validation widget in a form, click the label that appears in the design window when you place the cursor over a field to which the widget is attached. You can control a widget's properties in the Properties inspector.

The validation script of a widget is created by wrapping a <span> tag around the form element code. The <span> tag is used to apply properties and attributes to only a specific piece of content, such as a specific form object.

You can also use validation widgets to insert form elements with the validation script. When you insert a validation widget without selecting a form element (or after selecting a form element to which the specific widget does not apply), a new field is added with Spry validation already in place.

ADD TEXT FIELD VALIDATION

A text field requires the user to enter information manually — and that opens the door for users to enter *inappropriate* information in the field. You need to guard against inappropriate information being accepted by your form — and that's where validation widgets come into play.

Text fields are used to collect many different types of information. For example, a text field for a street address must accept all types of characters supported by the encoding type of the Web page. A text field for phone numbers, however, should be filled with numbers only. Dreamweaver's validation widget for text fields allows you to control the format of information that users are supposed to enter in a text field.

1. **With register.html open, select the First Name text field.**

2. **Click the Spry Validation Text Field button in the Forms Insert bar.**

Spry Validation
Text Field button

Selected field object

The text field is surrounded by a border (or widget) that attaches the validation script to the field.

This tab indicates
Spry validation.

3. **In the Properties Inspector, make sure None is selected in the Type menu.**

   This allows users to type any character supported by the page's encoding type.

4. **Make sure the Required check box is selected.**

5. **Select Required in the Preview States menu.**

   The message that displays when this form is left blank appears adjacent to the text field in the design window.

6. **In the design window, drag to select the red text that represents the error message, and then type "Required".**

Note:

You can check the encoding type by choosing Modify>Page Properties and clicking the Title/ Encoding category.

Change this text to
modify the warning
message for the
selected preview state.

Use this menu to preview
different warning messages
that will display for
different types of errors.

7. Choose Initial in the Preview States menu so the validation message does not appear when the form first loads in the browser.

The Text Field Validation Properties Inspector

The Properties Inspector controls the different attributes of Spry validation widgets. The following list explains the options for text field validation widgets.

- The **Spry Textfield** field displays the ID of the validation widget. By default, the ID is "sprytextfield," followed by a sequential serial number based on the number of same-type widgets in the form.

- The **Type** menu determines the format users must use when they enter data in the text field. If you select None, users can type any character that's supported by the page's encoding type. Dreamweaver provides validation for 12 formats. For some types (e.g., Date, Time, Credit Card, Zip Code, Phone Number), you can choose from a set of standard formats available in the Format menu. The Custom type allows you to specify your own pattern in the Pattern field.

- The **Format** menu is enabled when Date, Time, Credit Card, Zip Code, Phone Number, Currency, or IP address is selected in the Type menu. It contains a list of standard formats for the selected type, which forces users to enter the selected type of information according to the selected format.

- The **Pattern** menu is enabled when Custom is selected in the Type menu, enabling you to define your own format pattern for entering data.

- What you type in the **Hint** field (if anything) displays in the text field when the page loads in the browser. When users click in the text field, the hint disappears.

- The **Preview States** menu allows you to review and change the message that appears when different conditions are met (i.e., the user has not filled a required field). The Initial and Valid states display the field in its original appearance (that is, without a message).

- The **Validate On** group of check boxes determines when validation is performed. If you select Blur, the validation is performed when the user exits the field. If you select Change, the validation is performed only when a user exits a field after typing some text. Submit is selected by default, which means the validation is performed when the form is submitted.

- The **Min Chars** field requires a certain minimum number of characters in the field, such as a minimum of 10 characters for a phone number (to include the area code).

- The **Max Chars** field limits the number of characters that users can type in the field, such as no more than 16 characters in a credit card number.

- The **Min Value** and **Max Value** fields are enabled when you select Integer from the Type menu. You can specify these values to ensure that users do not type a number that is less than or greater than certain values. For example, to gather user birthdays using text fields, you might consider restricting the Max Value of the "month" text field to 12 and the "day" text field to 31.

- When **Required** is checked, users will receive an error message if they fail to enter a value in the associated field.

- If you specified a custom pattern for the text field entry, checking the **Enforce Pattern** box requires users to enter information according to your defined pattern.

8. Repeat this process to add validation to the following text fields. Follow the instructions listed for the different fields.

Last Name	Repeat Steps 2–7 as noted.
Company Name	Repeat Steps 2–7 as noted.
Address 1	Repeat Steps 2–7 as noted.
City	Repeat Steps 2–7 as noted.
State	Repeat Steps 2–7 as noted.
Zip	Repeat Steps 2–7 as noted.
Phone	Repeat Step 2 as noted. Select Integer in the Type menu to prevent users from typing anything other than numbers in this field. With Invalid Value selected in the Preview States menu, highlight the warning message in the widget and type "Please type numbers only." Repeat Steps 4–7 as noted.
Email	Repeat Step 2 as noted. Select Email Address in the Type menu to ensure users enter an address that contains the "at" symbol (@) and a dot. With Invalid Value selected in the Preview States menu, highlight the warning message in the widget and type "Please enter a valid email address." Repeat Steps 4–7 as noted.
Credit Card Number	Repeat Step 2 as noted. Select Integer in the Type menu. With Invalid Value selected in the Preview States menu, highlight the warning message in the widget and type "Please type numbers only." Type "15" in the Min Chars field and type "16" in the Max Chars field. Repeat Steps 4–7 as noted
Credit Card Name	Repeat Steps 2–7 as noted.
Password	Repeat Step 2 as noted. Type 5 in the Min Chars field. This will prevent users from submitting the form with a password that has less than 5 characters. Change the error message in the design window to "Type a password of at least 5 characters." Repeat Steps 4–7 as noted.
Retype Password	Repeat Step 2 as noted. Type 5 in the Min Chars field. This will prevent users from submitting the form with a password that has less than 5 characters. Change the error message in the design window to "Type a password of at least 5 characters." Repeat Steps 4–7 as noted.

Note:

Because countries other than the U.S. often have letters in their postal codes, you should not limit the Zip Code field to integers.

Note:

Although you can select Phone Number from the Type list and select US/Canada from the Format list to validate the phone numbers, selecting these options could restrict users from other countries from registering.

Note:

American Express card numbers have 15 digits and all others have 16 digits. Actual credit card number validation will be performed using a server-side script that processes and charges the card account number. You are adding this validation simply to make sure users enter the right kind of information — not to verify the account number itself.

Note:

The validation added for the Password and Retype Password fields is insufficient because it does not compare the values in the two fields. It is required to check that the same password is typed in both fields. For such validation, you will need to use scripts other than the ones Dreamweaver provides.

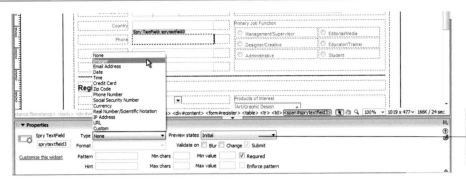

Different states (and messages) are available depending on the options you select in other areas of the Properties Inspector.

9. **Save the file. If you see the Copy Dependent Files message, click OK.**

   The Spry validation widgets are built around JavaScripts and formatted using CSS selectors; Dreamweaver automatically incorporates the necessary elements into your site when you use the Spry widgets.

10. **Continue to the next exercise.**

 ADD TEXT AREA VALIDATION

Although the text area in the right column is not a required field, you still need to control the amount of information users can type in the area. Validation is as much about guiding users to provide the correct information as it is about preventing invalid data from being submitted. Features such as character count and messages help the user to successfully complete the form.

> **Note:**
>
> *The Hint field in the Properties Inspector defines text that appears in the field when the form loads in the browser. The hint text disappears when a user clicks in this field.*

1. **With register.html open, click the text area in the right column of the table.**

2. **Click the Spry Validation Textarea button in the Forms Insert bar.**

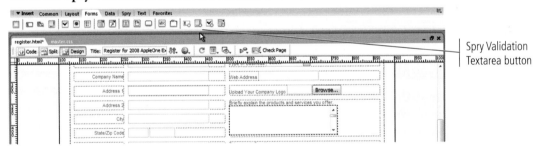

Spry Validation Textarea button

3. **In the Properties Inspector, deselect the Required check box (this is not a required field).**

4. **Type "500" in the Max Chars field.**

   This option limits the number of characters users can type in this field.

5. **Select the Block Extra Characters check box.**

   If this option is not checked, users can type more than the allowed number of characters, but the form cannot be submitted until the extra characters are deleted.

6. **Select the Chars Remaining option.**

   This option adds a counter that counts down the characters (from the maximum allowed) when users type in the text area.

7. **Make sure Initial is selected in the Preview States menu of the Properties Inspector.**

The widget shows where the counter will appear.

8. **Save the file and continue to the next exercise.**

The Text Area Validation Properties Inspector

The Properties Inspector controls the different attributes of Spry validation widgets. The following list explains the options for textarea validation widgets.

- The **Spry Textarea** field displays the ID of the validation widget. By default, the ID is "sprytextarea" followed by a sequential serial number based on the number of same-type widgets in the form.

- When **Required** is checked, users will see a message if they do not enter a value in the associated field.

- The **Min Chars** field requires a certain minimum number of characters in the field.

- The **Max Chars** field limits the number of characters that users can type in the field.

- The **Preview States** menu allows you to review and change the message that appears when different conditions are met (i.e., the user has not filled a required field). The Initial and Valid states display the field in its original appearance (that is, without a message).

- The **Validate On** group of check boxes determines when validation is performed. If you select Blur, the validation is performed when the user exits the field. If you select Change, the validation is performed only when a user exits a field after typing some text. Submit is selected by default, which means the validation is performed when the form is submitted.

- The **Counter** options enable you to add a character counter to the associated field. Using the Chars Count option, the counter displays the number of characters typed. If you specify a number in the Max Chars field, the Chars Remaining counter can be enabled to show how many characters remain in the allowable amount.

- The **Block Extra Characters** option, enabled if you specify a number in the Max Chars field, prevents users from typing more than the allowed number of characters. If this option is not selected, users can type more than the allowed number, but they will receive an error message when the form is submitted.

- What you type in the **Hint** field (if anything) displays in the text field when the page loads in the browser. When users click in the text field, the hint disappears.

ADD LIST/MENU VALIDATION

The Spry Validation Select widget ensures that users select an option (label) from a list, whether a drop-down menu or a scroll list. This type of validation can also prevent invalid labels from being accepted, such as the Select, Month, or Year options you placed at the top of the drop-down menus.

1. **With register.html open, click the Membership Level menu.**

2. **In the Properties Inspector, click List Values to open the List Values dialog box.**

3. **In the List Values dialog box, click in the Value column for the Select label and change it to "–1". Click OK to apply the change.**

    This value will be used to identify an invalid selection.

4. **With the menu selected in the design window, click the Spry Validation Select button in the Forms Insert bar.**

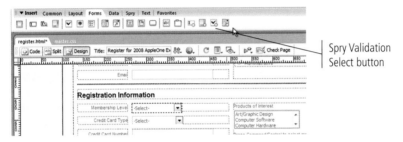

Spry Validation Select button

5. **In the Properties Inspector, check the Do Not Allow Invalid Value option.**

    The field next to the check box is activated, with –1 as its default value. Because this is the value now assigned to the -Select- option in the menu, the field will be considered invalid if the user doesn't choose a different option in the menu.

Note:

To achieve the same effect, you could leave the value for Select blank and check the Do Not Allow Blank Value option to make the default label invalid.

6. **Return the Preview States menu in the Properties Inspector to Initial.**

    The default message created by the widget is fine for the purposes of this project.

7. **Repeat Steps 1–6 for the Credit Card Type, (Expiration) Month, and (Expiration) Year menus.**

    In the case of the Expiration menus, change the values of the Month and Year labels to –1 since these menus do not have the Select label.

8. **Save the file and continue to the next exercise.**

DREAMWEAVER FOUNDATIONS

The Properties Inspector controls the different attributes of Spry validation widgets. The following list explains the options for list/menu validation widgets.

- The **Spry Select** field displays the ID of the validation widget. By default, the ID is "spryselect" followed by a sequential serial number based on the number of same-type widgets in the form.

- If you have a list label with no associated value, selecting the **Do Not Allow Blank Value** option prevents the user from submitting the form with the no-value label selected. This option is helpful when there is more than one label in the list that you do not want users to select.

- To prevent users from selecting a certain list item, you can check the **Invalid Value** box and type the value associated with the forbidden label in the adjacent field.

- The **Preview States** menu allows you to review and change the message that appears when different conditions are met (i.e., the user has not entered a value in a required field). The Initial and Valid states display the field in its original appearance (that is, without a message).

- The **Validate On** group of check boxes determines when validation is performed. If you select Blur, the validation is performed when the user exits the field. If you select Change, the validation is performed only when a user exits a field after typing some text. Submit is selected by default, which means the validation is performed when the form is submitted.

INSERT CHECK BOX VALIDATION

The Validation Checkbox widget provides two types of validation. The first is when a check box needs to be selected by a user, so the check box is marked as required. Usually, this type of validation is used when a user needs to agree to the terms of a service (as is the case in this form). The second type of validation ensures that users select a minimum number of check boxes.

There is a difference in how you make the widget work in these two scenarios. You can add the first type of validation after you have inserted the check box field. For the second type of validation, you need to first insert the Spry Validation Checkbox widget, and then insert the check boxes within the widget. In the Properties Inspector for the widget, you must then select Enforce Range (Multiple) and type the minimum or maximum number of selections that can be made from the available choices.

Note:

If the AppleOne owner wanted to require one or more selections in the group of check boxes on the right side of the form, you would need to use the second validation method.

1. **With register.html open, click the check box in the merged cell at the bottom of the form.**

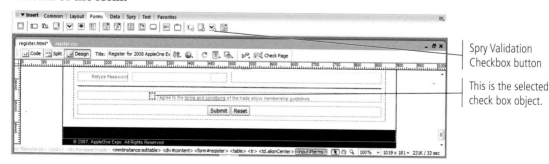

Spry Validation Checkbox button

This is the selected check box object.

2. **Click the Spry Validation Checkbox button in the Forms Insert bar.**

The checkbox validation widget is inserted.

3. In the Properties Inspector, make sure the Required (Single) option is selected.

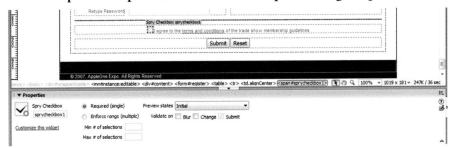

4. Choose Required in the Preview States menu. In the design window, change the warning message to, "You must check this box to submit your registration."

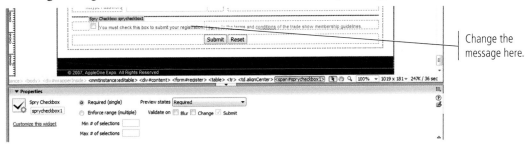

Change the message here.

5. Change the Preview States menu to Initial to hide the warning message in the design window.

6. Save the file.

7. Click OK in the Copy Dependent Files dialog box.

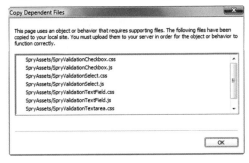

The Spry validation widgets include CSS styles that format the different warning messages. When you save a file that includes Spry validation, the necessary CSS elements are copied into the page where you placed the validation widgets.

8. Close the file.

Summary

In this project, you learned to add interactivity to your Web site by using forms. Forms are important tools that enable site visitors to communicate with Web site owners. An HTML form includes many elements that enable you to collect a wide variety of information from users, including name, company name, industry, address, phone number, and much more. Appropriate use of these elements can make the form easy to complete, as well as help you collect precise information. You also learned to add browser-based (client-side) validation using Dreamweaver's validation widgets. These widgets ensure that users provide all the necessary information in the correct format.

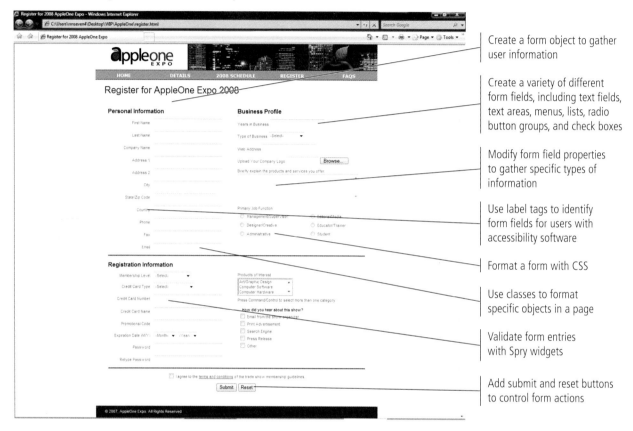

Create a form object to gather user information

Create a variety of different form fields, including text fields, text areas, menus, lists, radio button groups, and check boxes

Modify form field properties to gather specific types of information

Use label tags to identify form fields for users with accessibility software

Format a form with CSS

Use classes to format specific objects in a page

Validate form entries with Spry widgets

Add submit and reset buttons to control form actions

Portfolio Builder Project 6

Your client's conference is scheduled to occur next week, and they want to be prepared to gather exhibitor and attendee input as soon as the conference is over. They have hired you to build additional form pages for this purpose.

To complete this project, you should:

❏ Use the information and questions in the client-supplied documents (RF_Builders>AppleOne) to build forms that will gather the desired information.

❏ Use different form fields as appropriate to make the form very easy for users to fill out.

❏ Build each form on a separate page, maintaining the same look and feel of the overall site in each new form page.

"Because this is the first year for our new conference, we want to be prepared as soon as the show is over to gather as much feedback as possible while the event is fresh in participants' minds. Exhibitors and attendees will each receive a card with their registration packet inviting them to fill out the appropriate form, beginning the day after the show concludes. We want as many responses as possible, so we're even offering prize incentives for the first so many responses.

"We've sent you files with the questions we want to include in each survey. Most of the questions will be the typical 1-to-10 radio button options. Several questions will need fields where users can enter their own information. There are also a few questions that we want a 'choose one' set of options.

"Because we've already printed the cards for the registration packets, make sure you use the correct file names and method:

– The attendee survey page should be appleone.com/at_survey.html

– The exhibitor survey page should be appleone.com/ex_survey.html

– Form submissions should be emailed to thanks@appleone.com

"We don't have much time; these forms need to be ready in four days."

Animated Baseball Site

T & C is launching a baseball-coaching clinic to complement its existing football and golf clinics. You have been hired to design a Web site to provide information about their coaching programs and instructor profiles. They prefer the site to have dynamic rather than static content to make it more appealing to a young audience. Before you design the entire site, they would like to see a single-page demo.

This project incorporates the following skills:

❏ Designing layout elements for JavaScript animation
❏ Creating and controlling nested AP div elements
❏ Working with JavaScript to add visual interest
❏ Creating animation with JavaScript behaviors
❏ Creating animation with keyframes on a timeline
❏ Creating a Spry menu bar and formatting the elements with CSS

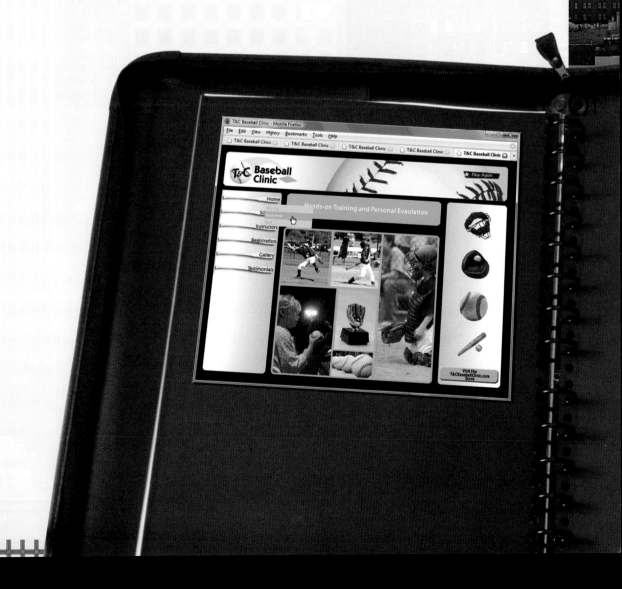

Client Comments

We are launching a new baseball clinic in the spring, and we want to make sure the new site is ready to go a few months in advance so we can accept early registrations.

There won't be much text on the individual pages because we want it to be very user friendly for both kids and their parents. We also want it to be engaging — make sure you include some kind of animation on each page.

The main pages in the site will be the Home page; Schedule pages for Spring, Summer, and Fall; Instructor pages for Coaches Jones, Ortiz, and Baker; an online registration page; a photo gallery page; and a page of testimonials from parents of our previous students.

As far as the overall look and feel, we really have no idea. We'll leave that up to you.

Art Director Comments

This stage of the site development is largely experimental because the client hasn't given us much information to work with. I only want you to create a single sample page for now; if the client likes the design, we'll move ahead and build a template from what you design.

I've had the junior designer prepare some images for different areas of the page. There are a number of indexed gif files that you can place into Dreamweaver without needing to adjust transparency settings.

Two different banners need to be animated. The top banner is an introduction to the T&C site, and the right animation is an ad link for the T&C online store. Although the majority of Web animations are created in Flash, you can use the tools in Dreamweaver to experiment and build samples for client review.

Even though you aren't building all the pages yet, I want you to include the site navigational structure. There are two levels in the site structure, so use a JavaScript menu to include the secondary pages in the menu

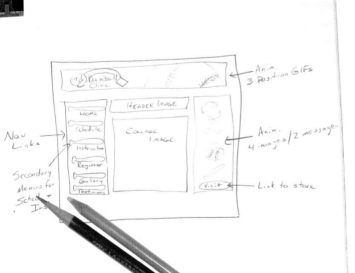

Project Objectives

To complete this project, you will:

❏ Design layout elements for JavaScript animation

❏ Create and control nested AP divs

❏ Create an image form field

❏ Create an animation timeline

❏ Attach JavaScript behaviors to the timeline

❏ Attach an interactive behavior to a form object

❏ Create a timeline for motion animation

❏ Animate timeline object properties

❏ Create a Spry menu bar

❏ Format Spry menu bar elements with CSS

❏ Adjust z-index to control object layering

Stage 1 Designing for JavaScript Animation

In the previous project, you learned how interactivity (in the form of an HTML form) can enhance the user's experience by enabling communication with the site owner. Animation is another dynamic tool for improving the user's experience because movement is likely to catch the visitor's attention.

In this project, you learn how to add animation effects to a Web page, making it more interesting and visually compelling. One of the primary skills you will learn is how to use **AP divs** or layers to design a Web page in Dreamweaver.

 ## DEFINE THE BASEBALL CLINIC SITE

As in the previous projects, the Baseball Clinic site must first be defined in Dreamweaver so the links between documents and images are created properly. The procedure for defining the site is the same for the Baseball Clinic site as for the sites in the previous projects.

1. Copy the Baseball folder from the RF_Dreamweaver folder into your WIP folder where you are saving your work.

2. Open the Manage Sites dialog box using the Directory menu in the Files panel.

3. If the AppleOne site is still available in the list of sites, export the site definition file into your WIP>AppleOne folder, and then remove the AppleOne site from the dialog box.

4. Click New>Site.

5. Create a new site named "Baseball", using your WIP>Baseball folder as the site root folder.

6. Click OK, and then click Done to create the new site.

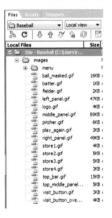

7. Continue to the next exercise.

INSERT AP DIVS

AP divs (also called **AP elements** or **layers**) are basically containers that exist in fixed locations to hold HTML elements. AP divs can be dragged to any part of the page, which means they can also be moved or modified using scripts.

AP divs are invisible if you don't define a background or border style for a specific div. This characteristic allows an object inside an AP div to appear independent of the container, which is essential for creating seamless animation. AP divs can also overlap, which is another key in creating animation. This characteristic makes it possible to include multiple objects at the same position, and then display them one at a time. The **z-index attribute** determines which div or layer appears on top of the stacking order; the layer with the highest z-index appears on top.

As you already know, the first step in building a Web page is defining the page structure. For better organization and control over the page content, you create each area of the page on its own layer. In this project, the top banner will be on its own layer (separate from the navigation bar), the main content will be placed on yet another layer, and each content area will be placed on a separate layer.

Note:

For this project, you will use AP (Absolutely Positioned) elements to create the different areas of the page.

1. **Choose File>New.**

2. **In the New Document dialog box, choose Blank Page. Choose HTML from the Page Type list and click the Create button.**

3. **Choose File>Save. Save the file as "index.html" in the root folder of the Baseball site (WIP>Baseball).**

4. **Choose Modify>Page Properties. In the Page Properties dialog box:**

    • **In the Appearance options:**

        – **Choose the Verdana, Arial, Helvetica, sans-serif combination in the Page Font menu**

        – **Define white (#FFFFFF) as the text color**

        – **Define black (#000000) as the background color**

    • **In the Title/Encoding options, type "T&C Baseball Clinic" in the Title field.**

    • **Click OK.**

5. **Choose Insert>Layout Objects>AP Div.**

    When you use the menu command to insert an AP div, the element is created at the location of the insertion point. In this case, there is no other element on the page, so the insertion point is positioned by default in the top-left corner of the page.

6. Click the handle of the AP element to select it.

New AP elements are automatically created with the name "apDiv", followed by a sequential number that represents the number of AP divs in the page.

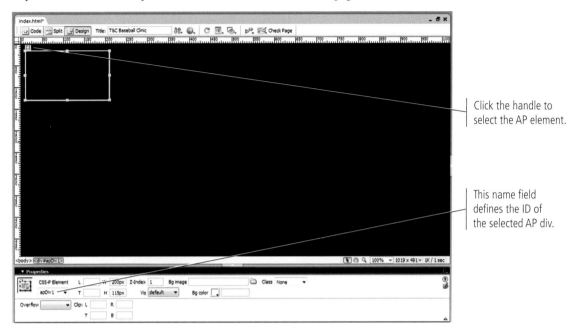

Click the handle to select the AP element.

This name field defines the ID of the selected AP div.

7. In the Properties Inspector, type "TopBanner" in the Name field. Press Return/Enter to apply the change.

This is the element ID, which is the name you will use to refer to this element. When you create AP divs, CSS ID selectors for the defined divs are automatically created as inline styles within the page code.

8. Open the CSS Styles panel and expand the <style> list. Click the #TopBanner selector in the CSS Styles panel to show the associated properties.

An AP div is still a div, except that it has an absolute (defined) position. As you learned in Projects 5 and 6, divs are controlled by ID selectors. Basically, when you create an AP div, you are visually defining the properties for the ID selector — even though the selector is being created for you behind the scenes.

Note:

The body selector has properties that were created when you modified the Page Properties dialog box.

Note:

The selectors for AP divs are created as inline styles in the code of the current HTML page.

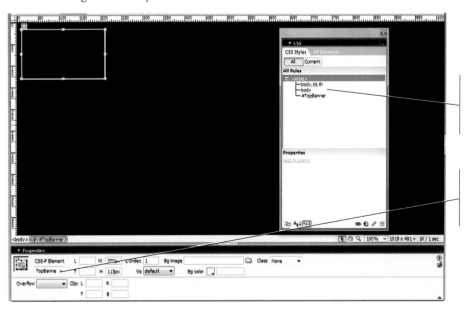

The two body selectors are created to apply settings from the Page Properties dialog box.

The new element name is also reflected in the related selector name.

9. **In the design window, click the div handle and drag the element to the middle of the page.**

Divs can be manually repositioned by dragging the div handle, or you can resize them by dragging any of the bounding box handles.

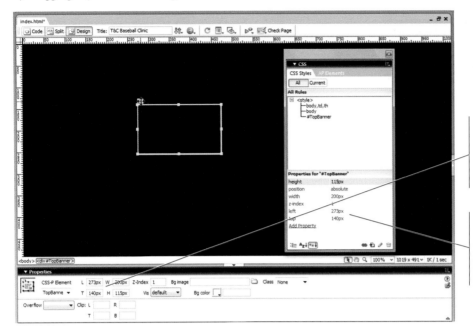

When you drag the div in the page, the L and T fields in the Properties Inspector reflect the element's new position.

In the CSS Styles panel, the left and top properties for the #TopBanner selector also show the element's new position.

10. **In the CSS Styles panel, change the left property to 15 pixels and change the top property to 18 pixels.**

Changing the selector properties affects the position of the object in the design window, as well as the associated values in the Properties Inspector.

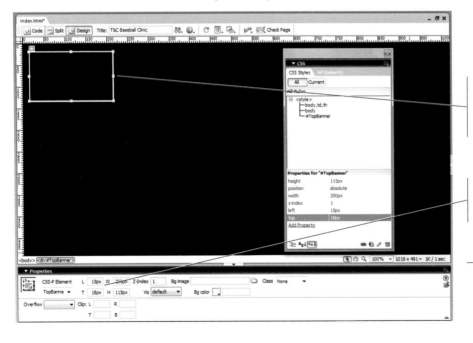

Changing the values in the CSS selector affects the selected element in the design window…

… as well as the related properties in the Properties Inspector.

Note:

Press the Arrow keys to move a selected AP div by 1 pixel in any direction. Press Shift and use the Arrow keys to move a selected AP div by 10 pixels in any direction.

11. **In the Properties Inspector, type "784px" in the W field and type "95px" in the H field.**

Make sure you type the "px" with the value, and don't separate the number and unit with a space. Since the CSS rules that correlate to the L, T, W, and H fields can have different units of measurements, you have to specify exactly what you want to accomplish when you define the AP div dimensions in the Properties Inspector.

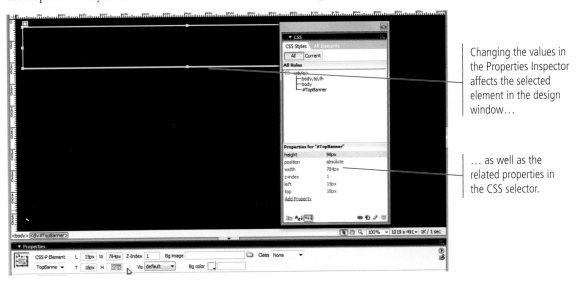

Changing the values in the Properties Inspector affects the selected element in the design window...

... as well as the related properties in the CSS selector.

12. **With the TopBanner div selected in the page, use the Properties Inspector to define top_bar.gif (in the site images folder) as the background image of the div element.**

The new background image is added to the div in the design window, and the background-image property is added to the #TopBanner selector.

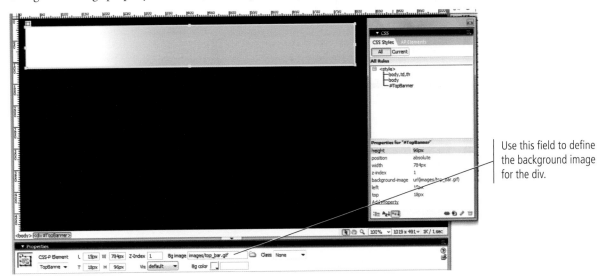

Use this field to define the background image for the div.

It is important to understand your options for adjusting an AP div. You can:

- Change the element visually in the design window
- Change the element numerically using the Properties Inspector
- Change the element numerically using the CSS Styles panel

All three techniques produce the same result because changing values in one location (design window, Properties Inspector, or CSS rule) changes the related values in other locations. You can use whichever method you find most suitable for a particular situation.

13. **Save the file and continue to the next exercise.**

USE THE DRAWING METHOD TO CREATE AN AP DIV

As with most software functions, there is almost always more than one way to create what you need. Creating an AP div element is no different. You can insert an AP div using the menu command (as you did in the previous project), or you can simply draw an AP div in the page. If you're comfortable with graphics applications such as Adobe InDesign or Illustrator, you might find it easier to simply draw the necessary elements, and then fine-tune the div parameters.

1. **With index.html open, click the Draw AP Div button in the Layout Insert bar.**

2. **Click anywhere in the design window and drag to draw a new AP div element.**

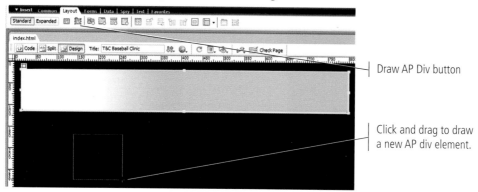

Draw AP Div button

Click and drag to draw a new AP div element.

Using the drawing method, the position and dimensions of the new div are defined based on the shape you draw.

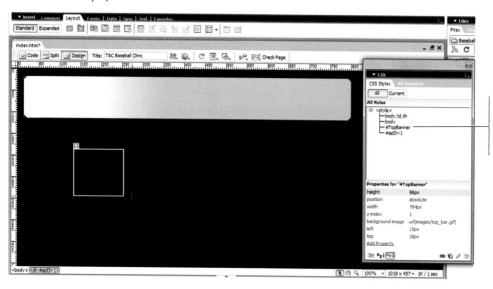

The new AP div automatically generates the necessary selector in the CSS Styles panel.

3. **Click the new div handle to select the element.**

4. **In the Properties Inspector, change the div ID to "LeftBanner".**

5. **Use the Properties Inspector to change the LeftBanner position and dimensions to:**

L: 15px	W: 165px
T: 125px	H: 478px

6. **Define left_panel.gif as the background of the LeftBanner AP div.**

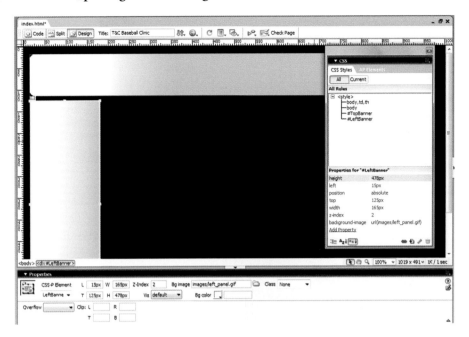

7. **Using whichever method you prefer, create additional AP divs for the rest of the main site areas. Use the following information to create the remaining page structure.**

Name	Distance from Left	Distance from Top	Width	Height	Background Image
RightBanner	635px	125px	165px	478px	right_panel.gif
TopMiddlePanel	190px	120px	435px	76px	
MiddlePanel	190px	213px	435px	394px	

8. **Click away from all div elements to deselect them.**

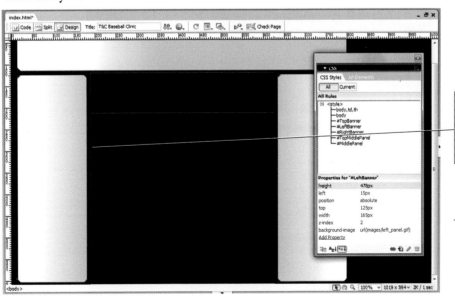

Note:

The LeftBanner div will contain a series of navigation buttons.

The RightBanner div will contain an animated ad for the Web site's store.

The TopMiddlePanel div will contain a graphic text heading.

The MiddlePanel div will contain the primary page content.

If you don't see the outlines of the empty div elements, choose View>Visual Aids> AP Element Outlines.

Note:

To hide AP div outlines, you need to turn off both AP Element Outlines and CSS Layout Outlines because an AP div is actually a type of CSS div.

9. **Click inside the TopMiddlePanel div to place the insertion point. Choose Insert>Image (or click the Image button on the Common Insert bar).**

The drag method for inserting images does not always work well with AP div elements. The Insert>Image menu command (or clicking the Image button in the Common Insert bar) is a more reliable method.

10. **In the Select Image Source dialog box, select top_middle_panel.gif (from the site images folder) and click Choose/OK.**

11. **In the Image Tag Accessibility dialog box, type "Hands-on Training and Personal Evaluation" in the Alternate Text field, and then click OK.**

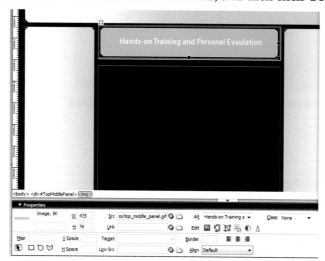

Note:

In this case, you are placing an image into the div as content rather than defining a background image for the div. Background images do not require alternate text, but content images do.

12. **Using the same basic process, insert the image middle_panel.gif into the MiddlePanel div. Enter "Photo collage" as the alternate text.**

13. **Save the file and continue to the next exercise.**

CREATE NESTED DIVS

In the previous exercise, you created AP divs to define the primary site structure. The two elements in the middle of the page are image placeholders that will remain static for the initial client presentation. The remaining three page sections (the top, left, and right banners) will contain dynamic content, which you will create using various techniques as you complete the rest of this project.

The top and right banner areas will both contain animation, which you will create using capabilities built into Dreamweaver. To prepare for those animations, you need to place a number of different objects that will be used in the animations.

Although you could simply place all of the different objects in AP divs at the same nesting level, that method might lead to management problems when you have more than a few AP divs. (In this project, for example, you are going to create no fewer than 19 AP divs.) It is much easier when you organize AP divs in nested groups wherever possible.

1. **With index.html open, click inside the TopBanner div to place the insertion point.**

2. **Chose Insert>Layout Objects>AP Div.**

   The new AP div is created inside the TopBanner div.

You should have clicked this div to place the insertion point before adding the new AP div.

3. **Click the handle of the nested div to select it.**

4. **In the Properties Inspector, change the div ID to "Pitcher".**

5. **Define the following position and dimensions for the nested Pitcher div:**

   L: 20px   W: 90px

   T: 3px   H: 90px

   When you place one div inside another div, the nested div's position is still absolute. The position (L and T) values, however, are relative to the containing element.

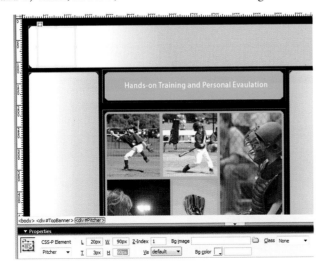

6. **Click inside the nested Pitcher div to place the insertion point.**

7. **Choose Insert>Image. Place the file pitcher.gif (from the site images folder), and enter "Pitcher" as the alternate text for the image.**

   Remember: the Insert>Image menu command, or clicking the Image button in the Common Insert bar, are more reliable methods for placing images into a nested div.

8. **In the CSS panel group, click the AP Elements tab to display that panel.**

   By default, the AP Elements panel is grouped with the CSS Styles panel. If your AP Elements panel is not available in that location, choose Window>AP Elements.

   The list includes all of the AP divs that have already been added to the page. In the list of AP elements, the Pitcher div is nested inside the TopBanner div.

9. **Click the Draw AP Div button in the Layout Insert bar.**

10. **Click inside the TopBanner div and draw a new div element.**

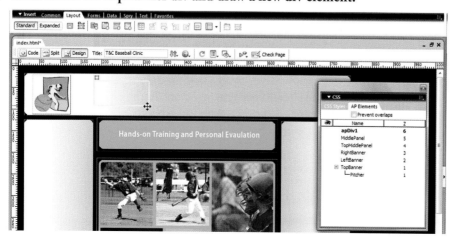

11. **Click the new div handle to select the element. In the Properties Inspector, change the div name to "Batter" and define the following position and dimensions:**

        L: 360px   **W: 70px**

        T: 8px   **H: 90px**

The new T value moves the top edge of the div above the top edge of the TopBanner div. The AP Elements panel shows that this div is located at the same nesting level as the TopBanner div. So, as you see from this step, you can't use the drawing method to create a nested div.

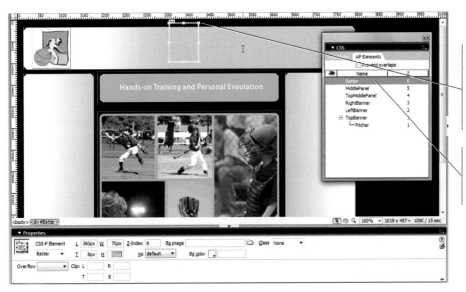

Even though you drew within the confines of the TopBanner div, the new L and T values show that the div is placed relative to the page, rather than the TopBanner div.

The position of the element confirms that the Batter div is not nested inside the TopBanner div.

12. **Insert the file batter.gif (from the site images folder) into the Batter div. Enter "Batter" as the alternate text for the image.**

13. **Click the Batter div handle to select the entire div element.**

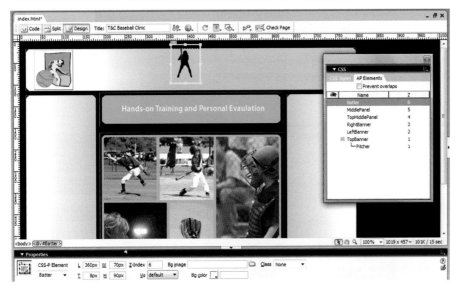

14. **Press Command/Control-X to cut the selected div to the clipboard.**

15. **Click inside the TopBanner div to place the insertion point.**

16. Press Command/Control-V to paste the Batter div inside the TopBanner div.

Even though you can't draw a nested AP div, you can use the drawing method to create AP divs, and then use the cut-and-paste method to nest those elements inside other elements.

When you paste the div as a nested element, the defined position properties (L and T) automatically adapt to be relative to the containing element; in this case, they define the positions from the top and left edges of the TopBanner div instead of the page body.

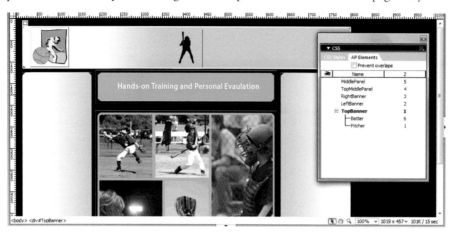

17. Using whatever method you prefer, create additional AP divs nested in the TopBanner div to contain the objects that will be animated in the top banner.

Name	Distance from Left (L field)	Distance from Top (T field)	Width	Height	Place Image Inside Div	Alt text
Fielder	700px	3px	65px	90px	fielder.gif	Fielder
BallMasked	270px	0px	520px	95px	ball_masked.gif	Masked Ball
Logo	10px	3px	200px	90px	logo.gif	T & C Logo

18. Save the file and continue to the next exercise.

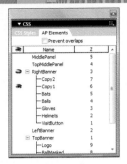

All AP divs in an HTML page are listed in the AP Elements panel (Window>AP Elements), which is grouped by default with the CSS Styles panel. Selecting an AP element in the panel list also selects the div in the page.

You can check the Prevent Overlaps option (at the top of the panel) to avoid different divs appearing in the same space on the page.

The Z column shows the **z-index** of each individual div, representing the element's order in the layer stack. The highest z-index value appears on top of the stack; other layers appear in descending z-index order (i.e., 3 is on top, then 2, then 1 at the bottom). You can change a div's z-index by clicking this column and typing a new value (or by changing the Z-Index field in the Properties Inspector when an AP div is selected).

Controlling AP Element Visibility

The left column of the panel can be used to toggle the visibility of specific divs. When the column is empty, the div is set to Default visibility; an open eye indicates a visible div, and a closed eye indicates a hidden div.

When first created, AP elements have no defined visibility setting, and thus, no icon in the left column of the AP Elements panel. If there is no eye icon for a specific AP element, the AP element inherits visibility from its parent container. (First-level AP elements are contained within the page body. For these elements, the Default and Inherit visibility options adopt the visibility of the page body — which is always visible.)

Clicking the Visibility column once hides the selected element. Clicking a closed-eye icon shows the element and sets the visibility property to Visible. Clicking an open-eye icon clears the element's visibility property and restores it to Default. (You can also click the eye icon at the top of the Visibility column to toggle all elements between Hidden and Visible.)

CONTROL PROPERTIES OF NESTED AP DIVS

In previous projects, you learned how elements within other elements adopt the properties of the containing element. For example, defining a label tag selector for a specific form (i.e., #form label) affects all labels in the form. The same concept applies to nested AP divs — properties of the containing div trickle down to all nested divs unless you override those properties for a specific nested div.

1. **With index.html open, create the following divs, nested inside the RightBanner div.**

Name	L	T	W	H	Place Image Inside Div	Alt text
VisitButton	1px	425px	163px	50px		
Helmets	45px	20px	80px	80px	store1.gif	Helmets
Gloves	45px	125px	80px	80px	store2.gif	Gloves
Balls	45px	235px	80px	80px	store3.gif	Balls
Bats	45px	340px	80px	80px	store4.gif	Bats

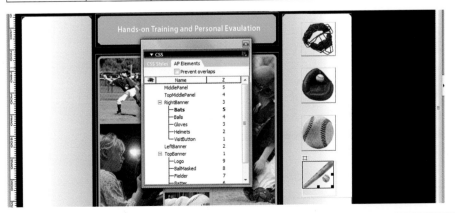

Note:

These elements will be part of a second animation (separate from the one in the top banner area).

2. Click inside the VisitButton div to place the insertion point. Add a rollover image (Insert>Image Objects>Rollover Image) using the following options:

Image name:	visitstore
Original image:	images/visit_button.gif
Rollover Image:	images/visit_button_over.gif
Preload Rollover Image:	Checked
Alternate Text:	Visit the T&C Store
URL:	#

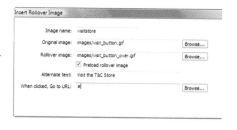

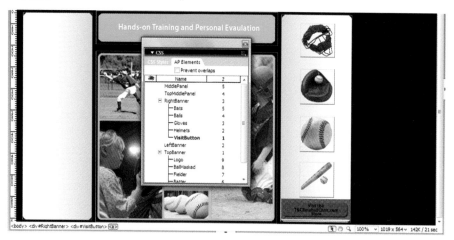

3. Using any method you prefer, create additional AP divs nested inside the RightBanner div.

Name	L	T	W	H
Copy1	10px	30px	145px	410px
Copy2	10px	30px	145px	410px

Note:

Make sure you nest these two elements within the RightBanner div, but not inside any nested divs that already exist in the RightBanner div.

The overlapping feature of AP divs allows you to display different objects in the same space (using behaviors to determine when and how each object becomes visible). This same feature, however, can make it difficult to create the different objects that occupy the same overall space. Fortunately, the visibility attribute of each AP element can be easily changed to make the building process easier to manage.

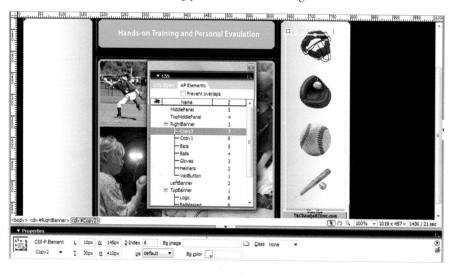

4. **In the AP Elements panel, click the empty column to the left of RightBanner to hide that element.**

If you hide an AP element, any nested elements with the Inherit or Default visibility setting will also be hidden.

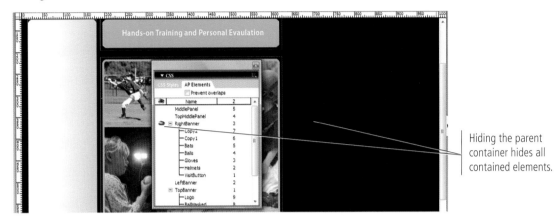

Hiding the parent container hides all contained elements.

5. **To the left of the nested Copy1 element, click the Visibility column twice to show only that element.**

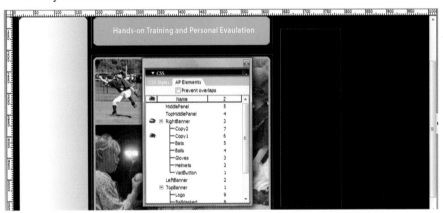

Note:

Clicking an element in the AP Elements panel selects the associated div in the page. This tool is useful when working with overlapping elements.

6. **Click in the Copy1 AP div to place the insertion point, and then type "We Meet All Your Baseball Needs". Press Return/Enter after each word so each word appears on its own line.**

7. **Click the eye (visibility) icon for Copy1 to return that element to the Default setting (inheriting the visibility of the containing div).**

8. **In the AP Elements panel, click the Visibility column twice for the Copy2 element to show only that element.**

9. Click in the Copy2 element and type "We Sell Everything But The Trophy". Press Return/Enter after each word so each word appears on its own line.

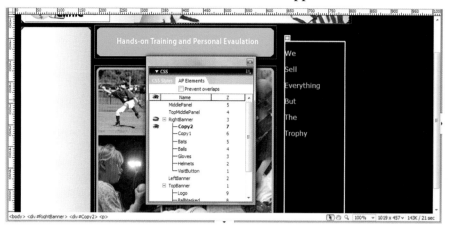

10. Restore the Copy2 and RightBanner elements to the Default visibility setting.

All the nested elements should again be visible.

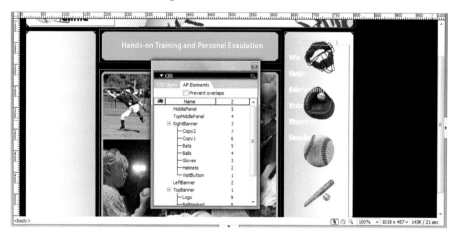

11. In the CSS Styles panel, click the #RightBanner selector in the style list, and then click the Edit Style button at the bottom of the panel.

- In the Type options for the selector, set the text size to 20 pixels, set the line height to 40 pixels, and change the text color to #3366FF.

- In the Block options, define center text alignment.

12. Click OK to change the selector definition.

Because both divs containing the type are nested within the RightBanner div, changing the #RightBanner ID selector affects the appearance of type in both of those nested divs.

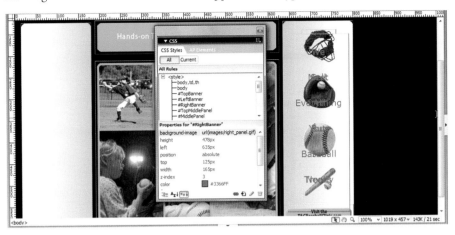

13. Save the file and continue to the next exercise.

 ## CREATE AN IMAGE FORM FIELD

At this point, most of the objects required to create the two animations are in place. The only remaining piece is the button that users can click to replay the top animation. The process for creating this div is the same as for the others you've already placed. The only difference is that to make the button interactive, you need to place the image as a form button.

1. With index.html open, create another AP div element named "PlayAgain", nested within the TopBanner div, using the following parameters:

L: 650px W: 120px

T: 10px H: 40px

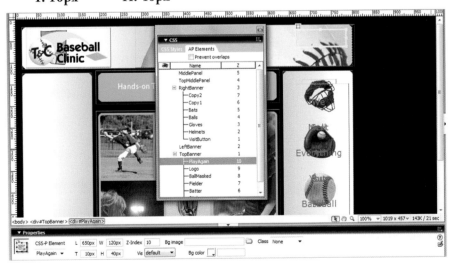

2. **Click inside the PlayAgain AP element to place the insertion point, and then choose Insert>Form>Image Field.**

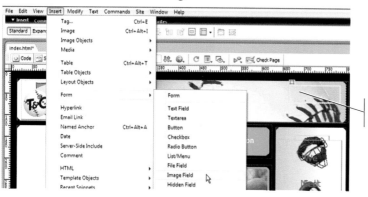

Note:

You can also click the Image Field button in the Forms Insert bar.

The insertion point should be inside this div.

3. **In the Select Image Source dialog box, select the file play_again.gif (in the site images folder) and click Choose/OK.**

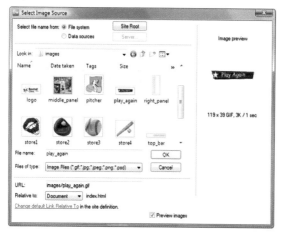

4. **In the Input Tag Accessibility Attributes dialog box, type "PlayTop" in the ID field. Select the No Label Tag style option and click OK.**

5. **When asked if you want to include the Form tag, click Yes.**

Whenever you place a form element without first creating a form object, Dreamweaver reminds you that the form tag is also required.

The red dotted line indicates the form tag that contains the form image field.

6. **Save the file and continue to the next stage of the project.**

Stage 2 Working with JavaScript

A script is a set of instructions that performs certain actions in response to an event (generally something the user does, such as clicking an object or typing certain information). JavaScript is one of the most widely used scripting languages because its simple syntax makes it easy to manage — even for non-programmers.

Here are a few examples of what you can do with JavaScript:

- Create rollover effects for images (as you did in Project 4)

- Validate form data before it is submitted to a server (as you did in Project 6 with the Spry validation widgets)

- Execute certain actions when a page finishes loading or when an HTML element is clicked (which you will do in this project)

- Feed dynamic text into an HTML page

- Detect the user's browser version and load a suitable page

- Store and retrieve information on the user's computer in the form of cookies

JavaScript scripts can be directly embedded into HTML pages using <script> tags. These scripts are interpreted by the Web browser to generate the desired result. You don't need to learn to write scripts to use JavaScript in your Web pages. Dreamweaver includes many built-in script snippets, and many free sources are available on the Internet. In some cases, such as animating behaviors, Dreamweaver adds the necessary code for you when you work entirely within the design window.

If a browser does not support JavaScript, the script displays as page content. To prevent this, the HTML comment tag can be added within the script:

```
<script type="text/javascript">
<!--
confirm("Would you like to continue?")
//-->
</script>
```

If you want to execute the same JavaScript on several Web pages, you can create the JavaScript in an external JavaScript file and save it with the .js extension. You can then attach the external file to an HTML page in the head section of the page code:

```
<script src="xyz.js"></script>
```

> **Note:**
>
> *JavaScript is not the same as Java (the programming language) despite the fact that both share some similar programming structures. JavaScript works in all the major browsers, and can be used without purchasing a license.*

> **Note:**
>
> *If the JavaScript is placed in the page head section, it will run only when an event associated with it is triggered. If the JavaScript is placed in the page body section, the script will execute while the page loads.*

DREAMWEAVER FOUNDATIONS

The Timelines panel (Window>Timelines) is used to create and control animation in Dreamweaver, either by changing object properties at specific points (keyframes) or by adding JavaScript behaviors that affect different objects.

A timeline consists of a series of frames; each frame represents a fraction of a second. You can define different object attributes (position, etc.) for each frame of a timeline which, when played in rapid sequence, creates the appearance of movement — animation.

The various elements of the Timelines panel are described below.

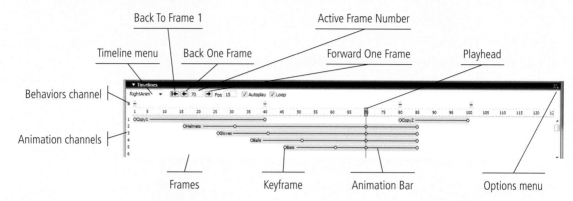

- **Timeline Menu.** This menu shows the different timelines that you have created (Timeline1, Timeline2, etc.). Dreamweaver allows you to create multiple animations; it is a good idea to create different animations on separate timelines rather than trying to manage multiple animations on a single timeline.

- **Playhead.** This indicates the current position in time that appears in the page layout.

- **Active Frame Number.** This field shows the number of the frame where the playhead is currently placed.

- **Back to Frame 1.** This button moves the playhead to the first frame in the timeline.

- **Back One Frame.** This button moves the playhead one frame to the left. (By clicking the Back button and holding down the mouse button, you can play the timeline backward.)

- **Forward One Frame.** This button moves the playhead one frame to the right. (By clicking the Play button and holding down the mouse button, you can play the timeline forward.)

- **FPS.** This field controls the number of frames that will play in one second. This setting controls the speed of the animation; the default fps of 15 is suitable for most types of Internet connections and browsers.

- **Autoplay.** This option enables the timeline to start playing automatically when the page loads in the browser.

- **Loop.** This option makes the timeline play continuously while the page is open in the browser.

- **Options menu.** Click this button to access a number of timeline features, including adding an object, behavior, or timeline, as well as removing or renaming a timeline.

- **Keyframe.** A keyframe, marked by a small circle, indicates the location where object properties change (new position, z-index value, etc.).

- **Behaviors channel.** This channel contains frames where JavaScript behaviors can be attached and activated. (Dreamweaver offers numerous kinds of behaviors that can be applied to objects on the timeline.)

- **Animation channel.** These channels contain animation bars for animating objects. (Each timeline contains 33 possible animation channels.)

- **Animation bar.** This area indicates the duration of a specific object's animation. A single animation channel can include multiple animation bars for different objects.

CREATE AN ANIMATION TIMELINE

Lightweight animation files can be produced in formats such as Shockwave for Internet viewing. Flash is another widely used digital animation tool. In addition, you can create some degree of animation directly within Dreamweaver.

The apparent speed of animation is determined by its **frame rate** (the number of frames that occupy one second of time). The optimum frame rate for Internet distribution is generally agreed to be 15 frames per second; lower frame rates cause the animation to appear slow or jerky.

The first step to creating animation in Dreamweaver is placing the objects you want to animate on a timeline. To complete this project, you need to create two different animations — one in the right banner that plays repeatedly, and one in the top banner that plays once and then displays a "Play Again" button. This means you need to create two separate timelines to contain the two different animations.

1. **With index.html open, open the Timelines panel (Window>Timelines).**

   In the Timelines panel, the default timeline is always Timeline1. (You can, however, create any number of timelines, depending on the requirements of your project.)

2. **In the AP Elements panel, click the TopBanner element.**

   Clicking an element in the panel selects the related element in the design window. Because you have so many different AP div elements, many overlapping in the same places, this is the easiest way to select the specific object you need.

The TopBanner element is selected.

All nested elements are also selected by default.

Note:

There is a difference between the term "frame" when referring to video and when referring to creating animation in Dreamweaver. In video terms, each frame is basically a separate image. But in Dreamweaver, a frame is a fraction of a second in which an object can have different properties from surrounding frames.

Note:

On Macintosh, the Timelines panel defaults to the middle of the screen. On Windows, the Timelines panel displays by default directly below the Properties Inspector.

3. **In the design window, click the square handle of the TopBanner element and drag the element to Frame 1 in Channel 1 of the Timelines panel.**

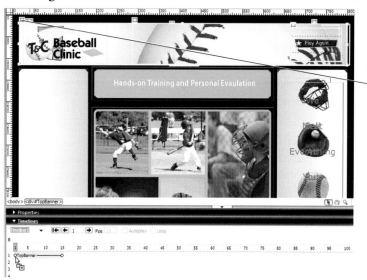

Drag the TopBanner handle to the timeline.

Note:

Because the TopBanner element contains all of the nested elements required in the animation, you don't need to drag each individual object onto the timeline.

4. **Click OK in the warning message.**

   When you create a timeline, Dreamweaver provides helpful tips about what you can accomplish.

When you release the mouse button, the object automatically occupies 15 frames (1 second at the default 15 frames per second) on the timeline.

5. **In the Timelines panel, click the keyframe handle on the right end of the TopBanner object and drag to Frame 75.**

   The overall animation will play over 5 seconds — or 75 frames at 15 frames per second. Dragging the right handle extends the object across the entire length of the animation.

Drag the animation bar's right keyframe to Frame 75.

Note:

By choosing Modify> Timeline, you can add or remove a frame and a timeline, as well as rename a timeline.

By selecting an animation sequence in the Animation bar, you can copy and paste the sequence into another area of the same timeline, into a different timeline of the same page, or into a timeline for a different page. You can also copy and paste multiple timelines at once. To select multiple sequences, hold down the Shift button.

6. **Click the timeline Name field and type "TopAnim".**

   It's always a good idea to use descriptive names for elements (including timelines) whenever possible. This will help prevent confusion later because you won't have to remember the difference between Timeline1 and Timeline2.

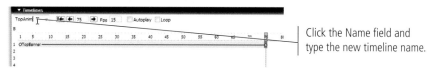

Click the Name field and type the new timeline name.

7. **Save the file and continue to the next exercise.**

ATTACH JAVASCRIPT BEHAVIORS TO THE TIMELINE

In the previous exercise, you created the timeline you will use to create the animation in the top banner area. In this exercise, you will attach JavaScript behaviors that will animate the different objects in the timelines.

1. **With index.html open and the Timelines panel visible, click Frame 1 in the B channel to select it.**

   The B (Behaviors) channel allows you to add animation effects to the objects in the timeline.

Note:

JavaScript behaviors can be used to add effects such as Show/Hide, Appear/ Fade, and Grow/Shrink.

2. **Choose Window>Behaviors to open the Behaviors panel.**

   The Behaviors panel provides a relatively easy way to attach complex JavaScript behaviors to objects, even if you know nothing about JavaScript code.

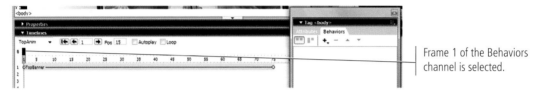

Frame 1 of the Behaviors channel is selected.

3. **Click the "+" button in the Behaviors panel to open the menu of behaviors.**

4. **Choose Show-Hide Elements from the menu.**

   Most available behaviors are controlled through dialog boxes, which open automatically when you choose an option in the Behaviors menu.

Click this button to add a behavior to the selected frame.

Note:

Some behaviors apply to only certain types of objects. If a menu object is grayed out, it cannot be attached to the selected object.

5. **In the Show-Hide Elements dialog box, click div "Batter" in the Elements list, and then click Hide.**

   Remember, Frame 1 of the TopAnim timeline is selected. The different objects in the banner need to appear sequentially over time, which means the first required behavior needs to hide all of the objects.

Note:

Unfortunately, you can't expand the dialog box to see the entire list of available elements. However, you can scroll through the list until you find the ones you need.

6. **Select div "Fielder" in the list and click Hide.**

   You can apply the same behavior to multiple elements within the Show-Hide Elements dialog box. You don't need to define different Show-Hide behaviors for each individual element.

7. **Repeat Step 6 to hide div "Pitcher", div "BallMasked", div "Logo", and div "PlayAgain".**

8. **Click OK to create the behavior.**

   The Behaviors panel shows that the behavior has been added to Frame 1 (onFrame1) of the active timeline.

   This column shows the event...   ...that initiates this action.

   Note:

   Double-clicking a behavior in the Behaviors panel opens the related dialog box so you can edit the properties of the behavior.

9. **Add additional Show-Hide behaviors to the timeline, using the following information. (Don't forget to select the correct frame in the Behaviors channel before adding the behavior.)**

   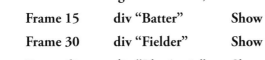

Frame 15	div "Batter"	Show
Frame 30	div "Fielder"	Show
Frame 60	div "PlayAgain"	Show

   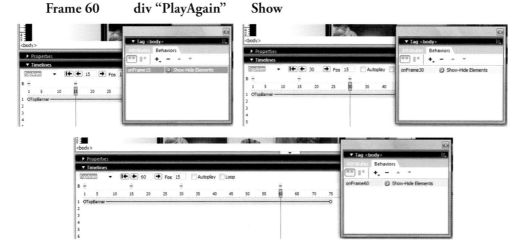

10. **In the Timelines panel, select Frame 2 in the B channel.**

11. **In the Behaviors panel, click the "+" button and choose Effects>Appear/Fade.**

The available effects can be used to add visual interest to the elements on the timeline.

Note:

It is not necessary to create behaviors in sequential order along the timeline. You can attach the behaviors to any selected frame on the timeline.

12. **In the Appear/Fade dialog box, choose div "Pitcher" in the Target Element menu. Review the options in the dialog box.**

By default, the effect will last 1 second (1000 milliseconds), fading out from 100% (fully visible) to 0% (hidden).

Note:

Choose Appear in the Effect menu to reverse the effect, causing an object to fade in (from 0% to 100%) instead of fading out. In this case, the Fade From and Fade To fields change to Appear From and Appear To.

13. **Change the Effect Duration to 1500 milliseconds and click OK.**

When the animation plays, the Pitcher object will appear and then fade out in 1.5 seconds. The Batter object will appear after 1 second and then begin to fade, so the visibility of the two objects will overlap slightly.

The Appear/Fade behavior is added to Frame 2 of the animation.

Note:

When the Fade effect is attached to an AP element, the element remains hidden throughout the timeline after fading out (unless you add a behavior to show it again).

14. **Apply the Fade effect two more times, using the following information:**

   Frame 16   Fade out div "Batter" in 1500 milliseconds

   Frame 31   Fade out div "Fielder" in 1500 milliseconds

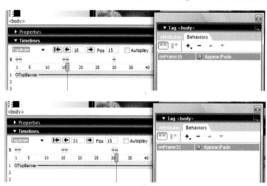

   Frame 40   Fade in div "BallMasked" over 1000 milliseconds

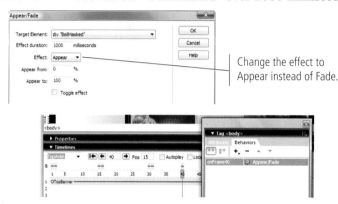

Change the effect to
Appear instead of Fade.

Note:

Because the BallMasked object is fading in, you didn't add a Show behavior to make this object visible before it fades in.

15. **Select Frame 45 in the B channel. Click the "+" button in the Behavior panel to open the Add Behavior menu, and choose Effects>Grow/Shrink.**

16. **In the Grow/Shrink dialog box, choose div "Logo" from the Target Element menu. Choose Grow in the Effect menu and leave the remaining options at their default values.**

17. **Click OK to add the Grow behavior.**

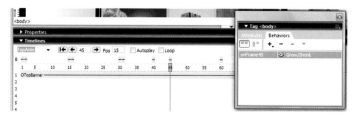

18. **In the Timelines panel, check the Autoplay box.**

    When this box is checked, the animation will play as soon as the page opens. Dreamweaver adds the necessary code to automatically run the animation, as you see in the warning message.

19. **Click OK in the warning message.**

20. **Save the HTML file. Click OK in the Copy Dependent Files message.**

    Dreamweaver behaviors rely on JavaScript functionality, which is stored in external files. When you save a page that includes behaviors, Dreamweaver copies the necessary files into your site folder.

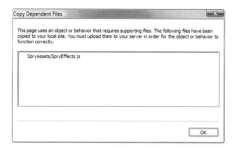

21. **Preview the page in your default browser to view the top banner animation.**

    If you use Internet Explorer, you might see a yellow bar at the top of the browser, warning you that some content has been blocked. If you see this warning, click the yellow bar and choose Allow Blocked Content so you can preview the animation.

22. **Return to Dreamweaver and continue to the next exercise.**

DREAMWEAVER FOUNDATIONS

The Behaviors panel provides access to ready-made JavaScript code snippets that you can use to add interactivity and dynamic functionality to Web pages. Even if you know nothing about JavaScript code, you can design a dynamic Web page using the behaviors included in Dreamweaver. Behaviors can be added to AP elements or to specific frames on a timeline. Following are brief descriptions of the behaviors available in Dreamweaver:

- **Call JavaScript.** This behavior helps you use a standard or custom JavaScript function in conjunction with an event.

- **Change Property.** This behavior enables you to alter the property of forms and form elements. In the Change Property dialog box, you can select the type of element, element ID, and property that you want to change. If a specific property is not available in the list, you can enter the property in the Enter and New Value fields.

- **Check Plugin.** This option enables you to query a user's browser to verify the availability of a required plugin. (It is important to enter the required plugin name exactly as it appears in bold, without including the version number.) Users without the required plugin can be diverted to alternative pages by specifying a URL. If the Always Go To The First URL option is enabled, users are directed to the initial page in case the plugin detection fails.

- **Drag AP Element.** This option makes your animation more interactive. It enables users to drag and drop AP elements anywhere on the screen. The Drag AP Element dialog box displays when this option is selected.

    - The **Basic tab** options enable you to select the AP element and movement from lists. You can specify coordinates of horizontal and vertical movements related to the drag-and-drop of an AP element.

    - The **Advanced tab** allows you to select whether an entire AP element or only part of it can be dragged. This tab also includes options related to JavaScript commands that can be used to control the drag-and-drop movements of an AP element.

- **Effects.** This option allows you to add effects to objects at different frames in an animation, such as Appear/Fade, Blind, Grow/Shrink, Highlight, Shake, Slide, and Squish. (You cannot add two effects on a single frame.)

- **Go To URL.** This option enables you to load multiple URLs into specific frames at the same time.

- **Jump Menu.** This option becomes active when you insert a jump menu on an HTML page. You can use this option to add or remove an element from the list, change the menu item names, and change the URLs associated with the menu items.

- **Jump Menu Go.** This option inserts an image or object link that can be used in cases when a link does not open the correct page. (For example, "If this page does not automatically load, click here…".)

- **Open Browser Window.** This allows you to set parameters for new windows, including window size, as well as visibility of the navigation toolbar, location toolbar, status bar, menu bar, scrollbars (as needed), and/or resize handles.

- **Popup Message.** This option creates a JavaScript alert box, where you can enter a message that displays when a user visits your Web page.

- **Preload Images.** This behavior enables you to upload files to the Preload Images list. Preload images display immediately in a Web browser, before the entire page downloads from the server.

- **Set Nav Bar Image.** This option turns an image into a navigation bar image.

    - In the **Basic tab**, you can specify images for different states. The Down Image displays when the user clicks the original image. The Over Image displays when the user's mouse cursor is over the original image. The Over While Down Image displays when the user clicks the original image and leaves the cursor over the original image area.

    - In the **Advanced tab**, you can change other images in the page (sometimes called a **disconnected rollover**) when users roll the mouse over an image.

- **Set Text.** You can use this behavior to change text in various areas of a page, using one of four options:

    - **Set Text of Container.** This options enables you to select and change the text in a specific container. The new content replaces the existing content.

    - **Set Text of Frame.** This option enables you to select a target frame, and change the text of the frame. This option replaces the content of the selected frame, but you can preserve the existing background color and text color of the frame.

    - **Set Text of Status Bar.** This option creates a message that displays in the bottom-left corner of the browser window. (Not all browsers allow this behavior by default. In Firefox, for example, users have to manually select a check box that is nested two levels into the browser's options.)

    - **Set Text of Text Field.** This option lets you select and change the content of a text field in a form.

368   Project 7: Animated Baseball Site

- **Show-Hide Elements.** This option enables you to show or hide specific elements on particular frames of an animation.

- **Swap Image.** The Swap Image dialog box includes a list of images. In the Set Source to Field menu, you can browse to locate the image you want to use in your animation. You can also swap one image for another when the mouse hovers over the first image.

- **Swap Image Restore.** This behavior is automatically added to an image when you add the Swap Image behavior. This option restores a swapped image to the original image.

- **Timeline.** This behavior has three options:
  - **Go To Timeline Frame.** In this dialog box, you can choose a specific frame number, and specify the number of loops for the timeline.
  - **Play Timeline.** This option includes a list of timelines in your file. You can select another timeline

to play when the playhead reaches a particular frame of the primary timeline.
  - **Stop Timeline.** This behavior stops an animation at a certain frame.

- **Validate Form.** This behavior ensures the user entered the correct type of data in a text field. (The behavior displays an alert box if the user doesn't enter the specified data in the field.) The Validate Form dialog box includes the following options:
  - The **Anything option** option allows any type of data to be entered in the field.
  - The **Use E-mail address** option allows the user to enter only email addresses in the field (by checking whether the entry contains the "@" symbol).
  - The **Use Number** option allows the user to enter only numerals in the field.
  - The **Use Numbers From-To** option allows the user to enter numerals in a specified range.

ATTACH AN INTERACTIVE BEHAVIOR TO A FORM OBJECT

Behaviors are not limited to timeline frames. You can also attach behaviors to specific objects (such as images) to control various aspects of an animation. In this case, you are going to add button control to the Play Again image so users can replay the top banner animation.

When you added the Play Again image, you created it as an image form field. The form container is necessary for any element that will accept user interaction — such as clicking a button to play a specific animation.

1. **With index.html open, deselect everything on the page and then click the Play Again image to select it.**

2. **In the Behaviors panel, click the "+" button and choose Timeline>Play Timeline from the menu of behaviors.**

3. **In the Play Timeline dialog box, make sure the TopAnim timeline is selected in the menu, and then click OK.**

The Play Timeline behavior is initiated by clicking the button (onClick).

4. **Save the file and preview the page in your default browser.**

5. **When the animation stops, click the Play Again button to test its functionality.**

6. **Return to Dreamweaver, and then continue to the next exercise.**

 ## CREATE A TIMELINE FOR MOTION ANIMATION

The next task is to animate the right banner. The following is a preliminary plan for that animation:

- The Copy1 div appears.

- After about half a second, the four product image divs move into position in the center of the RightBanner div.

- Each product starts moving at a different time, creating a staggered effect.

- All four product images move back to their original positions outside the RightBanner div boundaries.

- The Copy1 div disappears after the four product images start moving back to their starting points.

- The Copy2 div appears slightly before the product images are out of the RightBanner div boundary.

This second animation requires different techniques than those used to create the top banner. For this animation, you are going to use keyframes to change the properties (in this case, the position) of different objects at different points in time.

Although all of the right banner AP objects are nested within the RightBanner AP div, you need to add the individual objects to the timeline so you can change the properties of those objects throughout the animation.

1. **With index.html open, open the Timelines panel options menu and choose Add Timeline.**

A timeline with the name Timeline1 displays in the Timelines panel. When the new Timeline1 displays, you cannot see the TopAnim timeline and its animation objects.

Note:

Instead of using only one timeline to control all the parts of an HTML page, it's better to work with separate timelines, each of which controls a different part of the page. In this case, because the second animation will play continuously, you must create the animation on a separate timeline.

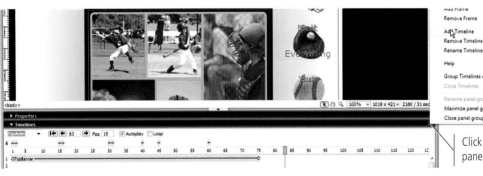

Click here to open the panel options menu.

2. Change the name of the new timeline to "RightAnim".

3. In the CSS Styles panel, click #Helmets to select it. In the Properties area, change the Left value to –100 pixels.

When you create an motion animation, the div objects that move need to be in their starting positions before you add them to the timeline.

The Helmets div moves to the left, outside the boundaries of the containing RightBanner div. The Helmets div should be invisible until it enters the boundaries of the containing div. To accomplish this effect, you use the overflow property of the containing div.

The Helmets div is now positioned at –100 pixels from the left edge of the RightBanner div.

Note:

Remember, the element selected in the AP Elements panel is what is selected in the design window.

The rule selected in the CSS Styles panel is not necessarily related to the element selected in the design window.

This can be easy to forget, and you might change properties for the wrong selector.

4. In the AP Elements panel, click RightBanner to select that element in the design window.

5. With the RightBanner element selected, choose Hidden in the Overflow menu of the Properties Inspector.

The Overflow setting determines what happens to content outside the div boundaries. By choosing Hidden, the content — including nested div elements — only appears when it is within the RightBanner area.

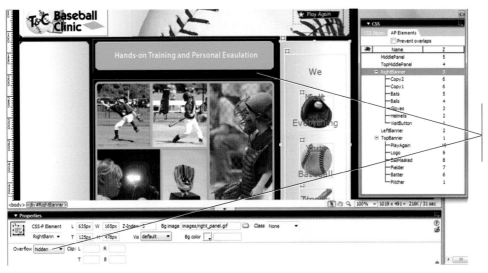

By hiding the overflow, the Helmets div is no longer visible at its current position (–100 pixels).

6. **In the CSS Styles panel, click the #Gloves selector. Change the Left property value to 175 pixels.**

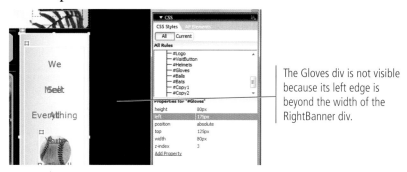

The Gloves div is not visible because its left edge is beyond the width of the RightBanner div.

7. **In the CSS Styles panel, click the #Balls selector. Change the Left property value to –100 pixels.**

8. **In the CSS Styles panel, click the #Bats selector. Change the Left property value to 175 pixels.**

All four images are now outside the div area, so they are effectively hidden. When you place the image divs on the timeline, they will assume the positions you set in Steps 5–8 (the default positions).

9. **In the AP Elements panel, click the Copy1 element to select it in the layout.**

Because the Copy1 and Copy2 divs are in exactly the same place in the page and both divs are visible, using the AP Elements panel is the only way to select the lower div in the object stack.

10. **Drag the element handle to Frame 1, Channel 1 in the RightAnim timeline. Click OK in resulting message.**

11. In the Timelines panel, drag the right keyframe of the Copy1 animation bar to Frame 40 (approximately 2.5 seconds at 15 fps).

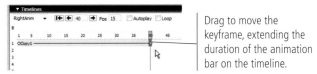

Drag to move the keyframe, extending the duration of the animation bar on the timeline.

12. Repeat Steps 9–11 to add the different right banner objects to the RightAnim timeline, using the following information:

Object	Location	Extend Right End of Animation Bar To
Helmets	Frame 16, Channel 2	85
Gloves	Frame 26, Channel 3	85
Balls	Frame 36, Channel 4	85
Bats	Frame 46, Channel 5	85
Copy2	Frame 80, Channel 1	100

The four product divs are not visible in the layout, and the Copy2 div is in the same position as the Copy1 div, so it is necessary to use the AP Elements panel to select each of these objects before you can drag them to the timeline.

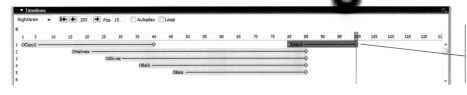

Because Copy1 and Copy2 will be animated with behaviors, you can place them on the same animation channel.

13. Save the file and continue to the next exercise.

ANIMATE TIMELINE OBJECT PROPERTIES

Your timeline now has six objects in five channels. The four object divs will be animated based on object properties, which is why each requires a separate channel on the timeline. The two copy divs will be animated with JavaScript behaviors (showing and hiding them at different points in the timeline), so they can be placed on the same channel.

1. With index.html open, make sure nothing is selected on the page and then select Frame 1 in the B channel of the timeline.

2. Using the Behaviors panel, add the Show/Hide behavior to hide the Copy2 div and show the Copy1 div.

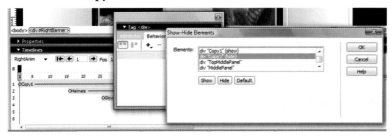

3. **Select Frame 40 of the B channel and add a Show/Hide behavior that hides the Copy1 div.**

Frame 40 is selected in the Behaviors channel.

4. **Select Frame 80 of the B channel and add a Show/Hide behavior that shows the Copy2 div.**

Frame 80 is selected in the Behaviors channel.

5. **In the AP Elements panel, click the Helmets element to select it in the page.**

6. **In Channel 2 of the timeline, click the keyframe at the left end of the Helmets animation bar.**

The Properties Inspector shows that this object is placed at X= –100. This is the same position you defined for the #Helmets AP div.

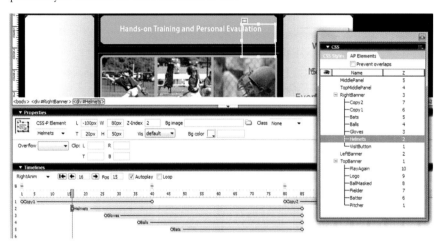

7. **Click the keyframe at the right end of the Helmets animation bar.**

By default, objects added to the timeline have keyframes at both ends of the animation bar. The object's properties default to the same values for each keyframe, so nothing is animated…yet.

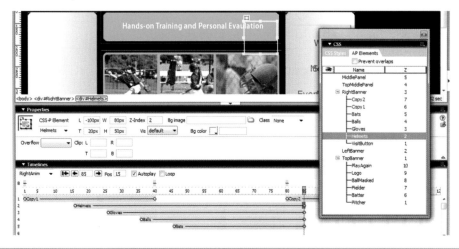

8. **Click Frame 31 in Channel 2 to select that frame of the Helmet animation bar.**

9. **Control/right-click the selected frame and choose Add Keyframe from the contextual menu.**

   As we mentioned earlier, a keyframe marks the place when something changes. In this case, you are defining the position on the timeline when the Helmets div will be located in the center of the RightAnim div.

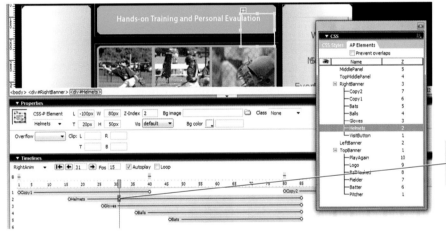

The new keyframe is indicated by the hollow circle.

10. **Control/right-click the new keyframe (at Frame 31) and choose Change Object from the contextual menu.**

    Remember, the position of an AP element is defined by the position values in the related selector. The Change Object command allows you to dynamically change the properties (position, etc.) of an object at a specific location on the timeline.

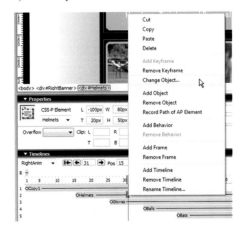

11. **In the Change Object dialog box, make sure Helmets is selected in the Object to Animate menu, and then click OK.**

In the design window, only the Helmets div should be selected.

12. **In the Properties Inspector, change the Left field to "45px".**

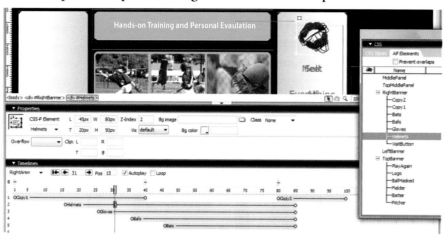

13. **In the Timelines panel, drag the playhead left to Frame 16.**

As you move the playhead, you can see the left position of the Helmets div move from 45 pixels to –100 pixels, which is defined for the Frame 16 keyframe.

When you change position properties of an object on the timeline, Dreamweaver automatically moves the object as necessary in the in-between frames so the movement appears as a smooth transition, instead of simply jumping from one position to the next.

As you drag the playhead to the left…

…the Helmets div moves from right (L:45px) to left (L:–100px).

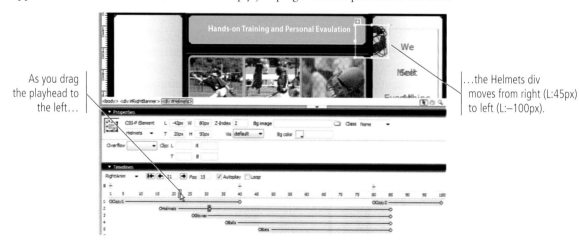

14. **Drag the playhead from Frame 16 to Frame 85.**

Based on the existing keyframes, the Helmets div moves from –100px at the beginning to 45px at Frame 31, and then slowly back to –100px at Frame 85 (the last keyframe).

Ultimately, all four of the product images should move out of the sidebar div at the same time, which means you need to define the starting point at which the second movement begins. This requires another keyframe.

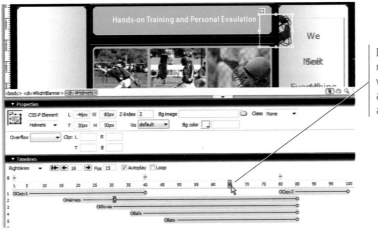

Dragging the playhead right, the object moves very slowly from L:45px at Frame 36 to L:–100px at Frame 85.

15. **Control/right-click Frame 70 in Channel 2 of the timeline (where the Helmets animation bar exists) and choose Add Keyframe from the contextual menu.**

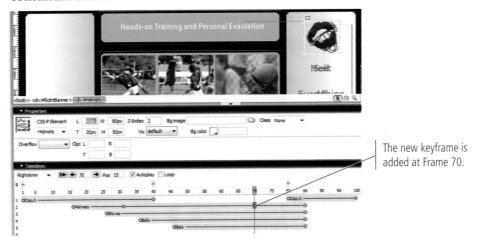

The new keyframe is added at Frame 70.

16. **Control/right-click the new keyframe at Frame 70 and choose Change Object.**

17. **Make sure Helmets is selected in the Object to Animate menu, and then click OK.**

In the design window, make sure only the Helmets div is selected. If any other element is selected, click away from everything to deselect all objects, and then click Helmets in the AP Elements panel to select only that div.

18. **Make sure only the Helmets div is selected in the page. In the Properties Inspector, change the Left field to 45px.**

This setting defines the object's position at Frame 70, which prevents the div from moving between Frames 31 and 70. Now when you drag the playhead across the timeline, the Helmet div will begin outside the sidebar container (Frame 16), move to the center (Frame 31), stay in place for a short time (Frame 70), and then move back outside the sidebar container (Frame 85).

19. **Using the same basic process, add motion to the three remaining product image divs, using the following information:**

Gloves	**Add keyframe at Frame 41 and change the Left position to 45px**
	Add keyframe at Frame 70 and change the Left position to 45px
Balls	**Add keyframe at Frame 51 and change the Left position to 45px**
	Add keyframe at Frame 70 and change the Left position to 45px
Bats	**Add keyframe at Frame 61 and change the Left position to 45px**
	Add keyframe at Frame 70 and change the Left position to 45px

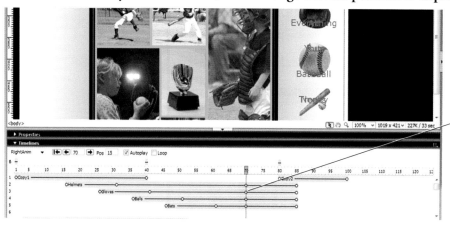

All four products will remain in place (L:45px) until Frame 70, when they all begin moving back to their original positions.

20. **In the Timelines panel, check the Autoplay box and click OK in the warning message.**

As with the previous animation, the necessary action is added to the page code so the animation will play as soon as the page loads.

21. **Check the Loop option in the Timeline, and then click OK in the resulting warning message.**

Looping allows the animation to play again as soon as all 100 frames of the timeline have displayed. At 15 fps, the entire animation will start over every 6.6 seconds.

To loop an animation, the timeline has to return to Frame 1 when it reaches the end of the animation. Checking the Loop box adds the necessary action code (Go To Timeline Frame), as you see in the warning message.

Note:

You can control the number of loops for a timeline. When you select the Loop option, the action is attached to the last animation frame in the B channel. By selecting that frame and double-clicking the Go to Timeline Frame behavior, the Go to Timeline Frame opens, where you can specify how many times the loop should repeat.

The Autoplay and Loop options should both be checked.

22. **Save the file, and then preview the page in a browser to see the animation.**

23. **Return to Dreamweaver and continue to the next exercise.**

 CREATE A SPRY MENU BAR

The Spry Menu Bar widget can be used to create a navigation bar with up to three levels of links. Second- and third-level links display as fly-out or drop-down menus (for vertical or horizontal menus, respectively).

These types of menus are useful for arranging pages into meaningful categories, as well as for saving space on the page. Users benefit by having direct access to information at deeper levels, instead of having to first navigate to section home pages.

When you insert a Spry menu bar into an HTML page, the required Spry JavaScript and CSS files are included automatically in the Web site's root folder when you save the page.

Note:

The Spry Menu Bar widget replaces the Pop-up Menu behavior of earlier versions of Dreamweaver.

1. **With index.html open, click inside the LeftBanner div to place the insertion point.**

2. **Choose Insert>Spry>Spry Menu Bar.**

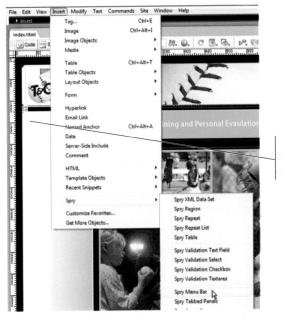

The insertion point should be in the LeftBanner div.

3. **In the Spry Menu Bar dialog box, select the Vertical option and click OK.**

A vertical Spry menu bar is inserted within the LeftBanner div.

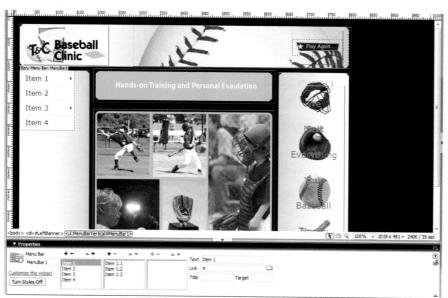

Note:

Clicking the title bar selects the entire widget, so you can modify the menu bar contents and properties in the Properties Inspector.

4. **In the Properties Inspector, select Item 4 in the first menu list and click the "+" button twice.**

The navigation bar you are creating needs to have six links; the default menu bar contains only four links. By performing this step, two new items are added to the first level of the menu bar (both in the Properties Inspector and in the page layout).

Note:

Click the Turn Off Styles link in the Properties Inspector to view the Spry menu bar as a bulleted list without the applied CSS rules.

Note:

To modify the list items in a Spry menu bar, you have to select the actual menu bar widget. If the widget is not selected, click the blue title bar of the widget to select it.

Click these buttons to add or remove menu items.

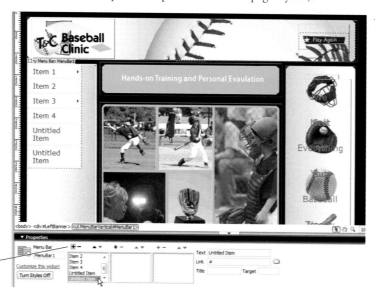

5. **In the Properties Inspector, click Item 1 in the first-level list of menu items and then click any of the items in the second-level list.**

By default, Dreamweaver includes secondary list items for Item 1 and Item 3. However, the Item 1 link for this page (which will be the "Home" link) does not require submenus.

When an item is selected in the second-level list (in the Properties Inspector) the secondary menu is visible in the page.

Click Item 1 to select it…

…then click any of the second-level items to show the secondary menu in the design window.

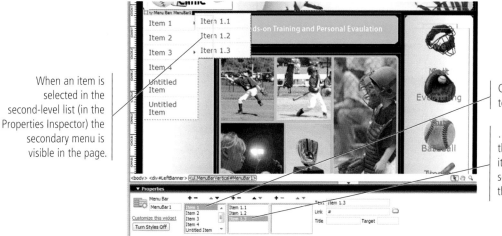

6. **In the second-level menu item list, select Item 1.3, and then click the "–" button above the second-level list to remove the submenu item from the list.**

Removing a menu item in the Properties Inspector removes the related item in the page.

7. **Repeat Step 6 to remove the two remaining second-level items from the Item 1 first-level link.**

After removing the secondary menu items, the arrow indicator is no longer included.

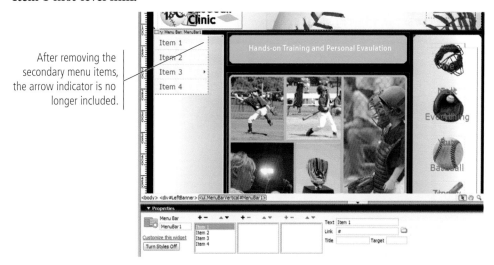

8. **In the first-level list, select Item 2.**

9. **Above the second-level list, click the "+" button three times to add three secondary menu items.**

10. **Select the first Untitled Item in the second-level list and type "Spring" in the Text field.**

    The Text field provides an easy way to change the words that appear in nested submenus. For first-level menu items, you have to change the text in the design window.

Note:

To add a third-level submenu, you have to select the appropriate second-level item and click the + button above the third-level list.

11. **Select the second item in the second-level list and change the item text to "Summer".**

12. **Select the third item in the second-level list and change the item text to "Fall".**

13. Repeat the same basic process to define second-level menu items for the remaining first-level menu items, using the following information.

First-Level Menu Item	(Will Become)	Second-Level Menu Items
Item 3	Instructors link	Coach Jones Coach Ortiz Coach Baker
Item 4	Registration link	None
Untitled Item (first)	Gallery link	None
Untitled Item (second)	Testimonials link	None

14. **Select Item 3 in the first-level list, and select Coach Jones in the second-level list. Delete all the third-level submenu items.**

    By default, Dreamweaver includes third-level menu items for Item 3.

15. **Save the file. Click OK in the Copy Dependent Files message that appears.**

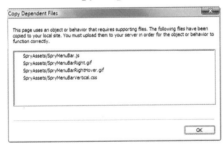

16. **Continue to the next exercise.**

REPLACE MENU TEXT WITH ROLLOVER IMAGES

The first-level menu items for this site need to display as rollover images rather than text links. The process you use here is basically the same as defining any other rollover image. You should, however, be aware of potential issues that can result from placing images into a Spry menu bar; you will discover those issues as you complete this exercise.

1. **With index.html open, select the text "Item 1" in the page layout and delete it.**

   This menu bar will use rollover images instead of text as the first-level links.

2. **With the insertion point in the space where you deleted the Item 1 text, choose Insert>Image Objects>Rollover Image.**

3. **In the Insert Rollover Image dialog box, define the following settings, and then click OK:**

Image Name:	home
Original Image:	images/menu/home.jpg
Rollover Image:	images/menu/home_over.jpg
Preload Rollover Image:	checked
Alternate Text:	Home link
When Clicked, Go To URL:	#

   After clicking OK, the rollover image for the Home link is inserted. (To see the image rollover effect, you need to preview the page in a browser.)

   The file defined in the Original Image field appears in place of the deleted Item 1 text.

4. **In the page layout, click the menu bar widget title bar to select the widget and display its properties.**

5. Click the empty space at the top of the first-level list.

When you replace a menu item with an image (static or rollover), that item appears blank in the Properties Inspector. The item is still there, but no text appears in the list of menu items.

Once you replace all six first-level links with images, the entire first-level list will appear blank — which can make it difficult to manage. That's why you defined the submenus *before* replacing the first-level text with images.

6. Repeat Steps 1–3 for the remaining menu items, using the following information.

Copy to Replace	Image Name	Original Image	Rollover Image	Alternate Text	When Clicked, Go to URL
Item 2	schedule	images/menu/ schedule.jpg	images/menu/ schedule_over.jpg	Schedule link	#
Item 3	instructors	images/menu/ instructors.jpg	images/menu/ instructors_over.jpg	Instructors link	#
Item 4	registration	images/menu/ registration.jpg	images/menu/ registration_over.jpg	Registration link	#
Untitled Item (first)	gallery	images/menu/ gallery.jpg	images/menu/ gallery_over.jpg	Gallery link	#
Untitled Item (second)	testimonials	images/menu/ testimonials.jpg	images/menu/ testimonials_over.jpg	Testimonials link	#

7. Save the file, and then preview the page in your default browser.

You can now see the rollover images for each first-level menu item, as well as the second-level submenus for the Schedule and Instructors links. The second-level menus, however, appear behind the photo collage (which is in the MiddlePanel div).

8. Return to Dreamweaver and review the AP Elements panel.

The LeftBanner div has a z-index of 2. The MiddlePanel div has a z-index of 5. When the page is viewed in a browser, objects with higher z-index values appear above other objects on the page. This is why the secondary menus (contained in the LeftBanner div) appear below the photo collage in the MiddlePanel div.

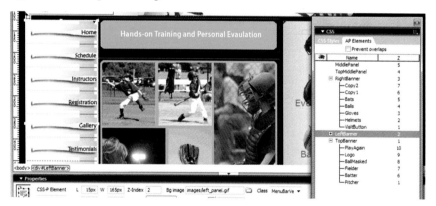

9. Click the LeftBanner div in the AP Elements panel to select that element.

10. In the Properties Inspector, change the Z-Index field to 20.

Changing the z-index to a number higher than all other elements means the LeftBanner element will be higher than the other elements in the stacking order.

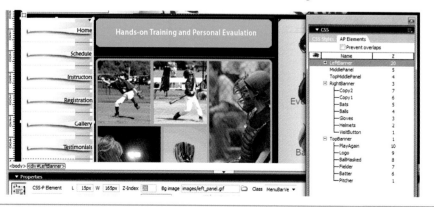

Note:

You can also simply change the z-index value in the AP Elements panel. On Macintosh, however, the Z column is not visible (a bug in the interface), so it is easier to use the Properties Inspector.

11. **Save the file and preview it in your default browser.**

The secondary menus now appear above the photo collage.

12. **Return to Dreamweaver, and then continue to the next exercise.**

FORMAT A SPRY MENU BAR WITH CSS

The Spry Menu Bar widget has a simple format by default, defined in a CSS style sheet that is automatically copied into your site folder when you save the page. To change the appearance of your Spry menu bar, you can simply edit the CSS selectors that are applied to different parts of the menu.

1. **With index.html open, display the CSS Styles panel. Expand the SpryMenuBarVertical.css list.**

When you insert a Spry menu bar into an HTML page, the required Spry JavaScript and CSS files are included automatically in your site folder when you save the page.

You can modify the appearance of the menu bar by editing the selectors that are available in the attached SpryMenuBarVertical.css file, but whenever you work with style sheets and selectors that you did not create, you should review the selectors and their properties before making any changes.

Keep in mind the following tags when you review the different selectors:

ul = unordered list   li = list item   a = link

Also, the a:hover pseudo-class controls the rollover behavior of link objects.

2. **In the CSS Styles panel, click the first ul.MenuBarVertical selector. Review the defined properties.**

For various reasons, multiple selectors with the same name might exist in the default style sheets. This particular selector has a number of different properties, as shown below.

Note:

Internet Explorer requires a couple of exclusive styles to modify the appearance of the links. The last two styles (respectively) implement the background and font colors of the links, and enforce the background color style of the second-level menu container.

3. **Click the second ul.MenuBarVertical selector. Review the defined properties.**

This selector defines only border attributes. Your menu should not have defined borders, so you can safely delete this selector. (If you wanted to add borders to the entire menu item, you could simply define border attributes for the remaining selector.)

4. **With the second ul.MenuBarVertical selector highlighted in the CSS Styles panel, click the panel Delete button.**

5. **Delete the second instance of the ul.MenuBarVertical ul selector.**

Like the ul.MenuBarVertical duplicate selectors, the second ul.MenuBarVertical ul selector defines only border attributes.

6. **Use the CSS Styles panel to modify the remaining selectors as follows.**

Selector	Category (in the CSS Rule Definition dialog box)	Property Settings to Change
ul.MenuBarVertical a	Type	Font: Verdana, Arial, Helvetica, sans-serif Size: 10 pixels Line Height: 20 pixels Color: #3BB44A
	Background	Background Color: #CCCCCC
	Box	Top Padding: 0 px Right Padding: 0 px Bottom Padding: 0 px Left Padding: 3 px
ul.MenuBarVertical a.MenuBarItemHover ul.MenuBarVertical a.MenuBarItemSubmenuHover ul.MenuBarVertical a.MenuBarSubmenuVisible	Type	Color: #FFFFFF
	Background	Background Color: #3BB44A

Note:

The first style modifies the attributes of the default menu and submenu items.

The second style modifies the rollover attributes of the menu and submenu items.

7. Save the file and preview it in your default browser.

8. Return to Dreamweaver, and then close all open files.

In addition to the Spry menu bar that you created in this project, Dreamweaver offers several other options for easily building common layout objects such as navigation bars and tabbed panels.

Image-Based Navigation Bars

The Spry menu bar that you already created uses JavaScript and CSS to create multi-level navigational structure. This option is primarily intended for text-based navigation links, although — as you saw — you can replace the link text with images.

The Insert>Image Objects>Navigation Bar command is another option for creating a navigation bar. This option creates a single-level, image-based menu with different rollover images for four different states of each navigation link. The entire navigation bar is created through a dialog-box interface, where you define the properties of different image links (including the alternate-state images).

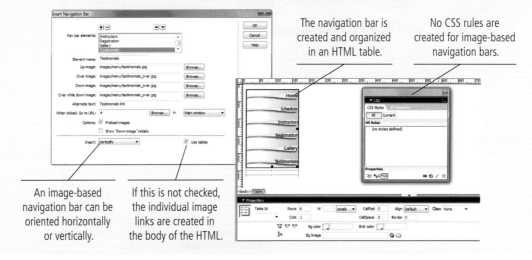

The navigation bar is created and organized in an HTML table.

No CSS rules are created for image-based navigation bars.

An image-based navigation bar can be oriented horizontally or vertically.

If this is not checked, the individual image links are created in the body of the HTML.

DREAMWEAVER FOUNDATIONS

Spry Tabbed Panels

Tabbed panels (Insert>Layout Objects>Spry Tabbed Panels) allow you to show a number of navigational tabs and a single content area that changes based on which tab is active.

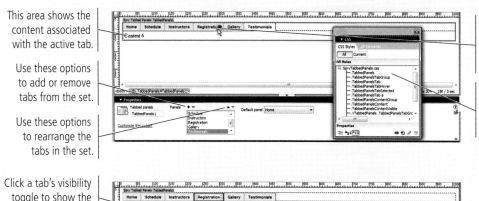

This area shows the content associated with the active tab.

Use these options to add or remove tabs from the set.

Use these options to rearrange the tabs in the set.

Roll your mouse over the right end of a tab to access the tab's visibility toggle.

The appearance of Spry tabbed panels is controlled by CSS selectors.

Click a tab's visibility toggle to show the associated content.

Spry Accordions

Like tabbed panels, accordions (Insert>Layout Objects>Spry Accordion) are another option for managing content for different categories in a single HTML page. In this case, the content panel appears directly below the active panel (unlike tabbed panels, in which a the content area remains static regardless of which tab is active).

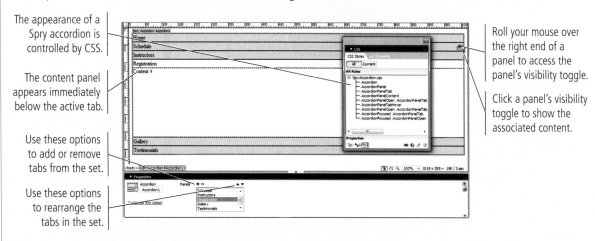

The appearance of a Spry accordion is controlled by CSS.

The content panel appears immediately below the active tab.

Use these options to add or remove tabs from the set.

Use these options to rearrange the tabs in the set.

Roll your mouse over the right end of a panel to access the panel's visibility toggle.

Click a panel's visibility toggle to show the associated content.

Spry Collapsible Panels

A collapsible panel (Insert>Layout Objects>Spry Collapsible Panel) is used to contain content that will only be visible when the tab is expanded.

When visible, the content panel appears immediately below the tab.

The appearance of a Spry collapsible panel is controlled by CSS.

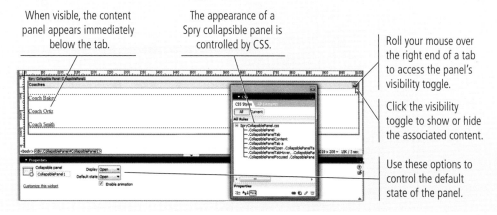

Roll your mouse over the right end of a tab to access the panel's visibility toggle.

Click the visibility toggle to show or hide the associated content.

Use these options to control the default state of the panel.

Summary

In this project, you learned how to use dynamic HTML and JavaScript to create animation on Web pages, which makes the pages more interesting for site users. Dreamweaver provides JavaScript snippets in the form of behaviors. These make it very easy to use JavaScript because they provide a panel-based interface to customize the snippets — even if you know nothing about JavaScript code.

In addition to the built-in options for creating JavaScript animation, Dreamweaver also includes easy-to-use tools to create multi-level, JavaScript-based page navigation. Combining these layout elements with CSS to format the different navigation elements, you can create sophisticated interactive Web pages with no existing knowledge of complex programming and very little effort.

Create AP div elements to structure the overall page layout

Use JavaScript behaviors to animate the visibility of different layout objects

Create an interactive form button to control an animated banner

Created nested AP div elements for easier layout management

Create a timeline animation to move different objects into place over a period of time

Create a multi-level JavaScript navigation bar using the built-in Spry widget

Adjust z-index to control the layering of different layout objects

Portfolio Builder Project 7

The City Zoo wants to bring its Website up to date with a more interesting, interactive design throughout the site but especially on the home page. They have asked you to build an entire new site layout, but want to first see your ideas for improving the home page.

To complete this project you should:

❏ Use AP divs to create the different areas of the page.

❏ Include the client's provided logo (in the RF_Builders>Zoo folder) prominently on the site.

❏ Use other client-provided images as necessary, or create or find other images to use as you develop the new home page.

"Our site will have five basic pages: Home, Animals Gallery, Animal Facts, About Us, and How You Can Help (links to vetted, animal-related charities around the world).

"The Animals section of our site divided into three rough categories: Earth, Sea, and Sky. The Earth group should be divided into separate pages for each continent. In the Sea group, we'll end up with fish and mammals. For the Sky, we don't know quite yet but we'll probably just leave that at the basic section page.

"Our primary concern right now is the home page, which we want to be far more interesting than it is now. We're open to anything. Just start from scratch and show us some completely new ideas that include animation.

"We sent you our logo file and some photos from our archives. The logo, of course, is a requirement on every page. We sent the photos just so you had some resources available. You can use any, all, or none of them — whatever you think works best.

"We also sent a couple of paw-print images, which we really like. We want to see these incorporated somehow into the site, but we'll leave the details in your hands."

Just Posters Dynamic Catalog

Just Posters, Inc. produces posters for professional office environments. It has a nationwide niche market, and it is backed by a strong distribution network. The company does not yet want to bypass its distribution network with a direct online store, but the owner does want an online presence to inform distributors about the company's products.

As the first part of that online presence, the company wants a site that showcases its latest poster collection. To make maintenance easy, the company wants you to build a database-driven site that can be maintained by anyone, without having to learn database technology.

This project incorporates the following skills:

❑ Setting up a MySQL database, importing a client's data, and connecting to the database from Dreamweaver

❑ Defining a Dreamweaver site for server-side processing

❑ Adding dynamic text and image placeholders in a PHP page and using binding to dynamically define alt text

❑ Repeating and limiting recordset display on a specific page

❑ Adding recordset navigation to the gallery

❑ Creating a dynamic page link using a URL parameter filter

❑ Using a filter to display data based on dynamic, user-defined form field values

❑ Showing and hiding page regions based on recordset contents

❑ Synchronizing the local and remote site files

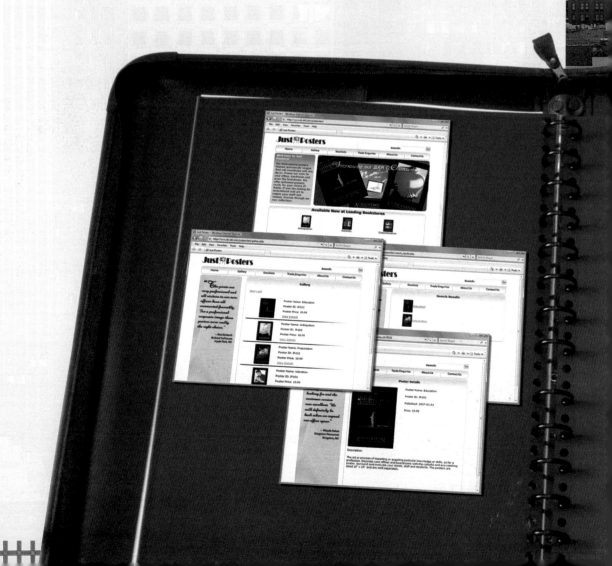

The Project Meeting

Client Comments

I started this company as a one-man thing in my garage, and it has grown over five years into a national supplier of quality artwork for office and business environments. We've got a strong network of national distributors for the business and office markets, and we're now considering the possibility of moving into the general retail markets as well.

Because everything has been fairly contained until now, we've always used print catalogs for product marketing. But if we move into retail, we need a Web presence that will show what we offer and, eventually, process online orders.

Until we move beyond our distributor supply chain, we want to maintain personal contact with buyers so we aren't going to offer online ordering yet. For now, we just want a Web site that can let users review the different posters that are available.

I exported our poster database, with all the information we need to display on the site. The file is in SQL format, and it follows the standards we got from your IT director so hopefully there won't be any problems.

Art Director Comments

I've had one of the designers build the pages for the site. The site is template- and CSS-based, so overall changes can be made easily as we move forward. When the designer built the different site pages, she defined areas that will hold the different items; you'll see the placeholders in the pages when you open them.

I need you, as our resident Web programmer, to take the prepared pages and build in the dynamic catalog functionality. Unfortunately, we're in the middle of upgrading our own server network. We won't have everything up and running for another week or so, so you'll have to use a remote server while you develop the dynamic elements.

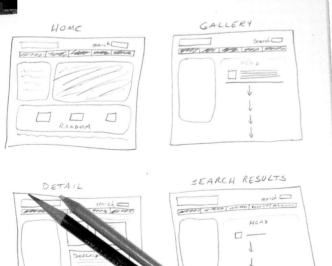

Project Objectives

To complete this project, you will:

- Set up a MySQL database and import the client's data
- Create the site definition for server-side processing
- Add data placeholders in a PHP page
- Use a binding to dynamically define alt text
- Repeat a recordset
- Add recordset navigation to the gallery
- Create a dynamic page link
- Create the poster details
- Troubleshoot dynamic pages for testing
- Add a search feature
- Show and hide regions based on recordset contents
- Display records with advanced filter criteria
- Synchronize the local and remote sites

Stage 1   Preparing to Use PHP and MySQL

So far, you have worked with Dreamweaver to create Web pages that contain the same code on the server where they reside as in the browser when they display to the viewer. The HTML code you view in Dreamweaver's code window is the same as what you can see in the source of the page. (Web sites that use unchanging code are called **static sites**.) You have learned how to use Dreamweaver's JavaScript tools to overcome some of the limitations of static HTML. For a site to be truly dynamic, however, it must display only the content a user wants see (rather than leaving the user to sort through all available content).

In addition to enabling user customization, dynamically displaying content also reduces the amount of maintenance required. It's much faster and easier to update pages, content and links with new information — as well as remove pages and links for items that no longer exist — when you use dynamic content rather than static.

Aside from the inconvenience of managing a large number of pages, they also require a lot of space on the Web server. Web hosting companies — especially free ones — provide limited storage space (unless you are willing to pay dearly for additional storage capacity). By creating a single page with a coding language that interacts directly with databases, you can program the page to display the details of any item in that single page.

Note:

Entire books have been written about building dynamic Web sites with server-side programming. We created this project to give you an idea of what you can do with Dreamweaver to build dynamic pages. However, we encourage you to read an advanced book on this subject if you want to continue your education beyond this project.

Databases

Databases provide an efficient framework for storing data in a predefined structure; this structure automatically forces you to organize content in a standard format. Many database platforms are available today. MySQL, Microsoft Access, and Oracle are among the most familiar database platforms. Each database platform has its own set of procedures for retrieving and displaying records from the database on a Web page. Each one also stores information slightly differently. MySQL is the most popular database platform because it is stable and is free of charge. It works on a relational database model, which designates the actual entries (records) as rows and the pieces of information for each entry (fields) as columns in a table.

Poster ID	Name	Price	Image Path	Alt Text
JP101	Education	19.99	posters/education1.jpg	Image for Education
JP102	Anticipation	19.99	posters/anticipation1.jpg	Image for Anticipation
JP103	Preparation	19.99	posters/preparation1.jpg	Image for Preparation

Database table   Fields for each record   Individual records

Server-Side Technologies

Browsers use HTML code to display the contents of a Web page; the HTML code is sent as-is to the browser. When you view the source code of an HTML page, the code you see is the code used to create the page. This leaves little flexibility for dynamic content.

A **server-side language** differs from HTML because the server-side code does not display in the page that appears in the browser. A server-side language such as PHP generates a Web page according to the arguments contained within the PHP code. To display a record from a database, for example, the code does not contain any actual record details. Instead, the code contains a reference, which is used to fetch a matching record from the database. Server-side technologies are not substitutes for HTML, but rather complement HTML. The page that displays in the browser still contains only HTML code.

Note:

PHP is just one of the server-side technologies that Dreamweaver supports, in addition to Active Server Pages (ASP), Java Server Pages (JSP), and ColdFusion.

Setting Up and Connecting to a MySQL Database

Unlike the Web sites of the previous projects of this book, a database-driven Web site cannot be created on a computer with a typical configuration. You need to have access to a computer with the languages and environment necessary to support databases. This means that either your computer or another computer on your network must have a Web server, a database application, and the coding language components installed.

If you are using a local server (a server on the same local network as your workstation), ask your network administrator what settings you should use to access and communicate with the local server.

Because we can't be sure that everyone has access to a local computer that meets the requirements of this project, we use a remote (online) server to explain the process of building a dynamic, database-driven Web site.

After extensive testing, we found problems with most of the "100% free" Web hosting sites:

- Many free hosting sites place banner or pop-up ads in your site's pages.

- Many free hosting sites do not include the necessary configurations (i.e., PHP and SQL).

- Many free services are slow, offer little or no technical support, and have a lot of downtime.

- The underlying structure of a free sub-domain (e.g., "mySite.FreeHost.net") sometimes causes problems when defining a testing server in Dreamweaver.

- Free hosting sites sometimes maintain SQL database files on a separate server from your site files, which can be problematic when you try to connect from Dreamweaver.

Based upon the results of our testing, we feel the best way to complete this project is to register a domain name of your own, which you can park at a Web-hosting server and use as the home of the Just Posters site. After you finish this project, you can (and should) later use the domain name to host your own personal portfolio site.

Choose a hosting provider that offers the following tools:

- Apache version 2 or higher as the Web server

- MySQL version 4 as the database application

- PHP version 5 or higher as the coding language pack

- PHPMyAdmin control panel for managing your database

For the sake of illustration, we registered a domain name "www.ek-atc.com" and parked the domain name at www.afmu.com. At the time of this writing, this company — Affordable Multimedia — provides a "free" hosting package with the necessary configuration as long as you register a domain name through their site. Including the domain name, the entire hosting package costs $27.95 for one year; it is well worth the expense — especially since you can later use the domain and hosting service as your personal site.

Note:

Even if you have access to a local Web server, you still need an online server to host your live Web site for the public to access.

Note:

Registering a new domain name can take several hours to days to process. If you follow our example, try to register the domain and set up a hosting account a day or two before you move forward in this project.

Note:

In on-the-job situations, the sites you design will use the clients' registered domain names — for example, www.againsttheclock.com.

Note:

When you move through the exercises in this project, we will point out where your information will be different, depending on the hosting service provider you use.

SET UP A MYSQL DATABASE

Dreamweaver provides a rich set of functionality for creating Web sites that connect to MySQL databases. However, the one feature Dreamweaver does not provide is actually creating a database or the tables it contains. You need to first use some other mechanism for creating the database tables, and then make the tables available on your server for Dreamweaver to access. (You can, however, use Dreamweaver to create an interface for adding data to the database on your server.)

The following exercise uses our hosting account for www.ek-atc.com as an example. If you use a different server (online or local) for this project, follow the instructions provided by your hosting company or network administrator.

Note:

Every hosting company will have a different configuration for creating a hosting site and for accessing and managing a MySQL database.

1. **Open your browser and log in to your Web-hosting control panel.**

2. **Locate and click the MySQL Databases link in the control panel.**

3. **In the MySQL Account Maintenance screen, type "jpdata" in the New Database field. Click Create Database.**

4. **When the browser shows that the database has been added, click the Go Back link.**

5. In the Current Users section, type a username and password in the appropriate fields, and then click Create User.

Most hosts append the site domain (excluding punctuation) to the database name that you define. In our example, the resulting database name is "ekatccom_jpdata".

6. When the browser shows that the user has been added, click the Go Back link.

7. In the Add Users To Your Database area, make sure the username (from Step 5) and the database name (from Step 3) are selected in the appropriate menus.

8. Make sure the ALL Privileges check box is selected, and then click the Add User To Database button.

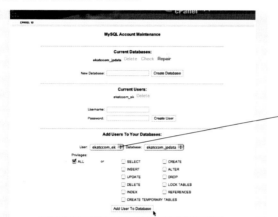

As with the database name, the domain name is also added to the username you define (in our case, "ekatccom_ek"). This information will be important later when you connect to the database from Dreamweaver.

9. When the browser shows that the account has been added to the access list, click the Go Back link.

10. Continue to the next exercise.

MySQL Privileges

There are four groups of privileges in MySQL — Data, Structure, Administration, and Resource Limits. If you are not the administrator of the MySQL installation, you might have access to only some privileges from these four groups.

- **Data privileges** are the most commonly used. In general, you need to provide only the SELECT, INSERT, UPDATE, and DELETE privileges to anyone maintaining a database table; these are typically sufficient to modify existing records, and to add or delete records. The FILE privilege allows users to copy files to a server using MySQL commands.

- **Structure privileges** allow the user to modify the structure of the tables. The CREATE privilege allows the user to create a new table or database, and the DROP privilege permits the user to delete a table or database.

- **Administration privileges** allow the user control over the use of the database, including creating users and granting privileges to other users (GRANT). SHUTDOWN allows the user to shut down the server.

- **Resource limits** are used to control the load on the server hosting the database. When a site has a lot of visitors, the load on the server might surpass its capacity, causing it to crash. By placing limits on the number of connections and operations that a user can perform, this load can be kept within manageable limits.

  MAX_USER_CONNECTIONS limits the number of simultaneous connections to the database. MAX UPDATES PER HOUR and MAX QUERIES PER HOUR limits can be used for database management accounts.

DREAMWEAVER FOUNDATIONS

IMPORT THE SQL DATABASE

Once you have created a database on your server, you can use the phpMyAdmin utility to manage the tables in the database, including adding new information manually or importing data from an existing SQL file.

As in the previous exercise, we continue to use our hosting account as an example. If you are using a different hosting company (remote or local), follow the instructions provided by your service provider or network administrator.

1. **If necessary, log in to your Web-hosting control panel and navigate to the MySQL Databases page.**

2. **Near the bottom of the MySQL Account Maintenance screen, click the phpMyAdmin link.**

    The phpMyAdmin utility is an easy-to-use visual interface provided by many hosting companies to manage SQL database files. You can use phpMyAdmin to create database tables from scratch, manage existing databases, and even export databases for use in another application. In this project, however, you must import the SQL database file that was provided by your client before you can build dynamic data into a Web page.

3. **In the phpMyAdmin screen, click the Import link near the bottom of the left column.**

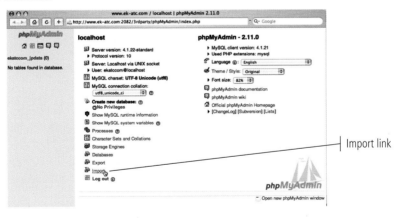

Import link

Note:

The phpMyAdmin screen might look slightly different from one hosting company to another. The functionality, however, should be the same.

4. **In the resulting screen, click the Choose File button in the File to Import area.**

5. **Navigate to the file justposters.sql in the RF_Dreamweaver>Posters>SQL Files folder (on your resource CD) and click Choose.**

Note:

You can also import data from a Microsoft Excel file with the ".csv" (comma-separated values) extension.

6. **When you return to the phpMyAdmin window, click the Go button in the bottom-right corner.**

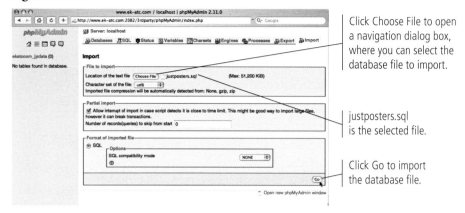

Click Choose File to open a navigation dialog box, where you can select the database file to import.

justposters.sql is the selected file.

Click Go to import the database file.

Two tables (adminusers and posters) are added to the database.

After the import is finished, two tables have been added to the database on your server.

7. **On the left side of the screen, click posters to review the structure of that table.**

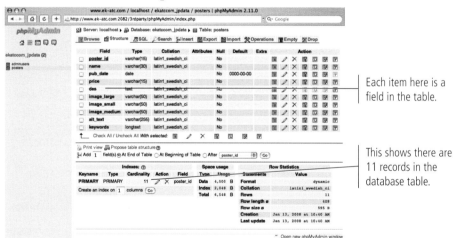

Each item here is a field in the table.

This shows there are 11 records in the database table.

The posters table has ten fields and eleven records. Each entry has:

- An ID for the poster (poster_id)
- A name
- The date of publication (pub_date)
- The poster's price
- A paragraph of descriptive text (des)
- Paths to poster images in three sizes (image_large, image_small, and image_medium)
- A description that will be used as the alterative text for the images
- A list of keywords for the poster

8. **Click the Browse link to review the contents of the posters table.**

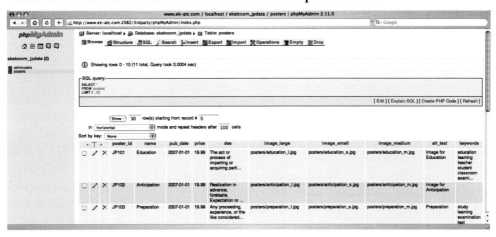

9. **Close the browser window.**

10. **Continue to the next exercise.**

Understanding MySQL Field Types

DREAMWEAVER FOUNDATIONS

PHPMyAdmin provides a simple interface to create a database table and define the attributes of its columns. Creating a table, however, requires some understanding of the column attributes. Fields in MySQL tables are columns; to create a table, then, you must define the fields. The following are some of the important attributes of a MySQL field:

- **Type.** This attribute determines the kind of information to be stored in the field, and can limit the number of possible characters (depending on the selected type). Although there are many different type options, the most common include:

    - VARCHAR can store any type of data up to 65,535 characters long.

    - TEXT can be used to limit the number of characters that must be stored by specifying the limit in the Length/Values field.

    - CHAR limits the number of characters that can be stored to 255.

    - INT stores numbers.

    - BLOB stores binary data such as images. (It is best, however, to not store actual images in a database.)

    - DATE and DATETIME are self-explanatory; note that MySQL stores date in the YYYY-MM-DD format.

    - TIMESTAMP stores the time when a record is inserted or modified in the table.

- **Attributes.** The UNSIGNED option is used along with the INT field type to ensure that only positive numbers are stored in the field. The ONUPDATE CURRENT_TIMESTAMP is used to ensure that the modification timestamp is stored. (Otherwise, only the record-creation timestamp is stored.)

- **Null.** The null option ensures that a value for the field must be provided for the record to be saved.

- **Primary.** This defines a unique value for each record, which can be used to identify records in the table.

- **Extra.** The auto_increment option is used to create records with an incremental, sequential value. When this is selected, values cannot be manually specified for the field. This can be used along with the Primary Key attribute, which requires the value stored in the field to be unique. (You can also click the Unique radio button to ensure the field's value is unique among all the records of the table without making the field the primary key.)

PREPARE THE SITE STRUCTURE

Most hosting providers require you to place public files inside a specific folder, such as public_html or htdocs. When users navigate to your URL, they see the index page located in the designated folder.

Using our example domain-hosting account, the hosting company requires public files to be placed inside the public_html folder. If a user types www.ek-atc.com in a browser window, the server returns the index page located at www.ek-atc.com/public_html/. The public_html folder name is not included in the site URL, but is required when you build, test, and upload files for viewing over the Internet.

Because we are using our own domain name for development and not the client's company name, it's a good idea to use a subfolder rather than placing the Just Posters site as the main www.ek-atc.com site.

1. **If necessary, log in to your Web hosting account control panel. (Make sure you are in the main screen of the control panel and not the phpMyAdmin screen.)**

2. **Click the File Manager link to review the file organization of your account.**

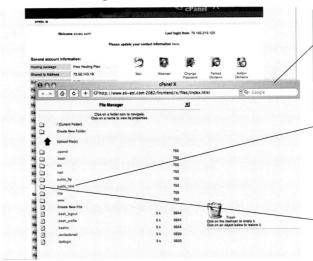

If you use Affordable Multimedia as your hosting company, the File Manager screen opens in a separate browser window.

Using this hosting company, any file that will be publicly visible must be placed in the public_html folder.

If you are hosting your site on the same server as in our example, you have to click the actual folder icon to open the folder.

3. **In the File Management screen, open the public_html folder.**

4. **Click the Create New Folder link to create a new folder.**

5. **Name the new folder "justposters", and then click Create.**

This folder will contain the live site, which you will upload after you finish development. You can then send your client a link to http://www.domainname.com/justposters/ so they can preview the completed site.

Add the justposters folder inside the public_html folder.

6. **Click the link to create another new folder. Name the new folder "test", and then click Create.**

   To accurately test dynamic, data-driven Web pages during development, you need a location that has access to your database and the processing functionality. You will use this folder to separate your working site (what you are developing) from the live site (the pages users see when they navigate to your domain name in a browser).

   Inside the public_html folder, we now have two folders with the following URLs:

   > http://www.ek-atc.com/justposters/
   >
   > http://www.ek-atc.com/test/

   The justposters folder will be used to upload the live site. The test folder will be used during development to make sure everything works properly before you upload the files for public viewing.

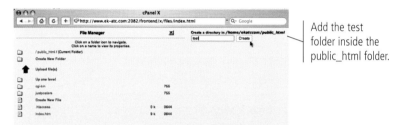

Add the test folder inside the public_html folder.

7. **Close the browser, and then continue to the next stage of the project.**

   This set-up process was required so you can use Dreamweaver to successfully build and manage a dynamic, data-driven Web site. The rest of this project focuses on Dreamweaver functionality.

Stage 2   Defining for Server-Side Processing

PHP (Hypertext Preprocessor) is a server-side scripting language. In other words, PHP pages *include* code that is read and executed by the server before a page is delivered to the requesting browser. PHP enables you to create dynamic pages that are assembled "on the fly," based on code in the page as well as user-supplied information (such as a search query).

CREATE THE SITE DEFINITION

Creating a site definition for a dynamic site is a little more complex than for a static site, especially if you are hosting the site on a remote server. You need to configure the site definition in such a way that it has all the requisite details for connecting to the database, using the correct programming language and including the correct authentication details.

1. **Copy the Posters folder from the RF_Dreamweaver folder on your resource CD to the WIP folder where you are saving your work.**

   This folder contains a Site Content folder, which will be your local site root folder.

2. **In Dreamweaver, open the Manage Sites dialog box using the Directory menu in the Files panel.**

3. **If the Baseball site is still available in the list of sites, export the site definition file into your WIP>Baseball folder, and then remove the Baseball site from the dialog box.**

Note:

You can define a separate server to use as the testing server, or (as in this project) simply create a secondary test folder on your existing server.

4. **Click New>Site.**

5. **Create a new site named "Posters" using your WIP>Posters>Site Content folder as the site root folder.**

6. **Make sure the Document option is selected in the Links Relative To option.**

7. **In the HTTP address folder, type the URL from which users will be able to access the site.**

   In our example, the address is http://www.ek-atc.com/justposters/. Make sure you enter the correct information for your domain name and server configuration.

8. **Check the Use Case-Sensitive Link Checking option.**

   The case-sensitive link checking option ensures that Dreamweaver looks for proper case in the links of the site. This option is required because most Web servers run on the UNIX operating system, which implements strict case-sensitivity.

Note:

Remember, the public_html folder name is not included in the actual site URL.

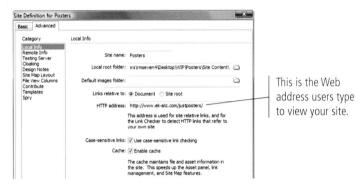

This is the Web address users type to view your site.

9. **Click Remote Info in the Category list.**

   The Remote Info category defines the location where your live site will upload so users can view it over the Internet.

10. **Assuming you are working with a remote server, choose FTP in the Access menu.**

    If you are using a local server, consult your network administrator for the settings to use.

11. **In the FTP Host field, type the hostname for your server.**

    In our example, the FTP host is ftp.ek-atc.com. Check your hosting account documentation for your FTP hostname and account information.

Note:

Consult your hosting company's documentation for specific information about the directory to use for pages that will be viewable on the Web.

12. **In the Host Directory field, type the location of your Web hosting account's site root.**

    This is the location that Dreamweaver's FTP capability targets to put or synchronize files (more on this later). In our example, the host directory is public_html/justposters/.

13. **Type your login (username) and password is the related fields.**

    This is the username and password for your actual hosting account, not the database you created earlier. (Again, consult your server documentation for the correct information; this was probably sent to you via email when you set up the hosting account.)

14. **Make sure the Save check box (next to the Password field) is checked, and then click Test.**

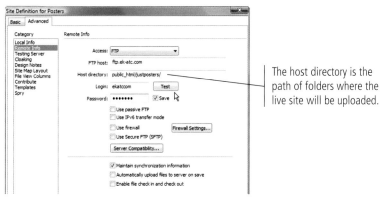

The host directory is the path of folders where the live site will be uploaded.

Note:

If you are working on a shared computer, you might want to uncheck the Save option. If you do, however, you will have to type your username and password when you upload files to your hosting account.

You must receive a message stating that Dreamweaver successfully connected to the Web server. If a connection with the Web server cannot be established, check your entries to make sure your Internet connection is active, and then try again.

Note:

The Check In and Check Out features of Dreamweaver are useful when multiple authors are working on the same site. If a file is checked out, only the author who has checked out the file can work on it. When you check in a file, it becomes available to other users for editing.

15. **Click Testing Server in the Category list.**

Dreamweaver must be able to access the database and processing instructions (software) to preview dynamic Web pages during development.

16. **In the Server Model menu, choose PHP MySQL.**

17. **In the Access menu, choose FTP.**

The FTP login details you provided in the Remote Info pane appear here by default.

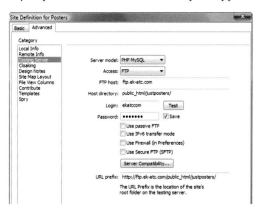

Note:

If you do not define a different testing server location than your Remote Info location, previewing your working pages from Dreamweaver will overwrite the pages in your main site directory.

18. **Change the Host Directory to "public_html/test/".**

When you use Dreamweaver to preview PHP pages in a browser, those pages will be put into the defined testing server directory.

19. Change the URL Prefix field to the correct URL for your test folder location.

In our example, the URL is http://www.ek-atc.com/test/.

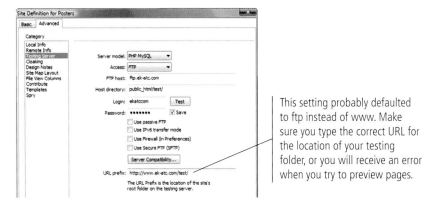

This setting probably defaulted to ftp instead of www. Make sure you type the correct URL for the location of your testing folder, or you will receive an error when you try to preview pages.

20. Click OK to accept the site definition settings.

21. If you receive a warning message about a mismatch between the URLs, click OK.

This message tells you that the different URLs could cause problems if you define site-relative links. Because you are using document-relative links to build this (and most) sites, you can dismiss the warning.

22. In the Manage Sites dialog box, make sure the Posters site appears in the list of sites, and then click Done.

23. Continue to the next exercise.

 UPLOAD FILES TO A REMOTE SITE

If you are working on a remote server, you can use the hosting provider's file management utility to upload the site files. However, Dreamweaver offers a number of options for moving files to a remote server from within the application. Dreamweaver's FTP functionality enables you to easily put files into the remote site folder (defined in the Remote Info pane of the Site Management dialog box). You can even synchronize all files on the remote and local sites — which is useful when you are ready to publish the site for public Internet access.

1. With the Posters site open in the Files panel, click the Expand button in the Files panel to show both the local and remote sites.

Click here to expand the Files panel.

2. **Above the Remote Files pane, click the Connect button to link to and show the remote site.**

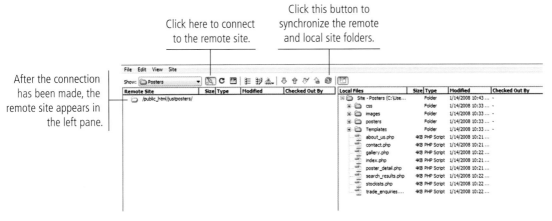

Click here to connect to the remote site.

Click this button to synchronize the remote and local site folders.

After the connection has been made, the remote site appears in the left pane.

Notice the "test" folder does not appear in the remote site. This is because the "test" folder is outside the host directory (justposters) defined for the remote site.

3. **Click the Synchronize button at the top of the expanded Files panel.**

4. **In the Synchronize Files dialog box, choose Entire 'Posters' Site in the Synchronize menu and choose Put Newer Files to Remote in the Direction menu.**

This utility enables you to synchronize an entire site or only selected files. You can also determine which version (local or remote) to synchronize from. (For example, if you accidentally delete files from your local site folder, you can choose to synchronize files from the remote site to the local site to restore the missing files.)

5. **Click the Preview button.**

After a few minutes, the Synchronize dialog box shows a list of all files that will be affected by the process. In this case, this is the first time you are uploading to the remote site, so all the site files need to be put onto the remote site.

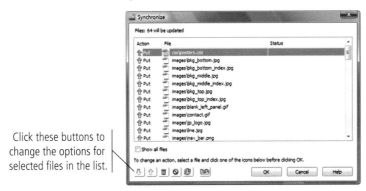

Click these buttons to change the options for selected files in the list.

6. **Click OK to put the files onto the remote site.**

   When you upload files to the remote server, Dreamweaver keeps a log of the different files that are affected. The Background File Activity dialog box shows a list of each file, including any potential problems encountered during the transfer process.

Note:

Dreamweaver will warn you if a file uploaded incorrectly or does not upload.

7. **In the Background File Activity dialog box, click the arrow button to the left of the word "Details" to expand the dialog box and show the progression of the synchronization.**

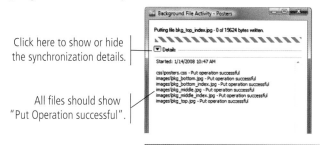

Click here to show or hide the synchronization details.

All files should show "Put Operation successful".

Note:

When you upload files to the remote server, Dreamweaver keeps a log of the different files that are affected. You can access this log in the FTP Log tab of the Results panel (Window>Results).

After the synchronization is complete, the files appear in the remote site as well.

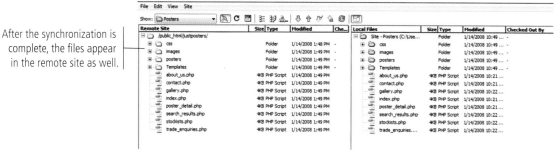

8. **Open a browser window. In the navigation bar, type the URL of the Just Posters site.**

   This will be the same URL you defined in the Local Info pane of the Site Definition dialog box. In our example, the URL is http://www.ek-atc.com/justposters/.

You don't need to type "index.php." This page is recognized as the default file for the defined path.

9. **Close the browser and return to Dreamweaver.**

10. **Continue to the next stage of the project.**

Stage 3 Creating Data-Driven Pages

Every page that needs to interact with a database needs the information required to access that database: the location of the database, its name, and the required user ID and password.

The PHP code required to access the database is generated automatically when you define the connection details. Since this code needs to be available in every page that accesses the database, Dreamweaver creates a separate page with this code, and places the page in a folder named Connections in your local site root. Using the **require function**, a reference to this page is automatically added to every page that needs access to the database.

CREATE THE MySQL CONNECTION

The Databases panel is the primary interface for connecting to and interacting with a database. Once the connection is created, the information is stored in a file in the site's Connections folder.

1. **With the Posters site open in the Files panel, collapse the Files panel to Standard view and make sure the local site is showing.**

2. **Double-click gallery.php to open it in Design view.**

3. **Open the Databases panel in the Application panel group (Window>Databases).**

   Before you can create a database connection, a file must be open.

Note:

You can edit or delete connection information from the included file by right-clicking a connection in the Databases panel and choosing from the contextual menu.

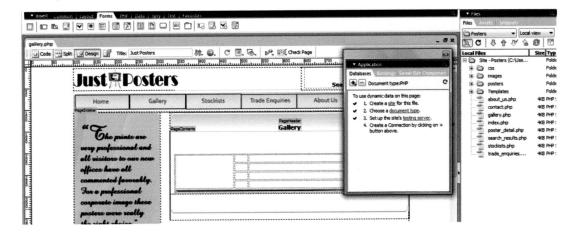

4. **Click the "+" button in the Databases panel, and then choose MySQL Connection from the menu.**

5. **In the Connection Name field, type "jpdata".**

This name is applied to the file in the connections folder; all database references in the other page files will refer to the file with this name.

6. **In the MySQL Server field, type the location of the database.**

In our example, the database is hosted on the same server as the site, as you saw in the phpMyAdmin screen when we imported the client's information into the database. The MySQL server, therefore, is localhost.

7. **Type the username and password for the database in the related fields.**

This is the name and password you defined when you created the database (probably including the underscore and the domain name as part of the username); it is not the same as the username and password for your hosting account.

Note:

Remember, when we created the database and username in the hosting control panel, the control panel appended the "ekatccom_" to our defined username (ek). So, the whole username for the database in our example is "ekatccom_ek".

8. **Click the Select button next to the Database field.**

The resulting Select Database dialog box shows the names of databases you can access.

You can simply type the name of the database you created, but clicking the Select button allows Dreamweaver to test the connection to your MySQL server using the details you provided in the previous steps.

9. **In the Select Database dialog box, select the database you created for the Just Posters site, and then click OK.**

After clicking OK in the Select Database dialog box, the database you selected appears here.

10. **Click OK to close the MySQL Connection dialog box.**

The posters connection is added to the Databases panel and a Connections folder is added to the local site files.

11. **In the Databases panel, expand the jpdata connection and expand the list of tables in the connection.**

12. **In the Files panel, expand the Connections folder.**

These are the two tables in the database file (as you saw when you imported the client's data).

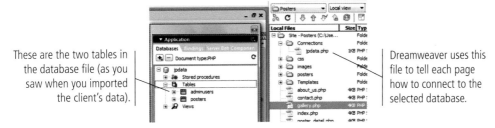

Dreamweaver uses this file to tell each page how to connect to the selected database.

13. **Continue to the next exercise.**

Checking Capitalization

When Dreamweaver creates the "Connections" folder for storing the connection details PHP file, the name of the folder starts with an uppercase C.

The file in this folder is used by pages in the site to connect to the database; each file that connects to the database uses the require PHP function to access the details in this file. The name of the Connections folder in the require code path matches what Dreamweaver finds in the site structure — in other words, the folder name in the file path starts with an uppercase C.

Many remote servers work on the UNIX operating system, which convert the case of file and folder names to lowercase and then enforce case-matching when looking for files. The references to the Connections folder in your site, however, will still contain the uppercase folder name.

To avoid this problem, change the name of the folder in the Files panel to start with the lower-case C; when Dreamweaver prompts you to update references to the file inside it, click Update.

DISPLAY RECORDS FROM THE DATABASE

Now that you have established a connection to the database, you are ready to add the data-driven elements to the site pages. The first page you need to build is a gallery of all the client's products. Each item in the gallery will link to a separate page that shows the details of a specific poster.

Working with a database to design pages is basically a matter of specifying which content (data) to display in the page. By designing pages around the database, you don't need to spend hours or days creating a large number of static pages for every conceivable need. This type of dynamic site also makes it easy to change the data in the database — for example, adding new products without manually generating new static pages.

1. **With gallery.php open in Design view, click the Server Behaviors panel tab in the Application panel group.**

If the Server Behaviors panel is not visible, choose Window>Server Behaviors.

2. Click the "+" button on the Server Behaviors panel and choose Recordset from the menu.

A **recordset** retrieves specific information from a database table. This dialog box enables you to specify the parameters for which records will be retrieved.

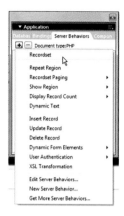

3. Make sure you are working in Simple mode.

Check the buttons on the right side of the dialog box; if the button above Help says "Advanced", you are working in Simple mode.

4. Type "getPosterList" in the Name field.

The recordset will be referred to as getPosterList in the page.

5. In the Connections menu, choose jpdata.

The connection tells the recordset the location and authentication details of the database from which records must be retrieved.

6. In the Table menu, choose posters.

This is the table in the database that contains all the poster details. Each recordset can retrieve details from a single table. You need to create a different recordset for each table from which you want to retrieve records.

Note:

Recordsets are instructions that a page contains for retrieving records from a table in a database. Unlike the connection details, which are stored in a separate file, recordset instructions are stored in the page that you are working on. A separate recordset is required to get records from different tables, and individual recordsets can include parameters for retrieving only those records that match certain criteria.

Note:

You can use only numbers, letters, and the underscore symbol (_) in recordset names. You cannot use spaces.

Note:

Dreamweaver's Recordset dialog box allows you to construct a MySQL query. While a basic query can be constructed (in Simple mode) without looking at the actual query code, the Advanced mode of the dialog box also allows you to modify the query manually. In Simple mode, you can create a query to retrieve records from a single database table; in Advanced mode, you can build a query that retrieves record details from across tables.

7. Click the Selected radio button above the Columns window.

When you define a recordset, you can specify the table columns (data fields) from which data must be retrieved. Remember: you don't necessarily need to display every field for a record on a given page. If you select All when all fields are not actually needed, the result could be an unnecessary delay in displaying the page because the page is downloading more data than it needs.

8. Press Command/Control and click the following columns to select them:

| poster_id | name | price |
| image_medium | alt_text | |

These fields will display for posters in the gallery.php page.

9. Make sure None is selected in the Filter menu.

As long as a recordset is not filtered, all the records in the database will display — which is what you want in this case. (You will later add a behavior to limit the displayed records to five at a time.)

10. Click Test.

The resulting Test SQL Statement dialog box displays all 11 posters, with the details from the selected columns.

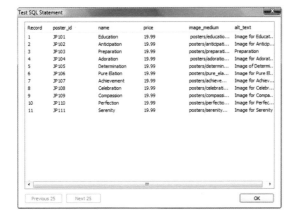

11. Click OK to close the Test SQL Statement dialog box, and then click OK to close the Recordset dialog box.

The getPosterList recordset is added to the Server Behaviors panel. You will use this recordset to display all the posters from the database in the gallery.php page.

12. Continue to the next exercise.

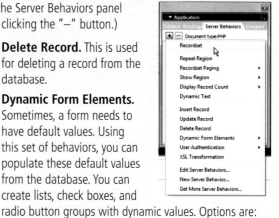

Available behaviors can be accessed by clicking the "+" button on the Server Behaviors panel toolbar. (Delete an existing behavior by selecting it in the panel and clicking the "−" button.)

- **Recordset.** A recordset is a query that contains the criteria for retrieving records from a database table.

- **Repeat Region.** This causes a selected region to repeat until all records retrieved by the recordset are displayed.

- **Recordset Paging.** This set of behaviors adds links that can be used to navigate through groups of records in the same set. Specific options in this menu are:

Move To First Page	Move To Previous Page
Move To Next Page	Move To Last Page

- **Show Region.** These behaviors can be used to either hide or display a region under certain conditions. Options in this menu are:

Show If Recordset Is Empty	
Show If Recordset Is Not Empty	
Show If First Page	Show If Not First Page
Show If Last Page	Show If Not Last Page

- **Display Record Count.** This set of behaviors displays the first, last, and total number of records displayed on the page. Options in this menu are:

  Display Starting Record Number
  Display Ending Record Number
  Display Total Records

- **Dynamic Text.** This behavior is used to show the contents of a specific database table field.

- **Insert Record.** This is used for adding a record to a database table by collecting values from a form.

- **Update Record.** This is used for updating a record in a database table by collecting values from a form.

- **Delete Record.** This is used for deleting a record from the database.

- **Dynamic Form Elements.** Sometimes, a form needs to have default values. Using this set of behaviors, you can populate these default values from the database. You can create lists, check boxes, and radio button groups with dynamic values. Options are:

Dynamic Text Field	Dynamic CheckBox
Dynamic Radio Group	Dynamic List/Menu

- **User Authentication.** This set of behaviors is used to restrict areas of your site to only those users who have permission. (Account details are saved in a database, and these behaviors match the user ID and password provided by users to the records in the database table.) Options in this menu are:

Log In User	Restrict Access To Page
Log Out User	Check New Username

- **XSL Transformation.** This feature is useful for collecting content received in XML files and displaying that content as an ordinary Web page. Content from RSS (Rich Site Summary) feeds is in the XML format.

- **New Server Behavior** and **Edit Server Behavior** are used for creating and modifying custom behaviors.

- **Get More Server Behaviors** directs you to a page that lists some free and for-sale Dreamweaver behaviors that are not available in the application as it is shipped.

Using the Data Insert Bar

All behaviors listed in the Server Behaviors panel can also be accessed from the Data Insert bar. A few other options also appear in the Data Insert bar.

- The Spry buttons are used to create dynamic areas with underlying Spry technology.

- The Dynamic Data button menu includes options for adding dynamic text, as well as the dynamic form fields.

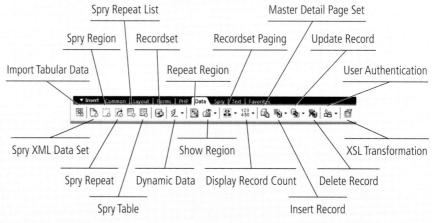

- The Recordset Paging button menu includes an option to create a Recordset Navigation Bar (which you use later to complete this project). The menu in the Server Behaviors panel only offers the individual navigation options.

- The Display Record Count button menu includes a Recordset Navigation Status option.

- The Insert Record button menu includes an option to open the Record Insertion Form Wizard.

- The Update Record button menu includes an option to open the Record Update Form Wizard.

ADD DATA PLACEHOLDERS IN A PHP PAGE

The gallery.php page has an empty table in the editable PageContent area. You will use this table to hold the information for each poster in the catalog, based on the data in the getPosterList recordset.

1. **With gallery.php open in Design view, click in the first row, third column of the table within the editable area. Type "Poster Name: " (including a space after the colon).**

   The labels for the dynamic content can simply be static text.

2. **In the Server Behaviors panel, click the "+" button and choose Dynamic Text.**

You should be working in the third column of the first table row.

   The resulting Dynamic Text dialog box lists the available recordsets, which you can expand to show the table fields that can be inserted in the page.

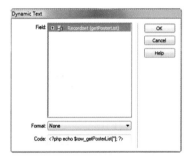

3. **If the getPosterList recordset is not expanded, expand it now. Click name in the list to select that table field.**

   The Code field at the bottom of the dialog box displays the code that will be inserted into the page to display the data. You don't need to modify this code.

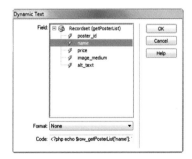

4. Click OK to close the Dynamic Text dialog box.

A dynamic text placeholder is added to the page, showing the recordset and column name that will display when a user views the page in a browser. The dynamic text definition is also added to the Server Behaviors panel.

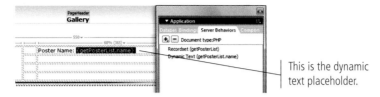

This is the dynamic text placeholder.

5. Repeat this process in the second row of the table to add a "Poster ID: " label and data placeholder.

6. Repeat this process in the third row of the table to add a "Poster Price: " label and data placeholder.

7. Click in the first column of the table and choose Insert>Image.

8. In the Select Image Source dialog box, click the Data Sources radio button.

A list of the available recordsets displays in the Fields pane. So far, you have created only one recordset, so only one is available.

9. Expand the getPosterList recordset (if necessary). Select image_medium and click OK.

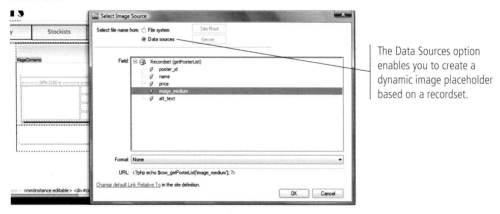

The Data Sources option enables you to create a dynamic image placeholder based on a recordset.

10. In the resulting Image Tag Accessibility Attributes dialog box, choose <empty> in the Alternate Text menu, and then click OK.

An image placeholder is added to the page. The database for this project does not contain any actual images. Instead, the records contain paths to image files of various sizes (small, medium, large).

When you insert the contents of a column containing an image path, Dreamweaver creates a placeholder for the image to be displayed. The definition in the Server Behaviors panel appears as a dynamic attribute definition.

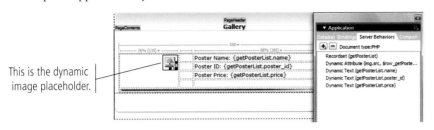

This is the dynamic image placeholder.

Note:

Although you can upload images to a database, it is widely considered bad practice because it bloats the size of the database.

11. **Save the file and continue to the next exercise.**

 ## USE A BINDING TO DYNAMICALLY DEFINE ALT TEXT

In the previous exercise, you added an image placeholder to the page. Because this placeholder will be an image in the served page, you need to include alternate text. By selecting the <empty> option in the Image Tag Accessibility Attributes dialog box, the appropriate code was added to the page. You will now add the alternate text dynamically.

1. **With gallery.php open, make sure the image placeholder on the page is selected.**

2. **Click the Bindings panel tab in the Application panel group.**

Displaying Images from a MySQL Database

Database fields of the BLOB type can be used to upload image files to a database table. While some designers find it useful to store a few images that are not too large, most caution against using this feature. Images have the potential to bloat the database and reduce its speed. The alternative to storing images in the database is to store the image name or file path. (This is what has been provided to you as part of the database file in this project.)

An important warning about this method: since the pages that use images might be at different locations in the site structure, the file path in the database might not be correct. For example:

image/pic1.jpg

refers to an image folder at the same level as the page calling the pic1.jpg file. If the calling page is in a subfolder, the path "image/pic1.jpg" will not find the correct image.

To avoid this problem, you can store only the image name in the database. When selecting the data source, the URL field displays the reference to the image field in the database that will be added to the page. At the beginning of this reference, you can add the correct folder path of the image. For example, if the code reference is:

<?php echo $row_getRecords['pic1.jpg'];?>,

and the file named in the database is located in the graphics folder, then modify the reference to:

graphics/<?php echo $row_getRecords['pic1.jpg'];?>,

DREAMWEAVER FOUNDATIONS

3. **Expand the getPosterList recordset and click alt_text in the list.**

4. **In the Bind To menu at the bottom of the panel, select img.alt, and then click Bind.**

   This associates (binds) the contents of the alt_text column to the Alt attribute of the image tag.

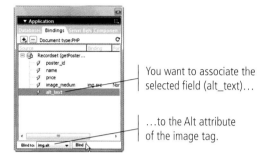

You want to associate the selected field (alt_text)...

...to the Alt attribute of the image tag.

5. **Save the page and preview it in your browser.**

6. **Click Yes when asked if you want to update the file on the testing server.**

7. **Click Yes again when asked if you want to upload dependent files.**

   To preview a file properly, the page's dependent files (images, CSS files, etc.) must also be added to the testing server. Knowing this, Dreamweaver asks if you want to put (upload) the dependent files as well.

   The Background File Activity dialog box shows the progress of the upload, including a list of the dependent files that were uploaded to the testing server.

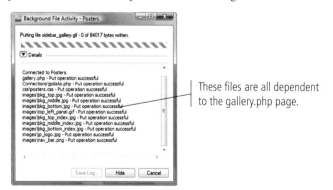

These files are all dependent to the gallery.php page.

When all the necessary files have been uploaded, the page displays in the browser. Two problems are evident. First, only one record appears in the page instead of the entire catalog. You will correct this problem in the next exercise. Second, the image placeholder appears as a broken link. When you upload a page to the testing server, the dependent files also upload. Because this is a dynamic image placeholder, however, Dreamweaver does not recognize the images that *might* be placed here as dependent files. In other words, the images referred to in the image_medium field of the database have not yet

Note:

If you or someone else has checked the Don't Show Me This Message Again checkbox, Dreamweaver rememebrs the last-used option. In other words, if someone checked Don't Show... and clicked No in the Dependent Files message, you will get an error when you preview the file in a browser because the dependent file with the database connection data (in the Connections folder) will not be uploaded to the testing server.

If you don't see the Update Copy on Testing Server or Dependent Files messages, open the Preferences dialog box and display the Site category. Make sure the Prompt On Put/Check In option is checked and click OK.

been uploaded to the testing server, so they will not preview. You could upload the image files to the testing server manually, but it isn't necessary for this project; just be aware that during testing, you will not be able to see the poster images.

The image does not appear, but the alt text does.

Only one record displays instead of the entire catalog.

8. **Close the browser and return to Dreamweaver.**

9. **Continue to the next exercise.**

 ## Repeat a Recordset

For the page to show the entire catalog, you must repeat the table for each record in the database. However, manually adding dynamic placeholders for each record would defeat the purpose of creating a dynamic page. Fortunately, Dreamweaver includes the ability to dynamically repeat a region to show more than one record in the recordset without the need to create additional data placeholders.

1. **With gallery.php open, select the entire table that contains the data placeholders.**

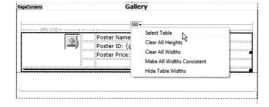

2. **In the Server Behaviors panel, click the "+" button, then click Repeat Region.**

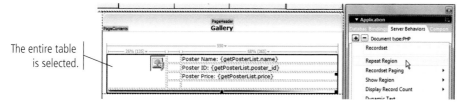

The entire table is selected.

3. **In the resulting Repeat Region dialog box, select the first Show option, type "5" in the associated field, and then click OK.**

The getPosterList recordset is selected by default because it is the only available recordset.

This server behavior causes the table to repeat to show more than one record in a database. In this case, you are also limiting the repeat to show only 5 records at a time.

It is important to understand that the Repeat Region behavior doesn't necessarily show all records in a database. Instead, the number of records displayed is limited by the number of records you allowed when you created the recordset. In this case, the getPosterList recordset has no limiting filter criteria, so the page displays all records.

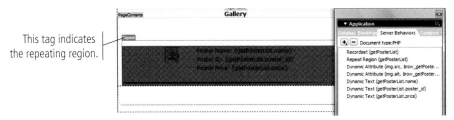

This tag indicates the repeating region.

4. **Save the file and preview it in your browser. When asked, upload any dependent files to the testing server.**

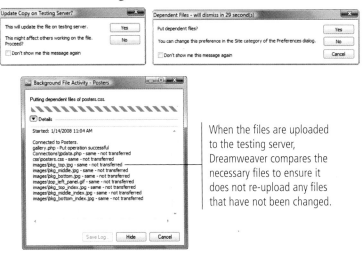

When the files are uploaded to the testing server, Dreamweaver compares the necessary files to ensure it does not re-upload any files that have not been changed.

The first five posters in the database display on the page.

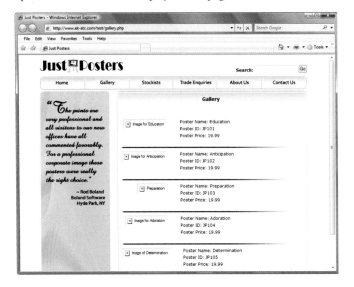

5. **Close the browser and return to Dreamweaver.**

6. **Continue to the next exercise.**

Add Recordset Navigation to the Gallery

To avoid the page from being overly long, many Web developers limit the number of records that can display on the page at one time. This is why you limited the Repeat Region behavior to show only five records. The way the page is currently designed, however, users cannot access the remaining records in the set.

Dreamweaver's Recordset Navigation Bar behavior allows you to create the navigation links that enable users to move between sets of records. The behavior does not create new pages, but simply retrieves the next or previous set of records, and then displays those records on the same page.

1. **With gallery.php open, place the insertion point in the empty paragraph above the repeated table.**

2. **Open the Data Insert bar. Click the drop-down arrow of the Recordset Paging menu, and then click Recordset Navigation Bar.**

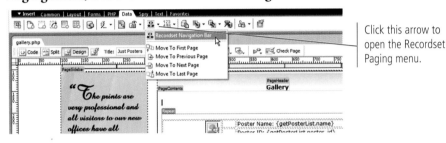

Click this arrow to open the Recordset Paging menu.

3. **In the resulting Recordset Navigation Bar dialog box, make sure getPosterList is selected in the Recordset menu, select Text in the Display Using options, and then click OK.**

Four links are added to the page (First, Previous, Next, Last).

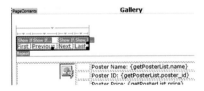

4. **Save the file and the preview it in your browser, uploading any dependent files as necessary.**

Note:

If you select Images in the Recordset Navigation Bar dialog box, Dreamweaver inserts images as the navigational elements. These images have the same functionality as text navigational elements. You can replace the default images with customized image files.

Note:

Depending on the length of your page, you might also consider adding these links at the bottom of the page, as well as at the top.

5. **Test the recordset navigation links above the repeating table.**

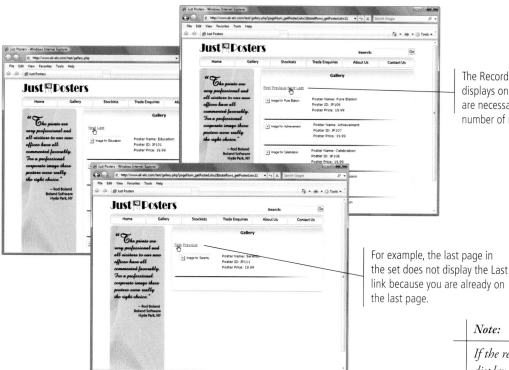

The Recordset Navigation Bar displays only the links that are necessary, based on the number of records to display.

For example, the last page in the set does not display the Last link because you are already on the last page.

Note:

If the records need to display in more than two sets, the first page will display only the Next and Last links. The second page will display all four links. The last page will display only the First and Previous links.

6. **Close the browser and return to Dreamweaver.**

7. **Continue to the next exercise.**

 ## CREATE A DYNAMIC PAGE LINK

The final piece of necessary information in the gallery page is a link to the full details of the selected poster. Because each link needs to open the poster_details page with the information for a specific record in the database, you need to pass the correct information — in the form of the poster ID — on to the poster_details page.

1. **With gallery.php open in Design view, type "View Details" in the fourth row of the third column of the table.**

2. **Select the text you typed in Step 1. In the Properties Inspector, click the Browse for File button next to the Link field.**

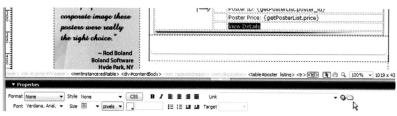

3. **In the Select File dialog box, navigate to the local root of the Posters site (WIP>Posters>Site Content) and single-click poster_detail.php to select it.**

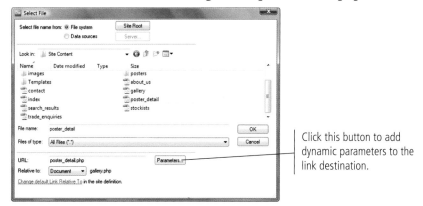

Click this button to add dynamic parameters to the link destination.

4. **Click the Parameters button next to the URL field.**

5. **In the resulting Parameters dialog box, click the Name column and type "poster_id".**

This is the name of the parameter that will be added to the link's destination URL.

6. **Click in the Value column, and then click the lightning bolt icon that displays inside it.**

7. **In the resulting Dynamic Data dialog box, expand the getPosterList recordset and click poster_id.**

8. **Click OK to return to the Parameters dialog box.**

9. Click Choose/OK to return to the Select File dialog box.

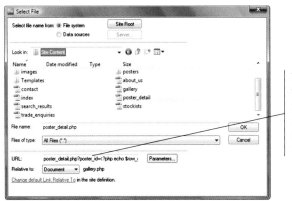

The URL field now shows that the link destination will open the poster_details.php page, using the poster_ID of the selected record to display the details for the correct link.

10. Click OK to create the link and return to the gallery.php page.

11. Save the file and continue to the next exercise.

 ## CREATE THE POSTER DETAILS

Clicking a View Details link in the gallery page needs to open the poster detail page, showing the detail information for the selected poster. In the previous exercise, you created a link that passes the poster ID of the selected record to the poster_detail page. Because recordsets are page-specific, however, you now need to create the necessary recordset and dynamic placeholders so the poster details page shows the correct information.

1. In the Files panel, double-click poster_detail.php to open that file.

2. In the Server Behaviors panel, click the "+" button and choose Recordset from the menu.

Each page that needs to connect to a table in a database must have its own defined recordset.

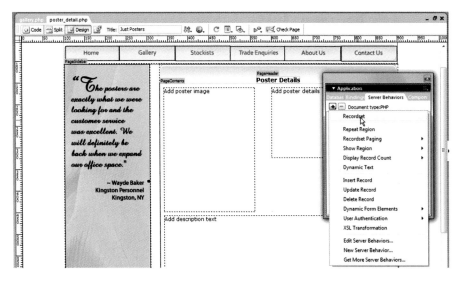

3. **In the Recordset dialog box:**

- **Type "getPosterDetail" in the name field.**
- **Select jpdata in the Connections menu.**
- **Select posters from the Table menu.**
- **Click Selected from among the Columns options.**
- **Press Command/Control and click the following column names:**

poster_id	name	pub_date	price
des	image_large	alt_text	

4. **In the first Filter menu, choose poster_id.**

This is the database field you want to search, so you are defining a filter based on that field.

The second filter menu defaults to the "=" sign. This menu determines the operator for the filter.

The third filter menu (on the second line) defaults to URL Parameter.

The fourth filter field defaults to poster_id because it is the only parameter you defined for a URL (poster_id is the name you assigned to the parameter in the link to this page from gallery.php).

In plain English, this filter statement tells the page:

> Look for the record where the poster_id is the same as the value of the poster_id URL parameter.

To get to the poster_detail page, a user has to click a link in the gallery page. When a user clicks a specific link, the value of the poster_id field for that record passes to the URL as a parameter named poster_id.

In the poster_detail page, then, the value stored in that parameter is used to filter the recordset and find the correct record in the database table.

Note:

Because the ID of a single record is sent to this page, the page displays a single record. There is no need to sort the displayed records.

5. **Click OK to create the recordset.**

   The getPosterDetail recordset is added to the Server Behaviors panel.

   Next, you add the dynamic content placeholders using the same technique as in the gallery.php page.

6. **Select and delete the "Add poster details" static text.**

7. **With the insertion point in the now-empty div, type "Poster Name: ".**

   Remember to add the space after the colon.

8. **In the Server Behaviors panel, click the "+" button and choose Dynamic Text from the menu.**

9. **In the Dynamic Text dialog box, expand the getPosterDetail recordset, select name, and then click OK.**

   A placeholder for the poster name is added in the AP element, and the dynamic text definition is added to the Server Behaviors panel.

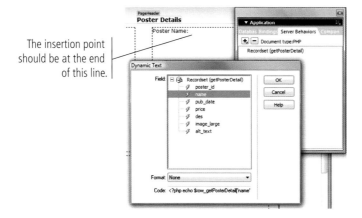

10. **After the dynamic text placeholder, press Return/Enter to start a new paragraph in the div.**

11. **Repeat the same procedure to add three more lines in the poster details area. (Don't press Return/Enter after the fourth line.)**
    - Poster ID: (use the poster_id field in the recordset)
    - Published: (use the pub_date field in the recordset)
    - Price: (use the price field in the recordset)

12. **Select the "Add description text" static text in the bottom div and change it to "Description: ". Press Return/Enter to add a new paragraph in the div.**

13. Add a dynamic text placeholder in the new paragraph, using the des column from the recordset.

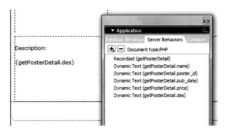

14. Select and delete the "Add poster image" static text in the top-left div. With the insertion point in the now-empty div, choose Insert>Image.

15. In the Select Image Source dialog box, click the Data Sources option. In the Field pane, select image_large and click OK.

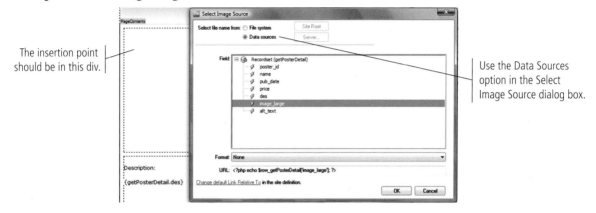

The insertion point should be in this div.

Use the Data Sources option in the Select Image Source dialog box.

16. In the Image Tag Accessibility Attributes dialog box, choose <empty> from the Alternate Text field, and then click OK.

You have successfully added placeholders for all the details that need to display on the poster_detail page.

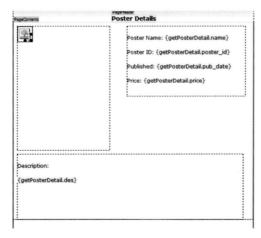

17. Save the file and continue to the next exercise.

TROUBLESHOOT DYNAMIC PAGES FOR TESTING

While previewing/testing dynamic pages is vitally important, it can also be troublesome. You already saw one problem in this type of testing, where images mentioned in a database field are not considered "dependent" to a specific page in Dreamweaver, so those images are not uploaded during the testing process. The only way to solve this problem is to manually upload the image files to the testing server.

A similar problem occurs when you test dynamic page links. In this project, you defined a link to move from one file to another based on which record a user clicks. The problem, however, is that dynamic links to other pages are not considered "dependent", so the linked page is not uploaded to the testing server. In this exercise, you learn how to work around this problem.

1. **Make gallery.php the active page in Dreamweaver. Preview that page in your browser (upload dependent files as necessary).**

2. **Click the View Details link of any record on the page.**

At this point, the poster_detail.php page simply shows a "File Not Found" message because the page that opens (poster_detail.php) should display the details of the record for the link you clicked. If you check the URL in the browser, the page name should be suffixed by a question mark, followed by a parameter name (poster_id), the equals sign (=), and then the ID of the poster for the link you clicked.

The immediate problem is that the page poster_detail.php does not exist on the testing server. As with the images used in dynamic pages, linked pages are not considered dependent files, so they do not upload when you test a page.

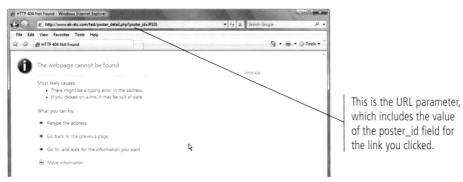

This is the URL parameter, which includes the value of the poster_id field for the link you clicked.

3. **Close the browser and return to Dreamweaver.**

4. **Make poster_detail.php the active page, and preview it in your browser (upload dependent files as necessary).**

The resulting page shows no records. By opening this page independently, no poster_id value passes to the page. The URL parameter "poster_id" is empty, so the filter cannot identify which record to display.

The important point, however, is that the poster_detail page has now successfully uploaded to the testing server.

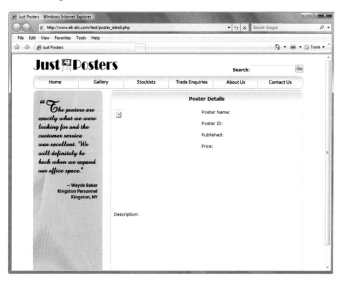

5. **Close the browser and return to Dreamweaver.**

6. **Make gallery.php the active page, and then preview it in your browser.**

7. **In the browser window, click the View Details link for any poster in the gallery.**

Because the poster_detail page now exists on the testing server, you can see the details for the poster you selected in the gallery page.

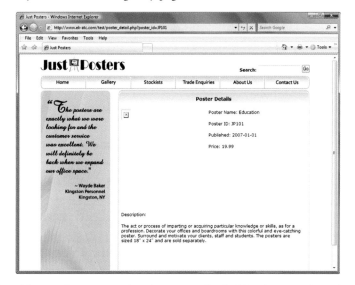

The final problem at this point is that the image placeholder does not show the correct alternate text. (It's okay that the image doesn't appear, but the alternate text should be visible.) This problem occurs because bindings are specific to selected recordsets, which are in turn specific to selected pages. For the images on the poster_detail page to show the correct alt text, you need to create the binding in the poster_detail page, as well.

8. **Close the browser window and return to Dreamweaver.**

9. **Make the poster_detail page active in the design window, and then select the image placeholder.**

10. **In the Bindings panel, expand the getPosterDetail recordset, and then click alt_text in the list.**

11. **In the Bind To menu at the bottom of the panel, select img.alt, and then click Bind.**

12. **Save and close both open files, and then continue to the next exercise.**

 ## ADD A SEARCH FEATURE

Using Dreamweaver, it is fairly easy to create a search feature that compares user-supplied keywords to the contents of a specific database column, returning only the relevant results.

In the client-supplied database, the posters table has a column named "keywords". For each poster record, this column contains certain keywords that users might enter when looking for that poster. In this exercise, you build the functionality to make the search feature look up the contents of this column and display the appropriate records.

1. **In the Files panel, double-click the design.dwt template file (in the Templates folder) to open it.**

   The Search text field has already been placed in the top-right corner of the page. This is where users will enter the keywords they want to search.

2. **Click the "Search" form field in the top-right corner of the page to select it.**

3. **In the Properties Inspector, change the TextField name to "userkeys", and then press Return/Enter to apply the new name.**

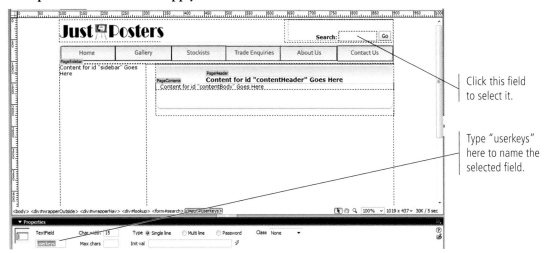

Click this field to select it.

Type "userkeys" here to name the selected field.

4. Select the entire form by clicking the <form#search> tag on the Tag Selector.

5. In the Properties Inspector, make sure Post is the selected method. In the Action field, type "search_results.php".

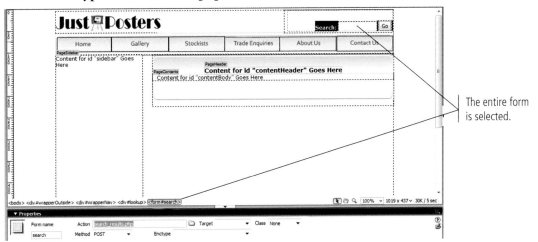

The entire form is selected.

6. Save the template page and update any files based on the template.

Close this dialog box when the update process is complete.

7. Close the template file.

8. In the Files panel, double-click search_results.php to open the file in Design view.

9. In the Server Behaviors panel, click the "+" button, and then choose Recordset from the menu.

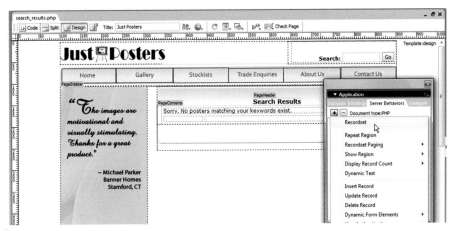

10. In the Recordset dialog box, type "getSearchResults" in the Name field. Select the jpdata connection, the poster table, and the following columns:

poster_id   name   image_small   alt_text   keywords

The first column (poster_id) needs to be retrieved so the value can be passed (as a parameter value) to the poster_detail page.

The second and third columns (name and image_small) need to be retrieved so those pieces of information can display in the results page.

The fourth column (alt_text) needs to be retrieved so the appropriate information can be bound to the dynamic thumbnail.

The fifth column (keywords) needs to be retrieved so the server can compare values in the database to user-supplied values passed from the search form.

11. Select keywords in the first Filter menu, and then select contains from the second-level menu.

You can filter a recordset based on a number of common logic operators.

12. Select Form Variable from the first menu in the second row.

You are using the Form Variable method because you want to filter this recordset based on what a user types in a form field.

13. Type "userkeys" in the adjacent field, and then click OK.

Remember, the input text field name in the search form is userkeys. This is the data you are passing to the filter by typing the form field name here.

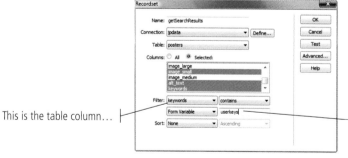

This is the table column…

…that you are comparing to the value a user enters in the text field named userkeys.

Note:

The "contains" operator ensures the search keywords need not exactly match the contents of the column. As long as the keywords are present anywhere in the column, the record will be retrieved.

Basically, you defined a filter that limits the getSearchResults recordset to only records where the contents of the userkeys field (in the search form) is contained in the contents of the record's keywords column.

14. **In the Page Contents editable region, click in the first column of the second row of the table.**

15. **Choose Insert>Image. In the Select Image Source dialog box, select the Data Sources option. Expand the getSearchResults recordset, and then choose image_small from the list. Click OK to insert the dynamic placeholder. Select <empty> when prompted for the alternate text.**

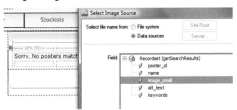

16. **In the Bindings panel, expand the getSearchResults recordset, and then click alt_text in the list. Select img.alt in the Bind To menu, and then click Bind.**

17. **Move the insertion point to the second column of the second table row.**

18. **Click the "+" button in the Server Behaviors panel, and then choose Dynamic Text. In the Dynamic Text dialog box, expand the recordset, select name in the list, and click OK.**

This page will display the poster thumbnail (image_small) and poster name (name) for the relevant records in the recordset.

19. **Save the file and continue to the next exercise.**

 ## Show and Hide Regions Based on Recordset Contents

You might have noticed that the first row in the search-results table says "Sorry, No posters match…". Obviously, you don't want this message to display if some posters *do* match the search results. In addition to defining a repeating region, you can also use server behaviors to determine whether a specific area will be visible based on specific filtering criteria.

1. **With search_results.php open, click in the first row of the table, and then click <tr> in the Tag Selector to select the entire table row.**

   This row contains the text that should appear only when no results are found.

2. **In the Server Behaviors panel, click the "+" button, and then choose Show Region>Show If Recordset is Empty.**

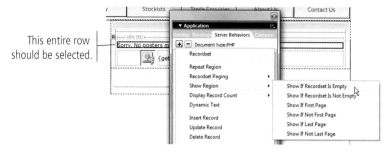

This entire row should be selected.

3. **In the resulting dialog box, the only recordset for the page is selected by default. Click OK.**

   This behavior ensures that this row (and its content) appears only if no matching records are found.

Note:

If there is more than one recordset on the page, then you must select the correct recordset in the dialog box.

4. **Click in the second row, and then click <tr> in the tag selector to select the entire row. In the Server Behaviors panel, click "+", and then choose Show Region>Show If Recordset is Not Empty.**

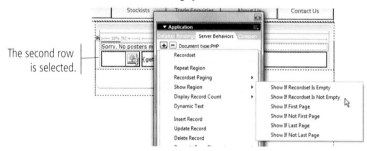

The second row is selected.

5. **In the resulting dialog box, the only recordset of the page is selected by default. Click OK.**

   This ensures that the row (and its contents) display only when matching records are found.

Two Show If… behaviors have been added to control the rows' visibility, based on the contents of the getSearchResults recordset.

6. **Select the entire table. In the Server Behaviors panel, click the "+" button and choose Repeat Region.**

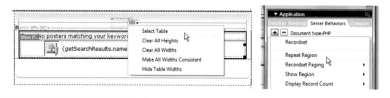

7. In the Repeat Region dialog box, choose the All Records option, and then click OK.

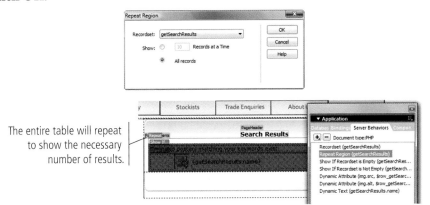

The entire table will repeat to show the necessary number of results.

Note:

If you are working with large database tables with numerous records, you might want to limit the number of search results on each page (as you did on the gallery.php page).

8. Select the name placeholder that you inserted into the second column of the table, and then click the Browse for File button in the Properties Inspector.

9. In the Select File dialog box, choose poster_detail.php from the site root folder. Click the Parameters button, and then define a parameter named "poster_id" with the value of the poster_id field in the recordset.

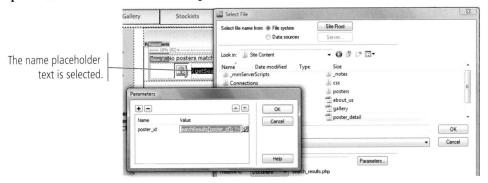

The name placeholder text is selected.

10. Click OK to close the Parameters dialog box, then Choose/OK to close the Select File dialog box.

11. Save the file, and then preview the page in your browser.

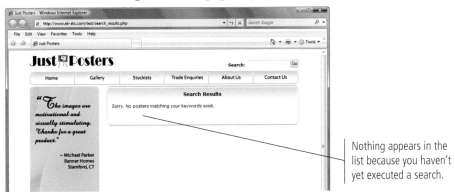

Nothing appears in the list because you haven't yet executed a search.

12. **Type "exam" in the Search field, and then click Go.**

The results page should display the Education and Preparation posters. (If you look at the keywords columns for these posters, they both contain the word "examination.")

13. **Close the browser and return to Dreamweaver.**

14. **Close the open file and continue to the next exercise.**

 ## DISPLAY RECORDS WITH ADVANCED FILTER CRITERIA

So far, you have displayed records without any specific filtering criteria. Dreamweaver creates MySQL **queries** — the means for interacting with the database file on the server — based on the options you select when creating a recordset. In this exercise, you modify a MySQL query to display a random set of posters every time the home page is refreshed.

1. **Double-click index.php in the Files panel to open the file in Design view.**

2. **In the Server Behaviors panel, click the "+" button and choose Recordset from the menu.**

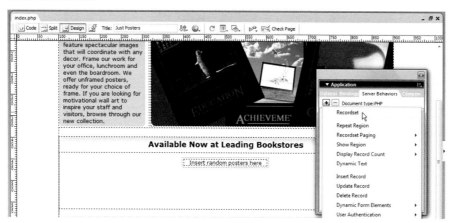

3. **In the Recordset dialog box, type "getRandomPosters" in the Name field. Select jpdata in the Connection menu, and select posters in the Table menu. Leave the All option selected in the Columns area.**

4. **Click the Advanced button on the right side of the Recordset dialog box.**

   The SQL text area displays the SQL query that is created when you select the table. The asterisk (*) in the first line indicates that the query will retrieve all records from the selected table (listed in the second line).

5. **In the SQL text area, click at the end of the second line and press Return/Enter. In the new line, type "ORDER BY RAND() LIMIT 3" (using all capital letters).**

   The RAND() command is used to arrange records randomly, while the Limit command is used to retrieve only a certain number of records.

Note:

The Database Items list and the Add to SQL buttons can be used to create complex MySQL queries. Except for Select, which is used to select a table from which records must be retrieved, you can use the buttons only after you select a field.

6. **Click OK to add the recordset.**

7. **In the index.php page, select and delete the static placeholder text from the table cell below the Available Now heading.**

8. **With the insertion point in the now-empty table cell, choose Insert>Image. In the Select Image Source dialog box, choose the Data Sources option. Expand the getRandomPosters recordset, select image_small, and click OK to insert the image placeholder. Apply the <empty> alternate text option when prompted.**

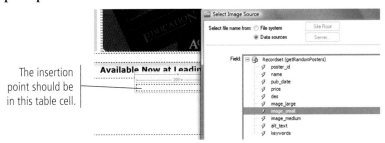

The insertion point should be in this table cell.

9. **In the Bindings panel, expand the getRandomPosters recordset and click alt_text in the list. Select img.alt in the Bind To menu, and then click Bind.**

10. **Press Shift-Return/Enter to add a line break after the image placeholder. In the Server Behaviors panel, click the "+" button and choose Dynamic Text from the menu. In the Dynamic Text dialog box, expand the getRandomPosters recordset, select name, and then click OK.**

11. **Select the entire table column.**

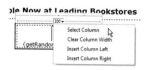

12. **In the Server Behaviors panel, click the "+" button and choose Repeat Region from the menu. In the Repeat Region dialog box, choose All Records, and then click OK.**

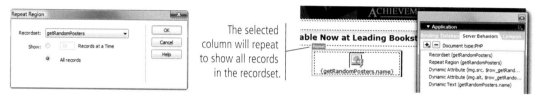

The selected column will repeat to show all records in the recordset.

13. **Save the page, and then preview it in a browser (uploading dependent files as necessary). Refresh the page at least once to see the effect of randomly displaying posters every time the page reloads.**

When you preview the page in the browser, it displays thumbnail images and names for three random posters. When you refresh the page, the posters different posters will be displayed. (A specific poster might repeat, but the combination of posters will be different.)

Note:

Although you selected All Records in the Repeat Region dialog box, only three records display because of the limit placed in the MySQL query.

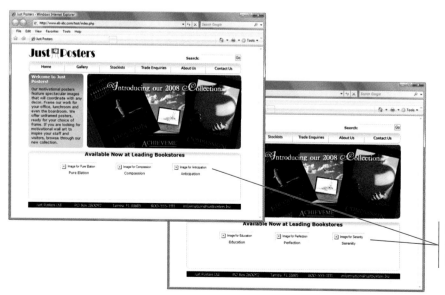

Different posters appear after refreshing the page.

14. **Close the browser and return to Dreamweaver.**

15. **Close any open files and continue to the next stage of the project.**

Stage 4 Preparing the Site for Going Live

Earlier in this project, you uploaded files to the remote server you defined in the Site Definition dialog box. Since then, you have made a number of changes to various pages. Although some files have been uploaded to the testing server, nothing in the actual online site folder has yet been changed — in fact, that's *why* you defined a different folder as the testing server location.

Now that development is complete, you need to re-upload the site files to the remote server location. Dreamweaver's FTP functionality makes this process easy.

SYNCHRONIZE THE LOCAL AND REMOTE SITES

1. **With the Posters site open in the Files panel, click the Expand button in the Files panel to show both the local and remote sites.**

2. **Above the Remote Site pane, click the Connect button to link to and display the remote site.**

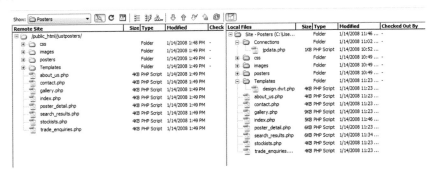

3. **Above the Local Files pane, click the Synchronize button.**

4. **In the resulting dialog box, choose Entire 'Posters' Site in the Synchronize menu. Choose Put Newer Files to Remote in the Direction menu, and then click Preview.**

5. **Review the information in the Synchronize dialog box, and then click OK.**

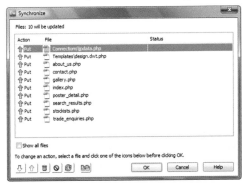

6. **When the Background File Activity dialog box disappears, review the files that have been placed on the remote server.**

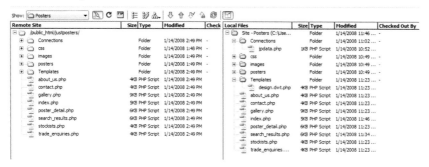

7. **Open a new browser window. In the navigation bar, type the URL of your Just Posters site.**

   In our example, the URL is http://www.ek-atc.com/justposters/.

8. **Test the links on the site, including the Search field.**

Note:

Because the image files have been uploaded to the remote site, the images now appear in the browser when you open the site pages.

9. **Close the browser and return to Dreamweaver.**

10. **Open the Manage Sites dialog box from the Files panel.**

11. **Export the Posters site definition file into your WIP>Posters folder, and then remove the Posters site from the list.**

12. **When asked, back up all settings including login and password information.**

   Dreamweaver includes this step to help prevent you from accidentally sending sensitive password information that you might not want to share with other users.

13. **Remove the Posters site from the Manage Sites list, and then quit Dreamweaver.**

DREAMWEAVER FOUNDATIONS

Throughout this project, you learned how to use Dreamweaver to build pages that find and display information from a MySQL database. In addition to simply displaying information, however, you can also use Dreamweaver to build pages that actually change the database — inserting new records, editing existing records, and deleting records — using only a PHP page in a browser (instead of logging in through phpMyAdmin). Say you have created an administrative page to display the contents of the database. This type of page typically contains three links:

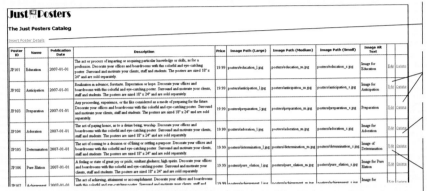

This link opens a page where users can fill in a form to add a new record to the database.

The poster_id of the relevant link must be passed to the linked page as a URL parameter.

This link opens a page where users can confirm the record deletion.

This link opens a page with a form that shows the current field values; users can change the values and to update the record.

Inserting or Editing Database Records Using Wizards

Although you can manually create an interface to add or edit records in a database table, Dreamweaver includes a Record Insertion Form Wizard and Record Update Form Wizard that make the process easier because you don't have to first create the form to display the record fields. (We use the Insert wizard as an example here; both have the same functionality.)

- **Connection.** This provides access to the available MySQL connections that are available in the site.

- **Table.** This lists the database tables that are available for the selected MySQL connection.

- **After Inserting, Go To.** You can use this option to define the page that will open after a user submits the form that will be created by this wizard (such as returning to the administrative catalog page).

- **Form Fields.** This box displays all the fields of the selected table for which form fields will be created. You can use the "−" button to not include a field in the resulting form, and click the "+" button to restore a deleted field. The arrow buttons can be used to change the order of fields in the resulting form. (Remember that some database fields might be configured as mandatory. If these are not included in the Insert Record form, users will be unable to add records.)

- **Label.** Dreamweaver automatically suggests labels for fields that will be added to the form. You can select a field in the list and change the related label using this field.

- **Display As.** For each field in the form, you can select the type of input that must be created. Depending on the type of field, you can also specify its properties.

- **Submit As.** This is the format in which the contents of the form field will be submitted to the database.

- **Default Value.** This is the value that will be displayed in the field when the page is opened in the browser. You can click the lightning-bolt icon to specify dynamic content as the default value.

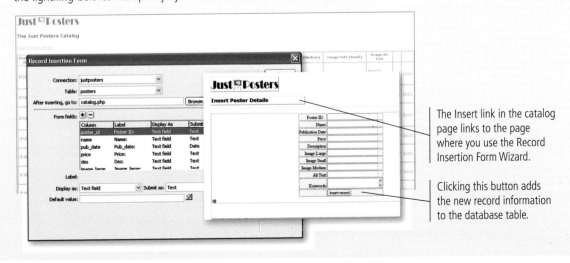

The Insert link in the catalog page links to the page where you use the Record Insertion Form Wizard.

Clicking this button adds the new record information to the database table.

DREAMWEAVER FOUNDATIONS

Inserting or Editing Database Records Manually

If you do not to use a wizard to automatically create a form for adding or updating a database record, you can use the Insert Record or Update Record dialog box to add the necessary behaviors to forms you have already created. (We use the Update Record dialog box as an example, but both dialog boxes have the same fields).

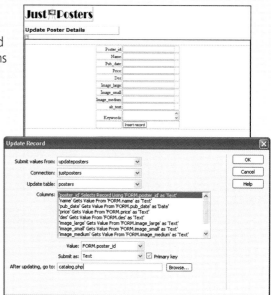

- **Submit Values From.** This lists the names of available forms.
- **Connection.** This lists the available MySQL connections.
- **Update Table.** This lists the available database tables.
- **Columns.** Each listing in this area shows the name of the table column, followed by the form field from which the column gets its value.
- **Value.** This lists the fields in the selected form. After selecting a column in the Columns box, you can select the form field from which that column will receive its value. (If the names of the database column and form field are the same, the same-named field is selected by default.)
- **Submit As.** This lists the formats in which the form field value can be submitted to the database.
- **After Updating, Go To.** You can use this option to define the page that will open after a user submits the form (such as returning to the administrative catalog page).

Clicking OK in the dialog box adds the appropriate behavior to the form. However, you still need a way to display the existing values of the record being edited. This is where Dreamweaver's Dynamic Form Elements behaviors are useful. Once you have added the Update Record behavior to the form, you can convert a standard form field to a dynamic form field (for example, select a text field and choose Dynamic Form Element>Dynamic Text Field in the Server Behaviors menu).

The Dynamic Text Field dialog box shows the selected form field (in the Text Field menu), as well as the dynamic value that will be displayed in the form field (in the Set Value To field). Clicking OK applies the dynamic value to the form field, so the field will show the correct information when the page is opened for a specific record.

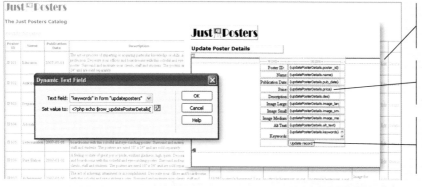

The poster_id of the clicked link must be passed to the Update page as a URL parameter.

Each field shows the value that was mapped in the Dynamic Text Field dialog box.

Submitting the form changes the appropriate record information in the database (on the server).

Deleting a Database Record

The Delete Record behavior inserts a form button that users can click to remove the related record from the database (without offering an option to confirm the deletion). Most developers map the Delete link on the catalog page to a secondary confirmation page, and then create a link from there to a third page that contains the Delete Record behavior.

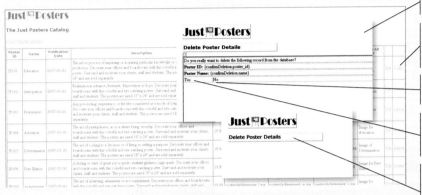

This page opens when a user clicks the Delete link in the catalog page.

The poster_id of the clicked link must be passed to the Confirm page as a URL parameter.

This returns the user to the catalog page without removing the record.

This links to the third page, which has a behavior that removes the selected record from the database.

This page will never be displayed in the browser. It only contains the Delete Record behavior and will redirect to the main catalog page.

In the third page (the one that will contain the server behavior), you can add the Delete Record server behavior. The behavior uses a **primary key** to identify the record being affected. (The primary key is a column in which each record has a unique value. In the posters table, each poster has a unique id so the poster_id field is the primary key.)

By passing the poster_id as a URL parameter from one page to another (from the main catalog page to the confirmation page to the page containing the behavior), the Delete Record behavior finds the appropriate poster_id and removes that record from the database.

Adding User Authentication

Administrative pages should not be accessible to just anyone. Dreamweaver offers behaviors that can be used to protect specific pages by ensuring that only valid users (based on usernames and passwords stored in a database table on the server) can access it.

Once you have built a login page with user ID and password text form fields, you can add the Log In User behavior to the containing form. The Log In User dialog box specifies the table and columns that contain the usernames and passwords, as well as the form fields that will be compared to the information in the database table columns. You can also determine pages to show if a user's login attempt is successful (such as the admin catalog page) or not successful (for example, an alternate login explaining that the entered username or password was incorrect).

The second part of defining the user login process is attaching the Restrict Access To Page behavior to pages that should be protected.

Summary

To complete this project, you used PHP coding to build a dynamic site that interacts with a MySQL database, including an interactive search feature that allows users to interact with the database to find only what they need. By incorporating different server behaviors, you have created only four Web pages that can dynamically display information for any number of products.

This site incorporated only a small part of what you can achieve with the dynamic-data tools that are available in Dreamweaver. If you plan to extend your career into Web development, we encourage you to find a book or class devoted specifically to dynamic Web programming.

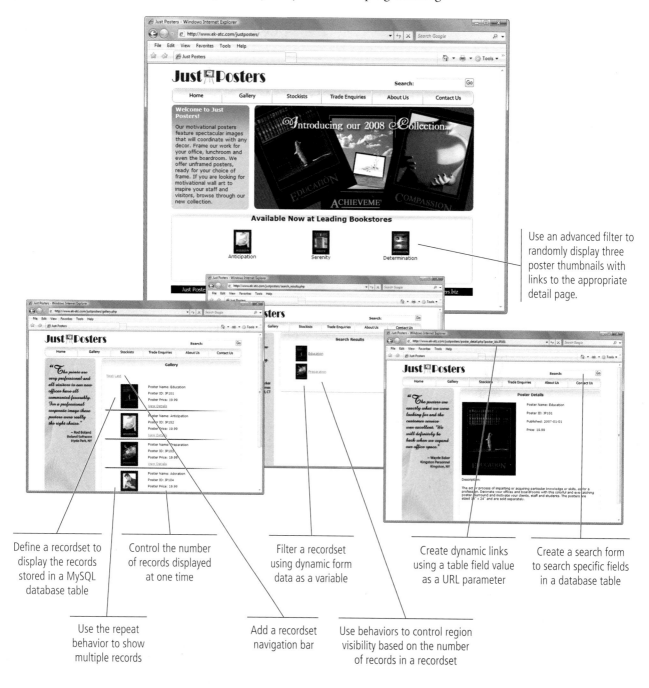

Use an advanced filter to randomly display three poster thumbnails with links to the appropriate detail page.

Define a recordset to display the records stored in a MySQL database table

Control the number of records displayed at one time

Filter a recordset using dynamic form data as a variable

Create dynamic links using a table field value as a URL parameter

Create a search form to search specific fields in a database table

Use the repeat behavior to show multiple records

Add a recordset navigation bar

Use behaviors to control region visibility based on the number of records in a recordset

Portfolio Builder Project 8

Every professional Web designer or developer needs a portfolio to display their work to prospective clients. If you've completed the projects in this book, you now have a number of different examples to show off your skills using Dreamweaver CS3.

The eight projects in this book were specifically designed to include a wide variety of skills and techniques, as well as different types of sites for different types of clients. Your portfolio should follow the same basic principle, offering a variety of samples of both creative and technical skills.

For this project, you are your own client. Using the following suggestions, gather your work and create your own portfolio.

❏ If possible, get your own domain name to host your portfolio site. If you can't get a personal domain name, use a free subdomain name from an established server company.

❏ If you use a subdomain or a free hosting company, make sure external ads are not being placed on your portfolio site.

❏ Include links to sites you have created, whether the pages are kept in folders of your own domain or posted on other public servers.

❏ If you can't include links to certain sites, take screen shots and post those images on your own site.

❏ For each sample site you include, add a brief description or explanation of your role in creating the site. (Did you design it? Build it from someone else's design? What techniques were used to build the site?)

❏ Be sure to include full contact information in a prominent location on your site.

Index

Index

Index

Index